NEW GENESIS

A
MORMON
READER
ON LAND
AND
COMMUNITY

"Here is declared the Creator of all that is good and beautiful. I have looked at majestic mountains rising against a blue sky and thought of Jesus, the creator of heaven and earth. I have stood on a spit of sand in the Pacific and watched the dawn rise like thunder—a ball of gold surrounded by clouds of pink and white and purple—and thought of Jesus, the Word by whom all things were made. . . . What then shall you do with Jesus that is called Christ?

"This earth is his creation. When we make it ugly, we offend him."

PRESIDENT GORDON B. HINCKLEY
The Church of Jesus Christ of Latter-day Saints

NEW
GENESIS
A MORMON READER
ON LAND
AND COMMUNITY

Edited by

TERRY TEMPEST WILLIAMS
WILLIAM B. SMART
GIBBS M. SMITH

SALT LAKE CITY

First Edition
02 01 00 99 98   5 4 3 2 1
Compilation copyright © 1998 by Gibbs Smith, Publisher
Essays copyright © 1998 by individual authors

Published by
Gibbs Smith, Publisher
P.O. Box 667
Layton, Utah 84041

Visit our Web site: www.gibbs-smith.com

Book designed and produced by J. Scott Knudsen, Park City, Utah
Cover illustration, *Autumn's Gold/Harvey's Pond,* by LeConte Stewart,
    courtesy Museum of Church History and Art.

Printed in the U.S.A. by Image Graphics Inc., Paducah KY

Library of Congress Cataloging-in-Publication Data

New genesis : a Mormon reader on land and community / edited by
    Terry Tempest Williams, William B. Smart, Gibbs M. Smith.
    — 1st ed.
    p.   cm.
ISBN 0-87905-843-9
1. Utah—Environmental conditions. 2. Environmentalism—Religious
    aspects—Mormon Church. 3. Human ecology—Religious
    aspects—Mormon Church. 4. Mormon Church—Doctrines. I.
    Williams, Terry Tempest. II. Smart, William B., III. Smith, Gibbs M.
GE15.U8N49   1998
363.7'009792—dc21   97-32750
                                                               CIP

CONTENTS

PREFACE

TESTAMENTS OF DIVINE CREATION

ON JULY 24, 1997, THE CHURCH OF JESUS CHRIST OF LATTER-DAY SAINTS celebrated the sesquicentennial of the Mormon pioneers forging the 1,300-mile trail from Nauvoo, Illinois, to the Great Salt Lake Valley in the name of religious sovereignty.

The reenactment of the pioneer trail was an emotional pilgrimage made in the hearts of each member of the church. Many of us joined the individuals who participated in the migration, and at times the modern-day pioneers numbered in the thousands. We thought about our own ancestors who had been part of the original trek, including members of the handcart companies who traversed the country in the 1850s. Most of us who live in Zion today are the beneficiaries of previous generations' sacrifices and commitments toward spiritual freedom. We carry their stories.

Throughout pioneer journals and letters, as well as in the firsthand accounts of those who retraced the steps of their kin, the overriding character remains the land itself: the weather, the wind, the rain, the heat of the summer sun; the swollen streams that had to be crossed, the tall-grass prairies that could hide a man's horse, the grandeur of the Rocky Mountains. It was the character of the land that shaped the character of the people. It was the pioneers' respect for the elements and all they had to endure that engaged them in daily dialogue with God. Humility and faith in their Heavenly Father were heightened literally mile by mile as they put one foot in front of the other toward the Promised Land.

And here we find ourselves now at the close of the twentieth century comfortably rooted in Zion.

Much has changed.

Compare a population of a few thousand residents in the Salt Lake Valley in the 1840s to its current population of more than a million individuals. Consider the density of homes climbing up the flanks of the Wasatch Mountains and spilling out of Emigration, Parleys, Big and Little Cottonwood Canyons to the urban sprawl stretching north to Brigham City and south to Nephi, not to mention the burgeoning growth centers of St. George, Cedar City, and Moab. Traffic is gridlocked on Interstate 15 as asphalt arteries are widened to accommodate the 2002 Winter Olympics.

Road rage has emerged as a new term in our vocabulary. Light rail is underway. Skyscrapers are raising the Salt Lake City skyline. Unlimited growth is our current story, progress is our theme.

Zion has become like any other place in America, a community of our own creation. But what about the creations of God? How do we fare as a people in relationship to a land ethic? We had an ethic of stewardship once. It is in the muscularity of our history, evident in Brigham Young's meticulous blueprint for the Salt Lake Valley carefully laid out through a pragmatic vision. He preached sustainable agriculture and dreamed a United Order while allotting time in LDS general conference for talks on appropriate farming practices and community vitality in harmony with the land.

This kind of leadership of Brigham Young, with an eye toward sustainability and ecological awareness, was impressive in the nineteenth century, but this kind of active vision within The Church of Jesus Christ of Latter-day Saints is even more necessary and critical today.

A report on the environmental positions of the thirty largest Christian denominations in the United States was undertaken in 1991. Denominations were grouped in one of five categories: a) Programs Underway—denominations with established national environmental programs in which laity can play a meaningful role; b) Beginning a Response—denominations beginning to move at the national level and in which lay assistance can help get programs underway; c) At the Brink—denominations poised on the brink of national commitment, where lay members' input might make the difference between inaction and action; d) No Action—denominations that have not yet begun to consider action; and e) Policies of Inaction—denominations formally committed to inaction.

The Church of Jesus Christ of Latter-day Saints was placed in the last category of "inaction."

We can change our behavior of inactivity toward the earth, personally and collectively, by first recognizing our past relationship to place as holy, tied to our religious sovereignty, and by honoring the Creator through his creation. This can take myriads of forms. We can begin to tell our stories to our families and neighbors as to why this land, even this state of Utah, means so much to us. The essays in this collection are an attempt to begin the storytelling of sustainability with our own spiritual tradition.

A few years ago, a conference on religions of the world and ecology was held at Harvard University. Overall goals included 1) the identification and evaluation of distinctive ecological attitudes, values, and practices of diverse religious traditions, making clear their links to intellectual, political, and other resources associated with these distinctive traditions; 2) description and analysis of the commonalities that exist within and among religious traditions with respect to ecology; 3) identification of the minimum common ground on which to base constructive understanding, motivating discussion, and concerted action in diverse locations across the globe; and highlight the specific religious resources that comprise such fertile ecological ground: within scripture, ritual, myth, symbol, cosmology, and sacrament; 4) outline the most significant areas, with regard to religion and ecology, in need of further study; and 5) articulate in clear and moving terms a desirable mode of human presence with the earth.

These are goals worth considering and reflecting upon within our own religion as members of The Church of Jesus Christ of Latter-day Saints. We are not alone in our reassessment of our relationship to Creation. There is a powerful and significant shift in religions all over the world regarding their relationship, their stewardship, toward the earth. Call it a "new genesis." The environmental crisis we face has become a moral crisis. Churches can no longer stand blindly with their congregations disengaged in the face of toxic waste dumps, air and water pollution, the degradation of soils due to pesticides, and the extinction of species. The global community of churches is beginning to open its eyes.

In November 1997, His All Holiness Bartholomew I, who heads the mother church of Orthodox Christianity, the See of Constantinople (now Istanbul, Turkey), declared that the degradation of the natural world is "a sin." The *Los Angeles Times* reported:

> *The remarks of the spiritual leader of the world's 300 million Orthodox Christians were believed to be the first time that a major international religious leader has explicitly linked environmental problems with sinful behavior.*
>
> *"To commit a crime against the natural world is a sin," Bartholomew stated. "For humans to cause species to become extinct and to destroy the biological diversity of God's creation, for humans to degrade the integrity of the Earth by causing changes in its climate, stripping the Earth of its natural forests, or destroying its wetlands. . . . For humans to contaminate the Earth's waters, its land, its air, and its life with poisonous substances—these are sins."*

Statements such as these by religious leaders that "lift the word sin" and place it in relationship to the spoiling of the earth raise theological inquiry toward "the cause, depth and dimension of human responsibility" in the plundering of the planet.

"The natural world is subject as well as object," writes Thomas Berry in his book *The Dream of the Earth.* "The natural world is the maternal source of our being . . . and the life-giving nourishment of our physical, emotional, aesthetic, moral, and religious existence. The natural world is the larger sacred community to which we belong. To be alienated from this community is to become destitute in all that makes us human. To damage this community is to diminish our own existence."

In our compassion toward all living things, we bow to the imagination, intelligence, and great love of God. Our stewardship toward the earth becomes our humility. Quite simply, through responsible actions toward the land, we return our love to the Creator and Creation.

Paul Gorman, executive director of the National Religious Partnership for the Environment, whose spiritual affiliation is with New York City's Episcopal Cathedral of St. John the Divine, says, "We have found again and again that when the issue of caring for creation enters people's hearts, it has incredible resonance in their lives."

The resonance for creation in the hearts of Latter-day Saints still burns brightly. The essays contained within this collection are evidence of this light. The voices are diverse, like the landscapes they speak from: Clayton White, a renowned biologist who formulated the link between the pesticide DDT and egg instability among peregrine falcons, addresses "the inarticulate speech" of his heart as a scientist who has spent time in deep solitude in the wildernesses of the world; Cordell Clinger, a member of the Tabernacle Choir, gives us a meditation on water and silence in Jerusalem; Natalie Curtis McCullough speaks about her own path toward the Promised Land both as a mother and as a woman who values her own sovereignty. And Natalie Taylor creates a moving eulogy to her baby by returning to a remembered place with her daughter and mother. They find their own healing grace in nature.

Surprising connections are made as former Salt Lake City mayor Ted Wilson shares how his passion for climbing in the Wasatch Mountains led him to a natural conversion to the gospel of Jesus Christ; and Donald Gibbons from Pittsburgh, Pennsylvania, also a convert, finds the same missionary spirit that moved him toward the truth of the Savior in his work with the Sierra Club.

Within this *New Genesis* there are moments of reverie: Marilyn Arnold declaring her love for the red-rock desert of southern Utah; Larry Clarkson merging with the ocean; Von Del Chamberlain's perception as an astronomer, reading the night sky with authority alongside his capacity to hear the music of creation.

There are simple acts recorded in pragmatism and beauty: Mike Alder discussing the process of composting; Ardean Watts watching his children build an earthen house; Kristen Rogers honoring the value and necessity of water in the American West.

There are stories rich in cultural diversity as Jane Hafen writes out of her Taos Pueblo tradition and what she knows as a woman with deep ties to the earth; Dorothy Allred Solomon creates a natural autobiography from her polygamist roots.

And these essays celebrating our spiritual ties to the natural world are strongly connected to family as written lovingly by Martha Young Moench in her creation of a butterfly quilt for her daughter; by the Bennion family in Spring City, Utah; and by Bonnie and Dan Judd, descendants of President Heber J. Grant, as they poignantly record how their family cabin in Brighton is alive with history.

These voices are representative of the power inherent in Mormonism, a sampling of the power within this religion that acknowledges a people's relationship to place, even Zion. We are a people who love our landscape in the heart of the American West. We are a people who have built communities here in arid country. We are a people who have chosen to stay put when others have simply moved on. As Emma Lou Thayne powerfully conveys in her essay, "The land sings through us."

It is our hope that these stories will inspire your own, that families, friends, wards, and stakes within the church will come together in the name of community and foster an ecological awareness as far-reaching as their strength and leadership within the Scouting program, youth development, welfare programs, international aid, and missionary work.

What might this "new genesis" look like?

It would involve the concept Brigham Young understood over a hundred years ago, that less is more. It would honor small-scale communities over corporate development. It would embrace water conservation and energy-efficient technologies. It would protect wild open spaces for the sake of wildlife, and the preservation of solitude, wonder, and awe, which is essential for soul renewal. It would be mindful of family planning.

The "new genesis" would be an exercise of compassion on behalf of all creation.

On Tuesday, January 21, 1998, President Gordon B. Hinckley addressed the St. George Area Chamber of Commerce. He noted that while St. George, Utah, now has a population of 47,000 and Washington County has a population of 76,000, "it may be foolish to say to any member of a chamber of commerce—and particularly to realtors—that I hope you won't continue to grow. If you do, then the culture, the spirit, and the ambiance of the community will change as it already has done so in a measure."

There is a renaissance among us. Perhaps it is not too much to dream that The Church of Jesus Christ of Latter-day Saints will exercise its organizational genius from the ground up on behalf of the earth, that we might return to our root nature of both pragmatism and vision, with an eye toward both heaven and earth.

The highest and truest progress in Zion would be the recognition and wisdom that saving souls and saving the planet are the same thing—testaments of divine creation.

THE EDITORS

"FOR IT IS EXPEDIENT THAT I, THE LORD, SHOULD MAKE EVERY MAN ACCOUNTABLE, AS A STEWARD OVER EARTHLY BLESSINGS, WHICH I HAVE MADE AND PREPARED FOR MY CREATURES. I, THE LORD, STRETCHED OUT THE HEAVENS, AND BUILT THE EARTH, MY VERY HANDIWORK; AND ALL THINGS THEREIN ARE MINE." (D&C 104:13–14.)

THE MAKING OF AN ACTIVIST

William B. Smart

S A KID GROWING UP ON THE THEN-OUTSKIRTS OF PROVO, I WASN'T the most responsible herdsman. Because we couldn't afford pasturage, I was supposed to watch our cows as they grazed along the country lane that would become today's crowded Eighth North Street. But there were distractions. Like searching for images in the clouds boiling across Squaw Peak and up toward Mt. Timpanogos. Or adventuring with Richard Halliburton or Jack London in books from the public library. Or the many World Series games I won by swatting rocks up onto the bench that today houses Brigham Young University. Or experimenting to determine which substance—cedar bark from the fence posts, the seeds of a weed we called Indian tobacco, or dried cow dung—could be rolled into the least evil-tasting cigarette. Meanwhile, the cows relished the neighbors' cornfields.

Simple times, with room enough for a kid or a community to grow pretty much unrestricted.

Times change. In the past half century, no issue has so torn apart my state as use of the land that once seemed so limitless. Preserving Utah's quality of life in the face of burgeoning population demands intelligent land-use planning and protection of open spaces. But because of powerful voices insisting on a man's freedom to use his land as he pleases, the issue is stalemated in the legislature and we continue to drift toward Californication.

With public lands the contention is more intense, more bitter. Determining the size and shape of BLM wilderness has increasingly polarized Utah the past decade to the point of threats if not actual acts of violence. President Clinton's September 1996 proclamation establishing the

Grand Staircase-Escalante National Monument set off a firestorm of antigovernment rhetoric from Utah officials and others, including words like "land grab," "felonious assault," "a treacherous move against our children and this state." Such attitudes are reminiscent of, and about as far-sighted as, that of Arizonans when, in 1908, Theodore Roosevelt created the Grand Canyon National Monument. For example, the Williams, Arizona, *Sun* editorialized that the monument was "a fiendish and diabolical scheme . . . the fate of Arizona depends exclusively on the development of her mineral resources." So much for editorial sagacity.

On such matters Utahns generally split along rural-urban lines, but there are other divisions. Republicans, Mormons, and longtime residents tend to resist government involvement in land-use issues, while Democrats, non-Mormons, and more recently arrived Utahns turn more to government for land-use planning and resource protection.

There are many exceptions. I'm one. Here am I, a lifetime Mormon and almost-lifetime Utahn, raised in a staunchly Republican home, an editor who early in a forty-year career with the conservative, Mormon-owned *Deseret News* campaigned, among other now-recognized sins, for construction of Glen Canyon Dam. But as I learned more about Utah and its growth problems and saw more of the world and the threats to its future, I changed. In 1968 I appointed a full-time environmental specialist—the first, as far as I know, on any newspaper between Chicago and the Pacific Coast. And today my retirement years are spent in conservation causes, as a director or supporter of such organizations as the Grand Canyon Trust, the Virgin River Land Preservation Association, the Southwest Heritage Foundation, and as an environmental representative on the Utah BLM Resource Advisory Council.

What experiences and influences nurtured this growing environmental ethic?

The good fortune of a journalism career has taken me to far places: the polar plateau, beautiful but frightening in its harshness, stretching out from our research station at the South Pole; terraced green mountains soaring into the clouds above the Yangtze; ceaselessly blowing sands of the Sahara beyond Timbuktu; Mt. McKinley wreathed in clouds and moonlight as seen from our campsite in Denali; emerald slopes of thigh-high grasses rippling in the winds sweeping off the peaks of South Africa's Drakensberg mountains; the richness and diversity of life—bird and reptile and sea, unmolested and unafraid—on the lava slopes and in the frothy surf of the Galapagos Islands; crimson forests of rhododendron trees climbing Himalayan slopes on the Nepal side, yak herds dotting Tibet's endless high plateaus on the other.

Such experience burned in me a conviction of how God must love his children to give them a home of such diversity and beauty, and of how profound is our stewardship to care for it. But I have also seen, in the rape of forest, range, and/or soil in places such as India, Nepal, China, South

America, the African Sahel, and in the unforeseen and unhappy consequences of dam-building on the Nile, the Columbia River system, the Colorado, and soon the Yangtze, how the pressures of poverty, overpopulation, or short-sighted development can warp that stewardship.

What has most indelibly stamped my soul with love of the earth, though, is the past half century of living and working in Utah and experiencing, close up and personal, this state's grandeur. I have lived at the foot of the Wasatch, daily lifting eyes to its Mt. Olympus and its Twin and Lone Peaks, frequently running its foothills, hiking its canyons, skiing its slopes. Spring and fall have found us in southern Utah's canyon country, hiking, jeeping, backpacking. Often in that ineffably beautiful country have I thought of the assurance of John Keats in his "Endymion" that "A thing of beauty is a joy forever . . ."

> *Therefore, on every morrow, are we wreathing*
> *A flowery band to bind us to the earth,*
> *Spite of despondence, of the inhuman dearth*
> *Of noble natures, of the gloomy days,*
> *Of all the unhealthy and o'er-darken'd ways*
> *Made for our searching: yes, in spite of all,*
> *Some shape of beauty moves away the pall*
> *From our dark spirits . . .*

Never has the beauty of the soaring cliffs, the hidden grottoes, the water-rippled sandstone of canyon country failed to expand my spirit beyond whatever pall it may have felt.

Good men blessed my life during those years. Men like Bates Wilson of the National Park Service, who on jeep trips to astonishingly beautiful places and around campfires under desert stars taught me to know and love southeastern Utah's canyonlands long before he helped create the national park of that name. Like Arnold Standing, long the assistant Intermountain Region forester, who through many years of show-me and deer-hunting trips to far corners of the state never stopped teaching about our dependence on the land and our responsibility toward it. Like, more recently, state BLM director Bill Lamb and others, who have worked diligently to educate me about the importance and complexities of managing our public lands.

In the mid-1950s a flash flood off Willard Peak roared through the little town of Willard, leaving rock-strewn gullies and ruined farms. With a few Forest Service men I rode horseback up the backside of the peak and over the top to study where, on its steep western face, the flood originated. The cause was obvious. Here, as all along the Wasatch Front, uncontrolled grazing, primarily by sheep, had denuded the watershed. My own grandfather, who ran sheep across the northern Wasatch, helped send that flood roaring down on Willard. Other sheep had denuded other slopes and, beginning in the 1880s, other floods devastated communities from Manti to

Brigham City. Responding to local pleas, the Forest Service and CCC terraced and reseeded many of the abused watersheds and closed some to grazing. That helped, but, as Willard learned, once-ruined land takes many years to recover.

As we munched sandwiches that day and looked over the orchards and farms spreading out toward the Great Salt Lake, Reed Bailey, the Forest Service's Intermountain Region range expert, spoke a sermon:

> I take my text from Psalm 121: "I will lift up mine eyes unto the hills, from whence cometh my help." All the beauty you see before you, the farms, the orchards, the towns, the lake you see out there—all this comes from these mountains. Help from the hills? Better had the scripture said life itself.

He went on to describe the inseparable connection between moisture collected in the mountains and life in the valleys below, and spoke with passion about our responsibility to protect the watersheds.

For me that was a defining day, a day of awakening consciousness. There were others. One was on the Paunsaugant Plateau where I stood with Arnold Standing on the sun-baked and cracked mudflat around the original Tropic Reservoir. Using teams and scrapers and enormous labor, the few families in Tropic Valley had carved out that reservoir and a thirty-mile canal around the Pink Cliffs to bring water to their fields. But over the years their livestock overgrazed the watershed, silt choked the reservoir, and not until federal agencies intervened did the land begin to recover.

Or I think of the rock-and-sand-and-cactus cemetery on the hill above Bluff. Buried there are the Hole-in-the-Rock pioneers who survived a desperate 180-mile struggle across the heart of the Colorado Plateau to establish a Mormon outpost on the San Juan. For a time, cattle gave Bluff the highest per-capita income in the West. But then the pattern repeated; uncontrolled grazing ruined the range. With livelihoods gone, Bluff became a near-ghost town. Today, not a single descendant of those pioneers buried on the hill lives in the area. Only the beauty of the landscape, the rock art and masonry remnants of its ancient Anasazi culture, and the romance and challenge of exploring the San Juan and surrounding canyons and mesas keep the town alive and well.

Bluff may be a paradigm for much of southern Utah. So much of present struggles over land use stem from perceived conflict between economy-based and spiritual/environmental values. Bluff has shown how those values can overlap. It's outsiders, though, who have restored the beautiful cut-rock pioneer homes there, built the tourist facilities and the river-running and backcountry outfitting businesses, researched and protected the Anasazi ruins and made them accessible for public education. The challenge for Utahns is to awaken to the value of what is all around them, the priceless resource of unspoiled land, and find creative ways not only to keep it unspoiled but to prosper in and from it.

4

Remembering Willard and Tropic and Bluff and so many other places, I feel profound gratitude for the stewards who through the years have protected our public lands for the sake of all who depend on, enjoy, and love them. It saddens me to hear fellow-Utahns belittle and berate public land managers as uncaring, arbitrary bureaucrats; those I know are knowledgeable, sensitive, hardworking men and women dedicated to use of those lands in ways that will pass them unspoiled to future generations. And it astonishes and angers me when members of Utah's congressional delegation propose to remove from federal management land that was saved by those same agencies from ruin imposed by the careless and incompetent practices of our own ancestors.

So these are some sources of my environmental convictions. Others are more deep-seated, more compelling. They concern the church I love, its doctrines I profoundly accept, the course I believe God would have his children follow.

When God created the earth, Judeo-Christian and especially Mormon doctrine teaches, he pronounced the seas and the land, the great rivers and small streams, the grass, the herbs, the trees, the fowls, the whales, the cattle, the fish, the creeping things, every living thing that moveth upon the earth—and ultimately man and woman—all good. In fact, all *very* good.

And then he gave man dominion over all his creations. Some seem to believe that means license to use all things for man's exclusive and short-term benefit. But I don't believe a God who pronounced his creations good gave man license to destroy them. Certainly, loving all the human family, he did not give one generation license to destroy the livelihood, the clean air and water, or the places of beauty of the next.

We think of the earth as unimaginably old. The shiny black schists in the inner gorge of Grand Canyon, the building blocks of the earth, have been there 2½ billion years; leaning against them in the sunshine to dry the whitewater soaking of the turbulent river, I have felt attuned to eternity's past and caught a glimpse of its future. The trilobites one chips from the shales west of Delta are 600 million years old. The shark teeth found while scrabbling on hands and knees in shaley clay flats west of Hanksville were dropped there when ocean covered this land 250 million years ago. Change takes aeons of time, and that's comforting.

But time is relative, and so is change. If the total time of Earth's existence is represented by one day, man's time on Earth is less than a second; since the industrial revolution started exploiting Earth's resources, the blink of an eyelash; my 75 years on Earth a tiny fraction of that. Yet, we are told, during my lifetime mankind has used up more of Earth's resources than were used in Earth's entire previous history—and among the vanishing resources I include natural beauty and opportunity for solitude and renewal. As Bill McKibbon has written, "It's as though someone has saved his entire lifetime, then spent everything on one fantastic night's debauch" ("The End of Nature," *New Yorker*, September 11, 1989). And remember, that use has been almost entirely in the industrialized world; the Third World is just beginning to get in the game. I don't believe such profligacy is what God intended.

What God did intend, and promised in Doctrine and Covenants 59:16, 18–19, is that if we live as we ought ". . . the fulness of the earth is yours. . . . Yea, all things which come of the earth, in the season thereof, are made for the benefit and the use of man, both to please the eye and to gladden the heart; Yea, for food and for raiment, for taste and for smell, to strengthen the body and to enliven the soul."

I like his priorities—that pleasing the eye and gladdening the heart and enlivening the soul are as important as food and raiment. If the fulness of the earth is to benefit the eye and the heart and the soul, surely it is to include unpolluted skies and water and landscapes. Surely it includes places of solitude and beauty where one can get in touch with self and with God.

God's people have always sought such places. Abraham, Moses, Elijah, Joseph Smith, the Savior himself all went to the wilderness to hear God's voice. Repeatedly, Book of Mormon peoples fled there for succor and redemption. It's not so different today. Our planet shrinks; people and technology crowd close. And the more closely they press, the more essential to our sanity and perhaps even our salvation are places of spiritual sanctuary.

In the spring of 1997, from the moonless dark of a wilderness camp on the California coast, I marveled at Hale-Bopp comet, whirling through its solar orbit, 85 million miles away, leaving a million-mile tail of ice, dust, gases, and ions. Five billion years, scientists tell us, it has been out there; in another 2,000 years whoever is then living on Earth may see it again. The power and majesty of such creation leave me in total awe and gratitude.

But then so do the clear descending notes of the canyon wren as it greets first sunlight on the cliff towering above my sleeping bag. So does the surge of current against my river raft, or the drip-drip of water from a hidden seep into my empty water bottle. Or the smell of Uinta Mountain meadows sun-warmed following the usual afternoon rain. Or clouds. Or desert varnish. Or Earth's silent music heard from a canyon rim.

These also are God's creation and, along with what strength I have left to enjoy them, his gifts. I am given stewardship for them; so are we all. We can't escape it, and Mormon scripture makes it clear that God will hold us accountable for our performance. That's sobering enough. But my grandchildren and their grandchildren will also hold me accountable. Loving them as I do and praying for them to enjoy in nature such beauty, peace, solitude, and soul-renewal as that with which the earth has blessed me, how can I fail to do my best?

William B. Smart is a founding director of Coalition for Utah's Future, director of the Grand Canyon Trust, and environmental representative on the Utah BLM Resource Advisory Council. He spent four decades as a writer, editorial-page editor, and finally editor and general manager of the *Deseret News*. His books include *China Notebook* (1978), *Old Utah Trails* (1988), *Messages for a Happier Life* (1989), *Lake Powell: A Different Light* (1994), and *Utah: A Portrait* (1995).

". . . AS I SAT PONDERING IN MINE HEART I WAS CAUGHT AWAY IN THE SPIRIT OF THE LORD, YEA, INTO AN EXCEEDINGLY HIGH MOUNTAIN, WHICH I NEVER HAD BEFORE SEEN, AND UPON WHICH I NEVER HAD BEFORE SET MY FOOT." (1 NEPHI 11:1.)

THE TRUTH OF GRANITE: A CANYON CONVERSION

TED L. WILSON

T WAS THE SPRING OF 1961. BOB STOUT AND I HAD DEFIED THE conventions of rock climbing in Utah and had ventured to Little Cottonwood Canyon to attempt the first climbing route ever completed in the canyon by modern climbers. We were the first to climb the walls since the Mormon pioneer quarriers had defied gravity and granite to cut blocks for the Salt Lake Temple construction.

High on the canyon wall, my teeth were becoming squeaky with the acid of fear. My feet, placed on tiny crystals and edges, began to shake. Taking three deep breaths allowed me to gain some composure, shift my weight to a more steady position, and use my fingernails on tiny dime-sized holds to scratch and claw to a tiny ledge. Once there, I shakily pounded two small steel spikes called pitons into a crack and yelled down, "Off belay, Bob."

That signal caused Stout to relax and eliminate the fear from his mind that I would take a long fall. We were connected by a rope 150 feet long. On the way up on the "lead," the first climber would pound in steel pitons, attach the rope to them with oval snap links called carabiners, and hope these running security points would stop a falling lead climber as he potentially fell twice the distance he was above his last piton placement before he hit a ledge or the ground. By using the rope and pitons, climbing could be made relatively safe.

Stout and I named our climb "Chickenhead Holiday." It was named so because the climb was festooned with the friendly protruding pieces of volcanic rock, embedded in the granite, called chickenheads. Chickenheads are comfortable to stand on and provide invaluable resting places for canyon climbers. It was called "Holiday" because climbing in those days sought to emulate the British stiff upper lip of Mount Everest fame ("Because it is there"), and we did not wish to let our friends know the climb should really have been called "We Almost Wet Our Pants" or "Shaking and Quaking Our Way Up the Granite."

We discussed our climbing with a sense of understatement so as to be cool with our friends in the Alpenbock Club, a collection of twenty or so climbers who had come together at Olympus High School long before climbing was to become a mainstream sport. Desperate to find others crazy enough to climb with in the sixties, the Olympus High climbers had relented and let interlopers like me join, even though I was a South High Cub.

Chickenhead Holiday was a lovely climb but was complicated by the fact that our equipment and climbing techniques were barely up to the task. We had avoided climbing in Little Cottonwood Canyon in the 1950s because its smooth, often-holdless rock and long cracks were technically challenging well beyond the sharp, friendly edge holds and cracks of Big Cottonwood Canyon. Only the cross-connecting we did with Yosemite climbers during the summer months in the Grand Tetons had given us the preliminary confidence to give the granite a try. Now it was 1961 and we were pushing the edge of the sport of rock climbing in Utah.

Such adventure requires confidence, not just equipment and technique. If my equipment and technique were poor in 1961, my confidence, which was essential to succeed on the smooth rock, was worse. I was twenty-one years old. My father had died when I was fourteen. I had been a mediocre high school student and was faking it through my first years of college and wondering if I would ever be any good at anything.

In spite of personal mediocrity in much of my young life, somehow I found the chutzpa it took to make a long and bold lead on the granite with just a couple of pitons in for security. I thought that adventures on the granite would transfer to long and bold adventures in my school life, with my friends, and with my existence in general. But as much as I returned to the granite and as much as my friends and my own ego congratulated me for succeeding with my fumbling bouts with fear, I did not become a better student; I did not do better in the world of work.

With personal frustrations at a high, September of 1961 was marked forever in history when the East Germans built the wall separating the grayness of communism from the excitement of a West Germany emerging with burgeoning capitalism after World War II. As the wall in Berlin rose, I was called by my hero John F. Kennedy to serve in Fort Hood, Texas, as part of the National Guard call-up designed to let the East Germans know America was serious about defending Germany.

It was off to Texas for ten months to a very shallow and lonely existence. The frustrations of Fort Hood were greatly exacerbated by the fact there was nothing to climb other than the cement beams of the Fort Hood bleachers at the post stadium. Even worse, I received letters from my Alpenbock friends describing the great climbs they were doing in Little Cottonwood Canyon. Texas was torture to me, a Rocky Mountain kid used to going to the mountains. My time in Fort Hood had evolved into one of those tough times of life when you are hating what you are doing and have no spiritual substance to fall back on. There was no belief in a cause, nothing that gave me a raison d'etre and lifted life to the point of noble sacrifice.

My active Mormon friends in my guard unit seemed to do well at Fort Hood, but for me—in spite of being born and raised in Salt Lake City, and being a fifth-generation descendant of pioneer apostle Orson Pratt, and having played starting guard as a kid on the Grandview Second Ward team—I had not taken to Mormonism. My father was a Southern Baptist and my mother was a jack Mormon, and they did not preach Mormonism in our home.

Then Fred Snow (name changed to protect the guilty) came along. Snow was a klutz. He was plump and was wired together in a strange way that caused him to look like a stringed puppet when saluting an officer. As his right hand lifted in salute, his left hand would also rise at least half as high in strange tandem. Once he changed a lightbulb in the barracks and could have been changing two.

Snow's breath was foul and he talked smack into your face. Worse, he had recently returned from a Mormon mission and must have won "missionary of the month" because he seemed hopelessly locked in the mission field even though he was now just another dog-faced trooper at Fort Hood. His failures at the rifle range and at running early in the morning, his sleeping in when he should have been at kitchen duty and other military malfeasances were compensated for, in his mind, by preaching Mormon gospel day, night, twilight—anytime. Snow's bunk was right next to mine so I was his main missionary target. The intensity of his attack was heightened by my own poor judgment in telling of my ancestor Mormons and the ward basketball team. Snow caused my suffering to seem eternal, like hell itself.

One night, I faked sleep while Snow droned on. Suddenly, he stopped talking somewhere in the fourth missionary lesson (without flannel board), and slipped a small book into my bunk next to my head. It somehow got into the pocket of the pants that I wore on guard duty the next night.

On guard duty, in spite of the general military order to "walk my post in a military manner, observing everything within sight or hearing," most of us at Fort Hood had developed various bug-out techniques. Mine was to look sharp until rounding the corner of Building 367-A; there, well hidden from the officer of the day, I would curl up in a little nook under a stairwell where there was a light above. Most often I would sleep, which would have deserved a court-marshal if I'd been caught, but no one I knew had ever been caught. When I sat down in my bug-out nook, the little book Snow had tucked under my pillow pinched the top of my leg. I pulled it out and, yikes!! it was the Book of Mormon.

Oh, well, I thought, becoming less defensive by having achieved a comfortable posture, I have left the lusty novel I had received from the "Satan of the Barracks" somewhere else, so, well, maybe I will just have a peek at this thing. I started to read.

Why have I roamed so far afield from my original subject—Little Cottonwood Canyon and spiritual deprivation? For under that soft night-light, in a dark Texas night, in humidity so thick you sweat through your battle fatigues under the arms, I began a spiritual journey that would take me back to Little Cottonwood Canyon where nature and God would combine to give purpose to my life.

I hid the book Snow had given me. I could not give Snow any idea I was reading the book regularly. He would have dragged me to the creek during field maneuvers and dunked me well enough to be a Mormon, something I wanted desperately to avoid. I read the book in the latrine when lights were out in the barracks, in my guard duty hideaway, behind trees and bushes while on field maneuvers, and lots of other secret places. I avoided mentioning it to my climbing buddy Rick Reese, also serving time at Fort Hood, who was an active Mormon. I could trust Reese with my life on a climbing rope, but I didn't know what his missionary spirit might be if he knew I was reading the book.

After ten months of active duty, I returned from Fort Hood and went back to college part-time, spending most of my spare time climbing in Little Cottonwood Canyon. One glorious climb led to another. Only a climber can conceive of the splendor of being the first to climb, along with a few friends, in a magnificent canyon such as Little Cottonwood. Imagine standing at the bottom of the canyon each visit and saying to your partner, "What new climb shall we do today?" Today, the new climbs are almost all gone and many of the classic climbs suffer lines of climbers waiting their turn.

There was much more than climbing going on with me right after my return from Fort Hood. Hanging around the Union Building coffee shop at the University of Utah, I had met Kathy Carling. She was taking more and more of my time and generally diverting me from what I considered the more serious aspects of life. Little did I know at that point that what we were doing was very serious. And as I write this thirty-two years later, we are still serious after five children, three grandchildren, many ups and downs, and a fantastically wonderful marriage.

Kathy did not understand then why I climbed. She still doesn't. I didn't understand her incredible artistic abilities. I still don't. We have always had this gulf between us. It is a difficult and troublesome gulf: me, the climber and mountaineer who will go off on occasion for weeks at a time; her, the artist who can still get so involved in her work that I just exist on the side.

We call this gulf the price we pay. The price for having individuality, for the right to be ourselves. In an ironic and strange sort of way it allows us to cherish even more the good stuff we do share and the bad stuff we would like to get rid of but never seem to be able to. One thing is for sure, we have stopped the suffering of trying to change each other. At least until tomorrow.

But Kathy had more to offer me than the irony of an independent dependency. Born and raised in a faithful Mormon home, she had a deep and uncompromising view of the gospel of The Church of Jesus Christ of Latter-day Saints. Not that she was self-righteous, she wasn't. And she was no prude. Kathy was just worldly enough to engage this Mormon investigator who didn't want to embrace the gospel. Had she been a gospel prude, she would have been no good as a missionary. Kathy and her four siblings married five non-Mormons. They converted every one of us.

On a spring day, I would gather my scratchy pitons and my rope, and head for Little Cottonwood Canyon in my blue Volkswagen beetle along with Rick Reese, Bob Stout, Curt Hawkins, or one of the Reams. I never let on to my partners how many crosswinds were blowing through my mind on those climbs.

I knew I was in love. But I was a junior in college, working forty hours a week to afford tuition, books, and car payments. I was a climber, and the independent lifestyle that demanded—I thought I would be a "world-class" climber—made me resent my love instincts and my college life.

My big conflict was spiritual turmoil. The guy with the bad breath and the preachy closeness at Fort Hood had started something (I still don't really want him to know that, he was so obnoxious!). Kathy and her family had aided and abetted Fred Snow. It was not the superficial quality of their Mormon life that attracted me, it was the fact that they seemed so deeply happy as a family. I had gotten in the habit of free food on Sunday afternoons at the Carlings', and they were a family that prayed, gossiped, talked, and laughed. Raised with a loving but alcoholic father, laughter had died at some point in my own family. It was wonderful to experience that laughter again.

My visits to Little Cottonwood, to climb or to just contemplate, were filled with the great questions of youth. Do I love Kathy enough to marry her? What about her family—would they demand I become a Mormon? Do I want to investigate the Mormon Church further? If I accept Kathy and Mormonism, how will that divert me from a career in climbing?

As I climbed in the canyon, the normal tug-of-war between fear and hope that is inherent in scaling vertical rock raged within me. That conflict went on near the center of my head. It raged where the spine meets the head, where the reptilian instincts abide. It was guttural and atavistic.

Overlaying these fundamental and basic mental struggles were the complicated questions of love, career, and religion. The outer brain, where hope and fear evolve to choice and thought and commitment, seethed with feelings and conflicts. My future life depended upon this struggle, for it would be the choices of the outer brain that would guide my life but the Cro-Magnon forces of the spine that might force the issue. We talk about crossroads, we read poetry by Robert Frost and others about choices, but there are really few times in life when it all comes down to a singularity of hope, purpose, desire, and commitment. I felt it deeply at that moment in my life's crucible.

My life was a black hole. All thoughts, feelings and emotions seemed to come rushing into the center like light itself. But nothing came out. I could not talk to anyone. If you had asked my climbing partners about such conflict raging within me, they would be puzzled. I said nothing.

It was mostly to Little Cottonwood Canyon that I took these passions. Partly because they were so powerful, I could not let them dominate my daily existence. I went about life rather calmly on a daily basis. Up early, off to school, lunch, off to work, and evenings for study was a routine that passed the days in automatic fashion. But the turmoil was never far below the surface, and when it rose like a Loch Ness monster, I had the presence to command it to the deep to wait for a climb in Little Cottonwood or a time when I would go to the canyon to contemplate.

I have often wondered why our surroundings shape us so. The human species survived because we have observed, internalized, and adapted to the demands of our environment. Had we not done so, we would not be here. Our species would have gone the way we condemn thousands of other species by imposing a change on them in the environment that they cannot adapt to. Our relationship to the places surrounding us is basic, internal, and fundamental to our survival as human beings.

The hard lesson of place is that we must adapt to our surroundings or die. We cannot cut corners. Eventually, if we do, the demands of the poisonous surroundings we build will outrun our survivability.

But the soft lesson of place is also true. That is, place can shape us in ways that put us in harmony with nature. The lessons of place can be instructive, beneficent, and loving in their scope. In Little Cottonwood Canyon the only hard lesson of place that I courted as a climber was the law of gravity. If I didn't follow the climbing rules, if I somehow cheated on the proper ways and means of scaling rock, it could kill me. I had been painfully reminded of that in October of 1965 when one of my best friends, Mark McQuarrie, in the midst of a gorgeous and artistic climb, had been killed on the cliffs of the canyon. Little Cottonwood and the hard lesson of gravity had demanded a payment.

For me, the thought that the canyon could be a killer entered my mind but never possessed it. Thank goodness for the kindness of the irrational concept we all possess: "It could never happen to me." Otherwise, we would be frozen in our tracks.

On a fall day, when Little Cottonwood was crisp with color and filled with rushing cool water in the stream, I sought solitude in a special place where the sound of water almost drowns out thoughts. Strangely, this noise acted as a mental filter; the thoughts that rose above the din were helpful ones.

On this day, as I contemplated my future with or without Kathy and with or without the Mormon Church, I began to think of the carving of the stream on the canyon bottom. Hundreds of thousands of years had caused the stream to erode to its present level, and that had occurred hundreds of thousands of years after the canyon was cut by the great Pleistocene glacier. Was time as important then? To an inanimate glacier, solid ice hundreds of feet thick and moving slowly only several feet a year, perhaps time is of no concern. The cycle of life is unimportant. No mouth to feed. No schoolwork to get done. No work to go to. No worries like mine—that a dad who had died suddenly of a heart attack at the age of fifty-one would pass on genetic junk that could cut my life short. No doubt, humans are different from glaciers.

If time is nature's way of making sure everything does not happen at once, my time on Earth had to be thought of differently than the kind of time my geology professor spoke of. That was my first thought, there by the stream. But the second thought was more powerful and more relevant to my existence. If I could contemplate the notion of time and the canyon couldn't, wasn't time *my* concept? The canyon could not utilize time, except to be a captive of it. I had control over my time, limited as it was. I was free to choose. The canyon just waited for the ice to melt, for its walls to erode and expose gorgeous granite, for trees and shrubs to take root, for water to run, for animals and then Indians to roam, for pioneers to carve stone. And, eventually, for anxious young people to come to climb and to contemplate.

My time on Earth, I thought, was terribly short. Yet, inside was a perspective that was boundless. Untamed by time was a realization that I possessed qualities and feelings that were not captive to the veil of tears of an earthly existence. No way to prove that one, I guessed. But every day my existence contained moments of timelessness. Just the ability to sit by a stream in the canyon and think was proof enough. But what of the timeless love I already had for Kathy? For the sheer joy I felt as I passed smoothly over the vertical rock of the canyon while climbing? For the feelings of goodness I had when I helped someone who needed my aid and thanked me sincerely? I thought of my grandmother's wonderful love when I took care of her in her terminal days of an Alzheimer's fog, of my mother's sacrifice of working two jobs to help me and my brother through school. And even the timelessness of a father, sometimes drunk and violent but more often kind and loving. Nights at Derks Field, watching the Bees and being timeless with my dad, now eternal.

The canyon was giving me an eternal perspective. In its solitary and timeless existence, it provided the contrast I needed to measure my own uniqueness. I began to feel that it would be a terrible shame to shape my life solely on the idea that I would be gone in just a few decades. That would lead to an empty existence, one dominated by short-term pleasures, by failure to have a family, by the danger of slipping into a narrow and selfish existence—even if it might be climbing. My nature revolted at that idea. The thoughts that had led to this startling and stunning conclusion had been started by a slow-carving stream surrounded by the colorful hues of the gold of autumn's Gambel's oak—and by the glory of Little Cottonwood.

On another climb in the canyon, perhaps two weeks later, I hunched on a comfortable ledge, securing my climbing partner Rich Ream with a rope as he climbed. It was an idle moment, punctuated by the hot sun glaring off white granite, when I began to reflect on the truth of granite.

I thought of the architecture of the great white rock. Blocks larger than houses hung and seemed suspended in space, defying gravity. Cracks split from the shifting forces of fault-block movement, and runnels of running water sometimes ran straight and true and other times took on the zig-zagged energy of a lightning bolt. Cracks offered climbers a path, a place for fingers and feet to climb. Cracks allowed the placement of climbing anchors and forged a link with sensibility and security in the irrationality of the vertical world.

Cracks, faces, slabs, overhangs, couloirs, ridges, and summits combined in the granite of Little Cottonwood to form truth. Gravity was responsible for this truth's formation. Truth was simple. If gravity was too much for the forces of granite architecture, rock simply fell to a place where gravity allowed it to remain. If water and wind eroded it, the granite simply yielded slowly over time. Perhaps nature is "beautiful" to us because it reflects this essential truth of physics. There is no room for deceit, only for the truth of gravity, wind, rain, snow, and glaciers.

Succumbing to the truth of the forces of nature made granite beautiful. Sitting on my lofty perch and securing Rich as he climbed up toward me ushered in a new thought, one that radicalized my brain. The thought was painful because it embattled my precious sense of unbridled individuality: "If granite and nature are subject to the laws of gravity and physics, and if the result is a symmetry and order that creates beauty, then doesn't the same principle apply to man and his desire to become personally beautiful? Doesn't man's beauty depend upon the same kind of submission to superior forces that carve granite, earth and sky? And shouldn't a person therefore submit to those things that cause beauty—aesthetics, ethics, love, hope, and—yes—religion?"

Finally, the culminating thought in my spiritual journey in Little Cottonwood Canyon was embedded in my head. Finally, the synthesis of a young life, of a life desiring independence, freedom, and expression, had occurred. I realized that I could find independence separate from religion but I could only find truth and beauty by submitting to heavenly forces. And, realizing that my life would demand a form of truth and beauty— powers necessary to love a wonderful woman, to have children, to teach, to contemplate—I was converted!

Returning from our Little Cottonwood climb that day with Rich Ream, I still could not vocalize, even to a dear friend such as Rich, what had happened. But that decision, coupled with the understandings achieved at other times in Little Cottonwood Canyon, was the axle of my life upon which all other forces have spun since that day.

I have come to learn that place is an arena of the soul. Since my formative years in Little Cottonwood, I have learned to love other places that have also given me spiritual sustenance through hiking, biking, skiing, climbing or just reflecting. Places such as Lupine Meadows, the Lower Saddle, Grand Teton, Leysin, Chamonix, Aquille du Midi, Denali, Baxter's Spire, the Thumb, Twin Peaks, Kliene Schiedegg, Storm Mountain, Meadow Shutes, Powder Park, Mount Superior, Lake Blanche, Mount Moran, Huana Potosi, Jungaraju, Hunter Canyon, the Needles, the Maze, and others reverberate in my mind as not only places of adventure and thrills but also holy places of contemplation.

Shouldn't we view God's handicraft as temples? Shouldn't we respect the few remaining places upon Earth that are wild, uninterrupted, and unblemished? Though it is true that we can and do occasionally improve on nature and that people must make a living, it is also true that the forces of development on an increasingly crowded planet threaten to tear down our temples of nature. We must seek wisdom and temperance that go beyond the equilibrium of the marketplace. For only there is found the spiritual essence of a place like Little Cottonwood Canyon. Shouldn't we offer a tithe to save God's natural handicraft on Earth?

Ted L. Wilson is the former mayor of Salt Lake City and is currently the director of the Hinckley Institute of Politics at the University of Utah.

". . . ADAM BEGAN TO TILL THE EARTH, AND TO HAVE DOMINION OVER ALL THE BEASTS OF THE FIELD, AND TO EAT HIS BREAD BY THE SWEAT OF HIS BROW. . . . AND EVE, ALSO, HIS WIFE, DID LABOR WITH HIM." (MOSES 5:1.)

SACRED GROUND

LYMAN HAFEN

T WAS A STEEP CLIMB UP THE SHINARUMP RIDGE. JOEY AND I clawed and hoisted ourselves toward the sky—closer and closer to the top of Shinobkaib. We hugged the rough conglomerate ledges as loose rock gave way beneath our feet, and stopped only for Joey to watch a lizard whip into a crevice, or for Joey to climb back into a cool recess of rock, or for Joey to pick up a smooth slab of shale that in his eyes bore some resemblance to the shape of Utah. Or for me to catch my breath.

I had wanted to make this climb since I was a boy. Had I been privileged to do it then, I would have seen it the way Joey was seeing it now: close-up, eyes fixed on the ground, his mind logging every detail within a short radius of his feet. For me, now, having just turned forty, it was a much broader experience, one with no dimensions in space or time. There was eternal significance in this climb for me. We were working our way to the top of the Mountain of God.

In Southern Paiute mythology, Shinob is the younger god, brother of Tobats. Kaib means mountain. This was sacred ground to the Shivwits and the Pahroos who inhabited this land when my Mormon forebears arrived here five generations ago. And it has held special meaning for me ever since a day more than thirty years ago when my father took me for a ride in the truck through the Washington Fields. We were probably on our way to look at a bull or a stud horse or somebody's stack of hay; all I remember for sure was Dad pointing at a huge mound of earth that lifted out of the landscape and stood inclined like a monument against the horizon. "They call it Shinobkaib," Dad said. "It's a sacred place for the Indians."

I was entranced by the big mesa. It looked like it had just one day up and lifted out of the earth—like the upper plate of a giant's dentures yawning into wide-open position. The top of the mountain was a flat, inclined table sloping upward toward the southeast. Not until much later would I learn that Shinobkaib is a remnant of the Virgin Anticline, an isolated piece in a complex geologic puzzle that has been scrambled here where the Great Basin, the Mojave Desert, and the Colorado Plateau meet in a collision of rock. I wondered then, as I have ever since, how you would get to the top of it, and when you did, what you might find up there that was so sacred.

Joey was seven, still a year shy of accountability in our Mormon culture where baptism is offered at age eight. He knew nothing of the significance of this climb to me. He was only vaguely aware of his own place in this landscape. It means nothing to him yet that he belongs to the sixth Utah generation, that all thirty-two of his great-great-great-grandfathers and grandmothers came to this place with nothing more than their faith and what they could carry in a wagon—to make it blossom as the rose. He does not yet understand that he is treading sacred ground.

I let Joey pick our way up the lower talused slope. Before long, we'd gained enough altitude to begin taking in the vast broken landscape around us. A beautiful pattern of hay fields lay like a quilt immediately below us. One field was cut in fresh windrows and in another, hay haulers were loading a pickup as it idled down the rows. Between fields snaked freshly oiled black streets with building lots marked out along them. Intermittent new homes in various stages of completion sprouted from the freshly turned earth. Beyond the fields rose the jostled and random sand hills, lava-capped ridges and sandstone bluffs that form the distinct and chaotically beautiful landscape of Utah's Dixie.

As we rose higher above the valley floor we saw more and more rich color. The town of Washington lay washed in green below us. Pine Valley Mountain rose powerfully blue out of its pink sandstone base to the north. The Arizona Strip stretched off like a wrinkled blanket to the south. The soft flowing Virgin River rolled around green tamarisk bends below us, and to the southwest, the Virgin Gorge opened like a ragged wound in the earth.

I looked over my shoulder to the west and discovered that the black ridge separating St. George from Washington blocked the view of the valley where I'd grown up. I would not be able to see the white iceberg of a temple smack in the middle of that valley. How strange, I thought, since the temple seemed always to be part of the view from any place I had stood during my life in this country.

Maybe it was fitting, though. Maybe it was only right that this ridge, called the Mountain of God by the Paiutes, and that building, called The House of the Lord by my people, did not stand within sight of each other. After all, the sacred stories of the Paiute had grown naturally out of this ancient landscape, just as naturally as this ridge had lifted out of the earth and onto the horizon. The hallowed stories of my people had been carried here from somewhere else, from a sacred grove in upstate New York, and imposed upon the landscape, just as our handsome white temple had been imposed upon a basalt foundation pounded into a swampy alkali slope in the neighborhood where I had grown up.

When we finally reached the top of Shinobkaib, Joey and I sat on the edge of a long shinarump slab. Our shoes dangled in the air 300 feet above the crusty alkali floor. Joey's eyes were full of wonder. I began to tell him of his great-great-great-grandfathers. Of John G. Hafen, who left his verdant home at the base of the Swiss Alps and came to this desolate place in 1861 to grow grapes and melons and peaches along the Santa Clara Creek. Of Samuel Knight, whose family had been close to the prophet Joseph Smith from the beginning of the Restoration. Samuel had accompanied Jacob Hamblin here to make peace with the Indians in 1854. Of Robert Dockery Covington, who joined the Mormon Church in Mississippi before the Civil War and came to the town of Washington to oversee a fledgling cotton industry.

Joey listened intently, his eyes fixed on the landscape, the only landscape he has ever really known. I asked him if he thought it was beautiful and he looked at me with a crooked grin. I wondered how he actually perceived it. Was it forbidding and ominous, or was it beautiful and inviting? Did it make him feel small and insignificant in the world, or did it swell his heart with joy?

I knew this sight, so overwhelmingly moving to me in such a comfortable moment, had not appeared so beautiful to my forefathers when they first laid eyes on it more than a century ago. They had all come from places where beauty presented itself in shades of green rather than gray and rust. They had all been cast out of Edens eastward—from the foothills of the Alps, the hardwood forests of New England, the rolling plantations of the South. From Mother England herself.

I wondered if I had passed on to Joey the same genetic connection to those faraway landscapes that I felt—the feeling of familiarity and longing that pictures of those places awaken in me. I must have inherited those connections from my ancestors, from people of faith who left behind their beautiful places of birth and came to this desert to build a new life from nothing. No, it was not beautiful to them. It did not become beautiful until the second or third generation when it began to be seen through the eyes of those with full stomachs, reliable water supplies, comfortable homes, passable roads, and hearts buoyed up by hope.

There was little rain to settle that dusty existence. Instead, the parched earth heartily accepted a continuous stream of tears, blood and sweat. Perhaps Charles Walker, an Englishman of noble descent and the acknowledged poet laureate of Dixie, reflected the thoughts of those early Mormon settlers best in an 1862 journal entry:

This was the hardest trial I ever had and had it not been for the gospel and those that were placed over me I should never have moved a foot to go on such a trip. . . . Traveled over mountains and vallies, thro rivers, dust, sand, rain and snow for 26 days. Arrived in St. George on the afternoon of the 9th of Dec. 1862. . . . St. George is a barren looking place. The soil is red and sandy. On the north ranges a long high red rocky bluff. On the east is a long black ridge of volcanic production. On the west the same.

On the south runs the Virgen river, a shallow, rapid stream. . . . To look on the country it is a dry, parched, barren waste with here and there a green spot on the margin of the streams. Very windy, dusty, blowing nearly all the time. The water is not good, and far from being palatable. And this is the country we have to live in and make it blossom as the Rose. Well its [sic] all right; we shall know how to appreciate a good country when we get to it. . . .

This from one of St. George's most romantic citizens. This from the man perhaps best equipped of all those early settlers to perceive beauty in the landscape. But beauty is hard to see through shimmering waves of scorching heat and wilted crops and dying children. A pristine sandstone canyon was nothing more than one more obstacle to cross. A billowing white cloud was one more false hope.

Joey and I were both entranced by the sheer power of the scene before us. I showed him where Utah ended and Arizona began. I stretched my finger to the southwest and explained to him that at the foot of those mountains, the Beaver Dam Mountains, some of the oldest rocks on earth were exposed. Vishnu Schist. I swung my arm to the east and showed him the ancient Hurricane Fault where the Colorado Plateau begins its eastward sweep. I pointed out the moenkopi in the clay hills below us, the shinarump member we were sitting on, the chinle layer below the lava-capped ridge to the west, the moenave of the rusty bluffs behind us, the kayenta of the red mountains to the northwest, the white and orange Navajo sandstone of Snow Canyon and the Zion towers, the Temple Cap at the top of Zion's West Temple on the far eastern horizon, and the pink Wasatch formation at the base of Pine Valley Mountain. I told him how the flat black ridges snaking all around us had once been the bottoms of stream beds where molten lava had coursed like rivers, then cooled, solidified and remained constant to this day; how erosion had washed and blown away the loose earth, leaving only those ridges protected by hardened caps of basalt and shinarump and sandstone.

Joey listened closely. He looked off toward the northeast at the high plateau in the distance where hints of pink and red peeked out of the blue. "What's that?" he asked.

"It's Kolob Mountain," I said.

"What's Kolob mean?" he asked.

"It's a very high place," I said. "Kolob means the place where God lives."

"I thought Shinobkaib means the place where God lives," Joey said.

We sat suspended in the bright desert morning, surrounded by sky, anchored to the earth only by its gravity. I told Joey two stories that morning on Shinobkaib.

Long ago, before the trees and the rocks had been made, there were only Tobats and Shinob, the two gods. They're the ones who the Indians say made the rocks and the trees and the people.

Tobats and Shinob were standing on a tiny speck of land, and everywhere else there was water.

"We must make more land," said Shinob. "Tuweap, the earth, must be on top of the water. It must stand up high so the living things can find it."

"Go and make more earth," Tobats said. "Call someone to help."

Shinob called to wootentats, the hummingbird, who was small but could stand in the air while he worked.

Shinob asked wootentats if he could build and the hummingbird told him to call swallow who builds with mud. Shinob sent wootentats to bring swallow.

"Can you build land out on that water?" Shinob asked swallow.

Swallow said he could make a place out on the water for the earth to rest.

"Do it now," said Shinob. "Do it quick."

Swallow plucked a leaf from beneath Shinob's feet, flew outward, and dropped it on the water. He plucked another and laid it beside the first, then another and another and another. He worked for many days and hummingbird helped him.

Shinob watched their progress and one day raised a strong wind loaded with sand. It came across the sky like a great storm cloud. When the wind reached the blanket of leaves, it lay down to rest. The sand dropped down upon the blanket and spread everywhere. Some of it ran over the edge and tied the earth down so it could not float away.

With great excitement hummingbird and swallow flew back to the somewhere they had come from. They met the robin and told him of the place where he could take his family and live. They went to the eagle, to the crow, and to all the other birds and animals and told them the earth had been made so they could have a place to go and make their homes.

But all of this movement came about too fast and too soon, for there was no food yet growing on the new earth. Tuweap was not ready yet for the living things to come. They soon grew hungry and they saw that they would perish unless the gods helped them.

Shinob heard their cries and went to see what was the matter. "There is nothing here to eat," they told him. "We are hungry. We will soon have to die."

Then the birds rose up like a cloud and began to swirl around in great flocks in the sky. They chattered and flapped as the animals huddled together in their hunger and sulked. The birds left Tuweap and flew far away into the western sky. They were gone for a long time.

When the birds finally came back they flew everywhere over the land, carrying seeds of grass, and seeds of berries, and seeds of trees. They scattered them all over the face of the land. Shinob sent strong winds to roll the sands around until the seeds were all covered.

Soon the earth began to crack and little green shoots came thrusting upward from the soil. In a little while the earth was green and there were *berries and fruits and grass and roots for the living things to eat. They grew fat and were once more happy together.*

Then I told Joey this story:

First God said, "Let there be light," and there was light. Then he divided the light from the darkness and called the light day and the darkness night. And that is what he did on the first day of creation.

Then God said, "Let there be a firmament in the midst of the water," and it was so, and this firmament divided the great waters under it from the waters above it. And he called the firmament heaven, and that was what he did on the second day.

On the third day, God said, "Let the waters under the heaven be gathered together unto one place, and let there be dry land." And he called the dry land earth and the gathering together of the waters he called the sea. And God said, "Let the earth bring forth grass, herbs, and fruit trees." And he saw that all things he had made were good.

Then, on the fourth day, God made two great lights, the lesser light, or the moon, to rule the night, and the greater light, the sun, to rule over the day.

On the fifth day, God said, "Let the waters bring forth the moving creature that hath life, and fowl which may fly above the earth in the open firmament of heaven." He created great whales and all the birds.

When it was the sixth day, God said, "Let the earth bring forth the living creatures." And there were all kinds of animals. Then He said to His Only Begotten Son, "Let us make man in our own image, after our likeness." And it was so. Then He said, "Let them have dominion over the fishes of the sea, and over the fowl of the air, and over the cattle, and over all the earth."

"Then he rested on the next day," Joey said. "I know that story."

He said he knew it because it was in the Bible and he had learned it in Primary. I told him it was also in the Pearl of Great Price, and I started to explain to him how the Pearl of Great Price also says God created all things spiritually before they appeared on the earth.

This was enough for Joey. He scampered off after a lizard and left me to contemplate on my rock in the sky. I recalled something I had recently read about the Paiutes being animists—how they believed that everything that moves has life, how they attempted to live in partnership with nature. The clouds, the breeze, water, and fire all were alive. They sought constantly to appease the forces of nature.

I thought about how my pioneer ancestors came to this place with a charge to subdue it and have dominion over it. They believed in a doctrine that assured them they would be punished for their own sins, and not for Adam's transgression. Nonetheless, they also knew they were heirs to Adam's legacy. They were heirs to ground that had been cursed for his sake, and in sorrow should they eat of it all the days of their lives. Thorns and thistles would it bring forth, and by the sweat of their faces would they eat their bread until they returned to that same dust from which they were made.

The indigenous Paiutes had earned their living by the sweat of their brow, with a reverence toward the deity that had created their existence, that had created this earth on which they lived and from which they took their sustenance. Then the pioneering Mormons entered their world. Jacob Hamblin and others, including my great-great-grandfather Samuel Knight, befriended them and taught them new methods of cultivation and planting, of diverting streams and controlling water and supplicating blessings from a Father in Heaven.

My ancestors built a temple, a great white edifice with a steeple that reached toward heaven and an endowment that taught them about the creation of the earth and their proper relationship with it. They built homes of rock quarried from the nearby ledges, and cut lumber from mountain forests scores of miles away. After years of failure they finally harnessed the Virgin River and spilt her waters across the white crusted soil. They lived in dire poverty for a full generation before the land finally and miraculously began to blossom as the rose. And it has blossomed ever since.

. . .

In 1942, Maurine Whipple published an article in *Look* magazine on the peculiar lifestyle of Mormons in southern Utah. I have a crackling yellow copy of that magazine on my bookshelf. In it is a photo of my grandfather's family kneeling at their chairs turned backward to the dinner table. My father is not more than ten years old in this photo. His fingers are clasped beneath his chin. The straps of his overalls run under the collar of a crisp white shirt. My grandfather is kneeling at the head of the table, his tie cinched tight, his spectacles in place, his head bowed as he prays upon a table brimming with food. Next to Grandpa is Grandma, kneeling near the cast-iron stove at the corner of the table nearest the kitchen. Eight of the family's twelve living children surround the table, each in a distinct, impatient praying position.

I am aware, whenever I look at the photo, that everyone in it played a part in getting that food from the garden, from the field, from the orchard, from the barnyard, to the table. They were literally reaping what they had sown, enjoying the bounties of the earth that sustained them. It also strikes me, as I consider my father in the picture, that he is probably not concerned with what his father is praying but more likely caught up in thoughts of his ranch of bony horses out back in the grape arbors. Bony horses were as close to toys as my dad came in those post-Depression, World War II days. They were white-crusted bones of cattle, individual vertebrae, leg joints, hoof bones, which—with a little imagination added—could be magically transformed into miniature animals. One dead cow could resurrect into a small herd. Death became life, refuse became wealth. Those simple bleached chunks of bone mystically transformed into elaborate ranches in the backyard dirt of a little boy's universe.

Even at that early age, my dad had grasped a sense of capitalizing on a natural resource that would otherwise go unused. It was an innate sense of productivity, of subduing the earth, of asserting dominion; and it was thoroughly reinforced by his culture and his religion.

The social, economic, and religious realities of my father's youth taught him that the practical use of the land and its natural resources—production—translated into survival.

That was the immediate concern of my Mormon ancestors: Survival. There was nothing romantic about their approach to the land. Their lives were zealously devoted to production. It was not only a physical imperative but a spiritual obligation. That devotion to productivity has carried through the generations. It is more than cultural. It is religious. For this reason, I believe, many rural Mormons approach today's environmental issues from a stance that does not seem politically correct to much of the rest of the country. We have a natural tendency to balk at the concepts of legislated wilderness, moratoriums on dam building, federal laws that show greater concern for certain species of plants and animals than for the lives of unborn children.

As I sat on that shinarump ridge and watched a hay truck idle down the row of a bright green field, I recalled early summer mornings when I pitched bale after bale of sweet-smelling alfalfa onto the truck bed, sweat rolling off my brow, arms aching, lungs straining. I had experienced only a token sampling of what it was to produce, but I had witnessed firsthand where my sustenance came from, and knew in my own heart that my survival as a human being was rooted in the earth that I walked on.

These fields will be gone, I thought. They'll be gone by the time Joey is old enough to lift a bale of hay. Neighborhoods will cover them and the water that once flowed over them—water still diverted from the river in the same place the pioneers finally harnessed it a century ago—will spill out of golden faucets and spray forth in perfect patterns from pop-up lawn sprinklers.

I looked down upon it now and realized that indeed my forefathers had succeeded. They made it blossom as the rose. They survived. They created, as Charles Walker once wrote in a song, a place which "ere long, everyone would admire." Brigham Young admired it as early as the 1870s when he built a winter home here. It was rediscovered in the early 1980s as condominium projects began emerging from the same ridges where the Anasazi built their own dwellings a millennium earlier. And now, it seems, people from all over the country have begun to admire it to the point they are moving here by the score.

As I sat there looking over it all, I came to another realization. I belong to a transitional generation. The last of the old-style producing Mormons are fading. They are clinging to their fields by the tips of their earth-blackened fingernails, baling $100-a-ton hay on acres worth millions. The new generation is turning away from production, and part of it is starting to lean toward preservation. My son Joey does not play with bony horses out back in the grape arbors. He sits before a computer and guides a sleek craft through cyberspace, while in the backyard, automatic sprinklers water nothing but lawn that is mowed weekly, packed in black bags, and set out for Monday morning pickup.

Somewhere between the poles of production and preservation lies the proper path. Stewardship has as much to do with the romantic concept of preservation as it does with the practical notion of production. We have succeeded in making the desert blossom; now we are faced with finding ways to sustain a quality of life far beyond what the pioneers ever envisioned. This means continued production. But it also means sincere and meaningful moves toward preservation. We need more water, but our hearts and our minds and our spirits tell us that there are places where dams should not be built. We need more electricity, but there are places where power lines should not be strung. We need more shelter, but there are spaces that should not be filled with homes. And there is ground, such as this, that should always remain sacred.

I do not worship the earth or the trees or the animals. I worship the God who created them, and out of respect to Him I am obliged to respect them. God cast Adam and Eve out of the garden with a charge to till the earth by the sweat of their brow. It is a charge that still applies these many generations later. If we are to survive, we must continue to till the earth and take our sustenance from it; yet tilling, to me, implies wisdom and reverence.

Joey's face reappeared over the edge of a rock. He had sneaked up on me while I was thinking. His smile nearly melted me and I was transfixed by his eyes. In those little-boy eyes I saw the joy and hope of the world. I peered deep into eternity and my heart swelled with a strange mixture of happiness and concern.

"Look, Dad," Joey said. He pointed over my shoulder toward the black ridge to the west. "What's that poking over the hill?"

I looked carefully and caught sight of the grey dome and needle barely visible above the black ridge. I noted the position in relation to the block "D" painted on the taller black ridge further west. It had to be. It was. The top of the temple's steeple was visible from the top of Shinobkaib. One sacred place connected to another.

"Come here, Dad," Joey said. "Come and look at this." I got up and followed Joey across the flat ridge of Shinobkaib. He led me to a point several yards away and showed me something very strange. It was a huge slab of weathered concrete. The first section was in the shape of a square as large as someone's living room. From there, a longer, narrower rectangular slab extended toward a final piece in the shape of a triangle. I finally understood that what I was looking at was a huge concrete arrow. Slight traces of yellow paint still clung to parts of the arrow.

I remembered hearing pilots tell of such arrows laid out at key points along the landscape. In the days before radar and radio contact, mail pilots followed the arrows from point to point, readjusting their direction at each arrow. Here, on this sacred ground of the Paiute, lay a signpost for latter-day travelers. Joey and I stood at the tail of the arrow and readjusted ourselves in the direction it pointed.

It pointed toward Kolob Mountain.

Lyman Hafen, a fifth-generation southern Utah Mormon, is a nationally published writer of fiction and nonfiction, whose family still ranches on the same land settled by his great-great-grandfather in 1869.

"YEA, ALL THINGS WHICH COME OF THE EARTH, IN THE SEASON THEREOF, ARE MADE FOR THE BENEFIT AND THE USE OF MAN, BOTH TO PLEASE THE EYE AND TO GLADDEN THE HEART; YEA, FOR FOOD AND FOR RAIMENT, FOR TASTE AND FOR SMELL, TO STRENGTHEN THE BODY AND TO ENLIVEN THE SOUL." (D&C 59:18–19.)

A DESCANT OF PRAISE AND THANKSGIVING

MARILYN ARNOLD

Y FEELINGS ABOUT THE NATURAL WORLD HAVE, FOR MANY YEARS now, been a mixture of affection and awe. In wilderness I have sought both excitement and repose, mystery and understanding, solitude and companionship, release and purpose. There, more than anywhere else, I find a perfect blending of the two sides of my nature ("And the spirit and the body are the soul of man." [D&C 88:15.]). I am a vigorous—though admittedly aging—physical being, and I am a quickened spiritual being whose heart has been undeniably changed in the manner described by King Benjamin and Alma. I cannot separate the love I feel for Father and Son from the earth they created. I think it is a gift, this love, like speaking in tongues or composing music. I have learned not to question it but to accept it gratefully.

I also believe that, like the capacity for languages or music, many have this gift to some degree. Something in mortals craves a home with a view, seeks a rocky shoreline, buries flower bulbs in the earth, longs for the smell of pine, picks up rocks and examines them, hones in on deep-cut canyons, irresistibly follows rivers, smiles at a bouncing cottontail, pauses at a band of red igniting the evening sky. At the last full lunar eclipse, for example, Kristine and Jerry Twiggs and I were pulled to the Arizona strip wilderness south of St. George, where we could watch the event far from city lights. Their teenage daughter, Aubree, wanted to go also, even though it was a school night, and both she and her parents would pay dearly for their indulgence the next day. Nonetheless, sleep can be made up, eclipses cannot. On finding a good observation spot, we hopped into the back of Jerry's pickup, settled ourselves with binoculars, snacks, cushions, and blankets, and watched, transfixed, while the whole event unfolded in the eastern heaven. The passing clouds, catching and letting go of the light, only enhanced the drama.

> *He that ascended up on high, as also he descended below all things, in that he comprehended all things, that he might be in all and through all things, the light of truth;*
> *Which truth shineth. This is the light of Christ. As also he is in the sun, and the light of the sun, and the power thereof by which it was made.*
> *As also he is in the moon, and is the light of the moon, and the power thereof by which it was made;*
> *As also the light of the stars, and the power thereof by which they were made;*
> *And the earth also, and the power thereof, even the earth upon which you stand.*
> *And the light which shineth, which giveth you light, is through him who enlighteneth your eyes, which is the same light that quickeneth your understandings;*
> *Which light proceedeth forth from the presence of God to fill the immensity of space—*
> *The light which is in all things, which giveth life to all things, which is the law by which all things are governed, even the power of God who sitteth upon his throne, who is in the bosom of eternity, who is in the midst of all things. (D&C 88:6–13.)*

I felt the reality of scripture powerfully that night, as I have on many other occasions. Although I am not a regular journal keeper, I have made occasional jottings in recent years. One of them proves that some days it is enough just to walk up Webb Hill, right here in my own neighborhood.

> *21 August 1994. Sunday night . . . I leave for Provo-Orem in the ayem, but tonight I buzzed up Webb Hill to move a bit and to take in the evening. Just as I reached the top and turned to come down, at dusk, a full moon began edging up from behind the far cliffs to the east. An involuntary "ahhh" sighed across my lips. It was magnificent—the biggest moon I've ever seen, perceptibly climbing the sky and popping free of the cliffs. The setting sun cast a glow on those red cliffs that was almost surreal, and the moon was a huge amber light above them. The very air was the color of the ruddy western sky, and every line was sharp and clear. No haze, no dust. I was torn between staying on the hill until dark—then stumbling down—or walking down and watching the moon change position in the sky as I descended. I came down, eyes fastened on that magnificent moon against a backdrop of horizontal lines. One small cloud brushed over the moon in odd pieces and configurations—now cutting off the top, now taking bites off the side. I am most aware of my aloneness when I have no one with whom to share such an experience.*

More dramatic, perhaps, were nights on the trail in the Sierra Nevada, above timberline, when we lay on our backs on cold granite slabs and picked out the constellations spinning their deliberate courses across the firmament. There were other nights when the skies were less friendly but no less awe-inspiring. I remember one night in particular in the High Uintas, when Joan Fisher and I hiked the last several miles to the accompaniment of approaching thunder and lightning. We arrived at a workable campsite near a high alpine lake at dusk, just as large raindrops began to fall. Hurriedly, we pitched a tent and crawled in with our sleeping bags. The storm arrived with a fury I have rarely experienced. The ground shook as the thunder and lightning moved up the mountain and directly over us. Rain drove at our tiny tent and drenched it in seconds while the merciless wind tried to rip it out of the ground. We lay there, huddled away from the soaked tent sides, too full of wonder to speak, the air crackling with great bursts of light that easily pierced the thin nylon sheeting above us.

Within an hour, the storm had tracked across us, and we emerged to greet stars and moon behind disappearing clouds. We did what we could to dry our bags, and after making a soggy supper, we crawled once more into our dripping, drooping shelter. A few hours later, we awakened to a distant rumble, and the whole process repeated itself. We lay there, watching and listening, feeling again the trembling of the earth before the might of its Creator. After our return, I happened to make a journal note about this particular experience. The hike was undertaken, I am now reminded, in celebration of a huge book completed after seven years of labor. The manuscript was on its way to the Connecticut publisher at last, and off I went for a change from the intense headwork of the last months. My hurried personal entry captures something of the event's immediate spiritual impact:

> 25 August 1993 . . . The mountains were incredibly beautiful—meadows full of flowers, streams, and ponds; lakes (we saw 40 in 3 days) deep and clear; snow fields; stony crags; and no people. That's all it took—I was reborn, restored, renewed. A huge thunderstorm Tues. evening and again in the night shook the ground and soaked the tent, but it was glorious. Exciting. We heard it approaching way below us, and it gradually moved right over us, with lightning so bright it hurt our eyes even behind closed lids. We were delighted with it. Joan is always pretty lively, but I have never seen her so animated. She was in heaven and pleased with everything. Life is good. How well I know it.

Our joy in the mountain storm reminded me of what Varua Cooper, mother of my friend Jan, said after experiencing a ferocious hurricane in Samoa several years ago: "I wouldn't have missed it for the world!" I believe she was eighty at the time, or close to it. I can also remember her joining us for a day hike to Pear Lake in the Sierra Nevada, when she was easily in her seventies. She was not a "hiker," per se, and had no boots or rough clothing. I can still see her in a cotton housedress, walking barefoot up that steep eight-mile trail, hands behind her back, torturous city shoes dangling from her wrists, face flushed with the effort. But she loved the earth and all living things, and no flower or bird escaped her sharp eye.

Much as I love the mountains, my soul's true home is the sandstone desert. What is it about stark horizontal and vertical lines in counterpoint that register their beauty in the pit of my stomach? There is a completion of me, somehow, in a deep red-rock canyon, a completion that I experience and express as worship. I remember many a lovely night when Molly Brog and I—Molly was as true a desert rat as ever lived—sat around a little campfire in the bottom of some deep sculptured canyon, leaning against our packs and singing every hymn we could think of. And Molly, who sings a lovely alto, always knew all the verses.

Wilderness, I have discovered, is not only about the natural world. It is also about the people who love it. And about the God who created it and seems to pour out his peace on those who love it. There are Jan Cooper and Renée Van Buren, botanists and birdwatchers of the first order, who have eagerly spent whole vacations and more than a month's pay for a glimpse of the California condor. There is Diane Chamberlain, who would drive a thousand miles for one silent conversation with a bear-claw poppy. There is the solitary Sierra Nevada flutist who sent his haunting melody shimmering to us across the highest of remote mountain lakes, easing our burden as we descended from a steep, craggy ridge, packs riding hard on sore hips and shoulders.

The longer I am acquainted with wilderness, the more I understand the need of Jesus, of Enos, of Joseph Smith, and others to leave the distractions of the workaday world in order to pray lengthily, to meditate, to seek guidance and resolve—or pardon—without interruption. Whether in desert, woods, or waterside, human beings—and even Christ himself—have communed with the Spirit and been blessed with instruction, commitment, and renewal. Many is the time I have sought out at dusk the hills southeast of St. George, sometimes with a troubled heart, to sit before distant bluffs aflame with the setting sun, there to offer quiet prayers both of gratitude and supplication. More than once, I have seen a gigantic moon squeeze from those same darkening cliffs and leap into a star-spangled sky. More than once, I have returned home with the assurance, as Robert Browning has said, that God is indeed in his heaven.

I remember hearing Dallin H. Oaks, then-BYU president, describe how he came to resolution about a particularly difficult decision facing Brigham Young University. After much discussion and prayerful consideration of the matter, he still had no clear idea as to what should be done. At last, he decided to leave the campus and take himself and the problem to the mountains where he could talk with the Lord, uninterrupted, for many hours. He did that, and when he returned, he knew what course the university should follow.

I am not much of a television buff—I suspect wilderness types rarely are. Books are more my line for indoor recreation. Nevertheless, twice a year, at general conference time, I do the unthinkable. I add a small radio to my bag of trail mix and head for the hills, careful to pick a spot where no one else is likely to appear. On those semiannual occasions, wilderness and technology merge compatibly for me. And if the choir happens to sing "How Great Thou Art," all the better. Out there, my mind and heart catch the wavelength of prophetic utterances, and I focus readily on matters of ultimate significance. The trivial, the petty, the material, drop off my brain like withered leaves. Henry David Thoreau went to Walden in an effort at self-purification. Something of that same impulse sends me into the wilderness at conference time. The difference between the Concord pilgrim and the St. George one, however, may be my consciousness of overwhelming debt and my deep need for divine help in the refining process.

2 April 1995 . . . Today is General Conference Sunday. As I often do, to get away from the distractions of the household, I took a portable radio and went out to listen in the sanctity of the bluffs and arroyos of my beloved desert. The morning session so moved me that I sat bowed on a rock for some time, dissolved in tears and prayer. I have decided that I want to live on a higher plane than I do now. I want to reach toward what the prophets have—that sweet combination of humility and spiritual certainty. I want to be totally loyal to the Church and its leaders. It is as if President Hinckley (newly chosen and sustained) has some special capacity to reach my stubborn heart. . . . I want to do as Lamoni's father did—give up all my sins in order to know God. I want to live more purely, more holily. Elder Maxwell made a stunning connection between ancient and modern requirements of sacrifice. We no longer are to sacrifice animals on the altar, he said; we are to sacrifice the animal within us and thus become the spiritual offspring of Christ.

Last autumn I enjoyed a rare, and relatively short, hike with a neighbor on Cedar Mountain in southern Utah. This is a woman with seven children ranging from four to twenty, and her opportunities for hiking are sorely limited. As we paused to take in the beauty of a mountain lake surrounded by meadow and trees, she exclaimed, "I can almost feel my soul healing." In the past two months, she had undergone a tonsillectomy, a nasal passage reconstruction, and emergency abdominal surgery. She had also seen three young daughters through tonsillectomies, and this was her first outdoor excursion in a long time. We talked about our very real need to reach beyond four walls, to leave concrete and blacktop and steel—and even tile and formica, not to mention computers—to get earth and rock under our boots, to breathe unpolluted air beneath a cloud-bannered sky, to give ourselves entirely to the natural day and to contemplation of God's purposes for his children.

Twenty-five yards down the trail on a backpacking trip, I can literally feel what I jokingly call "the poison" draining out of my system. It is a release like none other; it is also a homecoming, a reunion with the earth and its Creator, and a sense of returning to my real self, my better self, my spiritual self. I am not a pantheist, I do not believe God dwells in the flower or the rock. I believe he is a person. But just as I discover Eudora Welty by living with her eloquent words, and Georgia O'Keeffe by examining her extraordinary paintings, so do I move toward understanding the Lord by contemplating the natural world he created as well as the words he spoke.

On another note, almost academic (I am, after all, a university person), I remember seeing inside a magazine cover several years ago a "Genesis Checklist," with boxes before such items as "be fruitful," "multiply," "replenish the earth," "subdue it," "have dominion over the fish of the sea, and over the fowl of the air, and over every living thing." All the boxes were checked but the one beside "replenish the earth," and the checklist was illustrated with a picture of the earth shriveled like a prune. We have, indeed, been adept in the departments of exercising dominion and subduing, by our prideful misunderstanding of those terms. We have not done so well in the matter of replenishment. Although "replenish" once meant mainly "to fill," the prefix *re-* suggests "to fill again," that is, to restore to original fullness, or to replace that which has been taken out or used up.

A few weeks back, while working on another project, I ran onto an editorial written by Joseph F. Smith nearly a century ago. It was published December 15, 1905, in the *Juvenile Instructor,* once the official organ of the Deseret Sunday School Union. Although the essay's principal thrust is the value of commonplace things and daily life, these lines from the second paragraph confirm our obligation of replenishment:

> The great failure of many of our modern ways—for some day we shall see how mistaken and vain our ambitions have been—is that we substitute man's ways for God's ways. . . . We were created to inhabit, beautify, and replenish the earth.

The word "replenish," in the sense employed by Joseph F. Smith, refers to something in addition to "multiplying," to begetting and bearing children. We are to multiply, yes, but then something else, too. It has always seemed to me that the concepts of fruitfulness and replenishment extend and enhance the concept of multiplication, which is quite numerical. The animal kingdom multiplies by instinct, and the plant kingdom carries seeds for its own multiplying; but human beings, as gods in embryo, are blessed with understanding of the significance of procreation, and with the capabilities of fruitfulness and replenishment as well as multiplication. I think we are to practice a spiritual replenishment that extends into our families, society generally, and the natural world. Christ called it living more abundantly.

I am greatly impressed that an important and lengthy—and stunningly beautiful—segment of the temple endowment ceremony is the presentation of the Creation, in both its spiritual and its temporal aspects. Why, I have thought, is the beauty and magnificence of the Creation emphasized so grandly if it is not of immense concern to us, if we are not to take special care to conserve and tend it, even replenish it? And when we consider, as Moses learned, that "I, the Lord God, created all things, of which I have spoken, spiritually, before they were naturally upon the face of the earth" (Moses 3:5), the responsibility is increased. Forms in the natural world have spiritual as well as physical being. The language in the Book of Abraham does not lump members of the plant kingdom together, but attaches importance to each species individually. The Gods were concerned for "every plant of the field before it was in the earth, and every herb of the field before it grew" (Abraham 5:5).

Clearly, plants and animals have spirit and divine purpose: "And out of the ground made I, the Lord God, to grow every tree, naturally, that is pleasant to the sight of man; and man could behold it. And it became also a living soul. For it was spiritual in the day that I created it. . . ." The concept of "benefit" and "use," when applied to the natural world, is as much spiritual as temporal:

> Yea, all things which come of the earth, in the season thereof, are made for the benefit and the use of man, both to please the eye and to gladden the heart; Yea, for food and for raiment, for taste and for smell, to strengthen the body and to enliven the soul. (D&C 59:18–19.)

It is well for us to remember that the earth, like its inhabitants, has an eternal destiny that is part of our own:

> And the end shall come, and the heaven and the earth shall be consumed and pass away, and there shall be a new heaven and a new earth. For all old things shall pass away, and all things shall become new, even the heaven and the earth, and all the fulness thereof, both men and beasts, the fowls of the air, and the fishes of the sea; And not one hair, neither mote, shall be lost, for it is the workmanship of mine hand. (D&C 29:23–25.)

It is eminently clear to me that in reverencing the natural earth and the plants and animals that were carefully created and placed on it, we are reverencing "the workmanship of [God's] hand." We do not show our respect for the Artist by harming or dismissing the work of his hand. We should not miss the fact, either, that the Creator values the earth so much that he intends to restore the whole of creation in its fullness, with "not one hair" or "mote" lost. More than that,

> This earth, in its sanctified and immortal state, will be made like unto crystal and will be a Urim and Thummim to the inhabitants who dwell thereon, whereby all things pertaining to an inferior kingdom, or all kingdoms of a lower order, will be manifest to those who dwell on it; and this earth will be Christ's. (D&C 130:9.)

Although not by conscious design, in recent years, nearly all my meager attempts at poetry, at least those triggered by an outdoor experience, seem to end up as celebrations of Christ's redemption. That is what is affirmed for me in the natural world, with its cycling rebirth out of death, its resplendent light despite clouds and storm, its ability to renew me and restore sanity to life. Even now the earth is becoming a kind of sacred interpreter to me, perhaps in anticipation of its final destiny. It reminds me of ultimate truths; it clears my mind of daily clutter and quickens it to higher, sweeter realities; it enlarges my soul and increases faith and hope. The two personal pieces below—one a journal entry, the other a poem—were prompted by the same phenomenon in different years. Going to the south shore of Utah Lake for the annual event that the pieces describe became something of a ritual for me when I lived in that part of the world.

15 February 1987 . . . Storm threatening, but I was feeling restless, agitated in spirit. So I put my studies aside and asked Jan if she'd like to go out walking on the south end of Utah Lake. Although the snow is still pretty deep up here in Woodland Hills [home for many years], the valley is free of it— or was. We parked on the road and scampered through weeds to the shoreline where great piles of ice had blown and crunched against the meeting place of water (ice) and land. Some piles were as tall as houses, and the chunks were 7–8 inches thick, all crystalline and delicate despite their size. They shattered in long thin spears, like the finest chandeliers. A cute black dog adopted us, and we walked west while clouds lowered over the mountains to the east and south until we saw nothing but stretches of ice—hollow blue in its spiked depths—and gray water blending with the sky. It was like the north Atlantic, or Lake Michigan. The dog ventured out on a stretch of thin ice (thawed, then refrozen—we had walked on the lake where it was thick, hopping from chunk to chunk across thin connections) and broke through. Finally, after repeated efforts, he got onto ice that held him, but was afraid to move. When he stepped, the ice crackled and gave. So he stood, several feet from shore, and whimpered. Our encouragement didn't help much, but finally we coaxed him along to a sturdier spot, and he tiptoed to safety. I have never seen a dog walk so carefully. He was so happy to reach shore that he waggled all over, jumping on us and laughing with relief. Gradually the snow closed in, and we walked back by the road as darkness edged toward us. The dog, a resourceful mutt, caught and ate two or three mice. We were walking in the snow and wind, and were pretty wet by the time we reached the Blazer. A good, good feeling—happy and at peace.

EASTER THOUGHTS

For some ten days, now,
we have succumbed to the spectacular lure
of winter's splendid surrender,
the gradual breaking of the ice on Utah Lake

and the sudden flinging of it
in great bluish heaps of thick broken crystal
against the helpless south shore—
a miracle made by March wind and other
irresistible, conspiring forces of spring.
The same forces drove us also
to the south shore,
beneath heavy hanging skies,
in search of wonder
and the soul's salvation.
> *We climbed among the tangled,*
> *gleaming spires and domes, and*
> *walked, too, across the lake's doomed*
> *expanse to touch yet other shattered mounds*
> *and crumble a thousand icy*
> *needles in our hands.*
> *And as the snow took up again,*
> *we walked back through dampening*
> *lacy air and knew the desolate*
> *orchards above us would*
> *soon be hung with Housman's snow.*
More than ever, now,
I seek this symbol,
this contract with the universe
that ushers in the battering
and smashing of ice and
the trumpeting of waking waters.
It is His contract, wrought on Calvary
and notarized each spring, his word
that death's icy prison will crack
and crumble when struck by God's breath
and capsized by the well
of living water.

I had once thought to argue my point at some length by textual analysis of several scriptures, especially those in the Pearl of Great Price that relate to the Creation. I settled for taking a page from the late Joseph Campbell. It is a mistake, he said, for preachers to attempt "to talk people into belief; better they reveal the radiance of their own discovery."* I am no good at preaching anyway, and so I offer, with some misgivings, my own, very personal, discovery.

* Reported in Bill Moyers' Introduction to Joseph Campbell: *The Power of Myth* (New York: Doubleday, 1988), xvi.

Marilyn Arnold, BYU emeritus professor of English and dean of Graduate Studies, has loved wilderness all her life and is just now beginning to write about it.

". . . THAT [JOSEPH'S] SEED SHOULD NEVER PERISH AS LONG AS THE EARTH SHOULD STAND. WHEREFORE, THESE THINGS SHALL GO FROM GENERATION TO GENERATION AS LONG AS THE EARTH SHALL STAND; . . ." (2 NEPHI 25:21–22.)

THE BEING AND PLACE OF A NATIVE AMERICAN MORMON

P. JANE HAFEN

AM TAOS PUEBLO.

Taos Pueblo indicates my American Indian tribal identity, and designates a geographic location. Being and place are inseparable.

Taos Pueblo is the most northern Pueblo of nineteen along the upper Rio Grande in what is now called New Mexico. Two adobe structures embrace a plaza divided by the Rio Pueblo. The clear water of the river is frigid as it flows down from the sacred Blue Lake in the mountains above the Pueblo. The river gives life to the Pueblo people and the crops they have cultivated annually since before Columbus.

My people of the Red Willow, *Pueblo* (or "people" in Spanish), have lived in this specific location for over seven hundred years. When I stand on the north side of the plaza, I can observe the south Pueblo where my father was born. Just beyond the four-story, terraced, conjoined dwellings of the Pueblo, I can see the towering cottonwood tree that stands beside my grandmother's home, a separate adobe building. The Pueblo itself echoes the horizon of the mountains. I can barely distinguish the kiva poles that provide entrance to the earthen underground chamber where my father worships in his first language, Tiwa. On San Geronimo feast/harvest day, I stand on the north to survey the view and to hear better the old songs. My pulse throbs with the drums as I feel the ancient blood of my people flowing through my veins.

When I consider the genetic factors in my blood, I know that I have inherited a predisposition to gall bladder disease, high blood pressure and diabetes, an intolerance to the milk fats and sugars introduced by European contact. Nevertheless, the same blood that annoys my current life also endured the onslaught of virgin soil diseases carried by European domesticated animals: measles, smallpox, chicken pox. My particular ancestors outlasted not only virulent diseases but violent conflicts with Spanish conquistadors and American invaders. The Pueblo peoples were the only Native Americans to expel the Europeans successfully. In the Pueblo Revolt of 1680, initiated at Taos, the natives reclaimed their sovereign rights, their land, their religion. When the Spanish were readmitted twelve years later, it was according to the terms agreed upon by the Pueblos. Though I may not be the fittest, I know I have the genes of survival.

In addition to physical survival, Taos culture is among the most intact of native peoples. The ritual practices of the Taos people have weathered the influences of Hispanic Catholicism, American capitalism, inquisitive anthropologists, and the admiration of bohemian artists such as D. H. Lawrence, Willa Cather, Mary Austin, Frank Waters, Georgia O'Keeffe, Ansel Adams, John Marin, Andrew Dasburg, and other lesser known writers and painters. Native individuals have maintained their Taos practices despite systematic attempts to mainstream and acculturate them through government boarding schools, education, and missionary proselytizing. Undoubtedly, the traditions will also endure beyond the current fascination of New Age pseudospirituality and Santa Fe chic as well.

The nuclear age has brushed against the Pueblo, too. Los Alamos, the Manhattan Project, and Trinity site are not far from Taos. In desperate poverty, neighboring tribes have succumbed to economic temptations. The earth of Laguna Paguate is scarred by an abandoned uranium mine. To the south of Taos, the Mescalaro Apaches have contemplated accepting storage of nuclear waste. Taos has managed to persevere and keep their land from nuclear development.

However, the people have not remained untouched. After all, tribal member Tony Luhan married salon hostess and New York socialite Mabel Dodge, and became the model for the character Eusabio in Willa Cather's *Death Comes for the Archbishop*. For most Pueblos, the harvest feast and other seasonal celebrations fused with Catholic saints' days. Iconic symbols of tribal leadership include silver-knobbed canes given to the Pueblos by the colonial Spanish governor Juan Oñate, Abraham Lincoln, and, in 1980, Governor Bruce King of New Mexico. No culture can remain artificially preserved in the pristine past; accommodations ensure survival as a community keeps what is most sacred to them.

For the Taos people, the emblem of sacred endurance is the Blue Lake. Like the Pueblo itself, the lake and its surrounding lands have a history that reflects the land policies toward many native peoples in the United States. When the Treaty of Guadalupe Hidalgo procured Mexican territories for the United States government in 1848, the agrarian Pueblos were not accorded legal sovereign rights as Indian nations or land title because in the language of the treaty they were not "wild, wandering savages." Indeed,

Wilford Woodruff later declared that the Pueblos must have been Nephites because of their "advance[d]" civilization.[1] Nevertheless, through a series of court cases, the Pueblos won the right to be considered independent Indian nations with titled land. Taos' victory was short lived, however, as Teddy Roosevelt in 1906 seized the Blue Lake and 30,000 surrounding acres for the Carson National Forest, coincidentally named after Kit Carson, who forcibly removed the Navajo from their tribal lands. The sacred Blue Lake area was opened to public recreation. Taos people could use it for religious purposes only three days of the year, provided they advised the Forest Service in advance.

This land loss was more than simple transfer of title; it was the loss of ontological wholeness. Land seizures and exploitation from the United States government and individuals are not only illegal and immoral but they violate the very inalienable rights on which this country was founded. Elizabeth Cook-Lynn, Crow Creek Lakota author, explains how the loss of the land assaults the essential rights of native peoples:

> *The very origins of a people are specifically tribal and rooted in a geographic place, mythology, and land that are inseparable, and language is rooted in a specific place, in the discourse of American Indian nationalism.*[2]

Nevertheless, the freedom to practice religious beliefs and other aspects of the constitutional Bill of Rights are abrogated on Indian reservations.[3] Reservation lands, despite being sovereign nations, were viewed in terms of their usefulness, but "usefulness" only as defined by those in power. This particular land, the Blue Lake, and its interconnectedness with how the world is organized and life is sustained, rituals performed and language learned, transcends economic commodifications and legal definitions by a colonial power.

With the tenacity that has kept indigenous culture alive during 500 years of European contact, Taos fought fiercely to regain their land. Any expendable financial settlements were rejected. Finally, in December 1970, Richard Nixon signed a bill that returned the land to the tribe. To maintain the sacredness of place, public access is denied.

Taos is resolute in maintaining its tribal sovereignty. The Pueblo closes to the public during the winter season, losing substantial revenues earned from tourist visits. Tribal membership currently is restricted by requirements of residency and knowledge of the Tiwa language. Cameras, tape recorders, video cameras are forbidden at public ceremonies. The tribe charges fees for admission and daily camera access at the Pueblo. Certain areas of the Pueblo are always closed to the public. Regardless of the complicated effects of these policies, the tribe has the legal right to determine its own degree of involvement with mainstream society in whatever manner it deems will best preserve the integrity of the tribal community.

The good of the tribal whole exceeds the needs of the individual.

Individuals are defined in terms of tribal community. One of my children was assigned a family history project for school. He was given a four-generation chart. Besides personal information, he was to observe mobility in American society, occupational patterns, and European connections. We recognized that most of his predecessors are educators. Although my father was working away from Taos when I was born, everyone else we know in that genealogical line was born, lived, and died in Taos—no migratory pattern there. When my son asked about my grandparents' occupations, I told him to record that they were Indians. Their life had no compartmentalization for vocation, leisure, religion, and so forth. They did whatever the tribe expected them to do. Their tasks included ritual preparation of the youth, farming, hunting, baking bread in the earthen *hornos,* singing, dancing, and ceremonial participation, all determined by the natural cycles of the earth and whatever the tribe deemed necessary.

My own life is much more complex. Often, I am tempted to classify my life by the various identities I assume: race, gender, mother, wife, Christian, Mormon, middle-aged, urban, academic, professional. No matter the immediate role, though, these aspects are inseparable and comprise the whole of who I am. Nevertheless, race is omnipresent. One of the most complicated aspects of my life is that racial connection and Mormonism. Because I was raised with the label "Lamanite," which lumps all indigenous and Polynesian peoples together regardless of tribal differentiations, I combated and continue to confront basic theological, racial, and cultural misunderstandings. I am no longer amazed to learn that most Mormons I know believe the "Lamanite" designates a racial category and the dark side of a good/evil dichotomy rather than, after generations of Nephite and Lamanite intermingling in the Book of Mormon, a political classification. The recent linguistic shift from "Lamanite" to "children of Lehi" is encouraging. I am aware of uncomfortable issues between the LDS Church and native peoples, just as I acknowledge the difficult racial history of this hemisphere. Despite my own inner conflicts, common areas of beliefs contribute to the wholeness of my existence.

"The Lamanite shall blossom like a rose" was the church slogan that saturated my youth. I was never quite sure exactly what the phrase meant, but I believed it to be a good promise and commitment. When read in context of the scriptures and verses that follow, a sense of place emerges:

> But before the great day of the Lord shall come, Jacob shall flourish in the wilderness, and the Lamanites shall blossom as the rose. Zion shall flourish upon the hills and rejoice upon the mountains, and shall be assembled together unto the place which I have appointed. (D&C 49:24–25.)

My Mormon historical sense tells me that these verses are about Salt Lake City and the Mormon settling of the American West. My literary native sense reads these lines to indicate some familiar concepts: Zion is both a state of being—pure in heart—*and* a geographical designation; identity is inextricable with place; flourishing and rejoicing are coupled with hills and mountains—nature; establishing the house of Jacob in the wilderness is linked to whomever may be classified as "Lamanites." Indeed, the house of Jacob will be accountable for its relationship with "Lamanites."

It is impossible to consider Native American issues and Mormonism without considering the Book of Mormon. I do not have a clue whether my people are literal descendants of Book of Mormon peoples, nor do I think it matters. For me, the Book of Mormon offers precepts for living rather than historical accounts. Some basic tenets are recognizable, however. Nephi promises survival contingent upon place for his descendants: "[Joseph's] seed should never perish as long as the earth should stand" (2 Nephi 25:21). These descendants may be literal or metaphorically may include indigenous peoples. As heirs of Columbus,[4] not all native peoples encountered the explorer, but all were impacted by his actions; not all native people may be Book of Mormon-connected, but they may be affected by the cultural context of the book and its promises of survival. At the beginning of the twentieth century the native population of the United States was less than 200,000, diminished from an estimated population ranging from 10 million to 100 million at the time of European contact. This decrease, as Ojibwa writer Louise Erdrich observes, would be comparative to the United States population diminishing its current size to the city of Cleveland.[5] Considering the history of disease, violence, and assimilation, it is miraculous that any natives have physically survived and that the population is flourishing. Even more amazing is that we have retained our languages, cultures, and identities. Perhaps we have not perished, in part, because we have clung to our identities through the places we are and despite systematic efforts to remove us from those places.

A second familiar ring from the Book of Mormon is the idea of a promised land. While this premise has troubling accouterments of ideological and political supremacy of essentialism, it nonetheless demonstrates the significance of place. In cultures where livelihood depends on the earth rather than labor in the marketplace, the promise of a place is crucial. The idea of a covenant place cements state of being with location. Indeed, the only one of the Ten Commandments that predicates a blessing on a behavior is the fifth commandment:

> *Honour thy father and thy mother: that thy days may be* **long upon the land** *which the Lord thy God giveth thee. (Exodus 20:12, emphasis added.)*

The promise is not necessarily a long life but a continuance upon the life-sustaining land. That land neither an acquisition nor a commodity but a gift from God. A stewardship of that gift includes a responsibility to the earth. To honor our earthly mothers and our fathers, our heavenly mother and father, our mother earth and father sky, is to acknowledge our heritage, the community of our genetic lineage, and the sacredness of place.

As a sacred place, the temple evokes for me the familiarity of ritual worship, rites of passage, and an erasure of the divisions of our worldly existence. The elements of temple ceremony have the spirit of tribal cultures, yet do not replicate precise practices. Washings and annointings acknowledge the integral wholeness of body and spirit. The endowment reminds us that the natural earth is a gift. Sacred ritual clothing is required to worship. The promises made within the temple integrate our spiritual commitments into all aspects of our lives. We enter celestial rooms, dressed alike, hierarchies erased, rejoined in a communal whole.

The community of Mormonism is one of the most appealing aspects of my faith. I have hope in the ideal, as represented in the scriptures, that all are alike unto God (2 Nephi 26:33), that no one is esteemed above another (D&C 38:24–25), that we charitably care for one another without qualification or seeking our own (Moroni 7:42–48). The diversity of our spiritual gifts and individual callings contribute to our communal wholeness, just like the ritual responsibilities of my grandparents contributed to the tribal whole. This idealistic hope consoles doubts and soothes pains of history and racism.

Being a Native American Mormon is not without trials and absurdities. Because our chapel's street address is on Arrowhead Trail, I live in the Arrowhead Ward. When I was the Arrowhead Relief Society president, I was identified with place, calling, and some type of ironic native identity. I try to reconcile many apparent conflicts of the separate spheres of my life: being an indigenous person in an urban, mechanized society; a female in a male-dominated church; a person from the earth living in a society that has little regard for the earth; being Taos and Mormon. In his great vision, Black Elk, Oglala holy man, describes a sacred hoop that demonstrated the paradox of diversity and unity:

> And I saw that the sacred hoop of my people was one of many hoops that made one circle, wide as daylight and as starlight, and in the center grew one mighty flowering tree to shelter all the children of one mother and one father. And I saw that it was holy.[6]

I do not consider my Taos heritage to be mutually exclusive with my Mormon beliefs, but regard them both as part of a greater whole of all circumscribed truths. I am Mormon, and I will always be Taos Pueblo.

ENDNOTES

1. "I view my visit among the Nephites one of the most interesting missions of my life, although short. I say Nephites because if there are any Nephites on the continent we have found them among the Zunis, Lagumas (Lagunas), and Isletas, for they are a different race of people altogether from the Lamanites." Wilford Woodruff to President John Taylor and Council, 13 September 1870, in *The Lamanite: Past, Present, Future,* compiled by Jeffrey L. Simons and John Maestas (Provo, Utah: Brigham Young University, n.d., typescript), 121.

2. Elizabeth Cook-Lynn, "The American Indian Fiction Writer," *Wicazo Sa Review* 9, no. 2 (fall 1993): 31.

3. For a full discussion of a history of the relationship between American Indians and the Bill of Rights, see John R. Wunder, *Retained by the People* (New York: Oxford University Press, 1994).

4. Anishinabe writer Gerald Vizenor coined this phrase to refer to native peoples who have been influenced by Columbus's navigational error of 1492. See Gerald R. Vizenor, *The Heirs of Columbus* (Middletown, Connecticut: Wesleyan University Press, 1991).

5. Louise Erdrich, "Where I Ought to Be: A Writer's Sense of Place," *New York Times Book Review,* 28 July 1985, 1, 23–24.

6. John G. Neihardt, *Black Elk Speaks,* with an introduction by Vine Deloria Jr. (Lincoln: University of Nebraska Press, 1979), 43.

P. Jane Hafen (Taos Pueblo) is an assistant professor of English at the University of Nevada, Las Vegas.

"WHERE THERE IS NO VISION, THE PEOPLE PERISH." (PROVERBS 29:18.)

THE MORMON VILLAGE: MODEL FOR SUSTAINABILITY

RON MOLEN

HERE IS NO SINGLE STRATEGY THAT DEALS MORE ADEQUATELY WITH full resource use, an abatement of pollution, and even the search for more labor-intensive activities than a planned and purposive strategy for the human settlement."
—BARBARA WARD AND RENE DUBOS, *Only One Earth*

My first trip to Utah was in 1936 when I was seven years old. A hot, July trip from Chicago took three days, and we arrived just as the sun set and the vast green valley opened up. Evening lights sparkled like fireflies, and the air was fresh and cool. My father had grown up in Springville and felt the excitement of returning after a long absence. We stopped for a moment in front of the night-lit temple and tears came to my father's eyes. I somehow understood that this was a special place, a holy place.

We visited my great-aunt, Olive Anderson, the wife of the early Utah photographer. She lived in Mapleton, which at the time was still a classic Mormon village. She lived on a one-acre plot in a small adobe-and-stucco house with a flat-roofed front porch used for drying apricots. An unpainted fence enclosed the front yard filled with wildflowers. The rest of the land was used for orchard, vegetable garden, and chicken house. Even at seventy, my aunt claimed she raised most of her food. The irrigation ditch out front, with a bridge across for each house, was lined with huge cottonwood poplars, creating an umbrella over dusty, unpaved streets. At the time I could not imagine a more exciting place to live. Water. Dirt. And great trees to climb. A special place. A holy place.

During the rest of my childhood in Chicago, I thought of Utah as a kind of utopia. I read about the building of villages throughout the Great Basin in priesthood manuals that even suggested someday we would build cities again. I was fascinated with the whole idea of community, particularly after I read *The Mormon Village,* written by my father's cousin Lowry Nelson.

I later came to Utah and studied, then practiced architecture, but I did not find a culture interested in planning or architecture. Somehow that tradition had been lost. And today as I look over the same valley that inspired me as a child, a sea of brown air often hovers over the land, and the wall of high-rise buildings that dwarf the temple have grossly demeaned the sense of place. The question repeats itself over and over again: What have we done?

We have yet to earn the right to live in this exquisite mountain setting. Yes, we have made the desert blossom, but we have paved more of it, and worse, we seem to have no idea where we are going.

Brigham Young had a clear concept of how the Great Basin should be developed. Based on Joseph Smith's model, the self-sufficient Mormon village was replicated over and over again. A commonwealth of villages was the result, a community of communities. Each village controlled its own water, food, and fuel resources, and population did not exceed the carrying capacity of the surrounding land. Irrigation systems developed through cooperation were responsible for the success of these dynamic new communities. The Mormon village exerted a strong influence on other planned communities in the West that somehow never achieved equal success.

Despite the success of the Mormon village in an agrarian society, it never made an adequate adjustment to the industrial society. Unlike the Amish who held fast to their agrarian roots, the Mormon culture moved toward mainstream America and abandoned its agrarian tradition. Today, Utah is like any other western state; its main crop is hay for feeding cattle. Virtually all of its food and much of its fuel is imported, and fresh water in the mountains is no longer safe to drink. Self-sufficiency is a thing of the past.

Like the rest of America, there exists an uneasy feeling among the people here, a sense that something is amiss, that we are headed in the wrong direction. Gridlocked traffic on the freeways, pollution alerts, crime, drugs, violence, and political corruption are constant reminders that Utah suffers from the same problems as other highly urbanized states. And for good reason. Utah is the sixth most urbanized state in the nation.

What would Brigham Young think of a strip city from Brigham City to Payson that included three million people? Certainly that is the direction we are going. And there is every reason to conclude that traffic, crime, and pollution will also double if not triple. A drive through the urban sprawl along I-15 shows development not at peace with the land. It shouts greed and hostility, not cooperation and community. Little wonder there are so many mentally disturbed people in this grotesque environment.

In the cycles of nature, we observe birth, growth, then decay and death. This cycle also exists for communities. They spring up, grow, then begin to decay when there is no longer space for new life, and some die when the quality of life is so negative that they need to be abandoned or destroyed. Sensing we are in that cycle, many feel a strong need for change. But what should we do? How should we change?

Fortunately, there are some exciting new concepts that have a great deal in common with early Mormon community traditions. Sustainability is the label for a dynamic new philosophy that proposes well-defined solutions to the current malaise. A 1987 United Nations Conference Report called "Our Common Future" defined sustainability as "Not a fixed state of harmony, but rather a process of change in which the exploitation of resources, direction of investment, orientation of technological development, and institutional change are made consistent with future as well as present needs."

One hundred and fifty years, or seven generations, should be the new basis for all decisions. This is a far cry from a corporation's focus on earnings per quarter, a metaphor for a way of life that is clearly not sustainable.

A sustainable system must guarantee continuity, and a sustainable way of living must nurture the environment, focusing on the air, water, soil, and fuel necessary for life support. A sustainable system must also provide a solid economic base that serves the community first, a vital social order that achieves authentic community, and a healthy democracy that empowers all its citizens.

Unfortunately, modern cities where the great majority live don't begin to live up to these qualifications, and that is true of Salt Lake City, Ogden, and Provo. Air and water pollution, remote sources of food and fuel, political paralysis, and mindless sprawl make these cities vulnerable.

This condition is unique to this century. Cities in the past were sustainable because they had to be. Nineveh, a city in the Fertile Crescent around 800 B.C., had enough water, food, and fuel in the immediate environment to support a population of 800,000 citizens. The Paris that Benjamin Franklin visited had enough food-generating capacity from the surrounding farms to support over a million people.

The Mormon village was an extraordinary example of a sustainable community. The pioneers knew well the critical systems on which they survived. Water from winter snow, stored in some form of reservoir, fed the planted fields in the hot dry summer. Fuel was harvested from the surrounding forest. Life was organized around the resources of the countryside, and population did not exceed the carrying capacity of the land.

When the nation shifted from an agrarian to an industrialized society, the modern city lost immediacy with its life support. Water, food, and fuel often came from remote and not always dependable sources. Much of Salt Lake City's food presently comes from Florida, California, even Mexico. Fuel is imported from the Near East. No military general would accept so tenuous a supply line. We have learned to accept and trust a system that is not sustainable.

There are many levels of sustainability, but only a new planned community could mine the full potential. We need a model like the Mormon village, a model that could demonstrate how far we must go, how much we must change to achieve an authentic sustainable way of life. Once a working model was built and analyzed, many of the solutions could be applied to urban centers and small towns that are losing population. And like the Mormon village, the model could be replicated over and over again.

Sustainability requires community, a critical ingredient that has almost disappeared in this country. The self-centered, me-first "individual in society" would need to be replaced by a group-oriented "person in community."

Like the Mormon village, a sustainable community must have a clear strategy or master plan for survival, citizens who fully comprehend the strategy, and a dogged commitment to make it work. The community must also have control of life-support resources, maintain a scale that is comprehensible, achieve a social, political, and economic structure where people feel empowered, and develop technologies that respond to the needs of the community first. We need a model that fits the postindustrial society as well as the Mormon village fits the agrarian society.

The sustainable community must have a strong connection with nature and the sustaining land. Its members must have a strong connection with each other.

CONNECTION WITH NATURE

1. The Cycle

All life forms function in a cycle. Waste returns to the soil and generates new life, and the cycle repeats itself over and over again. Recently man has produced an enormous number of products (refrigerators and automobiles) that do not return easily into the system, some (industrial waste) that poison the system, and a small amount of waste (nuclear residue) that will take thousands of years before its toxicity no longer threatens life. The sustainable community will recycle products, minimize industrial waste, and reject any form of nuclear power.

Waste will be used as a resource. There will be virtually no garbage. Everything will be used in one form or another.

2. The Standard

Nature will be studied and used as the model. The house, yard, common areas, shops, schools, commercial buildings, and the community as a whole should be patterned after nature, like human settlements since the beginning of time that were often as organic as a beehive. Nature provides the discipline, the balance, the aesthetic. Every human settlement should be a special place, a holy place.

3. Protection of Natural Systems

The community should protect, even enhance the immediate environment. Natural systems violated in building the community should be restored. Lumber used for construction in the community should be replaced by planting on the perimeter a forest that would also reprocess

CO_2. Forests and wilderness are not only important environments for man but also for the animals that inhabit them. We share this planet with many creatures that have an equal right to life.

4. A Spiritual Relationship

In nature we find the source of life, and it is folly to continue to separate ourselves. Myths, traditions, rituals, and celebrations should set nature at the center of life. The change of seasons, the planting and harvest should be community celebrations.

CONNECTION WITH THE LAND

As we grow to better understand and honor nature, we will know how to use the land we require to survive.

1. The Sustaining Land

Each person requires so much air, water, and food. The land that provides these elements needs to be accounted for. The community has the responsibility to provide these critical resources. The community should be located in an area where fresh air and clean water are plentiful and sustainable, as well as a countryside capable of producing enough food for a vegetarian diet. Basic foods should not be supplied from great distances, and should somehow be controlled by the community. Farmers' co-ops and consumer co-ops could accomplish this.

2. Population

The life-generating capacity of the sustaining land should determine the population of the village. Citizens should agree to limit children to the carrying capacity of the sustaining land. Local taxes would be based on numbers in a household. Population management is critical for a sustainable community.

3. Permaculture

A new, high-density organic agriculture should replace the high-tech chemical agriculture of the present, which is a total violation of nature. Permaculture uses nature as a model and produces much higher yields. Farms would be much smaller, more labor-intensive, and with the use of greenhouses could grow fresh produce for much of the year. One farmer could support twelve families on six to ten acres. The Amish have much to teach us in this area, as do many experiments in Australia and England. For Utah, it would mean a major shift from growing cattle feed to crops for humans.

CONNECTION WITH EACH OTHER

1. Person in Community

The sustainable community requires citizens who understand that working together can yield more benefits than the individual acting alone. The Mormon pioneers were committed to the community ideal, and the success of the early settlements in hostile environments attests to their wise application of cooperation.

2. Scale

The entire community should be no larger than one and a half square miles and contained in an area with a one-kilometer radius. High-density housing would occur in clusters of single-family homes and town houses, yet one-third of the space would be dedicated to open space and parks. Neighborhoods with a population of 5,000 would have a center with a grade school, library, convenience stores, and clinics. Four neighborhoods would comprise a village of 20,000. While this scale is not arbitrary, ample sociological and planning data validate the one-kilometer radius and the population of 20,000. This was the optimum population for the Greek polis, planned cities of the Renaissance, the Mormon village, and communities in the English Garden Cities movement of this century.

3. Habitat and Workplace

The home and workplace should be no further than one kilometer apart. The need for commuting, or even the daily use of the automobile, would no longer exist. The community would be walkable, and as a result would have healthier inhabitants. An office and industrial park along with a commercial village center would be the source of employment.

4. Security, Identity, and Stimulation

The community would be a vital, exciting place to live. Research into new and improved sustainable systems, the development of a local economy with its own currency that served the community first, many opportunities for participation in the arts, and a strong emphasis on continued education would create a dynamic society. The community would also be kind and caring. The aged and infirm would have a secure place to live, and children would be given the highest priority. Social problems are difficult to solve for a nation, state, or metropolis but are very manageable in a comprehensible community.

5. Democracy

Village government would be fair and equitable. The basic plan of the community would give clear definition to the political structure. Houses would occur in a cluster, which would be part of a common. The cluster would have representation on the common council, and the common would have representation on the neighborhood council. The four neighborhoods would choose their representative on the village council. Democracy would function both from the citizen up to the leadership at the top and from the leadership down to each citizen.

The sustainable village would not be socialistic nor hopelessly utopian: it would simply be the kind of sustainable community that existed a hundred years ago.

A commonwealth of sustainable villages could be an intelligent alternative to the existing urban center. Assuming the Salt Lake Valley has approximately 200 square miles of usable land for development and agriculture, it could support a commonwealth of fifty sustainable villages of

20,000 people, and still have two-thirds of the land in forest or agriculture. One million people could live compatibly in a green and pollution-free environment. A good public-transit system could speedily handle travel between villages, reducing the need for automobiles and the resulting pollution even further. A community of communities could support museums, professional sports, the arts and sciences just as well as a large urban center.

Unfortunately existing cities and small communities have many built-in barriers to achieving sustainability. Yet they can be improved immensely. Seattle presently has a long-range plan for dividing into small, sustainable villages; the cities on the Wasatch Front should do the same. Throughout the country many existing smaller communities and new communities are being planned to reduce the need for the automobile. If they are not a sustainable village, they are at least headed in the right direction.

We need the model village to demonstrate to existing cities and small towns the full potential of sustainability.

Population growth should not occur in the cities but rather in the small towns that would greatly benefit from increased numbers and that could achieve sustainability quickly. The agriculture of the state would have to shift dramatically, and the obsession with large families would have to stop. The Wasatch Front does not need more freeways and brown air. We can add lanes, but we can't add more biosphere. We need self-sufficient communities where commuting is not required. And the small town, once successful as a Mormon village, needs to be revitalized. Life again must relate to nature, the sustaining land, and to community. Life should be lived in a special place, a holy place.

America needs resettling, not through greed and exploitation but through good planning and common sense. It is time for a change in the way we live, and the models of the Mormon village and Amish agriculture set an excellent example. We cannot continue to prosper in a dysfunctional society nor a polluted environment. If we allow uncontrolled growth of our cities and continue a selfish consumer-driven way of living that damages the biosphere, we could very well destroy the quality of life if not life itself.

The question then is, Will we change? Probably not until we are driven to our knees. But that might be sooner than we think.

Ron Molen was born in 1929 in Hammond, Indiana, attended Indiana University before an LDS mission in Switzerland and Austria, then graduated from the University of Utah with a BFA in architecture. He practiced architecture for thirty years in Salt Lake City, where he designed four communities and had a book published, *House Plus Environment* (1974), which deals with the social aspects of community.

"AND HAVING FOOD AND RAIMENT LET US BE THEREWITH CONTENT."
(1 TIMOTHY 6:8.)

A HOUSE OF MUD:
LIVING LIGHTLY
ON THE LAND

ARDEAN WATTS

N LIGHT OF THE IMPORTANCE MORMONS PLACE ON THE LDS Church being guided by living prophets, it is natural for them to look to their prophets, seers, and revelators for direction on important social issues. Although general public interest in environmental matters has risen dramatically during the past generation, there appears to be little sustained focus on them coming from church leadership. Positive references to environmental concerns in conference addresses and publications are offset, for example, by public denial that there is a global population problem.

Though the church often avoids taking sides on politically sensitive issues, it does urge its members to be anxiously engaged in political and community movements consistent with church teachings. Except on a few sensitive "moral" issues such as abortion, gambling, and pornography, a diversity of positions seems to be tolerated. We might, therefore, look to the actions and lifestyles of individual Mormon families for inspiration on how to fulfill "our sacred duty" on behalf of the environment.

Environmental positions are likely to be more powerfully determined by where one lives or what profession one follows than by Mormon doctrine or church policy. Compare the likely environmental position of a hypothetical stake president/rancher from a rural Utah community with an urban businessman counterpart. For these reasons I prefer to speak of one Mormon family's living experience that, in turn, might stimulate other equally valid responses in other families or individuals.

Our son, Marty, and his family live in a 4,000-square-foot hand-sculpted adobe house set in a thick stand of pinyon and juniper on the south slope of the Grand Mesa in southwestern Colorado. The south windows provide an expansive 180-degree view toward the 14,000-foot San Juan Mountains, framed by the West Elk Mountains on the east and the

10,000-foot Uncompagre Plateau to the west. Five miles up the hill to the north, the Grand Mesa with her hundreds of lakes and dense conifer forest stretches flat for almost 2,000 square miles. For me, he and his family of five are living models of one Mormon family's response to the environmental challenges being faced around the world.

The big events in Marty's life, before the really big event—meeting and marrying his wife, Terrie—included working in an Alaska gold mine fresh out of high school, a mission in Brazil, a round-the-world bicycle trip with two friends in 1978–79, and graduation from BYU with a degree in product design—choices consistent with his personality, abilities, and upbringing. Quiet and almost shy, he has a gift of curiosity—a passion to know how things work.

He chose San Francisco as a place to practice his profession and soon found challenging work, became a counselor to the bishop of a singles ward, married the girl of his dreams, and bought a fixer-upper home—all, within three years of graduation. The couple knew how to live in the city, taking full advantage of the amenities: libraries, museums, parks, beaches, concerts, restaurants, zoos, lectures. But with the advent of a daughter, Whitney, a vision of a different kind of life in a different place began to form.

Many of us dream dreams worthy of pursuit and never quite get around to making them materialize. Marty's approach has been that of a dream-maker—realization begins with being unafraid to try with all one's might. Although not a spectator, he was always a careful observer. He learned plumbing while working as an apprentice to make money for college, a skill that seven siblings and parents have to try hard to resist exploiting. As he and Terrie remodeled their California home he read books and asked questions of anyone with experience. He spent a few weeks learning woodworking from a Japanese temple builder. When it came time to remodel the kitchen he apprenticed himself to a master cabinetmaker. He and Terrie working together transformed an old shoe into a magic slipper and then sold it to provide a nest egg to sink roots in a place more suitable to their dream.

The model was the small dairy farm of Marty's maternal grandparents, Frank and Jennie Brown, in Liberty, Idaho. The love that emanated from those people was palpable even to a toddler. Marty spent several summers as a teen working on the farm. A feeling of warmth and acceptance greeted all who stepped through their door. It is no wonder that for forty years Marty and his siblings have been drawn like homing pigeons to the tiny valley bisected by North Canyon Creek a few miles northwest of Bear Lake. Two of Marty's children were brought back to that farmhouse to be blessed in a place hallowed by those who had lived there.

Frank and Jennie have been gone over twenty-five years and rest in the cemetery set on a hill that rises in the exact center of the valley. On Memorial Day Marty's extended family gathers there with violin, accordion, trombone, and saxophone, celebrating the memories that tie families together and to a landscape. On those occasions singing can be heard across the valley, and in the twilight the silhouettes of square dancers can be seen from Frank and Jenny's front porch over a mile away. Plates of pre-supermarket farm cuisine—fresh-baked bread and raw milk with green onions and watercress, a slice of sharp cheddar and a piece of homemade carrot cake—rest on a mantle of dandelion blossoms at the foot of a modest granite memorial. What is it that yearly draws families thousands of miles to spend a precious hour together? A landscape, a history, a feeling of belonging to a place made sacred with memories shared by many generations.

Upon leaving San Francisco, Marty and Terrie set out to create just such a place in the name of their own nuclear family. In addition to its natural beauty, Cedaredge, Colorado, lies about halfway between Salt Lake City, where Marty's parents live, and Showlow, Arizona, where Terrie's parents live, providing equal access to both families. They found a nine-acre parcel five miles up the hill from a town that has the necessities: post office, school, library, lumber store, gas station, groceries, and auto parts. They rented a little house in town soon after the birth of a son, Ben, but after a few months purchased an old thirty-foot Airstream trailer so they could live on the site and work together, taking full advantage of every daylight hour.

Hannah joined the family the second year in the trailer. Life with three small children in such confines had its challenges.

Initial plans for their house consisted of a model constructed of modeling clay. Details were in a software program housed in the computer kept in the back of their twenty-five-year-old truck. The design changed frequently as they incorporated new features and eliminated others. For the first year the computer was a way of supporting themselves by long distance. Marty continued to produce designs that could be sent electronically to and from San Francisco. The same tools that have played so prominent a role in the creation of our urban cement jungles provided them options for a large degree of freedom in the realization of their dreams as to where and how they wanted to live.

Their goal was to build a house with their own hands of materials available in the area, as environmentally clean as possible, with an eye to conservation of energy and low maintenance. With an almost endless supply of clay underfoot, adobe easily became the medium of choice. The economy of adobe continues throughout the life of the building, since it is the least energy-consuming of all building materials. The first batch of bricks, made of clay displaced from digging the foundation, cracked on drying. After a few tries they found that their clay worked best when mixed with approximately two parts sand to one part clay. Eventually, they found a variety of sand with sharp-edged granules that bonded well with their clay.

Making adobe bricks is backbreaking work. The ingredients are measured in shovelfuls and then mixed in a cement mixer. The thick mud is transported by wheelbarrow to a smooth, flat, sunny surface where it is poured into a wooden mold forming three 10" x 14" x 4" bricks, each one weighing about thirty-five pounds when dry. The mold can be immediately removed, washed clean of old mud and then laid down again for three more bricks; thus with two forms an uninterrupted cycle of brick making is possible. The bricks dry in the sun for two or three days and are then stood on their sides for more thorough drying before being stacked.

The children amused themselves by making mud pies in the ten-foot-high sandpile while mother and father put in sixteen-hour days mixing adobe. As they grew older they left their marks on the house. Handprints can be found here and there on bricks, as well as half-moon depressions on walls where the children's hammers missed their marks. Terrie would quit an hour early and magically produce gourmet meals to satisfy the most demanding tastes. She learned the art of cooking when, following her mission there, she returned to France "to absorb the culture." She reads, writes and cooks in French, and somehow manages to serve haute cuisine twice a day, making the most of produce from her garden and gifts from generous neighbors.

In the fourth year, they decided to move in for the winter with only a home-built fireplace for heat. The house is designed as a massive heating and cooling machine. The sun pours in through the two-story south-facing glass walls of the greenhouse over 300 days per year. Adobe retains the prevailing temperature very well, but a few stormy days in a row and the chill at the 7,000-foot elevation is easily noticed. That first winter rugs were used for doors and plastic for windows while the downstairs floors, except for the bathroom, remained dirt. Now, in their sixth year, the holes are mostly plugged, the insulation is tight, and this year they'll finish putting double-paned glass in the last seven of the sixty-six windows.

They seldom seem put out by what would be hardship to most of us. Instead of complaining about the unending heavy physical labor, they insist that they're only having "fun." Marty maintains that the same sweat moistens the body whether making bricks or biking, and that distinguishing work from play is mostly a mind game.

The way neighbors and friends help each other is reminiscent of a disappearing lifestyle. Scaffolding, tractors, cement mixers, power tools are passed freely from one neighbor to another. One day Marty called a wrong number and, thinking it was a friend from his ward, asked a total stranger if he could borrow a chain saw. Sometime later he discovered his mistake and called the man to apologize. The man expressed surprise that Marty had not come to pick up the saw. At harvest time the bounty of gardens and orchards does not know the usual categories or boundaries. Generosity flows so freely that the usual divisive distinctions of ethnicity, age, religion and economic class are greatly diminished compared to the prevailing norms of urban existence. There have been numerous occasions, such as installing the huge salvaged beams and spraying the exterior with stucco, when calls for help were necessary. The response from ward, neighbors, friends is not considered unusual by the many families who have sought out places such as Cedaredge for an alternative to the impersonality and commercialism prevailing in many of our cities.

Marty and Terrie took little thought for the morrow when they left well-paying jobs to move to a rural setting, feeling secure that they would find a way. Now in their sixth year, they can live comfortably in the house built with their own hands. Appropriate attention was paid to making every room aesthetically interesting. In addition, each decision was made with reference to sustainability, efficiency, and softness of environmental impact. Water is heated with solar panels supplemented by a traditional electric heater. Eventually, gray water will be recycled to the garden. Their heating bill consists of the purchase price of a used woodstove, a saw, and an axe. Their passive solar system and wall of glass on the south take advantage of nature's largesse.

Their home is a work in progress; I doubt it will ever be "finished." It will likely outlive all of its present inhabitants, not only because of how it is built but where it is built. They still have several rooms with dirt floors, but among their most successful experiments are mud floors as smooth as tiles. Many interior walls will remain adobe, with others earmarked for plastering (Marty's most recently acquired skill). They will eventually be hung with art, much of it of their own making.

They have postponed many interests during the building of their home, to be resumed gradually now that the pressures have leveled off. The number of hiking and skiing days is increasing. Terrie is a painter of considerable ability. She also anticipates returning to her pursuits in French literature. Photography is one of Marty's unrealized passions. Ready access to the scenic wonders of southwest Colorado and southeastern Utah was part of the game plan. Large colored prints from his round-the-world bicycle trip hang in the homes of friends and family, reminding us of what we have missed while he has applied his creative energies elsewhere.

By age five Whitney was reading at the second-grade level. They are now in their fourth year of home school, finding that balancing arts, science, and essential skills does not depend upon the school board or the legislature. The local home school support group is strong, and the local public school district has been cooperative in offering facilities and expertise for home schoolers. To them, prayer and the teaching of values are simply a part of everyday life, and learning—simply being alive. The parents know the value of socialization, so there are liberal rules for sleep-overs, and most of their family outings include friends. Going to church is a significant social occasion, anticipated by all.

Marty is now designing and building houses for others who share his convictions about blending sound engineering with beauty and sustainability.

He is building number three and designing number four for a friend who is allergic to many of the standard materials used in ordinary houses. While he and Terrie are admired by many, none of his siblings would likely wish to change places with them. A person must love hard physical labor and long hours, value highly being together as a family twenty-four hours a day, make material things a low priority, be willing to sacrifice styles and fads and physical comfort to live within their means. Their solution is an individual one suited to their combined abilities and sensibilities.

Their lifestyle is changing as their children grow older. They capitulated to owning a VCR because of the powerful educational resources it offers. Occasional visits to the city are opportunities to visit museums, zoos, parks, even a shopping mall. Nights are filled with foreign movies, concerts, theater made all the more delicious by the long waits between. They host a succession of guests who need a touch of country living. For anyone wanting to learn how to work, Marty is a formidable teacher.

Their lives, like their house, are works in progress. The end can't be predicted, nor the origins fully understood, nor the extent to which their LDS Church heritage figures in all of this. But there is power in the great enabling clause of LDS scripture—

> . . . it is not meet that I should command in all things; for he that is compelled in all things, the same is a slothful and not a wise servant; wherefore he receiveth no reward. Verily I say, men should be anxiously engaged in a good cause, and do many things of their own free will, and bring to pass much righteousness; For the power is in them, wherein they are agents unto themselves. And inasmuch as men do good they shall in nowise lose their reward." (D&C 58:26–28.)

—reminding us that much more is possible than can or should ever be commanded. Perhaps the strongest commandments ever given come as callings to individuals, families, and communities to go beyond that which is required of everyone by hearkening to the Spirit, who knows both our needs and our capacity and who can see the past, the present, and the future, who knows and bears witness of all that is virtuous, lovely, or of good report or praiseworthy and leads us to seek after these things.

Ardean Watts is best known as a former associate conductor of the Utah Symphony and a music educator at the University of Utah, as well as an active environmentalist.

"As the partridge sitteth on eggs, and hatcheth them not; so he that getteth riches, and not by right, shall leave them in the midst of his days, and at his end shall be a fool." (Jeremiah 17:11.)

POVERTY, POPULATION, AND ENVIRONMENTAL RUIN

James B. Mayfield

N THE WORLD TODAY NEARLY TWO BILLION PEOPLE LIVE IN ABJECT poverty. These poorest of the poor live in isolated rural areas that often lack electricity, potable water, and the basic social services related to health and education. They are vulnerable, have little or no status in their societies, are often ignored by their own governments, and even overlooked by most international organizations concerned with the plight of the poor. In fact, most resources available for the poor go to people living in towns and villages close to big cities. The real disadvantaged have little access to roads, marketplaces, or government services.

Today, concern and commitment are growing, both within the LDS Church and throughout the world, to create an earth free from severe poverty and malnutrition, debilitating illiteracy, and preventable diseases, a world in which the rain forests, the grasslands, and wetlands are protected, and an era in which cultural diversity, human rights, and democratization are encouraged. While an earlier generation struggled with the fear of insecurity and communist expansion, a new generation is waking up to the fact that world poverty and ecological degradation will be the challenge of the next century.

THREE MAJOR ISSUES FACING THE WORLD TODAY

What are the dilemmas and responsibilities that Latter-day Saints must face as they seek to understand these challenges of world poverty, population growth, and environmental degradation? Each of these issues has secular and theological dilemmas for members of the LDS faith. Let us first review the realities of these three problems and then consider various positions faithful Mormons might take.

The First Issue—The Realities of World Poverty

Looking at the data provided by Lester Brown in the *State of the World 1995*, one finds that in 1960, the richest 20 percent of the world's people (North America and Western Europe) absorbed 70 percent of global income; by 1989, the wealthy's share had climbed to nearly 83 percent. Meanwhile, the poorest 20 percent, villagers of Africa and Asia and Latin America, saw their share of global income drop from an already meager 2.3 percent to just 1.4 percent.[1] Throughout the world, according to the World Bank, more than 1.5 billion people live in chronic poverty, and of those, 630 million are "extremely poor," having an average per capita yearly income of less than $275 (roughly $23 per month).

Every year 20 to 25 million people die as a result of hunger and starvation. More people died from hunger in the past three years than were killed in World War I, World War II, and the Vietnam Wars combined. People living in less developed countries (LDCs) are chronically ill, suffering from various diseases, including malaria, diarrhea, and cuts and scratches that do not heal. Of every ten children born to poor parents, two die within a year, another dies before the age of five, and only five will survive to the age of 40. World Health Organization statistics on causes of death in LDCs in 1985 suggest that nearly 37 million people (23.3 million adults and 13.5 million children) died unnecessarily: 6.5 million adults died of infectious and parasitic diseases, 4.3 million from acute respiratory diseases, 3.2 million from diarrhea, 3 million from tuberculosis, 1.5 million from viral Hepatitis B, 1 million from malaria, 880,000 from measles, 550,000 from AIDS and 200,000 from schistosomiasis.

The Second Issue—The Relationship of Population to the Challenges of Poverty

We in the United States are blessed people overall. Few understand the contrast between us and the LDCs of the world. Americans are 5 percent of the world population but consume nearly 35 percent of the world's natural resources. The average American uses as much energy as 500 Ethiopians. U.S. population, 251 million now, is growing faster than in any other industrialized nation, but, *more than 90 percent of the world's population growth* is taking place in the LDCs. And while millions of acres of cropland are lost annually to soil degradation and erosion and to sprawling urbanization, industrialization, and modernization, statistics indicate global population is increasing at the rate of 100 million new mouths to feed each year.

The issue of poverty is largely a question of the relationship of people to available resources. To put it in its simplest terms, many are arguing that there are too many people on this planet, given the land and resources presently available. Currently, the number of the earth's inhabitants is rising by nearly one billion each decade. The agrarian nature of LDCs encourages large families, since children represent productive assets. They provide low-cost labor to the farm and may earn income from nonfarm employment. With the historical (and sometimes persistent) high infant-mortality rates, only a large number of live births could ensure an adequate number of living offspring. Further, since most LDCs cannot provide public care for their elderly, having a large number of children is a sort of old-age security system for parents. The pattern is perpetuated when parents in rural and disadvantaged urban families discourage their children from attending school. Time in school limits time for farm or other work and requires money for books and clothes that parents cannot afford.

The Third Issue—The Challenge of the Environment and Natural Resource Depletion

In many poor countries, rapid population growth, agricultural modernization, and inequalities in land tenure are creating increasingly large populations with little or no access to productive land. Without jobs and without productive land, poor people are forced into marginal lands in search of subsistence food production and fuelwood, or they move to the cities. Those who stay on the land are forced to graze livestock herds where vegetation is sparse or soils and shrubs are easily damaged, and to create agricultural plots on arid or semiarid lands, on hillsides, in tropical forests, or in other ecologically sensitive areas. It has been estimated that 60 percent of people in LDCs live in areas that are ecologically vulnerable. As more and more people exploit open-access resources in an often desperate struggle to provide for themselves and their families, the further their environment is degraded.

The toll on natural resources takes many forms, including soil erosion, loss of soil fertility, desertification, deforestation, depleted game and fish stocks from overhunting and overfishing, loss of natural habitats and species, depletion of groundwater resources, and pollution of rivers and other water bodies. This degradation further exacerbates poverty and threatens not only the economic prospects of future generations but also the livelihoods, health, and well-being of current populations. Women are particularly hard hit by the accelerating spiral of poverty and environmental degradation. When they have to devote more and more time to obtaining fuel and water, they have less time to devote to food production, to increase the household income, to pursue their own and their children's education, and to improve family welfare.

WEALTH AND WELL-BEING

Nor is the environmental crisis restricted to the LDCs. Signs of the planet's deteriorating health are all around us. Some, such as global warming and the thinning ozone shield, seem remote and can be understood only with the help of scientists. Others, including receding forests, contaminated water, and worsening air pollution, are painfully obvious. Progress and development as defined by modern economics are destroying the natural systems upon which we depend for health and prosperity. In the same way as an autoimmune disease, in which the body's own defense system attacks and destroys vital tissue, the world's consumer society is assaulting the very life-support systems that keep it functioning. That we persist in calling this "progress" is the grossest fiction—and one of the greatest dangers—of our time.

The scriptures suggest that the earth's resources are more than sufficient for our needs, but only if they are managed efficiently and carefully.[2] There is, in fact, enough food raised on this planet to feed every person, but the problem is unequal distribution. As Mahatma Ghandi said: "The Earth is sufficient to provide for everyone's need, but not for everyone's greed." Both poverty and affluence can cause environmental problems. In the industrialized world, at least 3,000 square kilometers of prime farmland disappear every year under new buildings and roads. In the LDCs the rural poor burn more than 350 million tons of dung and crop residue every year for fuel—material that should go back to the soil to restore nutrients. In the rich countries of the world, half the surface water and a significant amount of groundwater has been polluted with industrial waste; in the LDCs, 60 percent of the water sources are polluted with human and animal waste. At the heart of the problem lies ecological shortsightedness and commercial greed. What we need, to overcome the ecological crisis, is not more consumption but less, not more energy and growth but rather a profound change of values, attitudes, and lifestyles.

LDS THEOLOGICAL IMPLICATIONS CONCERNING THE THREE MAJOR WORLD ISSUES

Let us now consider these three issues from an LDS perspective. In the ideas now presented I will not be suggesting solutions but merely raising questions that thoughtful members of the LDS faith may want to consider.

The First Dilemma—Poverty and the Role of the Church

From its beginning, the LDS Church has been a missionary church, charged with the task of bringing the gospel of Jesus Christ to all peoples. In recent years, some have recognized an inherent dilemma in this charge when faced with the need to preach the gospel and the need to help the poor of this world. Many would say that there is no dilemma, that preaching the gospel must come first and the solutions for world hunger will come later. They would argue that we should only be concerned with those people who have the ability and capacity to accept the gospel, that the billion or so tribal and village people of the world who live in isolated and primitive areas are somebody else's responsibility. Others in recent years have begun to argue that the tasks are not mutually exclusive, that the church can allocate, and indeed has allocated, resources both for missionary work and for various humanitarian activities in other parts of the world where there are no missionaries.

What, then, should be our responsibility for those who are so poor, so isolated, so illiterate and superstitious that missionary work is neither appropriate nor possible at the present time? The scriptures give us some clues but no definite answers. Again I leave it to the reader to determine their meaning. In Mosiah 4:16–21 we read:

> And also, ye yourselves will succor those that stand in need of your succor; ye will administer of your substance unto him that standeth in need; and ye will not suffer that the beggar putteth up his petition to you in vain, and turn him out to perish. . . .
>
> And now, if God, who has created you, on whom you are dependent for your lives and for all that ye have and are, doth grant unto you whatsoever ye ask that is right, in faith, believing that ye shall receive, O then, how ye ought to impart of the substance that ye have one to another.

This kind of scripture raises significant questions about how we should help those who are less fortunate, how best to use our own resources for the benefit of the truly needy. If we as individuals only provide help to the poor who live in areas where the church already operates, we may be ignoring many opportunities to fulfill our responsibilities suggested in the scriptures. Many religious organizations and other private voluntary groups have developed programs and strategies to work with the poorest of the poor people of this world. We all are obviously encouraged to find ways to support such organizations with our time and resources. Such charity may be an important first step to raising standards of living and eventually reducing environmental damage in the LDCs.

The Second Dilemma—Population Growth and God's Admonition to Multiply and Replenish the Earth

The challenge of an ever-rising population, especially among the very poorest—the group least capable of caring for its children and preparing them for the challenges of adult life—has generated a great deal of controversy. If it is accepted that God wants us to multiply and replenish the earth, there is still the question as to whether this is true in all cases and in all situations. Writings of the prophets in this dispensation certainly suggest that healthy young LDS couples are encouraged to have large families. Couples who would postpone having children for selfish or unrighteous reasons are strongly urged to repent. But while it is physically possible for a couple to have 15 to 20 children, any careful reading of the brethren would not conclude that all couples must have all the children that they physically are capable of having, nor that there is no choice in this matter. The issue is not about numbers; it is about motives more closely related to the health and strength of the mother and the resources available to care for the children. If there is choice in this matter, the question must be: *What is the choice?*

The recently published *Encyclopedia of Mormonism* suggests:

Bringing children into a loving home is considered a sacred privilege and responsibility of husbands and wives. Given that context, birth control is a matter left to the prayerful, mutual decisions of a righteous couple, with the counsel that husbands must be considerate of their wives, who experience the greater physical and emotional demands in bearing children. A woman's health and strength are to be preserved in childbearing; thus, wisdom should govern how a husband and wife carry out the responsibility to become parents and to care for their offspring.[3]

Far more complicated is the question about people in the LDCs of Africa and Asia and what the church's stand might be for people living in these areas of abject poverty and misery. One could argue that God wants all these children born regardless of the tragic conditions into which they will be condemned, simply because there are a fixed number of spirit children who must come to this earth. Such a position is not without merit, but I want to suggest that other positions are possible within the framework of LDS theology.

Let us review three different positions that might be taken concerning the problem of overpopulation. There are those who would advocate a strong government-imposed system of family planning, easily available abortion, and imposed sterilization, arguing that the problem is so severe that drastic measures are needed. Such advocates of population control generally highlight two themes: First, resources are assumed to be limited. Since the human population must divide a finite stock of resources, more people means less for each person. Paul Ehrlich, a Stanford University biology professor, is a widely read contemporary advocate of population control. His book *The Population Bomb* combines hard scientific data with passionate advocacy for population control. His vivid description of Delhi, India, dramatizes his concerns: "The temperature was well over 100, and the air was a haze of dust and smoke. The streets seemed alive with people. People eating, people washing, people sleeping. People visiting, arguing, and screaming. People thrusting their hands through the taxi window, begging. People defecating and urinating. People clinging to buses. People herding animals. People, people, people, people.[4]

In contrast to this Malthusian nightmare are those who suggest an alternative scenario. Using a fairly persuasive mathematically based model with carefully collected empirical data, Julian Simon, professor of economics at the University of Illinois, argues as follows:

Why is the standard of living so much higher in the United States or Sweden than in India or Mali? And why is our standard of living so much higher now than it was 200 years ago? The all-important difference is that there is a much greater stock of technological know-how available, and people are educated to learn and use that knowledge.[5]

In a later piece of research he challenges the Malthusian argument that the world has only so much resource by suggesting:

Sound appraisal of the impact of additional people upon the scarcity (cost) of a natural resource must take into account the feedback from increased demand to the discovery of new deposits, new ways of extracting the resource, and new substitutes for the resource. And we must take into account the relationship between demand now and supply in various future years, rather than consider only the effect on supply now, of greater or lesser demand now. The more people, the more minds there are to discover new deposits, increase productivity, and improve technology, all else equal.[6]

In a second common theme in this debate, advocates of family planning insist that people have a right to something called "a better quality of life," and thus the needs of the living should take precedence over the yet unborn of this world.[7] Critics of population planning would obviously order these values differently. They see quality of life as less important than the right to human life and, thus, insist on the right of individuals to make their own reproductive decisions. They would argue that nothing can or should be done, either because the problem is just too great to solve short of some totalitarian scheme of control, or, equally important, nothing should be done that would interfere in the God-given processes of human procreation. Many theologians argue that birth control of any kind is prohibited by divine law. One cannot ignore this position as mere superstition or simply a conservative prejudice, for the power of scripture and religious traditions among all cultures and people is indeed persuasive and worthy of careful consideration.

Between the two opposing extremes, however, is a middle ground, made up of people who are concerned with the millions of families who simply have neither the resources nor the skills to take care of their children adequately. Such children are too often condemned to a life of poverty, illiteracy, disease, and misery. Central to the middle-ground position is the concept of human agency—the fundamental belief that people should be free to choose the number of children they want, based upon their cultural and religious values, their financial and educational resources, and the economic and social opportunities available to them. The tragedy is the millions of families who, because of lack of education or lack of awareness that alternatives are available, mindlessly increase the number of children who are doomed to the degradation and poverty we are describing.

Free agency is only possible when people have choices, and choices require opportunities, awareness, resources, and abilities in conscious decision-making. Teaching children skills, values, and proper attitudes is largely the responsibility of the women. Thus the best hope for solutions lies in strengthening the role and position of women in society, not through forced family planning and easily available systems of abortion, but by helping both men and women develop their levels of literacy and productivity to the point where they do have choices that are meaningful and fulfilling. There is a direct and observable correlation between the level of education of the couple and the size of their families.

Some might argue that education should not be encouraged for it tends to lead to smaller families. The logic of this position is defensible if you accept the notion that there is a finite number of children who must be born on this planet and that any effort to reduce population is counter to God's plan for this earth. However, the fact that God has created "worlds without number" suggests that there is plenty of space for an infinite number of spirit children in the larger scheme of things.

I believe that God wants people to make good choices, to use wisdom in determining the number of children they will have, and that in the long run, as systems of education and literacy are implemented throughout the world, the problem of overpopulation will take care of itself.

The Third Dilemma—Environmental Challenges and
Christ's Second Coming

Because many faithful LDS people believe that the millennium is just around the corner, there should be no need to be concerned with sustainability of natural resources, destruction of forests and wildlife, and pollution of our waterways. After all, such concerns have little meaning, one might argue, if the Savior will be with us in the near future. Neal A. Maxwell suggests a different perspective:

> *This concern with man's developing a more harmonious relationship with nature by abiding by its physical laws is timely and legitimate. When we interrupt or destroy the larger ecology of man's relationship to God and to his fellowmen, we are violating transcendental laws that are as immutable and as inevitable as those breached laws of nature for which we are now beginning to pay a terrible price. (Later installments will be even more severe.) That we do not fully understand these transcendental spiritual laws neither excuses us from learning of them, nor excuses us from their harsh consequences when we violate them.*[8]

In Malachi 4:5–6 we are told that the children must have their hearts turned toward their fathers and the fathers must have their hearts turned toward their children. In D&C 138:47, we are told that "The Prophet Elijah was to plant in the hearts of the children *the promises* made to their fathers" (emphasis added). Malachi (4:6) presents the Lord's warning if this turning of our hearts does not happen: ". . . lest I come and smite the earth with a curse," and D&C 138:48 suggests even more strongly: ". . . lest the whole world be smitten with a curse and utterly wasted at his coming."

I have sought to understand the meaning of these scriptures and how they might apply to us in this day and age. Obviously they refer to the importance of genealogy work, the need to identify the names of our ancestors, and to have their ordinances completed in the temple. Yet there might be another message, for scripture is given to us for our spiritual as well as our temporal good. Three thoughts came to me: First, we of this generation are asked to seek both our past and to look to our future. Second, we must create some special link with those of our past. And third, we have some special responsibility for those who will come after us. For just a moment, let us consider the third responsibility in more detail.

An Important Responsibility for Future Generations: Turning Our Hearts to Our Children

We live in a consumer-oriented society in which we are told that happiness only comes when we are buying, consuming, and spending for the latest fads, fashions, gadgets, and new toys. The media blasts us with enticements to spend, spend, spend. One social critic has pointed out that the great edifices of past civilizations were consecrated to God or the divine: pyramids, temples, pagodas, mosques, cathedrals. He then suggests that the present-day cathedrals of our civilization are the shopping malls—dedicated to self-indulgence and immediate gratification. The priests of these modern cathedrals are the advertising executives who spend nearly $130 billion each year convincing us that we must have the latest automobiles, trucks, televisions, clothing fashions, and all the other consumer goods that characterize our society. This obsession with ever-growing consumption is obviously having disastrous consequences for the environment, especially among our nonrenewable resources.

The scriptures previously mentioned suggest that this generation must also consider future generations, that we must be connected in some way with those yet to come. The key question here is whether we will be able to pass on to our descendants the same blessings and heritage that we received from our parents. When Joseph Smith lived on this earth, 75 percent of the landmass was covered with virgin forests, the major source of our oxygen. Today, that 75 percent has been cut to 30 percent, and an area of forest the size of the state of Connecticut is now destroyed in a matter of months during the year. During the last fifty years, more plant and animal species have been destroyed each year than in the previous two thousand years. It is estimated that 50 to 100 species are becoming extinct each year. Remember, after God had created this world with all its diversity and beauty, he declared that "it was good." Today, much of this destruction comes directly from our obsession for more consumer goods, which requires the cutting of our forests, the draining of our marshlands, the strip-mining of our hills, the overgrazing of our fields, and the mindless use of our nonrenewable resources. We justify such destruction of the beauties and resources of our planet in the name of progress, development, a better standard of living.

When the Lord suggests that we must turn our hearts to our children (our descendants), I believe this has a message with both spiritual and temporal meaning. Both are interconnected and together promise a solution to the problems that will otherwise cause the world to be "smitten with a curse." As the above scriptures suggest, if we do not link with our past, we will die spiritually, and if we allow this obsession for consumer goods worshiped in our present-day cathedrals to continue, the beauties and the diversity of our planet will be lost to our descendants. Indeed, the world will be smitten with a curse—both spiritually and temporally.

This generation runs the risk of believing that happiness comes from owning things, from exploiting the riches of the world for our own selfish wants, of losing spiritual and cultural values in the pleasures of the moment. Thus, this generation may well lose the blessing from knowing the promises that have been given, the sacrifices that have been made, and the meaning and purpose that can only come from our links to our past. Yet equally tragic will be the tendency to ignore the responsibilities we have for generations yet unborn. Happiness never comes from having or merely from consuming; it comes from being, from seeing why we should be grateful for what has come from the past, and from seeing why we must ensure that those who come later will enjoy the same beauties and diversity that we have enjoyed.

This is the great challenge of our generation. I do hope that we may be up to it, both short-term and long-term. In my opinion it does not matter whether the Lord's Second Coming is next month, next year, next decade, or next century. Preparation for that day is an ongoing individual responsibility for each of us. Concern for the environment is not an issue of time but of process and priorities. As Elder Maxwell suggests, our relationship with the beauties of this planet have both spiritual and temporal meanings, and man has been given a stewardship over the bounties of the world. How we manage that stewardship may be as significant a test as any related to the Lord's Second Coming. The problems of the environment, of world poverty and population growth are all closely interrelated. We each must consider these questions through thoughtful reflection and careful prayer. If "The Glory of God is Intelligence," if we are counseled to use wisdom and reverence in approaching the promises of the past, the challenges of the present, and the opportunities of the future, then each of us must not shrink from the task of confronting tough questions. The Lord, through his prophets, has taught us true principles by which we are to govern ourselves, true concepts of justice and mercy by which we are to judge our daily behavior, and true ordinances and teaching by which we may prepare for our futures. The time has come to stand up for what is right. May we have the wisdom and the fortitude to understand what our role in these issues may be. This is our challenge and our opportunity.

ENDNOTES

1. Lester Brown, *State of the World* (New York: Watch Institute, 1995).

2. D&C 104:14–18.

3. Daniel H. Ludlow, ed., *Encyclopedia of Mormonism* (New York: Macmillan, 1992), 116–17, s.v. "birth control" by Homer S. Ellsworth.

4. Paul R. Ehrlich, *The Population Bomb,* rev. ed. (New York: Ballantine, 1968), 1.

5. Julian L. Simon, "The Case for More People," *American Demographics* 1, no. 10 (November–December, 1979): 26.

6. Ibid., 28.

7. Paul F. McCleary and J. Philip Wogaman, *Quality of Life in a Global Society* (New York: Friendship Press, 1978), 25.

8. Neal A. Maxwell, *For the Power Is in Them* (Salt Lake City: Deseret Book Company, 1970), 10.

James B. Mayfield is a professor of political science at the University of Utah. He has thirty years of experience as a management consultant in third-world development with USAID, UNICEF, World Bank, and other international donor agencies.

THE FIRST RAIN

Kristen Rogers

ONIGHT, OUR WATER TURN BEGINS AT TWO IN THE MORNING, SO I'M stumbling around in the dark with a flashlight and a shovel. Yawning. It's kind of a game I'm playing; you get a little land and a couple of water shares, and you can pretend to be a farmer. My job tonight's not too hard. If I were a real farmer taking my water turn, I'd be here all night and then some— but all I have to do is make sure the water's here, adjust a couple of gates, and go back to bed. Beyond the trees I can see lights on at the neighbor's place. He's more serious about the game than we are. He stays with his water, pumping it onto his grass, working it down his rows. He wears rubber waders. I wear sandals.

Sometimes when it's our turn I get out to the gate and find the ditch empty. When it is, somebody has to get in the car, go find where the water's been diverted and turn it down the right way. It takes a long time after that for the stream to get through Brown's orchard, down the Hobbses' cement/rock ditch and under the lane to our garden. Whenever this happens, a little ball of anger ignites in the pit of my stomach. I need this water. I want to punish whoever stole it. No wonder more westerners have been killed over water than over gold or women or anything else! Murder could easily happen—especially back when life itself depended on the ditch being full.

But I guess our upstream thieves only work in the daylight, because the water's here now. My neighbor turns off his floodlight and goes in. I step into the small swamp that has collected around the closed gate—the cold on my feet slaps me fully awake—and tug at the handle. The gate's stuck. It takes a few heroic yanks to get it up. Water rushes down the ditch, and the swamp recedes.

North Mountain, where the water begins, stands dark against the stars. I listen to the gurgling of the water. I'm in an in-between moment—not the world of deadlines, electronics, and fossil fuels; not the world that doesn't depend on those and never did. I walk along the ditches, nudging here and there with the shovel. I can go back to bed now. But what with the white clouds drifting across the stars, the sound of quiet water, the pleasure of watching it nose through our sapling orchard, I'm not in a hurry to sleep. I'm the only person on earth. I stand and listen to the water.

I'm thinking about ditches and order. Reclamation. Deserts blossoming. The thing about irrigation ditches is how no-nonsense they are. How carefully planned, how orderly and efficient. In some of the towns the Mormon pioneers built, ditches still run along the roads. They practically define the geography. Irrigation grids shaped those towns and, in fact, an entire culture. They've probably shaped me, now, 150 years after my pioneer ancestors scratched out the first line in the dirt.

I'm thinking about my life. I look up at the mountain, the shape of it. The Big Dipper has swung below the horizon, out of sight. I wander around back, following the water. I have arranged my life in a certain type of order. It's a pleasing order, nourishing in some ways. There's a rhythm to it, like irrigation turns, as my attention flows in cycles: to children, to husband, to ideas; to computer or spirit; to car repairs, friends, ideas, music, chocolate chips, justice, or split ends. There are responsibilities that I have assumed, and I usually do what I'm supposed to. I help other people sometimes, and they help me. We share our lives. Generally, my days feel right.

And yet—for some time, waters have flowed through my dreams. Groundwater, hidden, moves through my writing. So do plumbers. The fluid keeps nudging me, disturbing my sleep. One night I dreamed that a neighbor baby fell into our pond. On another I dreamed of spring ditches, swift and flooding over. I'm out of sorts. My own monthly flows are heavy and insistent. I feel formless, as though something has dissolved who I am. When I walk in the mountains, I hear the streams speaking but I can't understand.

On my fortieth birthday, I hiked up to a waterfall. I watched the river shatter, the white spray, the pool below where the spray collected itself and became river again. This was Dry Creek, the cleavage between North Mountain and East Mountain. It's where we get our water. At the edge of the pool the water eddied, the creek rippling and folding in upon itself. Patterning and unpatterning. Flecks of light. Rocks below the surface, tawny in the sun. It seemed to me that my life depended on this water. Not the life that's in the food that we grow or the lawns we maintain. Not irrigation water. What I wanted was something else, something that I couldn't find among the garden beds or in my organized life.

"The waters symbolize the universal sum of virtualities," writes Mircea Eliade. "They are *fons et origo*, 'spring and origin,' the reservoir of all the possibilities of existence. They precede and *support* every creation. . . . On the other hand, immersion in water signifies regression to the preformal . . . a dissolution of forms . . ." Waters immerse me now, I think, even as I stand guard with my shovel over the dark streams of the night. I drift in the waters like a torn piece of moss.

Dry Creek runs behind our house—the very same creek that tumbles down the mountain, except that here and now it *is* dry. Stones line the bed—both round and razor-edged stones, white, black, pink, green. Bits of two mountains lie between the banks, as do random splinters of lives: old bricks, chunks of concrete, an occasional four-square ball from the school-yard upstream. This spring, snowmelt filled the creek bed. The rushing of it underlay our spring planting, our words to each other, our dreams at night. The voice of waters filled us.

Then one day the watermaster shut the flow off. The river went instead to the ditches, where it was parceled out according to the traditional system. In April we received our irrigation ticket in the mail, listing all the times—to the minute—that our water turn would start and end throughout the summer. But that piece of paper wasn't enough. We were empty. After the creek stopped running, we were stranded in silence, barren air, desiccation.

Mormons are proud to claim that they invented irrigation. Or re-invented it, anyway. My ancestors did this. They built towns in places where rain comes only in skiffs and cloudbursts. Everywhere they went they laid out their systems, their storage reservoirs and canals. They channeled the mountain streams into a framework of community.

But there's more than one way to make a life on the land. According to Frank Waters, the Hopi say that the Creator led them to their mesas in northern Arizona. He led them to a red-earth desert, and there he told them to end their wanderings. Because you'll learn faith by living here, he told them. You'll have to live by prayer and ceremony. If you forget the prayers you won't have enough water.

The story haunts me. I recognize God's voice speaking to a wandering people. The story is part of my own spiritual history.

> For the land, whither thou goest in to possess it, is not as the land of Egypt, from whence ye came out, where thou sowedest thy seed, and wateredst it with thy foot, as a garden of herbs:
> But the land, whither ye go to possess it, is a land of hills and valleys, and drinketh water of the rain of heaven:
> A land which the Lord thy God careth for: the eyes of the Lord thy God are always upon it, from the beginning of the year even unto the end of the year.
> And it shall come to pass, if ye shall hearken diligently unto my commandments which I command you this day, to love the Lord your God, and to serve him with all your heart and with all your soul,
> That I will give you the rain of your land in his due season, the first rain and the latter rain, that thou mayest gather in thy corn, and thy wine, and thine oil. (Deuteronomy 11:10–14.)

When the wandering pioneers arrived in Utah, they decided not to count on the rains of heaven. In 1856, Brigham Young said,

> [The Lord] could send showers to water our fields, but I do not know that I have prayed for rain since I have been in these valleys until this year, during which I believe that I have prayed two or three times for rain, and then with a faint heart, for there is plenty of water flowing down these kanyons in crystal streams as pure as the breezes of Zion, and it is our business to use them. (Journal of Discourses 3:331.)

Well, that's just common sense, and Brother Brigham was nothing if not businesslike. Heaven knows that it required a lot of conviction just to be Mormon, let alone to grow crops in Sanpete or the Salt Lake Valley or Santa Clara. If you've got a practical solution, why exhaust your faith just to water the crops? So—common sense is my history. Pioneer logic, order and practicality. It's not a bad heritage, but at times, maybe when I'm sitting on the mountain or maybe now while I settle onto the grass at two in the morning, I wonder where that practicality has led us. Where has it led me? The waters murmur through my mind. They soak into hard soil. The waters say this to me: You live in a land of hills and valleys, a land which the Lord cares for. But you have relied too much on form. You have not got your water by faith but by logic, as part of a system.

It's true. And what has that system brought about for our community? The hills and valleys are being sliced into grid upon grid. The mountain waters have been piped; they flow beneath asphalt, caged and invisible. Subdivisions spread, watered by sprinklers. Up on the bench, where before deer browsed in oak brush, huge houses receive water by pump. We have taken irrigation to the next step, and the next. We hardly think about water anymore. In fact, we no longer know exactly where the water comes from.

The waters say to me: This is you. Not just your town, but also your self. You have forgotten the source of water. You live most days as though faith weren't the essence of each moment. You have forgotten what you want and who you are, you live by schedule and authority. You can turn on a tap, turn on an ignition, turn on the news, and never have to remember that you're alive.

Last week I hiked with friends up to a lake on North Mountain. The mountain itself was fluid once. Of the igneous intrusions that pushed up the Wasatch Range, this was the lightest in density and therefore the earliest. We walked up the light rocks. High up, near a stand of limber pine, we stopped to breathe. Someone in the group told us that when molten igneous rock meets older metamorphic rock—as when a fluid North Mountain met the rocks of East Mountain—things happen. Chemical reactions. New minerals. Cleavages where water will naturally find a course, and thus new drainages and canyons. Where igneous meets metamorphic, veins of gold and silver come into being. When the fluid encounters the rigid, things change.

I looked at him uneasily, as though he knew the topography of my heart. I picked up a worn stone. I squeezed it and it crumbled, scattering its crystals on the ground. Water did this, over time. Water entered the rock, freezing, unfreezing, working the crystals loose. Water was tearing the mountain down.

In the beginning of all things, dry land emerged from the face of the deep. And then the rivers and rains dissolved the land and returned it to the sea. The cycle goes on, over and over. For me, now, immersed in waters, something might be born or something might dissolve. Something might change, if I don't try to control the flow of things. But how could I do that? I was born and raised by management; I have breathed it all my life. Management is how we do things.

A while ago, I went to a meeting of neighbors. Everyone was worked up about a new development on the foothills—proposed, and barreling toward city approval. We moaned and pontificated. How could we save our trails, our views? Where should the roads go? How many houses, and how far up the hill? Could we squeeze a park out of the developer? Passions flared. Everyone had a different best solution. The talk went round and round until late.

In the corner sat a man with a well-worn face, an outsider in a room dominated by Mormon men. For two or three hours he sat silent. Meanwhile, I had my say. We could solve this problem through intelligent regulation. Ordinance. Negotiation. By 11:30 everyone was tired but still at it. The man in the corner hadn't said a word.

We finally decided that everyone would give a closing statement, then we'd go home to bed. We went around the room, and when it was the corner man's turn he was slow to get started. "I don't know anything about all this stuff," he said finally. "Densities, trade-offs, cul-de-sacs, access, CC and Rs. I feel pretty stupid, but I just don't know all about that." I wasn't really listening. It was way too late. I yawned, and waited for the next person. But he went on. "All I know is, the land is sacred. It's holy."

The energy in the room immediately shifted. Tensed. There were a few sidelong glances.

"Every morning when I get up, I fall on my face and pray," he said. "For the land. I pray that we'll have wisdom, or that somehow we'll know what to do."

Another pause, then the next person took his turn. Said something about wildfire danger and increased traffic on First South. I sat remembering what maybe I once knew and have forgotten because I have given my faith to forms, structure, authority and logic.

Maybe it had to be that way. Maybe we needed irrigation ditches. Guttered water was the glue that held everything together. For better or for worse, it civilized the desert. And besides, ditches compensate for those of us who are faint of heart. But with all this efficiency, there's an absence. We live in communities that are not grounded in spirit but in commerce. We no longer perceive how the land and the people and prayer are one. We no longer sense the gaze of God. Once you can control nature, who needs God, anyway?

A lot of people I know are puzzling over what we've lost; they're floundering around, trying somehow to get it back. Most of the time, though, we don't really know what it is that we're trying to do. And almost all of the time, we have no idea how to do it.

This summer, after the watermaster had killed the creek and we nearly drowned in the silence, my husband had the idea of digging a pond in the backyard. At the time, we didn't recognize the connection. All he knew was that he wanted a water garden, with water lilies and a little cascade built from rocks, tubing, and an electric pump. I assured him that we neither had the time nor the money nor even the inclination for a project like that, but I came home one night to find that he and the boys had rented a sodcutter and ripped a big swath out of the lawn.

Well, I joined him. What else could I do? We dug. We stabbed at the earth—rocks, actually, from an old streambed—with a digging fork and spade. It didn't take long before I too became possessed with the need to gather water. An inch at a time, we dug down. When the neighbors learned what we were up to, they offered their tractor, a sturdy old monster. So then we took turns sitting high up on the tractor seat. The beast roared; the big shovel lipped up subsoil; the hole deepened. The tractor sweated up the incline with its loads.

Watching, I wondered if it could perhaps tip over. I'd barely dismissed the thought as paranoia when one of the wheels slid into a rut. The tractor teetered, my husband high up on the seat. Thousands of pounds of steel. In that moment between the world as I knew it and a blurry future, I prayed: Don't let it crush him. The tractor went over then, slow motion, slammed against the ground and lay there, growling and dripping diesel. It did not crush my husband. And yet—there it was, in front of our eyes, and I recognized it: our own arrogance. We'd thought that we could manipulate water without consequence.

But we were only living by the rules of our culture.

There's a company in south Utah County that makes explosives, and in the process has poisoned the groundwater with nitrates and explosive chemicals. The tainted water has migrated northward into agricultural and residential wells. It's moving toward municipal wells.

A lot of local people work at Trojan, descendants of the Mormons who first farmed this valley, working with the cycles of light and water. Now their children make dynamite. This is how they live, buy their food, keep a roof over their heads. Farming isn't enough to sustain a community anymore. Outside the Trojan plant, people, animals and crops have been drinking tainted water for some years. The best solution the state can come up with is to pump the aquifer. They pump the contaminated water into an irrigation ditch and let it run into Utah Lake.

This is our progress: As a spiritual community we began with faith, then marched faithfully into industriousness. At this point we could at least see the water in the ditches and follow it to its source. We recognized and lived within the cycles of the seasons, of drought and rain. Each person along the waterway bore responsibility for the water. But now it's different. Who bears responsibility now? Who knows the water's source, its paths?

There's talk of doing away with ditches and going to pressurized irrigation around here. It would be more efficient and less wasteful. I wince to hear the talk. I want the ditches as a last vestige of—something. Something that's going, even if keeping it alive sometimes seems like only a nostalgic pastime. When I see the water flowing straight and purposeful along the road, my heart follows it, the way the long ditch grasses are pulled into the current. The water looks so cool. This is my community, my history.

At these times it seems natural to me that the western settlers should have taken melted snow from the mountains and spread it across their fields. It seemed right to them. And yet, I wonder—what if we had lived by grace instead? If we depended on faith more than we depend on ingenuity? I wonder if our history as a people would have been different. I wonder if it's a natural progression or a result of arrogance that when we no longer need our fields we subdivide them in a way that brings profits but neither beauty nor community. I wonder if there could have been another choice.

Someone mentioned this week that pipes are being laid to carry Dry Creek during spring runoff. He said that the creek will no longer flow through its bed. Instead, pipes will carry water to Lehi, a town that wooed and won a microchip company with promises of tax breaks and cheap labor. They're out building the Micron plant right now, having bulldozed hundreds of acres of wheat and pasture. The plant will use enormous quantities of water every minute.

When I learned this news, I hiked up Dry Creek Canyon. I sat by the stream and watched how it braided and flowed around the dark boulders in its way. The water moved downward, shadowed, dark. Gnats above it rose into a sliver of sun and so became specks of light. Across the stream, horsemint grew, radiant. Somewhere below, I knew, there was a weir, and the stream would no longer make its own way.

And now I'm sitting in the grass, looking at North Mountain while the water floods the orchard, pools behind the grapes, slips into the dry creekbed. I'm shivering. I've set the shovel and the flashlight down somewhere, and it's too dark to find them. I'm miserably tired suddenly. I have to face myself: I have bought into a culture that employs water, air and soil in a way that strips them of all light. All these years, the voices of this culture have told me how to live, and I have believed them. The only way I could do this, I suppose, was by piping my own life force. The realization makes me indescribably sad.

I have done what Navajo Oshley, in a 1978 interview, accused all of us of doing:

People took up the land where the water was flowing and I have heard
these people got stingy with the water. . . . This thing called water is for
everything that is living, like horses and the birds. These people in
Blanding say that the water is to be paid for. I do not like this. . . . That is
why there is no rain. . . . The Mormons do not take the sacredness of the
land seriously and they are ruthless towards the land. . . . This causes the
drought. . . . If they practiced the sacred ways, we would have rain and
snow. They should offer prayers instead of drilling into Mother Earth.
(Robert S. McPherson, *Sacred Land, Sacred View,* p. 43.)

We're all ruthless toward the land to one degree or another, this land
that the Lord our God careth for. We're ruthless toward ourselves.
Collectively, we have no sense that God careth for the hills and valleys
around us. Yet there are now and always have been people who are trying
to establish a sacred connection with the land and the water that beautifies
it. And here am I now, in this hour between midnight and dawn, neither in
the practical world nor in the spiritual, hesitating between them, not quite
knowing how to abandon the system and live by heart and love and soul
on this land. Nobody has taught me how to do this.

But the deep waters still flow through my dreams. And the question I
hear is this: Will you let the waters flow where they will? Can you be fluid,
moving in faith, open to possibilities, willing to let something new emerge
from the waters?

It's a large question, too large for one night, and besides, there's still
time to go back to sleep before morning comes. The irrigation turn will be
over pretty soon. The ditch will be dry for a week and a little more. I get up
off the grass, hugging my arms to my body.

I look back at the mountain. I offer a faint prayer for the land, and for
me.

Kristen Rogers—writer, editor, musician, teacher, community leader, out-
doorsperson—lives in Alpine, Utah, with her four children. When her husband died
after completion of her essay, she learned that fluidity is not optional but essential.

"Thou shalt be diligent in preserving what thou hast, that thou mayest be a wise steward; for it is the free gift of the Lord thy God, and thou art his steward." (D&C 136:27.)

WATERMASTERS

Dennis Smith

UCKED INTO THE SOUTHEAST CORNER OF SALT LAKE VALLEY AT midcentury, the small town of Draper, Utah, was a typical example of Mormon culture. In the summer of 1942, when I was just a few weeks old, my Grandpa Smith, who was waging a losing battle with cancer at the time, stood in a close circle with several other men in front of the pulpit of the old Draper Second Ward chapel and performed one of Mormonism's most common and uniquely intimate ordinances. Before a hushed congregation, this cluster of simple farmers cradled me in their arms, and Grandpa Smith gave me my name and a blessing in a gravelly voice that God might well have heard.

Within a few months of that Sunday morning blessing and before I ever got a chance to know him, Grandpa Smith had died. My main impressions of him come from a family photo taken shortly before his death. Surrounded by his six daughters and three sons (including my father), Grandpa sits in the center of the photo next to Grandma. His face is pale and haggard. The cancer makes him look more like seventy than fifty-six. Still, there is a remnant of pioneer determination in the visage of this man in whom I see my father's face mirrored—and my own face, too, as I grow older.

These days, I am shocked to realize that I am within a year or two of the age Grandpa was when he died. With the passage of time I become ever more conscious of the bridges of culture our lives have spanned both together and apart—my grandfather, my father, and myself.

In his youth, Grandpa had homesteaded a farm in southern Idaho on the banks of the Bear River, along its broad arch from the northern slopes of the Uintas toward that great body of water with no outlet, the Great Salt Lake. The Idaho farm was the nest of my dad's earliest memories. With his younger brothers, DeVar and Kay, Dad would stand on the old steel bridge upriver from the house and watch the water slide beneath them. Sometimes, it felt as if the whole earth were moving instead of the water, which seemed strange because their image of the world appeared to be so immovable, so broad and endless beyond the minuscule scope of their tiny corner that it was hard to imagine the curvature of Earth's horizon, let alone its implied movement in the mirror of Bear River.

Our current vision of the earth, supplanted with complex color atlases and photos taken from outer space, has expanded our image of the globe to more comprehensible proportions than my father knew as a child on the Bear River bridge, a vision that has come upon us so gradually that we forget how enormous the world must have seemed to all who inhabited it before us. The earth was so immense, so endless, so overflowing with room to grow. Concerns for overpopulation or defilement of the planet were inconceivable. Beyond the setting sun there were always unexplored landscapes and exciting venues for expansion.

In my father's childhood, that vision of a constantly replenished landscape was still predominant in western America. From his vantage point on the Bear River bridge, the river beneath was always clear and drinkable. It came, uncelebrated, from mysterious and unquestioned sources, and flowed, pure and immaculate, toward a world of consistent renewal and constant opportunity.

When Dad was eleven, Grandpa sold the farm in Idaho and moved the family back to Draper, where he had lived as a child. Grandpa's own father had died on the old family farm, and he felt obligated to return and help his mother run it. In time, the Draper farm became his legacy, eventually to be split up among his own children, if they would have it. So my dad spent his teenage years in Utah learning patterns and places his father had known when he was young.

The west end of the Draper farm faced Relation Street, so named because almost everyone on the street was related. A good portion of the east side of town had been the property of Grandpa's grandfather, Lauritz Smith, who "took up" a large portion of land as one of the original settlers.

By my grandfather's time, Lauritz Smith's immense section of land had been parceled out from son to son. Grandpa's portion stretched clear to the mountain, where it melted away in the steep uncultivated slopes. In the collective mind, everything above that point, so to speak, belonged to nobody in particular and everyone in general. The mountains were the watershed, however, and the water was divvied out in shares to the farmers below in "water turns," which determined who would get how much and when they would get it. Needless to say, the politics of its possession could become quite heated.

Grandpa's father had been watermaster in Draper for many years. He often mediated conflicts over water between disgruntled farmers, and helped engineer and build the canal that brought irrigation water from the Jordan River Narrows. He was also in charge of the construction of a reservoir in the very tops of the mountains at the head of Bell Canyon, which made it possible for local farmers to realize an extra month of summer irrigation. For several years he orchestrated the teams of men who carried supplies up the narrow canyon to shape and fit the large blocks of granite that were used to build the dam.

Working together, the people of Draper had learned that even the work must be shared in order for everyone to benefit. Decades earlier, when timber was needed for building and firewood, gates were installed at the mouths of major canyons to exact tolls from anyone who would go into the mountains for wood. The laws of supply and demand were taking hold; the more people who came to the valley, the more valuable became the commodities that they needed—things such as water, wood, and land. But who determines such things? Who decides what part of the earth belongs to whom?

Such questions have become increasingly critical as the years have passed and as the population has increased. Most of our current regional environmental conflicts are rooted in the dilemma of who should have the right to diminishing resources in a climate of burgeoning population.

Across the low range of the mountains south of Draper in the northern corner of Utah Valley where my mother had grown up, maybe ten miles as the crow flies, a different scenario shaped a part of my perspective.

The reason Mom and Dad moved to Alpine was to help my mother's father, Grandpa Petersen, with his farm on the edge of town. He had contracted polio in the thirties and by the time of my birth, the farm had become too much for him to handle. We moved into Great-grandma Kristina's old log homestead, out behind Grandpa's house. The view from her front doorstep of high poplars along the East Field Ditch formed the essence of my earliest memories.

Out by the poplars, a makeshift bridge crossed over to Grandpa's barn, where a huge black-and-white holstein bull was kept in a side corral. My mother was terrified that if I didn't fall in the ditch and drown, I would be killed by the bull, or that if I caught a draft I might get pneumonia and die, as had happened to her little brother, Charles, many years earlier. Her corner of the world was very fragile. My parents' desires for a brighter world included making it broader. They have seen it become so broad that the old one has almost completely faded.

One summer in the 1950s when I was about eleven, I hiked with my dad from the Alpine side of the mountain to the top of Lone Peak, where we could look down the other side and see the town of Draper and the outlines of farms that were slowly being broken up into smaller and smaller parcels. He showed me the steep slash of Bell Canyon far below, curling up into the high glacial bowl where Bell Canyon Reservoir was located. It was his hope that we would be able to descend the steep north face of the peak to the reservoir, then find and follow the old trail that would take us down the other side of the mountain by nightfall.

Halfway between the peak and the reservoir on the steep northern face of the summit, we were hit by a thunderstorm, which came on us so suddenly that we weren't prepared for it. It was a bad place to be caught in a storm. Gushing water was loosening rocks all around and above us, and for a while things got pretty scary. Boulders the size of lunch buckets were careening down on either side of us, but we finally made it down to the fields of granite between the summit and the lake.

Under an overhang of rock, we waited for the storm to pass before going on to the reservoir. The lightning was terrible, and I remember water gushing over the edges of our cramped sanctuary. Looking back on it now, I realize that despite the brief terror of it, that afternoon at the head of Bell Canyon was a defining moment for me, a ritual of sorts, through which my dad introduced me to a portion of his life that I had not been aware of before.

After the storm, the sun came out as radiant in splendor as the storm had been ferocious. Massive banks of mist swept back from the ridges like curtains from a stage, revealing a sky twice as blue as it had seemed that morning. We trudged on toward the reservoir, stepping gingerly across wet boulders, and then, suddenly, we came upon it.

It wasn't large, maybe the size of a couple of football fields. But there in the palm of heaven's hand, its flat surface shimmered like glass. It was deep and cold. Huge slabs of granite thrust up from its depths, creating shelves where stands of pine hung out over the water like the masts of lonely immigrant ships. We walked around to the side where the dam was, and I was awestruck. Designed to span the glacial ravine as a slab of man-made wall constructed from hand-hewn granite blocks, it ranged from eight to twenty feet in height and was about two hundred feet across. The massive stones had been set in place with mortar made from cement that had been carried up from the valley on horseback by Grandpa Smith and his brother, Wilf, together with their father over a two-year period. For decades thereafter, going up to the reservoir for a summer outing became a family affair to be looked forward to by all the cousins.

So this was "the reservoir" my dad had talked about all these years, a part of his legacy—a part of his memories of Draper and the family inheritance he had stepped away from to move to Alpine when I was six weeks old. Choosing not to take his share of the Draper farm, his personal vision with my mother had taken him across the mountain to Alpine. Eventually, their dreams found root in a parcel of land adjacent to the farm where she grew up. And so it was that my father's forty-nine acres became the major landscape of my childhood.

Though I never lived in Draper beyond those first few weeks when I received my name in the old Draper Second Ward, the farm in Draper had become a part of my legacy, too, in its own way. When I was a kid, we drove around the Point of the Mountain to Draper to visit Grandma and my aunts and uncles and cousins almost every Sunday. The parents would sit on the porch and talk while the kids would go out back and play in the barn. Through those weekend visits, the landscape of my father and his father became a part of my awareness. Our hike to the reservoir over the top of the mountain served to weld that link even stronger.

Behind Grandma's house in Draper there was a big swinging gate that opened into the pasture behind the barn. Beyond the pasture was a grove of trees and a pond, which in the early days had been used for baptisms. On one side of the pond there was a concrete trough with a rusted pump and a pipe that brought water from somewhere beyond the trees. Maybe that was my ocean of mystery, a last remnant of pioneer passion drawing me forward to find out where the water came from. Who had piped it and why? Who had created this place, and who held possession of it?

But the pipe went through a fence and I was timid. Even then, a consciousness of boundaries was crowding in, restricting passage, defining ownership of land, water, and everything else that we now have come to define as unreplenishable resources. Since then, the obsession with possession within the realm of my world has only grown. Like a cancer, over time it expands from the base of the mountains outward, creating a tumor of cultural and environmental suffocation. Even the mountains are not spared. The lower hills are marred by meandering gashes, and pristine trails are becoming crowded. People who never knew the land the way we knew it are claiming it as theirs, just as we, who never knew it as our fathers did, assumed that it was ours.

These days when I pass through Draper, I sometimes drive up to the base of the mountain where Uncle Kay's final portion of Grandpa's farm has been split up into homesites. I study the people in their driveways, talking with neighbors while they watch their children play on the tightly manicured lawns. In turn, they study me with distrusting eyes. Who is this guy driving past our place, they wonder, making note of my license plate. How sad a state our lack of trust has fallen to. We have drawn the borders of our lots so fine that even the most innocent gestures are suspect.

It starts with the establishing of edges, with a mind-set of "us and them," with a need to define what belongs to whom. I can't help but feel that what the people on Grandpa's Draper farm assume is theirs is really mine in a way, or was, and always will be, while still acknowledging that it is theirs. The heart of my wondering is to try to understand why this is so.

Early Mormons, driven from pillar to post in Missouri and Illinois, developed an acute fixation of "us and them." Their quest westward was an attempt to find footing in a new and more secure environment. Embedded within the core of their doctrine was the concept of stewardship, the idea that nothing is really owned by anyone. Explored in several communities after they had settled in Utah in what was called the United Order, all local lands and possessions were held in common and meted out as stewardships according to individual need, a truly democratic concept.

But the idea never caught hold.

Is it a flaw in human nature that they were not able to make such a concept work? Are we destined, as seems to be the case in our current more-republican structure, to continue to chop and define the borders of possession into ever-diminishing parcels? These are major questions, and the way we respond to them in future generations will determine the structure of future lives and, possibly, of survival itself. Our ability as humans to preserve and protect, to provide and conserve, to sacrifice for the common good—our ability to trust and be trusted—will ultimately determine whether we live as savages or brothers.

Today, Dad adjusts his glasses with one hand and with the other fiddles with the remote that controls his cable channels on the TV. He can pick up black-and-white memories of the thirties on the movie station or, at his leisure, switch to CNN to see what is happening in the current world.

Like many of his contemporaries, he often comments that things are much different than they used to be. Almost as often, I find myself doing the same thing. Looking back on seemingly less complicated times, we imagine that things were more stable then, encased in simple virtues and pristine landscapes.

Looking back, would we be more assured if we could realize that the past was not so pretty as we tend to paint it? Would it help to remember the cholera, the thin and fragile shoes, the cold winter nights in dark houses under several blankets, and the summers with no air conditioners? By the turn of the century, Utah's canyons were all but denuded by the demands of construction and firewood. Black soot from tens of thousands of coal stoves added a thick tarry soot to the gloomy haze that would make our current freeway smog seem thin.

Before asphalt, our roads were quagmires, and myriad trails into the mountains cut gashes that would make Sierra Clubbers shudder. Cattle herds let loose for summer range wandered free on the high slopes, and there was no concern for the damage caused to the ecosystem. There was no such thing as an ecosystem. Herds of sheep tore up mountain grasses by their roots so thoroughly that by the early 1900s the once-luxuriant slopes were feeling the strain of unnatural erosion. Only now, after decades of careful land management, are they beginning to recover.

Faced with the problems of our generation, our grandparents would not have fared any better than we have done. In fact, given their lack of comprehension of the fragility of the land, they would probably have fared much worse. At fifty-four, I am old enough to remember and be a part of that mind-set of a constantly replenished earth and engrossed in the American vision of manifest destiny, a perspective to which the founders of Mormon culture in Utah were enthusiastic proponents. To those who followed Brigham Young into the Great Basin kingdom, the land must have seemed endless just because of its sheer immensity. It was a land of unending breadth, a place of new beginnings.

Yet, by our time we are feeling the opposite.

When I was a teenager, Utah seemed to be the drabbest edge of the planet. If you wanted to see any part of the world worth seeing, you had to drive a thousand miles before you came to anything of substance. To the north was Yellowstone and Idaho and Montana, with moose and elk and hot pots, and Yellowstone Lake and the surging wonder of Old Faithful, which went off at constant intervals, a dependable symbol of mystery and power. To the east was Denver, first stop on the way to the rest of America and everything else "Back East." The movies told it all in images formed from hopes and passions fostered in dreams from the depression; night clubs, flashy cars, people who lived in large apartments with doormen, and people who smoked cigarettes in long cigarette holders and wore tuxedos and sequined dresses. Southward were the drab and struggling towns of old Deseret, overrun by sand and scorpions. More exciting were the orange groves of California, the lore of Hollywood and Hopalong Cassidy. Like skirts of virgins, the floats of Pasadena's Rose Parade tempted us to imagine a scented world far fairer than anything we had in Utah. Reno waved with the long arm of a neon cowboy. San Francisco, surrounded by water and brightly colored bridges, glowed like a cluster of scattered diamonds on the edge of the Pacific.

Everything, it seemed, was everywhere else. We had lost our sense of the fragile beauty of home. That we lived in a world that anyone else would envy was hard to believe.

But the West has been discovered again. A new breed of visionaries are planting hopes in Utah soil. As the world seems to fold in on us, we have started, with jaws ajar, to take a second look at ourselves. Through the eyes of these new Utahns, the land takes on a new appearance. Through their eyes, the mountains seem more majestic, the deserts more unique. All in the same moment, we find ourselves confused, jealous, and appreciative of growth's advantages. Balanced between our nostalgic and progressive natures, we struggle to preserve that which has been, while attempting to assimilate a growth that promises to change us forever. And that can be difficult.

While the seemingly suffocating rush of new blood into Zion might, at first glance, seem to be crushing everything that was, the dangers might be similar to boulders loosed on a steep slope by a summer storm. We have been to the summit of pioneer expansion. Mormon culture as a "Utah" phenomenon has had its moment of glory, a moment rich with ongoing heritage. But the view we have gained since then includes a more complex landscape than we ever could have imagined from our narrow perspective on the valley floor.

Caught in a cloudburst and filled with angst, we tread ground that seems slippery indeed. But abandoning the mountain is not an option. We must trust in the prevailing reservoir of human spirit that guides our more charitable nature, and have confidence that the vision guiding the first pioneers might be rekindled through the vision of Utah's new generation.

Watermasters of the past knew the value of limited resources, and though imperfect, they were able to establish guidelines that assured everyone a proper share when fairly followed. What we need again are watermasters—watermasters aware of the value of the water on the land and considerate of the people's needs. Confidence in the positive traits of human nature leads me to believe that just and evenhanded watermasters are always available if only we have the good sense to choose them and the courage to create the necessary cradles of conservation.

For as long as there is water—water to cleanse, to purify, to replenish and renew—and the careful concern of caring watermasters, we will be all right, and there will be an even richer inheritance to pass on to our children and grandchildren, which they, too, might savor from the verdant and not-too-crowded edge of a never-ending stream.

Dennis Smith is a professional artist and writer living in Highland, Utah.

"For the earth is full, and there is enough to spare; yea, I prepared all things, and have given unto the children of men to be agents unto themselves." (D&C 104:17.)

GOOSEBERRY CREEK:
A NARRATIVE
OF HOPE

Eugene England

 HARLOTTE IS OUR OLDEST GRANDDAUGHTER, NAMED FOR HER grandmother. When she was baptized just after she turned eight four years ago, I promised her that the summer after her twelfth birthday I would take her on a day-long trip into the wilderness and teach her to fly-fish. We will go on Monday, August 17, 1998. This is how I imagine the trip, my vision of how I hope she will remember it:

We drive south from Provo on U.S. Highway 89, through Spanish Fork Canyon and the ghost town of Thistle, to Fairview at the head of the San Pitch Valley. As we turn east up Cottonwood Canyon, we are quickly surrounded by stands of scrub oak and mountain maple. Even after we drive into the shadow of the steep range of the Wasatch Mountains ahead of us—the western edge of Utah's high plateau country—the greens of the oak leaves stand out rich and varied, a few branches shading off toward copper and red though it is still summer. We are silent, climbing slowly along the deep cuts the dugway makes in the north side of the canyon and glancing far down to our right at the groves of aspen and darker spruce and fir that gradually increase to fill the south side of the canyon as we climb.

Finally, the road levels out into a gentle valley that slopes toward the ridge, and the sun reappears, blinding us with yellow and flooding the valley with a clear light that flashes from the little creek we can see occasionally through the dense willows and chokecherry bushes. We continue up over the ridge, make a sharp left onto Skyline Drive, and then after only 100 yards take a right onto a dirt road that leads down through two campgrounds in small clusters of blue spruce and aspen and out through sagebrush and other low shrubs to Lower Gooseberry Reservoir. Just as we turn along the shore we pass a man riding a sorrel mare, with a small black-and-

white springer trotting to the side. I slow to avoid spooking the mare and notice the man's large dark face under a black Stetson that reminds me of Navajos I have met. "Looks like a sheep man going out to check his herd," I say, and Charlotte slips out of her safety belt and turns to look back.

When she was very young, Charlotte developed an unusual passion about protecting wilderness. Her mother, Jody, remembers they were watching a program on the Amazon, which showed native people and animals living in balance with the forest, when the scene changed to recent clear-cutting of huge areas and talk of extinction of species of animals and plants and possibly tribes of people. According to Jody, "Something clicked in Charlotte, right then. She asked, 'There used to be a forest there?' and when I said Yes, she got up and started for the door: 'We've got to stop them.' I calmed her down by talking about things we were already doing, like recycling and sending donations to Nature Conservancy, and suggested we write a letter to our congressman, Wayne Owens. She dictated the letter and drew two pictures about how she felt to send with it, one of a lush forest, with animals and a little girl playing happily—and one, of course, of a clear-cut patch with sad animals and a little girl crying."

Jody thought that would be the end of Charlotte's enthusiasm, but Owens wrote back in a way that got her solidly hooked: "I am proud of a five-year-old who thinks about rain forests and whales thousands of miles from her home, but she also acts to save the environment by recycling. . . . Charlotte, I hope you will always remember your love for this earth and the creatures that live here. I know as you grow older you will think of new ways to help save the whales, forests, and all the creatures living on this earth."

According to Jody, "After that letter Charlotte seemed permanently called on a mission. She went ballistic when four 100-year-old sycamores were suddenly ripped out down the street, and she pushes us on planting everything we can and even got a friend to help her make up a flyer on recycling and circulate it throughout the neighborhood—and then sent a copy of it with a letter to President Clinton!"

Jody sent me a copy of that letter ("I am 7. I want to have the earth clean and the forests growing and animals safe and clean air and clean water. . . . I am giving this blue paper to my friends so they will help me clean the earth. Will you please help me too?") and Clinton's rather stiff, form-letter reply ("Thank you for your thoughtful letter and for sharing your suggestions. . . . You can do your part by improving your community and striving to be an example to others"). But Charlotte was enchanted with a letter signed "Bill Clinton" and took the assignment from the president of the United States very seriously. When I spoke at her baptism, it seemed right to review some of the LDS scriptures about our divine assignment to be stewards of the earth and the covenants we make to care for it; when I conferred the Holy Ghost on her after her baptism, I blessed her that she would continue to be a valiant defender and protector of the earth and would be guided by the Spirit in doing so.

As we drive along the edge of the reservoir to the parking lot that overlooks Gooseberry Creek where it flows north out of the reservoir and then turns west for a while along the side of the long earthen dam, Charlotte pulls herself up from the seat of my Toyota 4-runner so she can better see what her grandfather's wilderness, which she's heard so much about in story after story, is like. Charlotte is bright blond like her father, fairly tall, and quite thin, with her mother's quick intensity and her own calm passion to do right—hard to keep focused on one thing, quick to see what needs doing and help. When we stop she runs to the rock barrier to look down on the stream and cry, "What's that big tower over there?" but then, looking a bit embarrassed, comes back to help with the gear.

I help her rig the new eight-foot Garcia rod, which I have bought her, with a small Cortland reel, #4 line, and a six-foot tapered leader I think she can handle, then tie on a #14 Parachute Adams fly, large and with enough white hackle that she can see it well as it floats. As she puts her nylon jacket and our lunches and water bottles in her small backpack, I rig up my nine-foot Sage rod with a stepped eight-foot leader and tippett and put on a smaller fly, a #16 Renegade. Then I check my fishing vest for all the supplies we might need, including needle-nose pliers, small forceps, and first-aid kit, and hoist it over my shoulders. I show her how to hook her fly through the little wire loop next to her reel and tighten up the line so it won't snag on bushes, and we set off.

The trail soon brings us down to the creek and under the concrete tower, which is about the size of a large silo, perhaps fifteen feet in diameter and fifty feet high, with a series of corroding twelve-inch-diameter cast-iron pipes coming out of the side at two-foot intervals, each immediately turned up to make a flat-topped elbow and the whole series forming a perfect spiral from base to top—a strange sight in any wilderness.

"That tower used to be under water," I tell her. "See that line of pipes that stick out of the side?" Charlotte stands looking for awhile, then I point down the creek to the huge slabs of concrete tumbled along it and broken-off buttresses in the canyon walls where it starts to narrow. "A dam was built here in 1915 to stop the water from running off so quickly in the spring. Then farmers down in Price could use it for irrigating their crops in the summer as the water was let out gradually through each pipe in turn. But it was built poorly and the first year a huge spring runoff went over the top and washed under the bottom of the dam until it all just caved in and caused a flood that killed one man in Price. Then in 1925 they built a much bigger irrigation reservoir at Scofield, about ten miles down this canyon."

We follow the trail next to the creek down through the Mammoth Narrows that gave the original dam its name—a canyon, with steep walls right to the water, that turns north for a quarter mile, then east for a half mile, and north again to where the canyon opens out a bit. I know there is an excellent fishing hole there that has a low, grassy bank where Charlotte can cast without too much trouble and that has enough riffle all along its surface so she won't be seen too easily by the fish.

As we walk, I talk about the bare-looking hills around us. "All this mountain area down past Manti and up to Spanish Fork Canyon once had nearly two feet more of topsoil than it does now. It was covered with shrubs and flowers and grasses and lots more trees, and the flat meadows around the reservoir were filled with grass as tall as you are that the elk and deer fed on, and by the creek there were masses of chokecherries for the bears."

She stops and looks back at me. "Yes, bears," I said, "hundreds of them until most were shot or trapped and moved out. And people killed wagonloads of deer to take down to Ephraim and Manti, just used the hides to make gloves. And then, when the Indians and bears were gone, people started moving their animals up the canyons to graze until there were nearly a million sheep in summer range up here. And, of course, the sheep stripped the ground bare and ate everything green as high as they could reach and turned all this area into a dustbowl. People in the towns below could see where every flock was located by the dust clouds rising above the mountains. And by about 1890 thunderstorms in the summer began to run right off into the valleys. The floods ripped out the streambeds and filled the irrigation canals with soil and gravel and then washed down through the streets of the towns."

The trail takes us up over a hogback to where the creek turns north again, and I take the lead and angle down to the creek where it spreads out over a long table of rock, shallow enough for us to walk across. Then I lead Charlotte up over a little ridge on the east side of the creek and down to the special hole I have picked for teaching her. I show her how to use my small pliers to flatten the barb on her hook so it can be easily removed from a fish's mouth and then how to squeeze the fly floatant from its little bottle and spread it through the hackle with her forefinger and thumb; then we wade out into the shallow water over the long gravel bar at the bottom of the hole.

We practiced on the lawn in front of my house in Provo the night before, with a piece of wool tied on the end of her leader. I put a book under her arm and held her wrist while we counted out the 1-2-3-4 rhythm of classic fly-casting over and over: (1) pull the rod straight back to a two-o'clock position while stripping line out from the reel with the left hand; (2) wait one count while the line continues back past the rod tip and pulls the three feet of newly stripped line with it for added length; (3) using only the wrist, power the rod forward to a ten-o'clock position that carries the line out to make a huge figure eight; (4) pause with the fly stopping a few feet above the water before starting back as the 4-count is repeated—for as many such "false" casts as necessary, stripping out extra line from the reel each time on the 1-count until the fly is pausing just short of where you want it to land and then stopping at ten o'clock on the next cast for a soft float down to the water, ideally with the fly landing before the leader. Sounds easy, and Charlotte mastered it quite well on the bare lawn.

Now, she hooks some sedge on the bank behind her on the second false cast, then retrieves her fly and starts again. She gets nervous and forgets the 2-count, so *her wrist is uncocking too soon for the line to catch up and she is whipping it down on the water just ten feet ahead of her.*

I stop her and offer to hold her wrist again like last night, but she shakes her head. She is trembling a bit, and I almost laugh but catch myself. She manages to get the line out farther and let the fly drop, where a fish takes it immediately and then heads straight for her. She yells with excitement, and I yell at her to pull the line tight with her left hand, but instead she tries to reel in, and the fish comes too fast and shakes the hook from its mouth.

She starts to whip the line out again, not keeping her arm in and still not remembering the syncopated 2-count, and I can see she is near tears. I begin to notice how cold the water is on my legs. "Let's sit here on the bank a minute and warm up a bit," I suggest. "The fish can wait." After we get out, I say, "I can hear a rock chuck; let's see if we can see him." Across from us on the hillside are clumps of bitterbrush and alpine gooseberry, with a few orange Indian paintbrush growing in the clumps. Near the creek is a rock outcrop, and soon we see the inquisitive nose of the marmot leading it up into view so we can see its yellow underside. I point and then whisper, "They do well here, despite the coyotes, because they've learned to build their entrances between buried rocks and can't be dug out." Charlotte watches a while and stops trembling, then spots a ground squirrel skittering along the trail just below the marmot. "Let's try again," she says.

This time I stay on the bank and Charlotte wades out slowly, looks back self-consciously and grins, then plays out the line well with four false casts and lets the fly down to the water about twenty feet upstream. It floats slowly over to the left towards the main current, and I can see she is about to lift the fly and cast again, but I whisper, "Wait!" The fish strikes just at the edge of the current; she lifts the rod to hook it and this time holds the tension as it darts twice across the creek, then she gradually strips the line back with her left hand until the fish is hanging in the air in front of her. I quickly unhook the forceps from my vest, move out beside her, show her how to lower the fish back partly in the water, reach into the open mouth, and clamp the shank of the hook with the forceps; with a quick twist of my wrist, I remove the unbarbed hook from the fish's gristly lip and release it without touching it. She hugs me just for a moment and says, "I knew I could do it. Can I catch one more?"

She catches three more, all from that same hole. After she catches each one, I tell her to lengthen her cast a few feet to move up toward the head of the hole where the fish, which are all facing upstream, have not yet been spooked by those she caught earlier and played back downstream. The last one, I can tell, is larger than the others, and she almost loses it as it takes a run down past her over the gravel bar and into some strong current below her. But she moves to the side and keeps the tension well, playing the fish back up to stiller water. I reach down and grasp it behind the gills and hold it up for her to see. It is about fifteen inches long, perhaps a pound—a cutthroat with deep red smudges below its gills and the same red continuing in a bright stripe down its brown-and-green sides. I unhook the fish and it stops gasping, lying perfectly still in my two hands as we admire it. I say, "A gift to us, this strange, beautiful creature to come into our world for a moment." I lay the fish back in the water, facing upstream; its gills fill and it slowly starts to breathe. After a moment it suddenly darts back up to the deep hole.

I suggest we hike down the canyon a ways and try the fishing below where Silver Creek joins Gooseberry. There might be larger rainbows that have worked their way upstream from Scofield Reservoir. As the creek turns east, the grasses in the flattening valley increase, but the side hills remain quite barren, the vegetation mainly in clumps under low shrubs and sagebrush, and some erosion still continuing between the clumps. As we approach the point where a steep valley brings Silver Creek in from the north on our left, we can hear and then see a few sheep on the opposite side hill, and when we get there we can see hundreds of them scattered all the way up to the trees on the ridge. Dozens of sheep are in the stream and have turned it and the banks into a muddy wallow for two hundred yards. We can see fishing won't be any good for a long way below so we turn back.

Then I see the man on horseback we had passed on the road in to Gooseberry Reservoir; he is riding up Spring Creek, and I say, "He probably has a small camp up there to stay at while he checks these sheep. But maybe he has a trailer and a corral up on the Skyline Drive someplace, or maybe even down in Fairview, and a few more flocks scattered around."

We hike back up to our special hole, and Charlotte catches two more fish. After we eat our lunch, the clouds up over the ridge to the west have turned gray, and a light drizzle begins to fall as we finish the last crumbs. She looks disappointed as I pack up and get out her nylon jacket for her, but I say, "Let's hike back up to the dam, and if it isn't raining too hard, we'll try for some rainbows that may have slipped over the spillway from the reservoir." I know the large clear pools there will probably be too difficult for her but think she might be reconciled to leaving by then if the rain gets worse.

During the long hike back through the light rain, I keep showing her new varieties of flowers—a few buttercups and alpine dandelions where snow has lain late on a steep north-facing slope. In the gooseberry clumps, protected from the sheep, we find yellow dime-sized cinquefoils and white pink-veined lewiseas, and in one large patch are some Colorado columbine with huge white blossoms and blue spurs. I show her the little berries forming on the gooseberry bushes: "This is one plant we know was here before the land was overgrazed. It stays around because the cattle, even sheep, don't like it—but the ruffed grouse love those berries in the fall."

Downstream a hundred yards from the tower is a pool that I have never been able to fish successfully because the water is so clear and still and the banks are so steep, with no brush or even grass to hide behind in order to make a reasonable cast without being seen. But as I go by with Charlotte, I notice the pool surface is broken up with the splashing raindrops, and I decide to try something new. Motioning Charlotte to follow behind me, I move up the steepest bank and rollcast my fly out to the center of the deepest part of the pool, which looks black and bottomless under the darkening sky. I see my fly floating clearly against that darkness despite the wildly dimpling water, watch for awhile, and am about to give up when I see a form moving up from deep in the hole. I barely resist striking too soon as the fish lazily rises to the surface—and then, in a sudden sideways turn, it takes the fly and dives.

I whoop and lift the fish straight up in the air with my strike, then hold it there, laughing, while I reach out with my forceps, slip out the hook, and let the fish drop straight back into the edge of the creek. Charlotte laughs, too, but when I ask her if she'd like to try this new fishing style, possible only in a rainstorm, she thinks a moment, with her lips pursed to the side, then shakes her head, and I see she is getting cold and it is time to go home.

The rain stops as we drive back past the reservoir, and when we pull out onto Skyline Drive the sun breaks through to the west of us. I ask Charlotte if we can take a little detour and she nods, so I turn north along the drive for a mile until we can see off to the right a large patch of trees surrounded by a fence. "That's one of the 'exclosures' the Rangers built in the 1920s to keep out livestock and try to bring back the plant life so they could find out what is was originally; let's see what's inside." As we walk east through the hummocked clumps of brush, I watch the ground closely. Charlotte stops, and I look up as she points to a double rainbow that has formed to the south and east across the head of Gooseberry Valley where it is still raining.

When we get to the fence we can see immediately the huge difference protection from the sheep makes: The stand of spruce and aspen is the only one in the area, and under the trees the ground is dense with flowers and grasses, delphinium and tall bluebells, sweet anise and western valerian, mixed with all kinds of tall grasses and alpine foxtail. I show Charlotte the solid groundcover of lupines and vetches, especially the wild sweetpeas, and tell her how these nitrogen-fixing plants enriched the original soils so that this whole area was once even more luxuriant than even in the exclosure; I turn back to show her how the ground outside has only a few flowers hidden within the gooseberry bushes—and much bare ground between the hummocks.

She is very sober as we walk back to the car. "Do you think the earth would be better without people?" she asks.

I hope I will have a good answer for Charlotte when I take her on that fishing trip this year. I hope I can tell her how grateful I am for Teddy Roosevelt, who established the Manti National Forest in 1903, and the Forest Rangers assigned there who discovered how to stop the flooding and started to recover the vegetation and topsoil, and how I think the area will someday all look like the land inside that exclosure they built in their devoted, lonely efforts to understand. The grasses and wild peas will enrich the earth and the forbs and succulents will spread out until the topsoil builds up again. We'll find ways for people like that Navajo sheepman to make a good living without grazing these high meadows—or clearcutting the forests and strip-mining the hills and stinking up the air of the plateau with power plants.

What will be hardest, of course, is to teach Charlotte—in her passion for truth and justice, her anger at those who have injured the earth, even in ignorance or in their own desperate efforts to merely survive—to care about all the people involved. To love, as I do, J. W. Humphrey, one of the first Rangers in the Manti Forest, who lived with his wife and baby in a tiny cabin on the forest boundary and struggled for years with sprinkling cans and home-made irrigation systems to establish a nursery, raising hundreds of thousands of Ponderosa pine seedlings to begin the reforestation. To love Arthur Sampson, who in 1912 started the Great Basin Experimental Station over in Ephraim Canyon to study the plants and what the erosion had done and how to restore the land. To love A. Perry Plummer, who first convinced the sheepmen it was right to control the grazing so they could stop the erosion, by doing painstaking, backbreaking analysis based on building huge concrete collection boxes and comparing all the erosion for fifteen years from two similar watersheds, one protected and one not.

But I also hope to teach her to love the pioneers who killed the deer and bear, and the cattlemen, and the Navajo sheepman we will see. I hope to be able to explain the unusual Mormon concept that all God's creations—animals, plants, even, it seems, the rocks themselves—have a spiritual existence and identity that can be loved and must be respected, but that humans are the form of life that is most directly in the image of God and the form that God both created the earth for and gave the express command to care for the earth. I will try to explain how human life and freedom and creativity are thus the highest values, the ends that everything else, including the natural world, were created to serve. Thus preserving human life and opportunity to learn and love may sometimes require (or seem to) that parts of the natural world be sacrificed for those ends, as pioneer settlers often did, but that even then, as with the destruction of the Gooseberry Range, the costs are great and terribly long-lasting—and require repentance and restoration.

But most of all, I want her to love the earth as she tries to understand how it works, and to love all the people who try to live on the earth and use it for the best ends they can imagine—to be firm in her sacred duty to be a steward of God's world but patient and humble as she tries to learn better how to do that and to teach others to be such good stewards, to excite and inform their imaginations. I hope to give her reason to believe—and a convincing example—that the earth would not be better without people.

Eugene England is a professor of English at Brigham Young University, where he teaches Shakespeare and Mormon and American literature. He also authored *Making Peace: Personal Essays* **(1995) and coedited** *Tending the Garden: Essays on Mormon Literature* **(1996).**

"But behold, I have obtained a land of promise, in the which things I do rejoice; . . ." (1 Nephi 5:5.)

PROMISED LANDS

Natalie Curtis McCullough

Y FAMILY WENT SEA KAYAKING IN ALASKA ONE SUMMER. My husband, four children, and I flew into Anchorage, where we met our cousins, drove down to Portage, and took a train through a tunnel to Whittier. There we rented kayaks, loaded a little chartered boat, and set out for a six-man Forest Service cabin in a back bay of the Prince William Sound. We were dropped off on a rocky beach at high tide. We climbed a wooden ladder onto a thickly forested ledge to our campsite, situated with a view across eight or ten miles to College Glacier. We had our kayaks and our fishing poles, our sleeping bags, and some coolers. We shared stale-smelling mosquito-net hats. On one side of the cabin, down a steep weathered staircase, was a freshwater stream where we filtered our drinking water. In front of the cabin, a little circle of logs around a fire was our kitchen. A short distance from us was an island where our cousins set up their tent camp. We waved good-bye to the charter and settled in for a week of tides, which fluctuated twenty feet every six hours.

We shared our bay with a half dozen bald eagles fishing for the same salmon we ate. We passed a raft of sea otters with babies on their bellies, watched dolphins porpoise in front of a sailboat. Our bay was home to a pair of seals that played hide-and-seek with us in our kayaks. Up popped a head to see what we were about before it disappeared, almost without a ripple. Everywhere we paddled, they periscoped alongside us. Bear lived close by. We never got to see them, but several mornings we measured our feet beside the new tracks and noted fresh piles of scat. Steaming.

Because the summer sun in the Arctic does not seem to set, we were at the mercy of twenty-two hours of daylight. This changes some basic rhythms. I was surprised to learn how much the sun dictates my activity. Without the cloak of darkness, much of nighttime ritual stays in the shadowy places of sleep, just out of reach. It is harder to dream well in sunlight. I felt violated by the sense that I could always be seen. Although I gave up much in privacy, I gained much in perspective. In July the North Pole tilts toward the sun. This places the sun at such a low angle of incidence, we could chase the colors of alpenglow in the kayak for many minutes longer than the original onset of dusk at the cabin site, in the back of the bay. Many nights, between eleven-thirty and midnight, the water quieted so completely, it was impossible not to be lured back into our boats, seeking the farthest point of sunset from which we could still paddle back.

Sea kayaking is different than I imagined, and in a way, religious. Sitting so low in the water, I feel I am part of it. I feel securely weighted in its womb. Yet, everywhere I go happens under my own power. Because I use one long rod with paddles on either end, the oaring is very rhythmic and peaceful—unless I happen to be sharing a three-man kayak with my seventeen-year-old son and eight-year-old daughter. He tries to make her cry by tipping the boat dangerously low. She retaliates with a splash, and then, again, the rhythm changes. I fix a smile, thankful I am not able to move from my little hole in the fiberglass and cannot be responsible for the aberration of nature occurring behind me in the form of my children. Somehow in the wilderness setting, even the disruption of rhythm becomes rhythmic. The children quiet. The water stills. So do I. Stillness becomes a rhythm as dear as any.

Another remarkable rhythm is the fact of a twenty-foot tide that rises and falls twice every day. I cannot remember seeing the moon. If I did, I did not think to record it. Yet its influence directs tidal activity. I also feel a gravitational ebb and flow in my body. I know the gush and fill of longing to be on shore, rising to my family. I struggle with the equal pull away from the demands on shore, back out to sea. There is sweet terror in the wish to be a floating speck on open ocean. When the tide comes in, we paddle about the reefs in search of red starfish, purple urchins, and sea anemones. Jellyfish float beside us: brightly colored oranges and reds of nebulous-looking torn flesh. When the tide goes out, we walk the shoreline in steady slow motion, stooping to turn over every rock and shell. Every day the children make bucket aquariums brimming with sea life. I settle into an ethic both strange and familiar: insulated circular life.

What happens to me after a few days in the woods is that original cycles emerge. I leave fear and even the expectation of interruption as the primary life pattern. I center. I initially have the audacity to invade the wilderness setting to imagine myself conqueror. But I soften and become wary. What is possible in wilderness is the subduing of my own sense of importance. If I release myself to the ebb and flow, I have claim on the blessings of blending. I learn that belonging to the rhythmic forces is greater than controlling them.

One morning, I wake in the semi-light of the cabin, listening to the snores and dream murmurs of my family around me, feeling tired and claustrophobic. Even in wilderness, I feel trapped by sea, forest, and bodies. I yearn for the desert—strange longing to identify. From my side of our bunk, I hear the eerie cry of a loon, most ancient of birds. I do not see it, cannot be certain what it is. But I wish on the loon anyway, and imagine it flying in twilight overhead.

Again the loon calls. I do not see the source but am guided by the primitive voice. Whether to dive or to fly? It is lightly raining. Shall I adapt to this watery world, who was born dry-skinned in a desert? Can I be moonstruck, here where the sun stays so long? I will be crazy as a loon tonight. Take on her powers. Leaving my children to their own dreams, I rise against gravity to walk alone, afraid of night noises. In the dense undergrowth, leafy branches brush and encircle my neck. I sit alone atop a little hill and watch the sky slowly fill with a light it has hardly emptied. A part of me prays toward the growing light.

Landscape links me to spiritual rhythms and risks. Light divided from darkness, water springing from stone, even oxen blessed to live are experiences in the natural world that separate the created from the Creator. In the beginning of the apostle Paul's epistle to the Romans, I read about people

> Who changed the truth of God into a lie, and worshipped and served the creature more than the Creator, . . .
> [They] changed the glory of the uncorruptible God into an image made like to corruptible man, and to birds, and fourfooted beasts, and creeping things. (Romans 1:25, 23.)

The natural world is where my life's distortions are reshaped, and usually simplified, back into the "the truth of God." By my journeys in the wilderness, I awaken to the ancient call of my Creator and Redeemer, Jesus Christ. I have not seen Him, but believe I know His voice. And still I walk alone, afraid, in the night. Spiritual blessings and burdens ebb and flow. The forces that govern my tides are large, encompassing all my acts of belief and unbelief. Hope and despair naturally fluctuate. Ebb and flow.

Where do others hear His voice? Over and over the reply: in the garden, on the mountaintop, in the wilderness, over the long stretch of ocean sailing to a new world, in the desert and on the overland trail. The Promised Land always lies at the end of a wilderness expanse.

When I was a girl, my mother directed a lavish theatrical production called *Promised Valley*. It is the story of Mormon pioneers coming into the Salt Lake Valley to build a refuge from the world where they could worship their God and participate unhampered in His miracles. She cast me as an inconspicuous child in one of the families, more to be relieved of caring for me than to showcase my dramatic stage presence. I got to wear a pioneer bonnet and a long calico dress in which to act out the long westward trek. I still feel the impact of that archetypal journey. In a sense it was Mother who led me toward the ideal of a Promised Valley.

> I dream of a home in the valley,
> with fields in my mind flowing green,
> I long for a home in the valley . . .
> no lovelier place to be seen . . .

Crawford Gates, "I Dream of a Home in the Valley," *Promised Valley*

I was not an easy child to direct in any situation. I was as independent as I was invisible. As the middle child in a family of seven children, there was stiff competition for Mother's attention. This play was her way of paying attention to me. The project was enormous, my contribution was small. But I had a full uninterrupted view of Mother bringing her vision to life. From all those hours in the background, just watching her, something personal and precious happened to me, the ignored middle child. It felt like the tide coming in.

I am still governed by tides. The cycle of filling up and emptying out appeals to me. I experience tides as an emotional, physical, and spiritual gush and empty. I am drawn to the belief that they are necessary and natural, that they should not be fought against any more than the feminine cycle. What a relief to see that the swelling of old fears, hurts, even hopes are only high tide and low tide, balancing each other. How to release myself to the ebb and flow? I frequently forget to love and acknowledge the pale and changing moon—thinking my purpose is to work for evenness, for constant balance, that my goal is to fight the fluctuation. I have to be reminded there are reasons for seasons.

Hiking in the heart of Capitol Reef with my daughters has become a seasonal ritual in preparation for the dark of winter. The desert rock looks liquid in formation. The curves and swells of sandstone seem essentially feminine. I feel surrounded by a woman's body. I cannot pass without touching the swirls of stone, a tactile following of woman's flow. I forget to worry about where I sag and bulge, feeling only how dear and loved are the maternal circles. Blood, bloat, birth, babies, beginnings. In the heart of this feminine presence, I fill with wonder and belief. I have part in the circle. I am brought to believe in forces both reminiscent of and superior to my own. The "mother" in Mother Nature is very real to me. She is circular and rhythmic, even as I am. Living out the day-to-day luxury of my life's dream of mothering, I see the responsibilities and details that accompany it keep me from other dreams. Some women find the stamina to follow competing dreams. I am a seasonal woman. The feminine, maternal dream is large enough, strong enough to sustain my searching for this season. It will direct which dreams stay mere possibilities, dead-end side canyons, and those that eventually trickle into the headwaters with power to shape the earth.

We walk in mud, my daughters and I, streamside. We battle to be heard over the rush of water funneling into stone canyon. A few yards downstream, the canyon widens and water's rush diminishes. Our own voices ascend and echo back. Step by step we fill with dreams, influenced by patient water's path. We cluster together in spirited discussion, we string out, separate in our thoughts. Here in in the belly of the desert, we remember our love of mountain and sea.

I think back to the day in the Sound when we climbed from sea level to a mountaintop glacier, perhaps 2,000 feet high. We bushwhacked heavy undergrowth, walked the perimeter of a glacier-fed pond, followed a series of streams, took pictures of the children crawling through flowers in a hilly meadow. As we reached the last bluff before significant snowpack, my height-anxiety started its paralyzing grip. One by one, my family members, children, cousins, and adults moved upward to the final peak where they could glissade down the snow. I wanted to follow, as much to say the lovely word *glissade* as to enjoy foot-skiing from the heights. But I was gut-empty scared, my breath coming in painful bursts. I felt too exposed. I needed to hug earth. When even my youngest child scrambled up a yellow-white cornice, tottering on the ridge for effect, calling, "Come on, Mom! Don't be scared!" I turned back toward camp, wiggly-stomached, and walked home alone.

It had been many days since civilization. I wore layers of mosquito repellent, campfire smoke, and the stale air of a sleeping bag. We perspired in the kayaks and on the steady recent ascent. I was alone in camp. I went down the back staircase to the freshwater stream fed by the glacier my family was playing on. I stripped off mosquito netting, vest, sweater, shirt, underwear. Too timid to sink in the frigid waters, I only splashed, soaped, and splashed again, exhilarated by arctic air on wet skin. I submerged my head, shampooed, and submerged again. The rush of cold headache comes. Wet hair dripping down my back, I wrapped a fish-stained hand towel about me and climbed shivering to the cabin before the onslaught of shouts and laughter closed in. I stubbed a numbed and frozen toe on one of the wooden steps. It throbbed to life, completing my purification rites.

Cries from my daughters draw me back to the red-rock canyon. They have given up the hope of hiking with dry feet, and their sounds at the shock of cold water delight me. I adapt. I follow them into the river. Gradually, we veer onto a high plateau where the canyon widens. We walk under a delicate arch of willows, and come upon the body of a dead cow in the early stages of decay. We cover our mouths and noses. Flies swarm and feast in black clouds. Dried eyes stare back. Patches of hide pull away from distended ribs. There in the glare of stinking sun is a half-born calf wrapped in placental blue, still umbilically attached. One hoof pierced through to life; head and shoulders bound by the birth canal.

She died giving birth, I told them. The calf died being born.

We stayed there looking at her a long time but we did not cry. We all belonged here—the cow and her calf, my daughters and I. This, too, is part of the promise.

We listen for a voice crying out in the wilderness. We call back. We are called forward. Each wilderness journey builds reverence for the rise and sink of forces beyond our own. Promised lands.

Natalie Curtis McCullough was born and educated in Salt Lake City where she and her husband now raise their children.

"WHEN [HE] HEARD THAT IT WAS THE LORD, HE . . . DID CAST HIMSELF INTO THE SEA." (JOHN 21:7.)

HE DID CAST HIMSELF INTO THE SEA

LARRY CLARKSON

N O [HUMAN] ARGUMENT, NO [HUMAN] REASON CAN OPEN THE MINDS of intelligent beings and show them heavenly things; that can only be done by the Spirit. . . . When the Spirit inspires a man, his mind is opened to behold the beauty, order and glory of the creation of this earth."
—THE PROPHET BRIGHAM YOUNG

He passes through the door. Feet shuffle from shadowy tile onto wooden deck, raised grain and warmth caressing his steps. The light outside is harsh and he squints. The pound of the surf is incessant. He closes his eyes and listens as the next wave rises—water heavy with salt and slurry, heaving and building, balancing on the edge of sky. He sucks in a short breath and anticipates as the wave teeters.

The shriek and squawk of children and gulls break the thought and he opens his eyes. He watches the free fall of the celadon curl careen downward and onto itself with a boom. A gurgle of water and sand and air skims onto the beach with the rhythm of the next impending wave. The beating of a heart much larger than his.

When [he] heard that it was the Lord, he . . . did cast himself into the sea. (John 21:7.)

He jumps off the deck into a blanket of hot sand, catches himself, and stumbles toward the surf. His footing turns hard and wet, and he splashes through the hiss of receding foam. He kicks his knees high, straining hard against the increasing resistance and depth. Then, with legs coiled, arms and hands pointed, snorkel and fins flailing, he uncocks and hurls himself, piercing the rising wall of water.

Time seems suspended, the quiet below almost deafening. His body stiffens, then reacts. Fighting the wave, he kicks hard while losing flight, then suddenly shoots forward with the receding surf, gliding until he arcs to the surface and breaks water, gasping and gulping for air. A familiar shock of immersion swirls around him, uncovering what he thinks is a long-lost remembrance of water.

. . .

Naked, he treads the cobalt blue, adorned only with his feeble attempt to imitate the animals he has dominion over—a plastic snorkel, black rubbery fins, and a mask with a large glass lens. He slips his toes into the hollow cavity of each fin, stretches then hooks the slippery strap over his heels. He kicks softly to keep his head above the surface while the faraway beach bobs on the horizon in sync with the swells. He spits into the mask and smears sticky saliva inside the lens, forming a thin barrier against condensation from the warm air of his lungs and the cold water outside the glass. A quick rinse and the mask is donned. He checks the fit, sucks in air through his nose, and seals the soft edges of the mask against his forehead, cheeks, and upper lip. He inserts the fleshy flange of the snorkel into his mouth and takes a short cautionary breath. Seawater gurgles in the stiff plastic tube and he blows hard, dips his head below water, and swims off into the sea.

And God created great whales, and every living creature that moveth, which the waters brought forth abundantly, . . . (Genesis 1:21.)

One hundred feet from shore the water and waves are still turbulent. Sand and debris swirl off the ocean floor and surge with the constant motion of the waves and tides, hampering visibility and reducing line of sight from thirty feet to three. The smooth bottom is punctuated with large solitary rocks—harbors of loose coral, shells, and detritus of stones and pebbles that attract fish and scavengers looking for refuge while patrolling the waters for food carried in from the depths or out from the shore. Colors and shapes, forms and textures appear and disappear from his view with each rocking of the waves. The shallows are full of batfish, angelic phantoms with barbed tails like pitchforks, kicking up puffs of sand as they scurry away. A menace only if inadvertently stepped on, they are more concerned with his looming presence than he with theirs. A larger shadow quickens his pulse. The mottled brown and deceivingly languid silhouette of a guitarfish resembles a tiger shark but is a toothless bottom feeder, a vacuum cleaner picking up fishy debris. He notices dozens more as visibility increases and he drifts into deeper waters.

Three hundred feet offshore a small limestone reef floats into view, an oasis of old sea grass and young kelp dancing in a desert of open water and rippled sand forty feet below the swells. Garibaldi dash in and out of green swaying fronds like liquid flames. A distinctive Neanderthal hump above each fish's eye accentuates its territorial aggression, its pouty mouth like a predator's beak, ready to peck and scrape the rocky outcropping for food or to nip at intruders. Agitated by his human presence above, the golden fish swirl and flicker in warning below. He resists their fiery temptations to dive deep, to tease, to spiral down and around giant stalks of kelp to the bottom, then to bounce back to the surface like a sprung jack-in-the box. Instead he lies still, caught between water and sky. His head immersed and wet hair swirling, he pants through his snorkel and orchestrates his breathing until it is slow and deep and in cadence with the ebb and flow of the waves above and the undulation of the manes of sea grass far below.

> *. . . and the Spirit of the Gods was brooding upon the face of the waters. And they (the Gods) said: Let there be light; . . . (Abraham 4:2–3.)*

He floats like this, hypnotized by the repetition, the pulsating beat of blood rushing through his veins, no longer knowing where his rhythm ends and the ocean's begins. Legs dangling like tentacles, arms floating by his side like pontoons, he watches sunlight seep into the water and illuminate generations of plankton dancing in the void. The light underwater is diffused. The liquid mass filters out reds and yellows. The rough surface of the waves dapples the light, and the underwater world is bathed in a soft flickering blue that grays and deepens with depth. Dark masses of rock and kelp and bottom-feeding fish suck in the light, allowing little to reflect, revealing shadowy form but hiding intricacies of color and texture. While surface fishes with their gowns of glassy prisms reflect and refract the light, tiny transparent scales play with sunbeams—scatter highlights, break up shadows, isolate texture, and accentuate color—visually separating parts of the fish from the whole.

Mesmerized by the shadow dance on the ocean floor, his eyes catch flickers of light as schools of anchovies appear. A shimmer of silver and deep purple, the mass envelops him. He twirls his body in slow wide circles, shrouded by flash and sparkle as individual fish dissolve into a single mass of movement and light. Then startled by the beauty, overcome by the wonder, he dives, yearning. The school darts and he follows, kicking frantically, hands ripping through the dense nothingness. Countless writhing fish come into focus as he gains speed, and for a fleeting moment he thinks he sees the shadow of himself reflected in their bottomless eyes. The school banks to the left and he is alone, hovering like a bird in a darkening sky. He turns slowly, kicks, then slides above the water, needy for air.

> *. . . them will I visit with the manifestation of my Spirit; and they shall be born of me, even of water and of the Spirit— (D&C 5:16.)*

He is tired—muscles famished by lack of oxygen, energy sapped by the cold. He inhales a slow deep breath and lowers his head below the surface. Bending hard at the waist, he thrusts his legs high above his head and the weight of his body pushes him down. He pulls hard and breaks through the resistance of the first twenty feet where buoyancy disappears. The deeper he dives the faster he descends. Sand, dappled and alluring from above, turns to a dull gray ten feet from the ocean bottom, wrinkled like the skin of a long extinct creature. Spreading his arms and arching his back, he slows his descent. His upright body lands softly, puffs of sand billowing around his feet. With his arms stretched outward, he fights to stay stable in the ponderous and shifting current.

> . . . *the light of Christ . . . is in the sun, and the light of the sun,* . . .
> *(D&C 88:7.)*

A radiant orb floats soft and shimmering on the surface high above. Cascading pillars of luminescent greens and yellows catch his eye and pull his gaze upwards, becoming a clerestory of light, a cathedral in this nation of fishes. Time dissolves as he feels the soft caress of sea grass, glimpses the blurred flame of the Garibaldi as they turn, and passes into a deep state of mind. Receding into the womb, he drops through the geologic layers of his genes into a oneness with water while the currents rock him. Like Jonah, "the waters compassed [him] about, even to the soul: [and] the depth closed round [him] about" (Jonah 2:5).

All mortal thoughts are now drowned and his sins are washed away.

. . .

He hangs in this liquid space—a man on a cross, caught between death and resurrection. Bubbles trickle from the crease of his mouth, break loose, and seek repose sliding up the contour of his cheek. Struggling against the beauty, they try to cut through the mindless tether, and belch out a silent scream as they shimmer and rise.

> *And Jesus, when he was baptized, went up straightway out of the water: and, lo, the heavens were opened unto him, and he saw the Spirit of God . . . (Matthew 3:16.)*

The piercing burn in his lungs awakens him. Instinctively his body cocks; his thighs coil then release, hurling him upwards. He suppresses his panic, the pressure building as he ascends, his gaze transfixed on the orb. Legs scissor madly, arms flail as he struggles to escape the depths, up through the shafts of light, drawn by the pull of the sun. Body fighting soul. Ascension.

He breaches like a whale, breaks the surface into what feels to be the thin seam that binds earth and heaven. Engulfed in the siren chatter of the beach oblivious to his ascension, he is suddenly aware that his was not a flight into eternity but a journey, perhaps, back to his mortality.

> *Sometimes during solitude I hear truth spoken with clarity and fresh-ness; uncolored and untranslated it speaks from within myself in a lan-guage original but inarticulate, heard only with the soul, and I realize I brought it with me.* (Hugh B. Brown, *Eternal Man*)

Larry Clarkson is an award-winning graphic designer and a Utah backcountry vagabond who likes to paint and write poetry about the landscape.

"BUT THIS IS NOT ALL; YE MUST POUR OUT YOUR SOULS IN YOUR CLOSETS, AND YOUR SECRET PLACES, AND IN YOUR WILDERNESS." (ALMA 34:26.)

EXCERPTS FROM A JOURNAL IN ISRAEL

CORDELL CLINGER

 THINK OF THAT DAY OFTEN, EVEN THOUGH IT WAS TWENTY YEARS ago. I think of the hot desert sun, the seemingly lifeless topography, the bleached rocks and soil. It was all the color of cracking, except for the brilliant blue sky, cloudless and endless, and the cool water of the waterfall that fell over smooth rocks into many small pools. I had come to know this *wadi,* or small canyon, by conversing with Israeli students in Jerusalem. On the map, the small stream from the natural springs fed into the Jericho Valley. If I followed the stream from its source, it would lead me to the ancient city of Jericho, one of the many ancient cities in the Middle East. And one that I recalled from childhood because the walls fell down at the command of Joshua.

Israel attracted me because of its antiquity. But my college professor in Russian history ignited my desire to study Hebrew, archeology, ancient history, comparative religions, and modern political science on location. It was an adventure of a lifetime.

After living in Israel for five months, I realized there are many voices that are competing to be heard. It can be a very noisy place. There are voices of various religions claiming racial and doctrinal superiority, contentious political voices vying for land to live on at the expense of cultural and historical longevity.

The newness of the country, the juxtaposition between ancient and modern landscapes, was very exciting to me. But the noise was becoming too intense. There was too much to digest. I needed a break from the commotion of political double talk, contending religious thought, holy shrines, and the jarring contrast of modern twentieth-century interloping over, around, and on top of layer upon layer of past cultural civilizations. I needed to breathe. I needed silence. I wanted a clear space void of shrines, organized stones, blocks, rails, traffic, and people. I wanted to listen to what the ancient people in this land had listened to—silence.

And so it was with this in mind that I found myself drawn to the designated wadi with the waterfall. I started one early spring morning with the intent of finding the wadi and spending the day there in solitude. It was my first attempt of really trying to listen and connect with a landscape. To my great delight, there was no one at the waterfall. I was alone. I was alone—at last. The water was soothing after hiking a few miles in the hot desert sun. It was quiet and serene. Ancient.

Instinctively, I took off my clothes and lay there on the sun-baked rocks, ear to the ground, listening, smelling. The smell of the rocks and ground was an old smell. Musty and dry. These rocks, this land was the pathway of shepherds who had watered their flocks here; these rocks were the paths of aesthetes who had communed with God in centuries past. My head shifted from ear to ear, eyes closed, trying to imagine who and what had happened at this oasis. I then turned flat on my back facing the sun directly. I had never been so fully exposed before. And yet, I didn't really care if someone might be watching me. My exposed state was between me and the elements around me, beneath me, over me, all around me. I had shed the modern noise of the twentieth century by removing my clothes. I was merging with something ancient, primal, eternal—merging with rocks smoothed with time and water that had supported other people from other eras, human like me. In that hour of nakedness in these natural surroundings, I realized that I am a fellow traveler with many on this planet who search for a deeper meaning, who are hungry to locate their own personal truths. My attempt to lay bare in the pathways of antiquity made me realize that I am a small part in the history of mankind who want to revere the past, to honor their relationship with God and the land that was created.

"BEHOLD, HE HATH HEARD MY CRY BY DAY, AND HE HATH GIVEN ME KNOWLEDGE BY VISIONS IN THE NIGHTTIME." (2 NEPHI 4:23.)

THE VIRTUES OF FIRE, NIGHT, AND SILENCE

PAUL H. RISK

ROM MY EARLIEST YOUTH, I HAVE BEEN AWARE OF AND AWED BY the changing, stimulating, ever-interesting play of events in the outdoors. The electric thrill preceding a thunderstorm led by jousting, turbulent winds and accompanied by distant thunder drums. The leaves of elm and maple rolling upside down and curling, their undersides white against inky clouds. Deep in my soul something was stirred and a feeling of spiritual closeness and relevance began to grow and take shape. The world was more than mere leaves and clouds, plants and animals. The outdoors, I felt, was a conduit to a yet-undefined relationship with deity. The feelings developed and took clearer form as I matured, and with them came a firm assurance that my destiny was somehow tied to helping others feel and understand as I did.

After I began work as an environmental interpreter in the early 1960s, first at Descanso Gardens in Southern California and then as a Park Ranger Naturalist at Grand Canyon National Park and later at Lassen Volcanic National Park in Northern California, the drama of the natural environment became a vital focal point in my life. Rock patterns and ravens, fossils and freshets, wind and water have all intrigued, puzzled, and soothed me. The stark beauty of deserts, the open vastness of prairie, the somewhat intimidating emptiness of mountain crags have shaped and honed my desire to be able to communicate to others the feelings they generated in my heart and mind.

In teaching environmental interpretation at four universities over almost thirty years, I have striven to help students gain environmental sensitivity, awareness, understanding, and appreciation for the outdoors and learn to talk with others of these things. But there has been an ongoing frustration that so few seemed to feel the "magic" of it all, and of those who did even fewer were able to communicate their insights to others. Why, I have asked myself over and over, was that intangible element missing? I have concluded that part of the problem is that many, perhaps most, have simply not felt or experienced enough events to build a repertoire of sufficient richness and depth.

Simultaneously, as a twenty-one-year-old convert to The Church of Jesus Christ of Latter-day Saints, and later in leadership positions, including bishop and stake president, I have pondered the deep mysteries of the gospel, the meaning of our staggeringly brief sojourn in mortality. Why was it so hard for so many to feel the love of God, His closeness to us? Why did so few catch the vision and reality of grand promises stretching into the eternities with loving families timelessly united? I have found, as many before me, that the answers to life's deepest questions were most easily sensed away from the rush and breathless hustle of cities, where solutions were too often temporal and temporary. A wondrous peace, I found, could be mine as oft I prayerfully knelt beneath the sky, in my ears the whisper of evening's gentle conversation with itself. Monumental and simple, gospel truths smoothed their convolutions, and prayerful searches were answered clearly, unequivocally, yet with gentle power and permanence.

As I write these words, I am camped near the Royal Gorge in Colorado, and I wonder still, as darkness wells up from the valleys, spreading like a calming, secure blanket up the pinyon- and juniper-covered hills. Birds, in last frantic territorial flurries, dart hither and yon, raucously proclaiming the limits of their boundaries. A waning moon serenely, slowly descends the western sky, silhouetting black branches against its white crescent. The wind, so swift during the day, dies; crickets, silent during the heat of the day, begin their leisurely chirping in the evening coolness.

Carefully arranged dried juniper twigs are piled against a split pine log. Larger branches join them in a latticework of promised heat. A match's flame creeps greedily up the tiny twigs, growing and engulfing larger pieces. But there seems no rush. Slowly but deliberately, the fire grows, and we crouch closer in anticipation of the warmth and security it will bring. Tendrils of fragrant juniper smoke curl upward, chased by small orange flames.

Conversation slows. The silence of the night presses close, as does the darkness, while we stare moth-like into coals and flames that draw us back to early pioneer campfires and, farther back, to ancient family groups huddled close to the fire's life-giving warmth. Fires such as ours illuminated the otherwise-fearsome nights in dark caves of the prehistoric past, leaving on stone walls smoke smudges visible even today. Primitive eyes gazed hypnotically into fire's depths, their owners mesmerized by its whirling patterns, just as we are now. In awe and reverence and fear, thoughts turned to the eternal, the infinite, the unknown. Oral histories unfolded under star-studded skies as the brilliant celestial pinpricks looked down on the storytellers.

Then, as now, tales and histories, thoughts and dreams, expressed in hushed tones at the edge of a campfire's glow, took on special meaning and a depth of feeling that followed the hearers to the edges of their lives. So eloquently did those experiences speak to the depths of their being that later even the briefest whiff of familiar smoke could rekindle emotions of the past. No wonder ancient people felt so strongly that some kinds of smoke were sacred. Their fragrance, early Native Americans said, made their hearts grow good and helped their souls reach out to that Great Spirit who created us all. From such experiences we matured, our beings expanded, and our comprehension grew of our oneness with all the living and nonliving universe.

Today, we engineer genes, chase comets through the void, and, in almost godlike fashion, transplant organs. And still, we stand in uncomprehending awe of nature. An acorn yields an oak and an embryo produces an eagle, requiring the coordination of a myriad of extremely complex and sophisticated biochemical processes. Massive plates of rock slide snail-like over a plastic core of superheated magma at the center of our planet, and continents continue to rearrange themselves. Roots stretch inexorably toward earth's center while green shoots rise in the opposite direction, seeking the sun from which all energy and life are derived. Insects follow scent trails measured in parts per quadrillion as they seek others of their kind. Bats employ search-and-targeting systems similar to nuclear submarines as they "swim" toward their prey in the ocean of our atmosphere. The sun, seething at thousands of degrees Fahrenheit with yet-unduplicated nuclear fusion, slips above the eastern horizon each morning and descends in the west each evening. Darkness wells up around us and, like scattered, shattered diamonds, a panoply of stars, galaxies, and nebulae, "worlds without number," spreads in awe-inspiring grandeur over the sky. Ancient light, originating thousands, even millions, of years ago, sparkles against the black velvet of the night. How can one contemplate the universe and the infinity of space without wondering and finding disquieting questions and perhaps solace in the knowledge that the great God of us all is in control? However ill-prepared we may be to explain the mighty oak's transition from an acorn, or the miracle of worlds without end, He knows and understands, and we are comforted by that knowledge. As we comprehend the depths of our ignorance, we can seek to learn more of the myriad processes through which the apparent miracle of creation and life in the universe is carried out. And, in that quest, standing in His presence, we too may one day fully understand and appreciate.

The music of solitude has various themes—the rush of a mountain stream, a chickadee's plaintive cry, the wind whispering, fluttering, laughing through the trees. John Muir thought he could identify most of the trees in a forest solely by their songs, so unique were their voices as their wind-harp branches and leaves were gently touched by the fingers of the breeze. To me, though, three sounds—the howl of a wolf, the bugling of a bull elk, the call of a loon across northern lakes—especially evoke the call of the wild. The wilderness in their voices raises the hair on our necks and calls to a primeval self, to a kinship long forgotten or submerged in civilization's bustle.

There is in nature a gentleness as well as a sharpness that speaks, paradoxically, like the "still, small voice" of God, to an ill-defined part of the human psyche. It can best be felt where mankind's influences are nonexistent or, at least, nearly unobservable. Amid towering, glacier-mantled crags, beneath diamond-studded desert sky, on Grand Canyon's rim, its message is not heard but felt. Yet, unmistakable and vibrant is the message: There is a God from whose presence we have only recently departed. He loves us as surely as summer warmth and flower fragrance. He gave his Son for us, and prophets spoke and speak today that we might know his will. Angel choirs and angel trumpets might ring from the hills, but such is not necessary. The magic of our sojourn in mortality is best known through meaningful quiet, of solitude, of music we cannot hear. Clear and unmistakable it comes, touching harmonious chords within ourselves. Focusing a keen awareness of the immensity of the universe, it triggers a vibrant humility as our soul reaches achingly to the distant horizon. As a to-me-unknown author wrote, "The silence roared. I staggered back and heard my varnished ego crack."

The "roar" of isolation's silence, the gentle tranquility of solitude in nature are therapy for the spirit, wherein we can commune effectively with God, his answers coming clear and rejuvenating.

From time to time, islands of peace come into our lives that, once experienced, leave indelible life-changing images. I think of the deep blue of a summer sky on the Grand Canyon's North Rim, of stately ponderosa pines towering over crimson heads of Indian paintbrush nodding gently in vanilla- and terpene-fragranced breezes. Of ancient, twisted, weathered junipers rooted tenaciously but precariously in rock niches along the canyon rim. Of folded-wing ravens tumbling clown-like, toying with flight above the mile-deep abyss. Of the hiss of violet-green swallows swooping in impossible knife-edged, right-angle turns, shaming man's best efforts at jet-powered acrobatic flight. Of darkness rising from the canyon depths, pursuing sunset colors as they retreat from rocks to sky, and day gives gentle way to evening and night.

But times are changing. We are losing so much. Too often today, such magic experiences in nature are no longer accentuated by pungent campfire smoke. The Conservation movement and, later, environmentalism have proclaimed the sin of open fires, which, they contend, scar the landscape and scour it of available fuel. Instead of the quiet hiss and snap of burning wood, the rush and roar of stoves disposing of fossil fuels greet the night. Reminiscent of blowtorches and acetylene welding equipment, the tiny wonders will boil water in a few short minutes and never, ever blacken a pot. But they will also never, ever touch the human heart and close the gap between ourselves and the wilderness, between ourselves and our ancient past, between ourselves and our God. Where once aromatic smoke drifted on the evening air, we now have the hot breath of burned hydrocarbons and the pungent fumes of stove fuel. Even the intellectual satisfaction of being politically correct cannot make up for what we have lost.

When does the ethical purity of environmentalism so corrupt the very thing it purports to preserve that it becomes not a blessing but a curse? Would Emerson, Thoreau, or John Muir have ever passed on to us the power of their sojourns away from civilization had they not coupled their daylight ventures with the tranquilizing glow of a nighttime campfire?

And what of the salving, gentle blackness of the night? The profound silence bespeaking eternity? Mercury and sodium vapors and incandescent filaments now automatically illuminate the darkness, driving away our urban-imaged demons and chasing even the stars from the heavens. Silence, so conducive to inward and celestial journeys, is shattered by battery-operated stereos while the roar of automobile engines and, in the skies, jet aircraft severs our ties with the eternal and freezes us in the here and now.

How many generations yet unborn and cheated of the magic of fire, the beauty of night, the solace of silence will never know the rejuvenating power of nature? How many spirits yet unhoused in bodies will come less close to God? The answers are disquieting.

Yet, we are not left hopeless. Scattered remnants of wilderness still remain, islands of aloneness and peace where still sings the song of silence, where stars with their eternal fires still flame in the darkness. They may be found at a distant glacial lake riding high on a mountain flank, in the heart of a virgin forest, in the vast sweep of red-rock desert—or in small islands of natural beauty much closer to home. They are not all gone—yet. It is only for us to be committed enough to seek them, vigilant enough to preserve them, perceptive enough to open our souls to experience and savor them. Like many treasures, nature can be closer than we think—and so is He.

Paul H. Risk is currently professor of forestry and director of the Center for Resource Communication and Interpretation in the Arthur Temple College of Forestry at Stephen F. Austin State University. His teaching includes environmental interpretation and communication, environmental attitudes and issues, and environmental science. He writes a "Field and Forest Facts" column for two local newspapers.

"AND WORLDS WITHOUT NUMBER HAVE I CREATED; AND I ALSO CREATED THEM FOR MINE OWN PURPOSE. . . . FOR BEHOLD, THERE ARE MANY WORLDS THAT HAVE PASSED AWAY BY THE WORD OF MY POWER. AND THERE ARE MANY THAT NOW STAND, AND INNUMERABLE ARE THEY UNTO MAN; BUT ALL THINGS ARE NUMBERED UNTO ME, FOR THEY ARE MINE AND I KNOW THEM." (MOSES 1:33–35.)

JEWEL OF THE UNIVERSE

VON DEL CHAMBERLAIN

 GREW UP AT THE "HUB OF THE PARKS." THAT IS HOW THE PEOPLE of Kanab referred to our town when I was small. We could go to any of several of the most spectacular places on earth— Zion, Bryce, or Grand Canyon—just for an afternoon picnic. We would roll Easter eggs on what we called "the Sand," now a state park named Coral Pink Sand Dunes. While fishing on the Cedar Mountain, we could take a short drive to Cedar Breaks, visit an ice cave, watch water gush from the cliff at Cascade Falls, or visit a lava field that looked like it cooled yesterday. We went hiking, horseback riding, hunting in beautiful mountains and canyons. Until motion-picture people started coming every summer to make movies on our landscapes, we didn't really know they were that splendid to the eyes of the world. The planet seemed to me to be so gigantic in those days; even the part I lived in seemed huge as well as beautiful.

Now, when I think about that spectacular country, I tingle all over. We wandered among crimson sandstones under blue skies. These two colors, sandstone red and sky blue, have always been important to me, now more than ever. Reminiscing on this one day not so long ago, I said to my sister, "I think that red sand is in my blood." Nola replied, "Yes, and it's probably still in your socks as well."

The other "color" of my life seems to be black. There is something wonderful about blackness. At night, in a town unspoiled by light pollution, we could lie out under the most majestic vista of all—black sky from which starlight showered down, illuminating in our minds all sorts of questions. What are the stars? What do they mean to humankind? What do they mean to me? What is Earth? How did it come to be? How is it related to all that out there? How is it related to me? How am I related to all of those stars?

What am I? Who am I? Where am I? Why am I?

Very early, I knew I wanted a career in science. All around me was the most fabulous world to become acquainted with in the most intimate way I could. Wherever I went I picked up rocks. I loved to find books that would help me understand the stones I found. Always, however, my eyes turned back to the night sky. Although I did not know it then, my interest in stars and rocks would come together.

Another element that has become increasingly more important over the years is the power of words. As Lincoln said, "I can no more remember the books I have read than the meals I have eaten, but they made me what I am." Two particular books, both by George Gamov, still sit on my shelves: *Birth and Death of the Sun* describes how stars come into existence to make energy and the chemical elements that, in turn, make the world we know; *One, Two, Three . . . Infinity* tells how mathematics help make the world understandable in an organized and rational way. It was, however, still another literature that was most important of all.

> *There is no such thing as immaterial matter. All spirit is matter, but it is more fine or pure, and can only be discerned by purer eyes. (D&C 131:7.)*
>
> *And there are many kingdoms; for there is no space in the which there is no kingdom; and there is no kingdom in which there is no space, either a greater or a lesser kingdom. (D&C 88:37.)*
>
> *And worlds without number have I created . . . And as one earth shall pass away, and the heavens thereof even so shall another come; and there is no end to my works, neither to my words. For behold, this is my work and my glory—to bring to pass the immortality and eternal life of man. (Moses 1:33, 38–39.)*

The scriptures that my parents and friends taught me to study and respect had a sense of mystery about them that made me want to comprehend the spiritual as well as physical meanings of earth and sky.

Such feelings led me to study physics at the University of Utah. While on an LDS mission to California, I visited the Lick Observatory and decided I wanted to study astronomy. With a master's degree in astronomy from the University of Michigan, I found a job in an amazing intellectually sharing facility, a planetarium—one of the earliest forms of what we now call "virtual reality," created to make some of the greatest astronomical discoveries that have ever been made more easily understandable.

Life in planetariums took me from Flint (Michigan) Community College, to Michigan State University, to the Smithsonian Institution's National Air and Space Museum, finally back to Utah. Along the way came a life-changing experience.

On one of our vacations during the '60s, our family was headed west to visit relatives. It was summer and very warm. Our sights were on the cool Black Hills as a place to camp for the night, but the map showed we would pass close to the Badlands, a place we had never visited. We decided to drop down for a brief look before driving into the mountains to camp for the night. Once in this intriguing place, however, we could not leave so quickly. We pitched our tent where there were no trees, just grass and marvelously eroded rock formations. As day ended, the once-bright rocks and pinnacles turned to a myriad of imagined figures silhouetted against the darkening sky.

We attended the campfire program at the little amphitheater. The naturalist greeted us, as he did each arrival: "Where are you from?" "Did you enjoy your day here?" "What did you do?" "What will you do tomorrow?" This casual conversation flowed nicely into the program, which was about what we should have seen in the Badlands that day or what we should look for tomorrow. As I sat, listened, and watched photographs on the screen, I also marveled at the sky as it became more and more lustrous with stars. Here I was, a planetarium teacher—one who worked hard to help others appreciate and enjoy the stars—and here we were, a little group of people gathered together under the most spectacular starscape one can imagine, talking about the rocks around us. Almost all of us had spent most of our time inside cities polluted by lights that prohibited seeing the stars. Now they beckoned in all their glory, ignored as we focused on the screen.

In my mind, I yelled out, "Look at the sky! Look at the blazing stars! Have you ever seen such a sight?" But I kept my seat, wondering at the opportunity present at that moment, so much greater than any teaching moment I could possibly imagine in a planetarium.

I didn't sleep much that night. We arose early, broke camp, then drove over to the visitor's center to wait for it to open. At the desk, I introduced myself, and a few minutes later had the opportunity to thank the chief naturalist for the campfire program, then to ask if they had considered their exceptional opportunity to include the starry sky in such programs. His answer was, "Our assignment here is to interpret what is most unique and special about this particular place, and that is the geology and wildlife of the Badlands." Although disappointing, that made sense to me.

Driving westward, I thought about this experience: people from cities everywhere gathered here to learn about their surroundings; trained people assigned to help visitors understand and enjoy their brief time in a place with no lights and with blazing stars in an unpolluted sky. About ten miles out of the park I realized that the night sky *was* one of the things special to that place.

I continued to think about this opportunity and finally devised a plan to visit selected parks and introduce the concept of sky interpretation. In the summer of 1972, I took a sabbatical and visited a number of parks to conduct seminars presenting this concept. The idea caught on and has continued to spread since that time. The experience of working with people, out under the real stars, is so much more powerful than what happens inside the "virtual universe," the planetarium.

While visiting Mesa Verde National Park, I asked the question again: "Have you considered the possibility of interpreting the night sky?" The reply was, "Our job is to interpret what is unique and special here, and that is the Indian ruins and the people who lived in them." That answer sent me to the library to see if I couldn't find at least a few things to indicate what Native Americans had thought about the stars. What I found overwhelmed me. Every book on Indian mythology was rich with traditions that linked earth and sky. There are tales that "explain" how Sun, Moon and stars were put in the sky, why they move as they do, and how they govern the seasons. Stories present powerful lessons about human relationships to the natural world and to each other.

For example, the Skidi band of Pawnee Indians, who lived their traditional lives in what is now Kansas and Nebraska, believed that their hereditary roots went up into the sky. They looked to the stars for religion, for understanding their ancestry, and for a model of political leadership and social structure. Tirawahat, the supreme deity who was never seen, was thought of as residing at the zenith of the sky, where he could direct the forces of the universe. From that lofty place he had sent the male Great Red Star of the morning to the east, where all things would be planned. He placed beautiful female bright Evening Star in the west, where all things would be accomplished. Other star deities were sent to their stations to hold up the heavens and govern the cycles of nature. Morning Star took a difficult and legendary journey to the west to court Evening Star, and from their union the first human female was born and sent to earth. Sun and Moon gave birth to the first male. From this beginning the Skidi people came into existence. The star gods gave them sacred artifacts and directed them in how they should build their homes and in the ways they should perform ceremonies. All these things were symbolically represented in the patterns and movements of Sun, Moon, planets, and stars.

One group of stars, the "Council of Chiefs," consisted of a dozen or so stars in a circle that passed directly overhead, so that it could be observed through the smoke hole of the Skidi lodge, through which prayers were sent on smoke from the fireplace up to the ancestor-deities. The Chief's Council constellation (Corona Borealis plus a few other stars) set the pattern for political consensus by sitting in council. Another tiny group of stars, known to the Skidi simply as the "Seven Stars," and to most people today as the Pleiades, reminded the people of the importance of unity, a guiding principle for the Skidi. The "Chief Star," or North Star, set the example of stability for chiefs among the people, watching over the band just as the Chief Star watched over the tribe of stars. The lodge served as a basic observatory to monitor stars that could be seen through the east-oriented entryway as they entered the visible sky, and others that could be observed through the smoke hole, passing near the zenith at certain times of night and seasons of the year.

Studying the celestial mythology of the Skidi Pawnee reveals an astonishingly detailed foundation for living derived from observation of nature. When a pair of dim stars, the "Swimming Ducks" (Lambda and Upsilon Scorpii), first appeared in February, low in the southeast just before the light of dawn washed the stars from the sky, the Skidi priests became intently alert, listening for the sound of thunder that came from the west, rolling across the plains. When this new cycle of storms began, they took down the sacred bundles and began a series of ceremonial activities that lasted through the times of planting, hunting, and harvest. All this was keyed to the stars that represented the awakening of the ducks that migrated northward and the winds that brought renewal of life to the soil. The Skidi calendar system had all the features needed for successful subsistence, for it contained astronomical, meteorological, and biological elements. I am not aware of a better system to be found in traditional society anywhere in the world.

As I studied this and other Native American cultures, I began to wonder why we spend so much time pondering the mythology of the Greeks when there are so many equally provocative and interesting revelations of deep human intuition and perception of nature that originated right here in America. The more I researched, the more I realized the beauty of ideas that few people know about, and the more I wanted to explore and share them. This led me to become part of a growing group doing research in the new field of Archaeoastronomy, the study of astronomical traditions, practices, and knowledge of indigenous cultures.

One of the parks I visited in 1972 to introduce sky interpretation within the National Park Service was Canyon de Chelly National Monument. The superintendent and chief interpreter said they wanted to show me something in the canyon. We jumped into their jeep and drove into one of the most beautiful places I have ever seen, stopping at a number of curious sites. Inside rock alcoves formed by rock dissolving and falling away from cliffs—the places where one often finds Anasazi ruins—there were patterns of black crosses painted on ceiling rock. The little that was known about these "planetarium sites," as they had been named by an archaeologist, was that the painted crosses had probably been put there by Navajos, and that they represented stars. Starting that year and continuing to this, I have been studying these "star ceiling sites," as I prefer to call them. I have cataloged more than seventy of them, gathering lots of data, formulating many questions, and proposing a few interpretations.

The primary interpretation that keeps coming back to me in new forms as I continue my research is that the stars painted on the ceilings are part of ceremonial activity focused on protection. Most Navajo ceremony deals with protection and curing from illnesses believed to result from inappropriate or unwise behaviors. One medicine man told a park service employee that the stars hold up the sky, and that the star-crosses were intended to keep the rock ceilings from falling. Another seemingly related idea in Navajo mythology suggests that the stars had been put in the sky to watch over the people and to instruct them in the ways they should live. Believing—though certainly not knowing—that star ceilings were intended to make the places where they are found safe for use by the Diné—the Navajo people—I join these people in the hope that these beautiful canyons will remain safe for those who live there and those who visit. Such symbolic practices deepen my enjoyment of the magnificent world we live in and my fervent hope that we will do our part in protecting the canyons, mountains, deserts, oceans, and atmosphere that are so intimately intertwined and fundamental to our survival and well-being.

My study of star ceilings and other rock art has brought me into contact with many Navajo people. They are some of the finest friends I have, and have taught me a few things about how Navajos interpret the stars. Even though the star ceilings do not show recognizable patterns of stars, I have discovered other places in northwestern New Mexico where Navajos once made rock art that does include such patterns. Stars are most important to Navajo people, and I have learned some of the concepts concerning them. One region of the sky, for example, contains a star called "Fire Star" (the North Star). Moving through the night around the Fire Star is the "Revolving Male" (the Big Dipper) on one side, and the "Revolving Female" (Cassiopeia) on the other. For Navajos, these stars represent the importance of spending time with the family at home, in the hogan, around the fire, doing the things families should do together.

One thing I learned is that Navajos associate stars with crystals, and this brought me back to my love affair with rocks. Now, everywhere I go I tend to see the glitter that crystals produce in rocks. I see the sparkle of the Milky Way gleam across an outcrop of sandstone, within mineral grains in a streambed, or on the surface of a sand dune. One day, while in the company of a Navajo medicine man, I took out my hand-lens, scooped up a handful of sand, and asked him to look at it through the lens. "Wow, it's actually a bunch of little rocks," he said. "Yes, and in sunlight it looks like a bunch of stars," I replied. We continued to discuss Navajo philosophy, star ceilings, rocks, and sand, with focus on the overriding principle that any of us could adopt from Navajo teaching: everything we do should be directed toward achieving harmony and balance with the universe.

I am certainly not alone in my interest in Navajo people; they are one of the world's most-studied cultures. It is said that someone once asked, "Do you know what constitutes a typical Navajo family?" The answer: "A father, a mother, some children, several dogs, some sheep and goats, and an anthropologist." I believe the reason so many scholars find the Diné to be so interesting is their pivotal concept of harmony and balance in all things. "Walk in Beauty" is a phrase that is practically synonymous with "Navajo." Like all people, they seek long life and happiness, and Navajo ceremonial practice emphasizes that this is attained by achieving compatibility with everything around them. This tends to result in humility toward others and in the active belief that all things in nature are sacred. I thank my Navajo friends for this principle, which I attempt to adapt and follow.

Which brings me to what I most deeply feel about Earth, our home. Because I have studied astronomy, taught others about planets, stars, galaxies and the universe, and done some original research on how astronomy has come into the lives of people throughout time, I am frequently asked how I feel about the immense universe. What is it from all my study and thinking about the great cosmos that I would most like others to know? What one thing that I now understand do I have the most urgent passion to impart to others?

My answer: It is Earth that impresses me most! When one considers how infinitesimally small Earth is in the vast universe we can observe, measure, and describe, it seems miraculous that it exists at all. Even if every star were to have a planet similar to Earth, we would still realize that the share of the universe where we could live would be minute almost beyond comprehension. And when we consider the time and physical process that have provided the brief moment of our lives, we ought to feel the deepest appreciation for the fact that we are here. Planet Earth is the jewel of the universe: no more beautiful, more delicate, more precious gem exists anywhere as far as we know.

It is the realization of the smallness, the loveliness of this one body in the enormous universe that gives me an overwhelming appreciation for everything in nature. I could not bring myself to throw a piece of paper out the window, vandalize or destroy in any conscious way any part of the environment. Our Most High Father has given us the gift of mortal life; for me at least, that includes not only the opportunity to fully enjoy the beauty we see all around us but also the responsibility of stewardship to pass it unspoiled to future generations.

> The earth is the Lord's, and the fulness thereof . . . (Psalms 24:1.)
> . . . the earth is full of the goodness of the Lord. (Psalms 33:5.)
> When I consider thy heavens, the work of thy fingers, the moon and the stars, which thou hast ordained; What is man, that thou art mindful of him? and the son of man, that thou visitest him? . . . O LORD our Lord, how excellent is thy name in all the earth! (Psalms 8:3–4, 9.)

With the evidence of modern science that the materials of Earth are the result of many billions of years of astrophysical process, it seems appropriate to share the Native American view of the sacredness of our relationships to Earth and Sky:

> Oh our Mother the Earth, oh our Father the Sky,
> Your children are we, and we bring you the gifts that you love.
> Then weave for us a garment of brightness;
> May the warp be the white light of morning,
> May the weft be the red light of evening,

May the fringes be the falling rain,
May the border be the standing rainbow.
Thus weave for us a garment of brightness
That we may walk fittingly where birds sing,
That we may walk fittingly where grass is green,
Oh our Mother the Earth, oh our Father the Sky!
—TEWA, "Song of the Sky Loom"

Von Del Chamberlain, former director of Hansen Planetarium in Salt Lake City, is a naturalist by inclination, an astronomer by training, an educator by experience, and a romantic by choice.

"... I HAVE PROMISED ... THEIR RESTORATION TO THE LAND OF ZION. ...
NEVERTHELESS, IF THEY POLLUTE THEIR INHERITANCES, THEY SHALL BE
THROWN DOWN; FOR I WILL NOT SPARE THEM IF THEY POLLUTE THEIR
INHERITANCES." (D&C 103:13–14.)

STEWARDSHIP
OF THE AIR *

HUGH W. NIBLEY

ET ME SAY AT THE OUTSET THAT AFTER FORTY YEARS OF BREATHING the miasmic exhalations of Geneva, I must admit that things are definitely better under Mr. [Joseph] Cannon's supervision than they were in the days of U.S. Steel. We have all heard arguments on both sides in this affair. Recently Mr. Cannon publicly injected a religious note into the discussion with his declaration that the reborn steel mill is a child of divine intervention, an act of providence.

The connection between the sacred and profane is entirely a proper one, and I welcome the excuse for a philosophical course. For as we learn even from the Word of Wisdom, body and mind—the temporal and the spiritual—are inseparable, and to corrupt the one is to corrupt the other. Inevitably our surroundings become a faithful reflection of our mentality and vice versa. The right people, according to Brigham Young, could convert hell to heaven, and the wrong ones heaven to hell. "Every faculty bestowed upon man is subject to corruption—subject to be diverted from the purpose the Creator designed it to fill."[1] This principle meets us in the Law of Moses: "... ye shall not pollute the land wherein ye are: for blood it defileth the land: ... Defile not therefore the land which ye shall inhabit, wherein I dwell: for I the Lord dwell among the children of Israel (Numbers 35:33–34). And today we are told that "the whole world lieth in sin, and groaneth under darkness and under the bondage of sin. ... For shall the children of the kingdom pollute my holy land?" (D&C 84:49, 59). "... I have promised ... their restoration to the land of Zion. ... Nevertheless, if they pollute their inheritances, they shall be thrown down; for I will not spare them if they pollute their inheritances" (D&C 103:13–14).

Brigham Young explains:

114

You are here commencing anew. The soil, the air, the water are all pure and healthy. Do not suffer them to become polluted with wickedness. Strive to preserve the elements from being contaminated by the filthy, wicked conduct and sayings of those who pervert the intelligence God has bestowed upon the human family.[2]

And this is now brought home to us in the great bicentennial address of President [Spencer W.] Kimball:

But when I review the performance of this people in comparison with what is expected, I am appalled and frightened. Iniquity seems to abound. The Destroyer seems to be taking full advantage of the time remaining to him in this, the great day of his power. . . . I have the feeling that the good earth can hardly bear our presence upon it. . . . The Brethren constantly cry out against that which is intolerable in the sight of the Lord: against pollution of mind, body, and our surroundings.[3]

Brother Brigham states the problem in terms of a flat-out contest between the most vital necessity of life and pure greed, a principle as old as the human record, rooted in a fundamental fact of nature:

The world is after riches. Riches is the god they worship. . . . What constitutes health, wealth, joy, and peace? In the first place, good pure air is the greatest sustainer of animal life.[4]

The Lord blesses the land, the air, and the water where the Saints are permitted to live.[5]

As is well known, all metals are lifeless crystals arranged on a hexagonal plan, which can grow only by accretion from without—they are, so to speak, expansive, acquisitive, and dead by nature. On the other hand all organic life favors pentagonal forms (with the Fibonacci progression) and grows from within, reproducing itself in the life process.

Throughout the human experience, that strange dichotomy between the organic and inorganic meets us in parable, history, myth, and folklore. Brother Kimball referred expressly to the Destroyer. There is no more ancient, pervasive, or persistent tradition than that of the adversary, the Prince of Darkness, most often and most widely described as the lord of the underworld who sits in his Stygian realm upon all the mineral treasures of the earth, worked by toiling slaves amidst foul and pestilential vapors. Many years ago Jakob Grimm made a long study of the subject. Our lord of the underworld rules under many names—Satan, Loki, Mammon, Mulciber, Hephaestus, etc.; and his workers are the gnomes, trolls, kobolds, dwarfs, and other grimy hard-working creatures. The model is plainly taken from prehistoric mining regions such as the immensely old Varna works in Yugoslavia and others in Asia Minor and Cyprus. For the classical writers, Spain was his kingdom, with its blighted regions of mines, smelters, and foundries—all worked by starving, filthy, driven slaves, converting the landscape into barren wastes of slag and stunted vegetation.

Cyprus was early stripped of its forests to provide fuel for the copper and silver smelters.[6] Plato tells us that Attica in his day had become "the skeleton of a body wasted by disease." The abundant forests were gone; gone were the food for animals and the storage for water. "In the old days," he says, "the water was not lost, as it is today, by running off a barren ground to the sea."[7] Though that enlightened city passed an ordinance against throwing garbage into the streets as early as 500 B.C., today, 2,500 years later, Athens is strangling in smog, which is literally destroying those glories of Plato's day that have survived until the present.

The big boss is best known by far under his names of Pluto and Plutus, the one denoting his function as the lord of the underworld and the other as the god of riches.[8] The best-known public appearance of Pluto is his rape of Proserpine, the most famous rape in song and story.[9] She is the daughter of Demeter, Mother Earth, and represents everything that is fresh, beautiful, green, young, and growing. Pluto, in his black *quadriga*, or black stretch limousine, sweeps out of his subterranean realm amidst choking clouds of sulphur dioxide, carbon monoxide, and assorted particles, and snatches Proserpine away from the scene to go down and live with him as a very rich but unhappy bride. In northern mythology when the maiden goes down to live below, her name is changed to Hell. With her departure all the upper world becomes as dull and gloomy as Pluto's own busy factories, foundries, and smelters. This makes Pluto's claim to rule over the earth complete. He takes the treasures of the earth and with them creates the wealth and the armaments that enable him to rule through the ages with blood and horror.

The psychological side of the legends is significant. The Pluto figure is shunned and avoided by men; no ancient tribe claimed him as an ancestor. No cult paid him honor, for all the fear and dread his power inspired. His uncompromising enemy is Dikē—justice or righteousness. Theognis of Megara, a ruined aristocrat, lamenting his lost fortune, sings the praise of "Plutus, thou fairest of gods and most desirable of all things, through thee even the basest man can become a pillar of society" *(esthlos aner)*.[10] Shakespeare says the same when he has Timon of Athens, after losing his fabulous wealth, tell us how gold can make "black white, foul fair, Wrong right, base noble, old young, coward valiant,"[11] how it can turn scoundrels to senators; and, most to the point, how it can transmute the foulest stench into the balms and spices of an April day. Plutus is always selfish, always reluctant to share what he has with his brother Hyginus. His gifts to mankind are dullness of intellect *(anoia)*, boundless self-importance amounting to self-adoration *(megalopsychía)*, and the arrogance that guarantees ultimate ruin *(hybris)*.

In a fable told in the *Phaedrus*, when Hercules was received into heaven after completing his philanthropic labors among men, all the heroes and demigods gathered round to congratulate him on his arrival. When Plutus came to greet him, Hercules promptly turned his back on him. This shocked them all, and when he was asked why he did it, Hercules replied, "Because he makes men base and corrupts everything he touches."[12] But the best-known trait of Plutus to the ancients was his blindness, which is the main theme of the philosophers and poets. There is no proportion between merit and mischief, reward and deserts, right and wrong when Plutus bestows his gifts.

At first, in archaic times, Plutus was an agrarian figure, the reward of the hardworking farmer, but with advancing civilization he was given a new persona, wealth as such and no questions asked. "Plutus has become the common guide of life," wrote the poet Antiphanes, "because people think it will get them everything, and they are not particular how." When the schoolmen started to make the rules in late antiquity, they ordered Arete (virtue, honesty) to step down and yield her place to Pluto.

It is easy to recognize in Pluto the Cain figure. Cain began as a farmer; but when he followed Satan's instructions and made use of that great secret of how to murder and get gain, the earth refused him her strength, and he became a wanderer. Since time immemorial, that homeless tribe (the land of Nod means land of unsettled nomad) is designated throughout the East by the name *Qayin*, meaning a wandering metal-worker, the mark of his trade and his tribe being the face blackened at the forge; he is a skillful maker and peddler of weapons and jewels, the twin destroyers and corrupters of mankind. Long ago, Eusebius, called the father of church history, tells of an early Christian tradition of evil spirits who, constantly seeking to defile and corrupt human society, "move about in thick polluted air," a most fitting environment for their work. In a passage from a famous Hermetic work, the *Korē Kosmu* 23, the Air complains to the Creator, "O Master, I myself am made thick and polluted, and by the stench of dead things from the dump I reek to heaven, so that I breed sickness, and have ceased to be wholesome; and when I look down from above I see things which are too awful to behold."

Of the Sagas of the North, the one best known to us, thanks to Wagner, is the *Nibelungenlied*. The Nibelungs were hideous dwarfs who mined, smelted, and forged deep within the earth. They possessed the Rheingold, which gave any possessor infinite power but forced him to renounce love and doomed him to destruction. Freia, the goddess of youth, was bartered for the gold and carried away by the giants; whereupon the earth was covered with a pall of smoke, and all things, including the gods, began to age and wither. Note the Proserpine parallel. The story is an endless procession of tricks, lies, and murders for power and gain. We are introduced into a world of ringing hammers, glowing forges, warped and deformed dwarfs plotting their dirty tricks and murders, brainless giants knocking each other's brains out, men and women of high society plotting and poisoning, all of them after the same Rheingold—because the Rheingold of course made its owner the ruler of the universe. A recent production of the "Ring" in Germany, in which the protagonists are steel and munitions barons, departs not a jot from Wagner's intent.

The most famous passage relevant to our subject is from another medieval epic, the opening refrain from *Macbeth:* "Fair is foul and foul is fair: Hover through the fog and filthy air."[13] Shakespeare must have gotten the idea from the Bible, which calls Satan the Prince of the Air but also the Prince of Darkness—that kind of air. He is also called the Prince of this World, who promises power and gain to all who will make a pact with him. The theme of Shakespeare's tragedy is fraud and deception as a means of obtaining power and control; in the closing lines Macbeth admits that he has been taken in: "I . . . begin To doubt the equivocation of the fiend That lies like truth,"[14] i.e., the double-talk of the promoter that put him on top, the rhetoric of Madison Avenue: "And be these juggling fiends no more believ'd, That palter with us in a double sense; That keep the word of promise to our ear, And break it to our hope!"[15] The worst thing about the "filthy air" is that it turns out to be a smoke-screen; Macbeth is led on and put off from day to day until he is done in. It is a smooth, white-collar scam such as Macbeth half suspected from the beginning: "But 'tis strange: And oftentimes, to win us to our harm, The instruments of darkness tell us truths, Win us with honest trifles, to betray's In deepest consequence."[16] What kind of honest trifles? Such pleasant bits as those pacifying public relations assurances: "We are not monsters or ogres, we are people just like you. We love our families just like you, we go to church too!" Or to quote the scriptures, "I am no devil" (2 Nephi 28:22). That, of course, is all perfectly true—the workers are not the culprits but the pawn of owners, who use them to justify profitable pollution while hiring as few workers as possible and paying them as little as possible.

Not only Wagner but Ibsen, Shaw, and others call attention to the moral dilemma that beset the nineteenth-century industrial society, as it does ours today. When getting gain entails the destruction and degrading of life, what should we do? Undershaft, Shaw's super tycoon, replies with the simple motto, "Unashamed." The great fortunes that made America a world-class power were paid for by mill towns in which life was very near to hell. But the owners lived far away, and starving immigrants desperately competing for jobs were willing to submit to anything.

No more vivid description of that world can be found than one written in 1855 by a prominent Latter-day Saint living in England. I thought of his essay last fall; looking toward Provo from Redwood Road where it enters the valley at an elevation to the west, I paused to behold the dense, murky, brown fog jammed against the mountains right behind the Brigham Young University by the prevailing winds, and I remembered the opening lines of the composition:

> *All nature smiles, and teems with health and brightness and fragrance,*
> *where you are, but over the valley before you rests an awful, impenetrable,*

dark, black cloud, . . . approximating to a realization of your ideal of the
"dark valley of the shadow of death," . . . You walk down the hillside, and,
as you enter the thick, dark cloud, . . . you feel no more the invigorating
influence [of the sun], . . . a sense of oppressiveness falls upon you, and you
realize, to your unmistakable discomfort, that the darkness around [you]
can not only be seen, but felt and tasted. Suddenly, to your great astonish-
ment, you discover that this dreary spot is inhabited by human beings![17]

He contrasts the situation with that of the Latter-day Saints "spreading
themselves on the face of the earth, and carefully cultivating it," invigo-
rated by "the pure, bracing air, [and with it] health."[18]

For one hundred years Utah Valley was idyllic. Agrarian economies, as
we know, are the stablest on earth. They have existed for thousands of
years throughout the world and are still going strong. Industrial
economies, on the other hand, though surprisingly ancient, are expansive,
acquisitive, extractive, unstable, speculative, competitive, destructive. In
England it meant the Deserted Village, and the vast futility of empire. It has
kept any attempts at achieving a stable American civilization off balance
for two hundred years.

Our Latter-day Saint philosopher of the 1850s tells us what he found
when he entered the factory town: "Overpopulation—filth, want of
employment, destitution, moral degradation, physical degeneracy, disease,
untimely death."[19] Who would ever have thought 135 years ago that this
would be an accurate description of our inner cities today?

Men of science viewing such scenes deplore as possibly the worst
aspect of the whole thing the fact that people can adapt themselves to such
a life, especially if the alternative is starvation. How much can people live
with? Do you recall the last sentence of Orwell's novel *1984?* "He loved Big
Brother." Or how people could go on for years resigned to daily life in the
Gulag Archipelago? Or how the prisoner of Chilon finally refuses to leave
his rat-infested dungeon because he has become accustomed to it? Jake
Garn says that we should all learn to live with corporate pollution lest we
jeopardize the profits of big business. But where do you draw the line?
How much cigarette smoke should we tolerate, for example?

This brings up the question of degree of intent. To return to our
ancients, Aristotle told us that there are two kinds of goods that we are after
in this life—goods of first intent and goods of second intent.[20] Goods of second intent are good because they help us obtain other things. Thus a pen-
cil, a watch, shoes, a hammer, a stove, etc., are all useful for obtaining
something beyond their own value. Goods of first intent, on the other
hand, are good in themselves and need no excuse; they are not the means
but the goal. Thus millions of people take the plane to Hawaii—the plane
is a good of second intent and gets us there; but the delights of the islands
are goods of first intent, whose enjoyment needs no explanation or excuse.
People crave them for what they are and actually need them more than any

of the amenities. Goods of first intent: "All things which come of the earth
. . . are made for the benefit and the use of man, both to please the eye and
to gladden the heart, . . . for taste and for smell, to strengthen the body and
to enliven the soul" (D&C 59:18–19). Utah Valley without the steel mill
offers treasures of first intent. The mill is not beautiful and for most of us
has precious little utility. What is it then? It is a good of *third intent,* the one
and only thing that is not good of itself, and is not useful of itself, but is
prized above all else—it is money. Letters to the editor have been quite
frank in telling us to wake up and realize that those dark clouds to the west
mean just one thing—money.

Clear examples of third intent lie all around us today. Take the town of
Beatty, Nevada, for example. "The residents here," says the news report,
"are dusting off the welcome mat for something the rest of the country
abhors: a dump to house nuclear waste which will remain 'hot' for tens of
thousands of years. . . . Despite protests by Governor Richard Bryan and
others, . . . Beatty residents say they would welcome the dump, if handled
properly, because it would mean an economic boost." Only in southern
Utah could we top such eagerness to sacrifice forever values both of first
and second intent for number three, a quick monetary shot in the arm.
Where else but in Utah would you ever find an *Anti*-Wilderness Society,
composed of mining, lumber, and cattle interests? What? Making war on
the lingering remnants of our precious wilderness already in full retreat, as
people by the millions buy vans and camping gear, and take off to our over-
crowded parks and national forests in forlorn search of remaining open
spaces? Of course the object of the league is not to destroy the wilderness—
those are the very men who like to play Wild West; their behavior is
explained by one word—money.

Another example to convince you that there is such a thing as that
ruinous good of third intent: A Houston financier bought the Pacific
Lumber Company in 1985 by selling high-yield, high-risk corporate notes
through Dexel Burnam Lambert, specialists in what some people call "junk
bonds." To pay off the $795 million debt they are logging the largest stand
of virgin redwoods remaining. Instead of cutting some trees, the company
was felling all the trees in selected tracts. Maximum harvesting of these
trees, many over 1,000 years old, was to satisfy debts incurred. Needless to
say, "spokesmen for the company" assured us that this was only common
industry practice, and was not environmentally unsound.

They say production can be sustained indefinitely under current plans.
Just wait 1,000 years and the clear-cut will grow right back again. Here one
of earth's supreme goods of first intent, unsurpassed anywhere in its
haunting magnificence, exists merely to pay off junk bonds—third intent
pure and simple. Not long ago, a governor of California, championing the
cause of those who were bent on turning all the groves into cash, uttered
the famous one-liner: When you have seen one redwood, you have seen
them all.

I grant you that the product of the operation is useful, a good of second intent; but how carefully do we balance the value of one against the other? Should whales be slaughtered to make useful soap and shoe polish? Should the sacred Blue Canyon of the Hopis be strip-mined to light millions of bulbs glorifying the gambling dives of Las Vegas?

When U.S. Steel moved in during World War II, advertising its vastly profitable operations as a selfless patriotic contribution toward making America strong and free, the people cheerfully accepted the inconvenience. After World War II, a new excuse was needed for uncontrolled pollution, and the smelters came up with the slogan, "The Solution to Pollution is Diffusion." There would be taller smokestacks. But being still further pressed, they took the bull by the horns with a campaign brazenly proclaiming, "Mining is Beautiful!" adding "when it creates a common heritage." Brigham Young never ceased telling the Saints that the one thing that would disrupt the civilization of Deseret was mining in the Territory. What the company called a common heritage was temporary jobs for "Chicanos, Blacks, Native Americans, and sons and daughters of the immigrants," but I strongly suspect that the miners were as little aware of the heritage as the stockholders and owners were.

"Oh what a powerful argument human *self-interest* is!" said Tertullian.[21] Here is a bold headline: "Timber Spokeswoman: Environmentalists Gag Free Enterprise." But here is another by Jack Anderson: "Timber Firms Ax Free Enterprise."[22]

Within the past ten days we have had a classic example of the overpowering argument of third intent. Last autumn Congress finally got through a bill against the fierce opposition of the billboard interests, tightening restrictions on the industry. Billboards are not ornamental, and they are not useful; they are strictly goods of third intent. For years now, enlightened communities throughout the land have put increasing controls on the things. But what do we find now in Utah Valley? The *Provo Daily Herald* displayed a picture of "officials cutting the ribbon on a new billboard campaign," which is to adorn Provo and Orem with a rash of new giant signs, "hoping to encourage Utah County residents to keep dollars here." At the same time we learned that the authorities are planning to attract more retirees to the state. The people I know who have moved to Provo from both coasts have done so expressly to get away from the ticky-tacky urban clutter of billboards, remembering the mountains and the clear blue sky of their childhood—and we offer them billboards cunningly placed where the eye cannot avoid their impudent and offensive intrusion. And we think that is going to make us richer?

The first reply to complaints when the mill reopened was, "If you don't like it, then why don't you just move out?" Again we have Brigham's reply, "This is our home."[23] "This earth is the home He has prepared for us, and we are to prepare ourselves and our habitations for the celestial glory in store for the faithful."[24] "This is the habitation of the Saints; this is the earth that will be given to the Saints."[25] Again we have the support of the ancients. The earth, said Aristotle, was made to be a home for man, permanently, and for that he must achieve a stable balance with nature, harmonious and pleasant to all. Cicero echoed this sentiment when he said that the earth is a fit home for both gods and men, and man has his part to play in taking good care of the garden. This must be a stable, eternal order with man at the top of the animal scale, held most responsible if things go wrong.[26]

Notice that all these references are to one's local home as well as earthly habitation. They are now one—where do you move when pollution is universal? Now the dispute takes on a wholly new direction. It is a new ball game. Heretofore we have always heard that air is free, and it is a free country, and business cashed in on the boundless ocean as a free dumping ground for industrial garbage. But then Heyerdahl found his rafts floating in displays of garbage even in the remote vastness of the mid-Pacific and the mid-Atlantic. Last year we all held our noses as we watched the three-month odyssey of a scow loaded with 3,000 tons of waste, which it tried in vain to dump surreptitiously in various places. That no longer goes. If the ocean is finite, how much more so the limited airspace of the valley, an even less proper receptacle for tons of industrial filth, that must be inhaled by 250,000 people with every breath (taking in between 10,000 and 12,000 liters of air every day).

For nigh onto two hundred years, smoke-blackened skies were joyfully hailed as the sign of prosperity and progress, and still we hear the pious protests, "Are you against progress? Do you want to turn back the clock?" Again the answer should be seriously considered.

Before [World War II], one could not buy a watch that did not have a phosphorescent dial. The things were immensely convenient and economical, indispensable, we could not live without them, and their manufacture gave employment to thousands of poor people, for it was largely handwork. In spite of all those great benefits and blessings touted by the industry, you cannot buy one of those watches today. We have actually turned back the clock on progress, made a technological retreat, trashed an indispensable commodity. But it took Jane Addams a whole generation to bring about that drastic change. Her argument was the naively simple one that making phosphorescent watches killed people, since the worker had to tip the tiny phosphorus-bearing brushes with her tongue, dooming her to the deadly phossey-jaw. But of course the disease took years to show up, and so for long years, that was the franchise of the industry to continue. This is an extreme case, but the same delaying tactics are followed everywhere. You will recognize the likeness to the effects of breathing Geneva air. Maybe not so drastic and not so quick but granting the same license to pollute and jeopardize health.

But the problem is more serious than that. Every passing month brings forth new evidence from around the world that the physical danger entailed in the operation of such plants as Geneva is far greater than anyone had heretofore realized. The contribution of such combustion centers to acid rain, greenhouse effect, and damaged ozone is irreversible. Here an entire issue of the *National Geographic* (December 1988) asks on the cover, "Can Man Save This Fragile Earth?"[27] We have long known that there is something wrong, if only by the duck test: if it looks bad, tastes bad, smells bad, and sounds bad in duplicitous argument, then it must be bad.

"The respect that makes calamity of so long life" is always the time element, allowing for endless obfuscation: No definitive proof, requires further study, experts disagree, a complicated problem, we are doing everything in our power, or having done everything in our power (meaning in both cases we can't do more and intend to go on stalling), leaning over backwards, studying the problem, bringing in our experts to reject the findings, listing only a small sampling, working with figures out of date, taking it under advisement, etc. Along with this goes a swelling liturgy of praise for the benign effects, the lofty intent, and boundless benefits of the operation.

Imagine an official offering a sizable sum of money to a local institution with which I am associated. The head of that group says he would thankfully receive the generous donation the moment the company was ready to show him a letter from the EPA stating that EPA emissions standards, low as they are, were being observed at the plant. Being a lawyer, he knows the real nature of the offer and puts his finger on the spot, and there the matter ends.

A far better gift than cash handouts to our nature-loving Boy Scouts, and school children, and to the freedom-loving citizens attending the festival in July, would be "the clear blue sky [arching] over the vales of the free,"[28] the clearer the freer, including freedom from respiratory complications in later life. But of course there is one serious drawback to that. The clear blue skies cost much more than the highly publicized handouts.

I could be accused of being prejudiced and extremist, but I would not have taken my position at all if I was not forced into it by the bristling headlines that have suddenly emerged on every side; and the issue never would have reached the covers and front pages of staid conservative journals had it not been thrust upon *them* by the crushing accumulation of evidence sounding alarm in all quarters. I was brought up in an alarmist atmosphere first by my grandparents, then by the Axis Powers, and now by a sea of frightening statistics; but especially the scriptures kept me thinking.

I do not worry very much about Geneva anymore; it is only a small fumarole at the base of a mighty volcano that is now shuddering and groaning ominously. Anderson said that he hears the great waterfall roaring just ahead. So let us both end with the Book of Mormon:

> For behold, ye do love money. . . . O ye [polluters], . . . who sell yourselves
> for that which will canker, why have ye polluted the holy church of God?
> . . . Why do ye build up your secret abominations to get gain, and cause

that widows should mourn before the Lord, and also orphans . . . , and also the blood of their fathers and their husbands to cry unto the Lord . . . for vengeance upon your heads? Behold the sword of vengeance hangeth over you; and the time soon cometh that he avengeth the blood of the saints upon you, for he will not suffer their cries any longer. (Mormon 8:37–41.)

This talk was given 16 February 1989 in Provo, Utah, as part of a Clean Air Symposium at Brigham Young University. The following letter to the editor was written immediately after the original presentation:

February 16, 1989

Editor
The Daily Herald
1555 North 200 West
Provo, Utah 84601

Dear Sir:

People often say they do not understand me. They say it so often that I should have the sense to shut up in public. And now I have gone and done it again. Since it is a preacher's duty to make himself understood, when he fails he owes his hearers an apology. And I fail every time I step into the past, where I prefer to spend my days. There my students lose me. The past simply does not exist for us today, except in old costume movies revived on TV. So the idea of the age-old confrontation between agriculture and industry in days long past rings no bells.

For example, nothing is more beyond dispute than that people who worked in mines and mills have throughout history been underpaid and overworked, living in unspeakably dismal conditions. Most of them right down to modern times have, in fact, been slaves. I have written feelingly about them. But to interpret the above statement as a description of the workers at Geneva, where friends and relatives of mine have worked from the beginning at far better wages than I ever received, is about as far as misunderstanding can go. And to say that it depicts them as hideous and deformed dwarfs, forging the fatal Rheingold, either makes me the world's worst communicator or denotes a hair-trigger predisposition to jump at conclusions.

Then why did I bring up the subject at all? We have here a discussion that has reached something like a stalemate. Each side accused the other of being insufficiently informed, and both are right. I have the advantage of being equally uninformed on both sides, and look on only as a spectator. But what I see is a drama of immense age and impact, something that has been quite fundamental to the scenario of life on this afflicted globe. We are told that in cases like this, one cannot know too much about the subject, and in an impulsive moment, acting on that unproven premise, I agreed to bring ancient instances into the discussion. That was a mistake. It is rash and foolhardy to go out for the recondite and esoteric stuff unless you are prepared to take it all the way, which is hardly to be done in half an hour.

Recently, indignant citizens have been reminding me of "what has made this country great." Unfortunately they can only tell me what has made it rich—a very different thing, as Socrates would tell you. Every time the Nephites got rich they stopped being great. What has made us rich in the first instance is vast, natural resources. Just an hour before sounding off, I listened to Jack Anderson tell how the Japanese, with none of our fabulous resources, are able to run rings around us in almost every department, getting very rich indeed by all-out work and dedication. But that is not real greatness—the soaring Dow-Jones is not forever. To me the austerity, the "plain living and high thinking" of old New England, the devout wisdom of the Founding Fathers, and the studious and courtly ways of a handful of Southern gentlemen showed us the way to be great—a way we have not followed.

Time did not allow me to give the conclusion to the talk, which was to declare that I no longer worry much about Geneva, that the only time it really got to me was on those sweet spring nights when every breath from the west reminded me of what I was missing. Unfortunately, breathing was not optional or I could have escaped that prejudice too. Today I see in Geneva a smoking fumarole at the base of a mighty volcano that is just about to blow—Jack Anderson's talk left me in little doubt about that. I take small comfort in the conviction that before long circumstances are going to settle the problem for us.

Sincerely,
Hugh Nibley

ENDNOTES

1. *Journal of Discourses* 6:94.

2. Ibid., 8:79.

3. Spencer W. Kimball, "The False Gods We Worship," *Ensign* 6 (June 1976): 4 (emphasis added).

4. *The Latter-day Saints' Millennial Star* 22:738 (emphasis added).

5. *Journal of Discourses* 10:222.

6. Strabo, *The Geography of Strabo* XIV, 6, 5.

7. Plato, *Critias* 111A-D.

8. Ernst Wüst, "Puton," in *Paulys Realencyclopädie der Classischen Altertumswissenschaft*, 23 vols. (Stuttgart: Druckenmüller and Waldsee, 1951), 21:1:1000.

9. Ibid.

10. J. Zwicker, "Plutos," in ibid., 21:1:1035.

11. William Shakespeare, *Timon of Athens*, act 4, scene 3, lines 28–29.

12. Phaedrus, *Fables* IV, 12.

13. William Shakespeare, *Macbeth,* act 1, scene 1, lines 14–15.

14. Ibid., act 5, scene 5, lines 49–51.

15. Ibid., act 5, scene 8, lines 25–28.

16. Ibid., act 1, scene 3, lines 137–41.

17. *The Latter-day Saints' Millennial Star* 17:337.

18. Ibid., 17:338.

19. Ibid., 17:338.

20. Aristotle, *Metaphysics* V, 2, 3–4.

21. Tertullian, *De Spectaculis* II, 89–90.

22. Jack Anderson, *Provo Daily Herald,* 2 January 1985, 21.

23. *Journal of Discourses* 8:297.

24. Ibid., 8:294.

25. Ibid., 15:127.

26. Cf. Cicero, *De Natura Deorum* II, 39; 45; 53.

27. *National Geographic* 174 (December 1988): front cover.

28. Charles W. Penrose, "O Ye Mountains High," in *Hymns of The Church of Jesus Christ of Latter-day Saints* (Salt Lake City: The Church of Jesus Christ of Latter-day Saints, 1985), no. 34, verse 1.

• • •

This material also appears in The Collected Works of Hugh Nibley, Volume 13: *Brother Brigham Challenges the Saints,* eds. Don E. Norton and Shirley S. Ricks (Salt Lake City: Deseret Book Company; Provo, Utah: Foundation for Ancient Research and Mormon Studies [F.A.R.M.S.], 1994), 55–75. Used with permission.

Hugh W. Nibley is one of the most gifted scholars in the LDS Church today. His linguistic abilities, his concern with detail, and his brilliant mind combine to make all efforts productive and meaningful. He is a prolific writer and a gifted lecturer.

"THE LORD IS MY SHEPHERD; I SHALL NOT WANT. HE MAKETH ME TO LIE DOWN IN GREEN PASTURES: HE LEADETH ME BESIDE THE STILL WATERS. HE RESTORETH MY SOUL . . ." (PSALMS 23:1–3.)

EMBRACING
THE CALL

LARRY YOUNG

OR THOSE OF US LIVING IN MODERN SOCIETIES, THERE IS A PARTICULAR danger that we are guilty of participating in the destruction or degradation of God's creation without fully realizing it. The logic of late modernity, the logic of modern society and advanced global capitalism, is the logic of consumption and control and dominion. It is the logic of trusting in the arm of flesh and of genuflecting in front of the false idols of materialism. It is the logic that allows the most materially advantaged individuals in our global community, including the majority of North Americans and Europeans, to insulate themselves from many of the impacts or consequences of their actions.

Being wise stewards of God's creation, for example, can be challenging when we are not immediately impacted by the pollutants of unregulated industrial production that result in low-cost goods at our local department stores but create unhealthy living conditions for our brothers and sisters in developing countries. But because God has blessed us with intelligence, choosing to remain in ignorance does not absolve us from responsibility.

Upon reflection, we also realize the difficulty in justifying our modern standard of living since it is dependent upon a level of material consumption and pollution that cannot be sustained if all other human beings are to be afforded the same opportunity. The truth is that God's creation would collapse, its divine nature would be destroyed, if all the world were to live the way most of us do in America.

So where does the call of Christ take us? Do we choose to sustain a global distribution of life chances that deny some of our brothers and sisters the same blessings that we have? Should we deny those less fortunate than us adequate health care, housing, and nutritional food, as well as the opportunity for parallel levels of material well-being, in order to protect the sustainability and divinity of God's creation? Of course, this requires us to ignore the obvious, that God's economically disadvantaged children are also part of the whole of creation.

Or does the call of Christ lead us to consider different ways of living that allow for dignity and justice for all while also protecting the divine creation? The call of the wise steward seems to pull me in a particular direction. What seems less clear is whether I am faithful enough to embrace that call.

How do we sustain and nurture the whole of creation? I do not fully know the answer, but when I am spiritually alive it is clear to me that we must not seek to escape the question if we want to fully engage the sacred.

So how do we proceed?

At the very least, we must participate in a conversation and be faithful enough to understand that the call of Christ is a call to stand outside of the ordinary logic of our culture as we seek to live responsible, compassionate, fully aware lives.

At its heart, the call of Christ in relationship to God's creation is a call to live in tension—a tension that exists because most of us who read this book are guilty of living at least on some level of contradiction to what is necessary to protect creation and enable social justice for all humanity. The call to live in critical tension is a call to constantly reflect upon the implications of our beliefs and actions as they relate to the environment. If we assume that our beliefs and actions are always benign, we cut ourselves off from hearing the prophetic call of God. But we can begin to understand that the call into critical tension is a call to accept a divine gift. That is, as we struggle to discern God's call and live authentically in relationship to it, we will engage the spirit, and witness in every place that, at every moment, we are embraced by and participating in the sacred nature of creation.

Our actions can be transformative. We can act to protect that which is at risk. In committing to healing the wounded earth, we commit to healing our wounded selves. As we seek to fulfill the divine stewardship we have been given, we can act with hope and confidence because we will be acting in concert with the will and imagination of God.

In my own efforts to reject nuclear weapons and to protect what few wild places we have left, I have sought to act conservatively by encouraging policies that get us to slow down the negative, destructive transformation of creation. I have sought to encourage the communities I am a part of to avoid actions that could lead down paths of no return—paths that I sense would negate the sacred.

As we seek to act, our motives can be called into question. For example, I understand that there are people of good will who might disagree with my specific efforts, but I hope they would not question the decency and genuineness of my labors. I have been surprised when fellow Mormons (including members of Congress and others who serve in important policy and advocacy positions) have called me a "radical environmentalist" at public hearings and in the press. I suspect they have done this out of anger, frustration, and a true difference of opinion. I believe they have also engaged in this kind of rhetoric because they sought to use language as a political tool to delegitimize and disempower my voice as an ordinary citizen. Perhaps they were perturbed by their inability to exercise unrestrained power. Perhaps they misunderstood my intentions. But for me, one challenge is how to remain a person of dignity and moral force in the face of such attacks. I wonder whether I engage in similar unthinking acts as I seek to pursue what I understand and believe to be the proper course of action.

How, then, do we seek to influence policy without losing our humanity and integrity? We can reflect back on our own motives and ask whether we are prone to see the evil outside more quickly than the darkness inside. We can remember that our truest identity is reflected in the love of God. We can strive for a fair dialogue, a conversation, where we both listen and speak. Our words and actions, regardless of the ends we seek and the actions of those who differ from us, even oppose us, can always demonstrate our love.

Through all these reflections, I retain the naive belief that the more of us who seek to engage the question of what constitutes right living in relationship toward God's creation, the more likely we are as a human family to be wise stewards. We will come to see that exterminating species and degrading ecosystems is not wise stewardship. We will recognize that polluted water and air is not wise stewardship. And we will begin to understand that condemning people to live in conditions of environmental degradation is not wise stewardship. If sustaining our level of consumption dictates such brutal outcomes, then we are not engaged in compassionate living.

Within my own philosophical tensions, I am filled with hope. I am filled with hope because within the Mormon community there is already a foundation in place for the development of a land ethic that does not shy away from the hard questions of our time. Such a land ethic awakens us to God's presence in every place and every moment, issuing forth the prophetic call to experience the world fully, joyfully, and acknowledge our place within the divine creation. Our love is a sacred act. My prayer is that we will be brave and wise in our relations, that we will embrace the call.

Larry Young is cochair of the Utah Wilderness Coalition and associate professor of sociology at Brigham Young University.

"Teach ye diligently and my grace shall attend you, that you may be instructed more perfectly in theory, in principles, in doctrine, in the law of the gospel, in all things that pertain unto the kingdom of God, that are expedient for you to understand; Of things both in heaven and in the earth, and under the earth; things which have been, things which are, things which must shortly come to pass; things which are at home, things which are abroad; the wars and the perplexities of the nations, and the judgments which are on the land; and a knowledge also of countries and of kingdoms—"
(D&C 88:78–79.)

CONSERVATION VS. CONSERVATIVES: HOW THE GOSPEL FITS

Donald L. Gibbon

 AN I BE A MORMON AND STILL HAVE A PATRON SAINT? IF SO, THEN John Muir is mine. "When you try to pick out anything in the universe, you find it hitched to everything else," wrote Muir. Every natural thing was important to him. Given the Mormon dedication to studying the scriptures and the admonition to "liken them to ourselves," you would think that Mormons would be just as deeply committed to environmental protection as Muir was. We sing about such things in our hymns. For example, "In Hymns of Praise" speaks of God's being "concerned with every sparrow's fall." How about God's concern with every spotted owl or salmon? In Isaiah, we read about lions lying down with lambs. But that is a distant and theoretical concept. How about ranchers figuring out how to get along with wolves? The natural world seems to have little place in the panoply of things most Mormons worry or even think about. This isn't so different from most other Americans ... but aren't we supposed to be a peculiar people, different in important ways?

I think about these matters all the time, the contradictions between what we profess and say we value deeply and the way we act as individuals.

My wife and I recently saw the Zefferelli movie from the '70s *Brother Sun, Sister Moon,* the story of the conversion of St. Francis of Assisi in the late twelfth century. It fits in perfectly here.

Francis, the son of a wealthy, ostentatious merchant, went off to the Crusades as a young chevalier, only to return soon sickened in body and heart with the whole idea. He recovered from his wounds, rebounding with a total and explicit rejection of his father's capitalistic lifestyle, coming right out the other side with a vow of simplicity and poverty. He wanted to live as the birds live. He wanted to obey the admonitions of the Sermon on the Mount. And he did just that.

He went to the Vatican and preached the Sermon on the Mount to the Pope and all his cardinals, in an act of unparalleled effrontery. And the Pope responded, to his cardinals' disgust, with an embrace and the admission that "as a youth, I had your same courage," but power, riches, and politics had sapped his will. The Pope knelt down and kissed the bare feet of Francis while the cardinals plotted how to use the Pope's humility to further ensnare the poor.

I feel just like the Pope in this scene. I don't have the courage to truly "walk my talk." Few of us do. I sit in my office, making little contributions to our society, watching my fellow employees being unceremoniously sacked in the name of greater efficiency and lower expenses. I drive my car, fly across the continent, throw away my plastic, eat my beef, take the darned picnic on the paper plate and Styrofoam cup, and swallow the guilt.

Even the most environmentally conscious of us has to grow "line upon line, precept upon precept." Even John Muir didn't understand the full import of the developmental pressures in the Sierras when he first saw them, though he knew they were terribly destructive. It took decades before he realized what he would have to do to protect Yosemite. He first went into the Sierras in the late 1860s but didn't found the Sierra Club until 1892.

Let's back up and think about who we are as a "peculiar people," as a culture, and see how these peculiarities affect our relationship with the natural world. Let's try to unravel what is truly doctrinal and what comes from local tradition that becomes confused with the church itself. Let's look at what some thoughtful leaders have said about the place of the natural world and our relationship to it.

Confusion comes from the fact that so many of the leaders of the LDS Church for the past 140 years have come from the Intermountain West. Rather than speaking as church members, they speak out of their cultural and political biases, and these are often at serious odds with "environmental wisdom."

One of the great non-Mormons who sympathized with Mormon values was Wallace Stegner, the historian-author who wrote *The Gathering of Zion, The Mormon Trail,* and *Beyond the Hundredth Meridian,* a biography of John Wesley Powell. The import of that title is this: Powell recognized that agriculture "beyond [or west of] the hundredth meridian" would be basically impossible without irrigation. This has proven to be true (with some notable exceptions, such as the Willamette Valley in Oregon). Look at North Texas: as the aquifers have been pulled down farther and farther, farming becomes prohibitively expensive. The soils have become degraded, drained of all nutrients, and loaded with salts. I did my geology Ph.D. thesis in the area north of Big Bend National Park in West Texas. The topographic maps for that area are replete with names such as Paradise Valley and Green Valley. Today these places are moonscapes, totally destroyed by overgrazing and erosion from sudden rainfalls. Powell was right.

Traditionally, most land-based westerners, including church members and leaders, have been infected by the dream that they could do anything they wanted with "their" land because of what they saw as private property rights. They have not looked at their land as being that which the Lord declared to be good and admonished us to care for. Surely the first half of the LDS temple endowment ceremony, where the Creation of the world is so beautifully depicted, confirms that the gospel enjoins total respect for the material earth and all its inhabitants.

Anger is clearly not doctrinally appropriate when directed at environmentalists who advocate changing the way the human population relates to the nonhuman world. Elder Neal A. Maxwell said in an LDS general conference talk that "there may be relevant insight in reproof" (*Ensign*, November 1995, pp. 22–24), implying that all of us would do well to listen when we are chided for our behavior. The chider may be telling us something important. The recent rounds of criticism of ranching and mining practices in the American West may just contain some truth that would be valuable for the ranchers and miners to hear, if they want to "get right with God." But being humble and teachable are not well-known virtues of independent westerners.

The problem lies in an amazing lack of respect and sensitivity. Here's one of my favorite examples. At the time I took a Sierra Club backpacking trip down Slickrock Canyon in southern Utah in 1972, I had not yet joined the church. Ten of us were hiking along the bottom of the canyon, surrounded by the spirits and the physical evidence of the Anasazi. All around we found pit dwellings, granaries, woven sandals, pottery shards, the stunning walls of pictographs and petroglyphs. Rounding a corner, we saw in front of us a big bronze plaque honoring "Bishop Someone" for his dedication to the Scouts of his church ward. The plaque had been bolted into the sandstone, directly on top of a pictograph!

One of our hikers was a sixty-four-year-old Californian, hiking with a forty-year-old Trapper Nelson pack frame made of oak and canvas. He was outraged by what he saw. Shaking with anger, he picked up a large boulder, hefted it above his head, and smashed the plaque over and over, finally breaking it off the wall. He took the plaque up the canyon and buried it deep in the sand, never saying a word.

Clearly a good man had given of his time and energy for years to the boys of his ward. His efforts had been appreciated and ward members had sought for "the perfect memorial." They had raised funds to put up a memorial to this fine man, not realizing that at the same time they were desecrating the memory of *prior* inhabitants of that spot.

That's a Mormon example, but this scene could be replayed hundreds of times in our American culture, with different casts of the violators and violated. The violated are often nonhuman.

Elder Neal Maxwell also has said that we, as a people, must recognize the fact that the past few decades have been ones of unusual prosperity. They have also been unusually temperate. In other words, we've had exceptionally nice weather. He counseled us to prepare for harder times. Similar admonitions came from Elder L. Tom Perry in a recent LDS general conference: "As long as I can remember, we have been taught to prepare for the future. . . . I would guess that the years of plenty have almost universally caused us to set aside this counsel. I believe the time to disregard this counsel is over" (*Ensign*, November 1995, pp. 35–37). What this implies is that what worked marginally in the past probably won't work at all in the future. We've got to widen the margin for error in our relationships with the natural world. Floods in the Midwest, drought in the East, and earthquakes in the West show us that we simply cannot control earth processes at our will.

The leaders of the church clearly recognize the difficulty of providing for all the earth's people. The most tangible result of that recognition is the formation in 1975 of the Ezra Taft Benson Institute for Food and Agriculture at Brigham Young University. Unfortunately, the institute is invisible to most church members. Not a development agency per se, its function is to work with indigenous agencies in countries where hunger is a problem, to help them teach their people to feed themselves. The institute fits perfectly with the church's emphasis on personal and family preparedness. Its major program is devoted to family self-sufficiency and small-scale agriculture.

I recently wrote an article for *Dialogue: Journal of Mormon Thought* (summer 1995, pp. 101–9), entitled "Famine Relief, the Church and the Environment." In that article I considered the policies behind the church programs to help the people of the underdeveloped world feed themselves. These policies demonstrate that, at important levels, church leadership both understands the issues and also is open to new approaches. As an example, the Humanitarian Services Division of the Welfare Services Department was organized in 1985 to deal with world hunger issues. The division has four focal areas through which to deal with "relief and developmental work in Africa and other similarly distressed regions of the world" (quotation from the First Presidency message calling for the first church-wide fast in January 1985 to raise money for African relief). These areas include the following concerns:

1. The well-being and health of women and children, including such areas as employment and literacy, as well as physical health;

2. Agricultural production, processing, and marketing (small-scale and family-oriented);

3. Family productivity and employment (enterprise development); and

4. Emergency response.

These are clearly important ingredients for any program to deal with concerning world hunger. And they will also lead to environmental success *if* three other vital steps are also attended to. First, it is overwhelmingly important that agricultural production be independent insofar as possible from high-tech inputs. Dependence on synthetic fertilizers, big tractors, and pesticides will doom the projects to long-term failure, from lack of hard currency, if not from death of the soil itself. Second, every project must be planned with the long-term health of the environment in mind. Plants must not grow quickly and deplete the soil of nutrients, animals must not require exotic feed or breeding stock, and so forth. And third, every project must be designed to come to fruition *quickly*, at least to some important degree, so that local enthusiasm is maintained. And the Benson Institute realizes that the teaching function is perhaps the most important. The institute is a perfect example of implementation of Joseph Smith's precept: "Teach them correct principles and they will govern [or feed!] themselves."

In October 1995, I organized a regional Conference on the Restoration of Wildlife and Habitat in Pennsylvania, conducted at the Pittsburgh Zoo. Almost no one from the church came, but 150 other people did. It was an exciting day. The talks focused on the projects all across the state of Pennsylvania concerned with wildlife restoration, including river otters, fishers, turkeys, bluebirds, ospreys, shad, and even rattlesnakes.

One of the presentations was given by Blaine Puller and Ned Karga, district foresters for Kane Hardwoods, the second-largest private landowners in Pennsylvania. They spoke on the process of industrial forestry as their company practices it. Kane Hardwoods is a Pennsylvania subsidiary of Collins Pine, a family-owned lumber business that has been running its own mill for 140 years on the same large tract of timber in Northern California. Their remarkable record of responsible forestry shows that it can be done and done profitably. They are not perfect, but they are open to learning and are committed to staying in business for the long term. They know a lot about the forest, far more than most amateur "environmentalists" who spend a great deal of time criticizing Forest Service practices. Their lives depend on that knowledge, and most importantly, they *recognize* that, contrary to the cut-and-run breed.

In the mid '70s, shortly after joining the church, I took a job teaching geology at Guilford College in Greensboro, North Carolina. I quickly became known as an accessible scientist within the local church. The state geologist in nearby Raleigh, North Carolina, a wonderful old gentleman with a big white shock of hair, was also the LDS stake patriarch. A member called me one day to ask how a man in his position in the church could possibly make a statement to the effect that a fault running under a particular nuclear power plant was 160,000,000 years old when we know the earth was created in seven days! I was really put on the spot—here I was, a wet-behind-the-ears Mormon, also teaching historical geology, being called on to criticize a stake patriarch in the performance of his job!

What did *I* believe?

I don't remember how I answered the question, but I do remember getting on the phone to the BYU Geology Department and asking, "How do *you guys* handle these issues?" Ken Hamblin, a BYU geology professor who had authored the excellent physical geology text I was using in my classes, was most helpful. In particular, he directed me to a book in two volumes, now long out of print, called *Science and Religion: Toward a More Useful Dialogue* (Geneva, Illinois: Paladin House, Publishers, 1975). These volumes were filled with essays by predominantly Mormon scientists on all the relevant questions about the intersections of the scriptures and modern scientific thinking. It was a relief to discover that I wasn't struggling with these issues alone.

I was also helped in my struggles by two teachings, one secular, one religious. The first is that I was taught early to rely on the "method of multiple-working hypotheses." This requires that you accept as not frightening or threatening the fact that the data you have before you can be explained in several different and possibly quite contradictory ways. That's okay . . . just keep gathering data! The second is the teaching in the Doctrine and Covenants in which we are enjoined to study essentially all kinds of phenomena, freeing us from artificially limiting the types of knowledge we are willing to consider.

> *Teach ye diligently and my grace shall attend you, that you may be instructed more perfectly in theory, in principle, in doctrine, in the law of the gospel, in all things that pertain unto the kingdom of God, that are expedient for you to understand; Of things both in heaven and in the earth, and under the earth; things which have been, things which are, things which must shortly come to pass; things which are at home, things which are abroad; the wars and the perplexities of the nations, and the judgments which are on the land; and a knowledge also of countries and of kingdoms—. (D&C 88:78–79.)*

I have found that the most helpful book of all for Mormons trying to understand the relationship of their religion to the earth we live on is *The Creation*, published in 1976 by Frank B. Salisbury, a Ph.D. plant physiologist from Cal Tech, who has held leadership positions at many levels in the church. Salisbury takes the reader through current (1975) understanding by modern science of molecular biology, historical geology, paleontology, and human anthropology. The scientific findings of the past twenty years do not fundamentally change or diminish the value of this part of the book. Finally he takes on the big one—the theory of evolution. Here he shows that he supports the proposition that theories are simply proposed explanations of the data we have in hand. Theories are intentionally supple, changing all the time as new data are gathered.

Here is an example of that phenomenon from personal experience. When I took my first physical geology class in 1955, I distinctly remember the rather condescending superiority with which the "Taylor-Wegner" theory was mentioned in our text. Some rather odd German meteorologist had noticed the strangely coincidental "good fit" between continental outlines across the Atlantic, and had suggested in the early 1900s that perhaps they had been joined at some time long ago. Not much more was made of the proposal in my undergraduate classes, except for recognizing the correspondence of fossil distributions between southern Africa and South America. But when I returned to graduate school only a few years later in 1961, Vine and Matthews had already published their seminal papers on sea-floor spreading and the Mid-Atlantic Ridge. The academic geology world was *abuzz* with "continental drift," and this "new" theory was being used to explain virtually every puzzling geologic question of the past. But one of my colleagues at Penn State University, Dr. MacKenzie L. Keith, spent much of his last few years before retirement pointing out important problems *not* elucidated by the theory of continental drift! "Mac" was an exceptionally bright and sometimes ornery fellow who took great delight in popping pompous academic balloons, but his purpose was serious. He was upset with the rush to get on the scientific bandwagon without thinking through all the issues.

Salisbury suggests that insofar as the "theory of evolution" makes logical sense out of much of the data available, it is a useful tool. But there are huge holes in it, either major blocks of missing data or available data for which it does not account. So Salisbury attacks what he sees as the weakest link, evolution's statistical foundation. He finds that the "theory of evolution" as presently formulated is unsatisfactory in its ability to account for the number, rate, and timing of positive change—changes that produce successful descendants—in organisms over geologic time. The statistical realities of random chance cannot generate enough variation to account for what we see in the field and in the fossil record. And he presents excellent arguments in support of that contention. He accepts all of the "realities" of modern science but appeals to the Creator as the most vital player in the process of creation rather than random chance, which he says simply will not get the job done. And he leaves "multiple-working hypotheses," *including evolution,* out there for further study.

His closing section is interesting for Mormon audiences. He ghost-wrote a "Millennial Symposium" at which past leaders of the church are given a chance to state their case about Creation. He used his prerogative as symposium organizer to put himself on the program, closing with his own views. No matter what your scientific or environmental predilections, I believe most of us will respect this wise and gracious teacher for sharing this amazing depth of knowledge with us.

So what does all this imply for me as a Mormon and my relationship to the land? First of all, it enables me to return to the hymns and say with even greater conviction, "How great Thou art!" It helps me to take with even greater personal seriousness the charge made to mankind in Genesis to be stewards of the land for which we have been given responsibility. It gives me even more energy with which to work to convince my fellow members that the gospel requires their attention to the natural world.

But I am not waiting for them to join me in this vital work. If I did, I would be missing major opportunities to "magnify my calling," which I hear very clearly. I believe I have been given talents and energy that must be applied to the protection of the natural world. I must be "anxiously engaged" in *this* good cause. Contact with "nature" in all its manifestations gives me immense joy, and I am delighted that my wife, Linda Bazan, not only shares that joy with me but teaches me new sensitivities. Call us missionaries: together, we devote large portions of our time and substance to "charging our batteries" and helping others charge theirs, traveling, organizing conferences and gatherings, teaching, and supporting others who share these commitments. I have no shred of doubt that this is God's work.

Donald L. Gibbon is a Senior Research Fellow for Calgon Corporation in Pittsburgh, Pennsylvania, where he lives with his wife, Linda Bazan, and two amazing Cardigan corgis.

"AND IT CAME TO PASS THAT ENOCH LOOKED UPON THE EARTH; AND HE HEARD A VOICE FROM THE BOWELS THEREOF, SAYING: WO, WO IS ME, THE MOTHER OF MEN; I AM PAINED, I AM WEARY, BECAUSE OF THE WICKEDNESS OF MY CHILDREN. WHEN SHALL I REST, AND BE CLEANSED FROM THE FILTHINESS WHICH IS GONE FORTH OUT OF ME? WHEN WILL MY CREATOR SANCTIFY ME, THAT I MAY REST, AND RIGHTEOUSNESS FOR A SEASON ABIDE UPON MY FACE?" (MOSES 7:48.)

THE HANDIWORK OF GOD

VAUGHN J. FEATHERSTONE

SEVERAL YEARS AGO I WAS IN A YOUNG MEN'S GENERAL BOARD meeting. I cannot recall whether I was the Young Men's president or a counselor to Robert L. Backman. At the close of the meeting we had invited one of our general board members, Terry Nofsinger, to give a spiritual thought. In essence he said that when he was a young Scout about thirteen years of age he was on a winter Scout camp at Tracy Wigwam. There were several feet of snow on the ground. This particular night the whole troop was in the cabin. He recounted:

My scoutmaster came to me and said, "Terry, let's go for a walk." We put on our heavy coats and went out into the clear cold night. There was a full moon. The pines were laden with snow, and we walked on top of the snow, which had frozen solid enough to do that. When we were about fifty yards from the cabin, my scoutmaster said, "Terry, would you feel all right if we kneel here and have a prayer?" I agreed. We knelt and my scoutmaster offered a prayer. When he finished he said, "Terry, do you pray?" I said that I didn't. The scoutmaster then said, "Don't you think it is a good idea?" Terry said he thought for a moment, then said, "Yes, I think it is a good idea." The scoutmaster then said, "Terry, will you pray every morning and night the rest of your life?"

Terry said that he never made a commitment unless he intended to keep it. Even as a young man this was a quality in his life. He thought for a long moment and determined that praying was a good idea and he ought to do it. He continued: "I promised my scoutmaster that night, after kneeling in the snow under a full moon, that I would pray morning and night the rest of my life."

Then Terry turned to the Young Men's Presidency and said, "I want my scoutmaster, Vaughn Featherstone, to know that I have prayed every morning and night since that experience."

I have often wondered how important the setting was—beautiful white snow, a full-moon night, great pines laden with snow. There is something about nature that brings out the very best in us.

As a young Scout, I went to that same Tracy Wigwam Camp with our scoutmaster Bruford Reynolds. To this day, I remember a sign on the cabin door that read, "A Scout does not wantonly destroy property." As a young man I knew that also included the trees and nature's beauty in the canyons. When we went camping, we were trained to return everything to its natural state so that no one could tell if anyone had camped there overnight. Now, the Boy Scouts of America call it "No-Trace Camping."

Another time when I was scoutmaster (Terry Nofsinger was still in the troop), we went to Camp Steiner. We took some of the older young men and hiked in to the Four Lakes Basin. As you can imagine, it was only a short time before the troop began to stretch out. The older stronger boys were setting a pretty good pace. The younger boys were sagging a little behind. I was in about the middle of the pack. I had memorized the Sermon on the Mount and began to quote it as we hiked down the trail. The boys out front began to slow down and the boys at the rear picked up the pace. Soon we were walking down the beautiful High Uintas Trail in a large cluster. As you know, the Sermon on the Mount includes chapters 5–7 in Matthew. It is fairly long.

Through the years I have always known that it was the great spiritual, natural, clean wholesome setting of a high mountain trail, beautiful lakes, meadows and pines that gave me the perfect backdrop to share the Sermon on the Mount with the Scouts. I could have shared it in a classroom at the ward meetinghouse, and it would have been okay; they may have listened some, but out in nature in the magnificent Uintas it was a very special teaching moment.

These beautiful lines are quoted from Elspeth Huxley's 1959 novel *The Flame Trees of Thika:*

> *The best way to find things out is not to ask questions at all. If you fire off a question it is like firing off a gun—bang it goes and everything takes flight and runs for shelter; but if you sit quite still and pretend not to be looking, all the little facts will come and peck around your feet, situations will venture forth from thickets, and intentions will creep out and sun themselves on a stone; and if you are very patient, you will see and understand a great deal more than the man with a gun does.*

It seems you can always identify those who love the out-of-doors and the grand designs in nature. They seem to draw a special strength and character from the soil, the wondrous creations of God, as well as the wild birds and animals. This is a glorious earth upon which we live. There is a healing that takes place when we spend time in the lofty mountains, beholding the beautiful, clean sparkling rivers and streams and watching eagles and other mighty birds in flight. Who does not stare in awe at a great monarch pine that stands in the forest, or wonder at how anything could be so beautiful as you drop down over a mountain pass and behold an emerald- or turquoise-colored lake resting among the pines. Over the years I have watched boys turn into men during a one-week campout in the High Uintas Wilderness.

George Dawson was a great Canadian engineer and explorer. He was small in stature, and had serious respiratory diseases that took his life in his early fifties. He worked summer and winter surveying, exploring, and doing engineering work in the vast cold northern wilderness of Canada. The northern city of Dawson is named for him.

After he died his community eulogized him in these words, which comprise a special and wonderful tribute:

And tell him the men he worked with
Say, judging as best they can,
That in lands that try manhood hardest
He was tested and proven a man!

The ways of nature are not always easy but we learn valuable lessons and gain every time we experience them.

There is a Scout council in the Midwest called the Dan Beard Council of the Boy Scouts of America. Another great Scouter, Hamblin Garland, paid the following tribute to Dan Beard:

Do you fear the force of the wind,
The slash of the rain, go face them
And fight them, be savage again.
Go hungry and cold like the wolf.
Go wade like the crane.
The palms of your hand will toughen,
The skin on your forehead will tan,
You'll be rugged and swarthy and weary;
But you'll walk like a man.
—VAUGHN J. FEATHERSTONE, *Man of Holiness*

What a blessing is the great out-of-doors. The Boy Scouts of America has a large Scout ranch called Philmont, located just outside of Cimmaron, New Mexico, in the northeastern area of the state. I believe that, with recent acquisitions, it is approximately 139,000 acres of land. Each year, about 18,000 Scouts and Explorers visit the ranch to take high-adventure backpacking treks in the Rocky Mountains. They are exposed to nature and taught all about the wildlife, as well as the flowers, shrubs, and trees. They sit around a campfire and look at the stars and the constellations, and all nature seems to come alive for them.

As a boy working on my Eagle Scout, the most exciting and most difficult merit badges for me were Bird Study, Camping, Pioneering, Lifesaving, etc. However, they were those I learned from the most. Now the Scouting program has expanded to include Nature as well as Earth and Environmental Science merit badges. Our Scouts of today are being trained to respect and care for planet Earth.

The Lord said, "I, the Lord, stretched out the heavens, and built the earth, my very handiwork; and all things therein are mine" (D&C 104:14). And, my, oh my, what a handiwork it is. A great scoutmaster helped me to appreciate nature and the out-of-doors. I have taught and modeled what I learned from him.

In his book *Self-Renewal*, John Gardner states:

Young people do not assimilate values of their group by learning words (truth, justice, etc.) and their definitions. They learn attitudes, habits, and ways of judging. They learn these in intensely personal transactions with their immediate family or associates. They learn them in the routines and crises of living, but they also learn them through songs, stories, drama, and games. They do not learn ethical principles; they emulate ethical or unethical people. They do not analyze or list the attributes they wish to develop; they identify with people who seem to them to have these attributes. That is why young people need models, both in their imaginative life and in their environment, models of what man at his best can be.

I learned this from Bruford Reynolds, and learned it in intensely personal transactions with a few boys and a great leader. I learned to emulate an ethical nature-loving leader of great substance. I could identify with him "of what a man can be at his best."

For fifty-four years, since I was taught as a Scout, I have not thrown papers, cans, or garbage from the car as we traveled. Our sons always carry out the nonbiodegradable trash when they float the river. In fact, our family loves to float the white-water rivers, and we carry everything out. We practice to this day "No-Trace Camping." We don't kill the birds, cut down or carve on the trees.

The Boy Scouts of America is a worldwide organization. It has over 5,000,000 men and boys registered. In the oath that a boy repeats every week, he promises to do his duty to God and his country. The country, this country, and all other countries are part of God's handiwork. A man who reverences God and country will be a model for boys as Bruford Reynolds was to me. A reverence of God is a reverence for all his creations.

My wife, Merlene, made an interesting observation. A couple of years ago our family, including some of our grandchildren, about twenty or so, floated the main Salmon Rivers. One morning early, all six of our sons and our son-in-law and our grandsons were sitting together on an outcropping of rocks. We had one of the brothers, my oldest son, teaching. Merlene said that as she looked over and saw this group of Aaronic and Melchizedek Priesthood bearers—all six sons and son-in-law Eagle Scouts, the oldest grandsons Eagle Scouts, the others deeply involved in Scouting—"I have never been more grateful or pleased in my life for what you have done for our sons and family." I thought, *I owe it all to a great scoutmaster who was a model of living in all dimensions of life.*

Let me conclude these thoughts with a very relevant scripture from Moses 7, verses 48 and 49:

> *And it came to pass that Enoch looked upon the earth; and he heard a voice from the bowels thereof, saying: Wo, wo is me, the mother of men; I am pained, I am weary, because of the wickedness of my children. When shall I rest, and be cleansed from the filthiness which is gone forth out of me? When will my Creator sanctify me, that I may rest, and righteousness for a season abide upon my face?*
>
> *And when Enoch heard the earth mourn, he wept, and cried unto the Lord, saying: O Lord, wilt thou not have compassion upon the earth?*

Enoch asked the Lord two more times when the earth should rest, and then the Lord gave this promise: "And the day shall come that the earth shall rest, . . . And righteousness will I send down out of heaven; and truth will I send forth out of the earth, . . ." (Moses 7:61–62).

All that is grand and magnificent about this beautiful earth shouts the truths of the glories of nature and the handiwork of God. May we have appropriate reverence for all the creations around us and do our part to help our Mother Earth find peace and rest.

Vaughn J. Featherstone was called as a General Authority in the Presiding Bishopric of the LDS Church in 1972 and sustained to the First Quorum of the Seventy in 1976. He has been a registered Scout for fifty-four years, and has served on the National Executive Board of the Boy Scouts of America and the National Advisory Council, having received the Silver Beaver, the Silver Antelope, and the Silver Buffalo Scouting Awards, as well as the distinguished Eagle Award. He has also served on and chaired many other committees.

"AND IT CAME TO PASS THAT WE DID TAKE OUR TENTS AND DEPART INTO THE WILDERNESS." (1 NEPHI 16:12.)

WILDERNESS PEOPLE

RALPH H. TINGEY

I

HE BLOOD THAT FLOWS THROUGH MY VEINS IS THE BLOOD OF MY Mormon ancestors, tough people who pushed handcarts across the West to settle a desert wilderness. I was raised by special people who instilled in me a love of these wild places. As an adult I have lived in wilderness areas of the West and the Arctic as a preserver of the land and our culture.

We tend to think of wilderness as land devoid of people; however, human beings have lived in these places for a long, long time. The Utah deserts were inhabited aeons before my forefathers came. I have lived in wilderness areas most of my adult life, and the people who live in and near those places have been my mentors. But how did my journey begin?

My great-grandfather William Hurst was the first supervisor on the Dixie National Forest in southern Utah. My grandfather William Hurst was a forest ranger on the Dixie; I think they started together, the year the Forest Service was created. My uncle, William D. Hurst, who was called Dee to distinguish him from the rest, was a ranger on the Ashley National Forest when I was a young boy. He retired as the Regional Forester in Albuquerque. His sister Margaret, my mother, was born in Panguitch, Utah, and spent her young life at the Harris Flat Ranger Station on Panguitch Lake. Forests are in my blood.

Each summer my parents would send me to live with my Uncle Dee and Aunt Dolly in Vernal, Utah, to play with my cousin, William J. Hurst, (whom they called Bill J. for obvious reasons). Those summers in the wild still burn brightly in my memory. I remember how we would bounce in a pickup truck up the narrow dirt road out of Vernal, over the pass to the ranger station in Manila. From there we would take pack trips into the Uinta Mountains, the horses loaded with tepee tents, grub boxes, and a cast-iron Dutch oven. Uncle Dee would bury the oven in the coals of a campfire and make baking powder biscuits. The smells from those campfires, the biscuits, the cutthroat trout frying in butter, and from lodgepole pines and horses on the shores of the lakes in the High Uintas took root in my fertile young soul and grew like wildfire.

My father, a doctor in Salt Lake City, grew up just a block from the Salt Lake Temple, a city kid. But every Saturday in season he would take me fishing or hunting. This ritual became as regular as religion. All summer we would fish the clear trout streams of the Uintas. Those tiny brooks filled with little fishes were his secret refuge from a hectic life as a family doctor. At eighty-three he still seeks his peace there. In the fall he would wake me before dawn and drive to the marshes of the Great Salt Lake to be ready for the ducks at dawn. As winter approached we would join Uncle Dee and Grandpa Hurst for a deer hunt in the High Uintas. My early life revolved around school, church, and the mountains, and there wasn't a clear distinction between them. I'm not the first person to see wilderness as a metaphor for life and religion, but in my case it was not artificial. They were fairly integrated.

In 1957 at age fourteen, I discovered mountaineering. With my friends from the East Ensign Ward, Milt Hokanson and Frank Rippon, I climbed Lone Peak south of our home in Salt Lake City. We and probably every other fourteen-year-old boy in the ward were Boy Scouts in Mike Coles's great Troop 179. Mike had taken the troop on a high adventure every summer: in 1955 we spent a week in the Uintas; in 1956, before the dam was built, we floated the Glen Canyon. Over the next few years mountain climbing consumed my life and continues to be a driving passion to this day. The seeds sown by a caring scoutmaster grew among the other wildflowers in my soul.

Growing up Mormon in Salt Lake City offered me the opportunity to serve a mission to Finland where I, like all missionaries, learned the language. It was one of the most fascinating and rewarding experiences of my life and convinced me to study foreign languages. So, I spent the next three years studying classical Greek at the University of Utah. But I was used to spending my summers out of doors, so in the summer of 1965 I got a job as a ranger in Grand Teton National Park where I had climbed in the late '50s and early '60s. In the winter I would study Greek, and later Arabic and ancient Near Eastern languages in graduate school at Johns Hopkins University in Baltimore. Each summer I would migrate back to the Tetons to my job as a ranger. Finally, in the middle of writing my Ph.D. dissertation, I spent a winter in the Tetons, and those wild roses of my heart bloomed. I never went back to the university but began a career protecting parks, those wild places that my parents, relatives, and church leaders had taught me to love.

II

My boss, Tom Milligan, was the ranger's ranger, the ultimate hard man. Tom was the South District Ranger in Grand Teton National Park; I was the Jenny Lake Ranger. The Jenny Lake climbing rangers, men such as Jim Olson, Bill Conrod, and Bob Irvine, were the iron men of the mountains. Yet even after ten years of climbing the hardest routes, hundreds of dangerous mountain rescues, and daily trips into the mountains, we still looked up to Tom Milligan as our paragon. Seventeen years my senior, he was the fittest of us all, and we were tough!

Tom's philosophy of managing parks took the long view. We lived for the mountains, the patrols, and the mountain rescues. But after a rescue Tom would remind us, "You guys did good today, but in twenty years, no one will remember this rescue. But if you don't clean up the fire pits in the backcountry, twenty years from now we won't have any wilderness." Even after living in Yellowstone and dealing with stock for nearly twenty years, he didn't believe that horses were ultimately compatible with park wilderness preservation and a good visitor experience. He believed people should hike into the Teton backcountry.

In midsummer of 1979, the park superintendent planned a horse trip along the skyline trail between the forest and the park with the Targhee National Forest supervisors and district rangers to discuss cooperative management of the common boundary. Tom and I were invited on the pack trip. Sheri and I owned two horses, so Tom asked me just to ride up for an overnight with light gear in contrast to the group's heavily laden pack train. I rode Talker well over twenty-five miles that morning. When we got to the beautiful meadow near Sunrise Lake, I dismounted and shook hands with my forest ranger friends from Ashton and Driggs, across the range. They all stared at my horse and gear; I was riding a twelve-pound English saddle and carrying red nylon saddlebags filled with bivouac gear. I took off the saddle and draped it over a log, brushed Talker, and picketed him in the meadow. Out of the corner of my eye I saw the guys lift my little saddle and discuss it in hushed tones. I looked at their large Spanish saddles and eyed the sore spots on the backs of a couple of their horses.

About that time, Tom Milligan walked into camp. He was dressed in shorts, his ranger shirt, running shoes, and a baseball cap, carrying a small backpack. He had hiked eighteen miles up the trail to prove his point about the horses. After greetings and expressions of astonishment at the distance he had covered that morning, the conversation turned to the management of the area. Tom waxed eloquent on the impact of the horses grazing the small, grassy clearing, the short growing season for the alpine plants, the changing visitor expectations, pollution of the only alpine lake in the area, and other impacts from people and horses.

By late afternoon everyone wanted to build a big fire and cook the slabs of beef they had packed up for the occasion. I hauled out a head of lettuce, fresh fruit, and gourmet foods, and joined the campfire. Tom opened a reused cat food sack and ate with us. It soon became obvious that Tom hadn't carried a sleeping bag, so the rangers asked him what he was going to do for the night. "Well," he replied, "I've got to hike back down home this evening. I've got a tennis match with my wife."

The conversation was wrapping up and the subject turned to Tom's imminent retirement. "What are you going to do when you retire, Tom?" someone asked. Tom slowly passed his eyes over each one of the generally overweight crowd, their middle-aged bellies starting to hang over rodeo buckles. With a twinkle in his eye and in his admonishing baritone he replied, "I'm gonna get in shape!"

III

Fast-forward through fifteen years in the Tetons, working, climbing, fishing, kayaking, skiing, marriage and a family, to Denali National Park in Alaska. Sheri, Thor, and I had come up when the new parks were created in 1980 under President Jimmy Carter. Denali had been tripled in size, and I was hired as the management assistant to help solve the problems of the new park areas. Sheri and I fell in love with the vast, raw beauty of the land, the solitude, moose, bears, and caribou. Every hike, every trip was an adventure. The "Lower 48" seemed so tame in comparison, and after a two-week winter trip through the Brooks Range in the Arctic, our minds were settled to make Alaska our permanent home.

We found a piece of land near the park at the mouth of the Yanert Valley. The Yanert drains Mount Deborah and is a dog-sled highway in the winter—the perfect location. We had a pile of logs delivered, and Sheri and I peeled and planed their inside surfaces to build our own cabin. It was small, with one big room downstairs and a sleeping loft. It had no running water, no electricity, and few neighbors. But the view from the loft was magnificent: Denali Park to the west, where we could see Dall sheep with our telescope, the Healy Range to the north, and Pyramid Peak and the Yanert Valley to the east. The Nenana River flowed north through the canyon a few hundred yards and a steep drop-off to the west.

Distances across the Alaskan wilderness are tremendous. Only two major arteries connect the cities; the rest of the state is essentially roadless. Daphne was born a year after we arrived and our son, Thor, was just a young child; travel with them posed a problem. But the lure of pure wilderness was strong, so we bred a dog team. Thirty dogs lived in front of the cabin.

Our closest neighbor, Dennis Kogl, also had a dog team, and taught us everything he knew about mushing dogs. He is a man of few words, but a harder worker I have never met. The quintessential Alaskan, Dennis had traveled everywhere by dog team. The year we arrived in Denali, he and Laura Larson set off from Denali Park with a dog team pulling a freight sled towards the Iditarod Trail. Dennis snowshoed about 300 miles, breaking trail for the dogs across the wilderness to McGrath, the next village west. From McGrath they caught the Iditarod Trail to Nome, another 600 miles. At Nome the team picked up more supplies and journeyed up the Arctic coast to Kotzebue, Point Hope, Wainright, finally arriving at Point Barrow, the northernmost point in the country, about three months later. Spring had arrived, the snow was melting, so Dennis and Laura hitched a ride down the Alaska Pipeline Road with the dog team, back to Denali Park. For us this was a tale of high adventure; for Dennis it was another day in Alaska. I chose Dennis as my Alaska mentor.

For ten years, Dennis and I shared three Yukon Quest dogsled races, house-building, political discussions, salmon-fishing expeditions, midnight adventures up the Yanert Valley, and auto-mechanics sessions. He was the closest friend a man could have. So it was only natural that in the spring of 1989, Dennis would go with us on the spring dogsled trip from our house ninety miles through the heart of Denali National Park to Wonder Lake.

We put the dogs in harness at park headquarters, packed the sled with a week's food, and stuffed Daphne deep into sleeping bags and caribou skins to protect her from the cold. Sheri, Thor, Dennis, and I each took off with a loaded sled and team of dogs in a long canine procession across the barren, rolling, snow-covered hills. The first day we traveled fifty-five miles past Savage River, where the first concessionaire set up a tourist camp in 1921. Past Sanctuary River, up which we had driven the dogs to the Refuge Valley years ago. Into the Teklanika River where the archaeological sites on the river bluff show the rich history of early Native Americans who hunted the caribou in the valley. Up Igloo Creek where the Dall sheep are sentinels on the high cliffs. Down into the East Fork River where Adolph Murie, the famous biologist, studied the wolves. He and Louise, his wife, raised a small daughter in the cozy cabin; each visit Thor and Daphne giggled at the small hole in the outhouse built for her.

We spent our first night in the most famous site in the park, the Toklat Ranger Station. Sitting in the cabin that evening we spoke of Harry Karstens, the first superintendent of Mount McKinley National Park and the first person to climb Mount McKinley. Talk about a tough human being. The rumor was that Harry had left Chicago at age sixteen after a bad fight with his brother in a barn. He arrived at the gold camps on the Forty Mile River as a dog driver, carrying mail and freighting supplies to the camps. His toughness was legend, so he was nicknamed "The Forty Mile Kid." He gravitated to Fairbanks, and then Kantishna, where in 1906 he was hired as a guide by Charles Sheldon, the famous hunter-naturalist. The two spent the winter of 1906 at a small cabin on Cabin Creek from which Sheldon hunted the spectacular game animals of Alaska: Dall sheep, caribou, moose, and grizzly bear. Being a member of the Boone and Crockett Club, which keeps the big-game animal-trophy records, Sheldon was concerned about the survival of the great trophy animals on the Toklat.

Sheldon returned to the east with a mission: the creation of Mount McKinley National Park ". . . as a game preserve. . . ." Congress created the park in 1916, the first park established under the new National Park Service Organic Act. Although it includes the tallest mountain in North America, its purpose was to protect the caribou and Dall sheep from professional meat hunters who were shooting them to supply the gold-mining camps just north of the Toklat in Kantishna, where gold had been discovered in 1904.

History flooded my thoughts and our conversation. I, the park ranger, with my best friend, the toughest Alaskan I knew, was sitting at the Toklat. Almost every day for ten years, I had been hiking, climbing, traveling the park by dog team, working on subsistence hunting issues, mining issues, visitor concerns, management plans, and ways to protect the park. Yet tonight, I was just a mile from where Sheldon and Karstens had spent similar nights seventy-five years earlier, planning a national park. Sheldon's dream had come true. The Dall sheep and caribou roamed freely, their gene pools unaltered by the guns of the trophy hunters. My children could still sit in a meadow surrounded by full-curl rams, or watch a grizzly bear chase a ground squirrel. During the summer, tourists could watch the wolves stalk the migrating bands of caribou from Polychrome Pass above us or, from the windows of the shuttle bus, see a grizzly take down a moose.

We walked out into the minus-thirty-degree air, which bit our skin. The snow crunched under our mukluks. We each lugged a five-gallon bucket of hot meat and broth, which we poured into each dog bowl. The dogs wolfed down the supper, and we collected the bowls and checked the dogs' feet. I called Sheri and the kids out to listen to the silence, watch the stars and mountains collide, and be at peace for the night. The dogs broke into the nightly chorus, a long howl lasting about thirty seconds. When they were finished, the East Fork wolf pack replied with the most famous hallmark of the Arctic wilderness. The sound of wolves howling in the winter darkness always thrills me, and this particular pack has special meaning, like I am truly home. We looked up to see a brilliant aurora explode overhead like fireworks on the Fourth of July. Red and green curtains and showers of light covered the sky. It was the climax of the greatest day of dog mushing in my life, the grand finale of ten years of our lives in the wilderness of Denali.

IV

In August 1990, with twenty sled dogs, a Labrador retriever, and a cat, Sheri and I and our two youngsters landed on the minuscule Kotzebue runway on the northwest coast of Alaska, thirty miles north of the Arctic Circle. After Denali National Park, I had taken a position as superintendent of three immense parks: Cape Krusenstern National Monument, Noatak National Preserve, and Kobuk Valley National Park. They total about nine million acres of the western Arctic, or roughly the size of Massachusetts, Connecticut, and Rhode Island.

From Kotzebue, the parks loom on the distant horizons. On a November day as we walked along the beach in front of our house, the coast of Cape Krusenstern was visible ten miles across the sound; Mount Noak sat a soft purple on a sea of phosphorescent blue while the clouds reflected the brilliant pinks, oranges, and yellows of the sun, and the pastel

Arctic sky merged green into the crimson horizon. Nature here is harsh, but its colors are spectacular.

For centuries, the windswept shores of Cape Krusenstern National Monument have been a summer fishing and trading site for the Inupiaq Eskimos. The horizontally stratified beach ridges record a thousand successive generations of Eskimo ingenuity and dependence on both land and sea. The physical remains of house pits, harpoons, and graves define the chronology for the occupation of Northwest Alaska, from the sites of early man to those of modern Eskimos. Even today fishing and seal hunting camps dot the shore seasonally. Sitting on the prehistoric cliffs above the beach we could imagine the ancient shaman's eyes beckoning the whales.

To the north lies the Noatak National Preserve, where the Noatak River flows out of the ancient valleys of the Brooks Range. The Noatak, 425 miles long, flows westward from the Gates of the Arctic and empties into Kotzebue Sound in front of town.

To the east, Kobuk Valley National Park is a ringed mountain valley complete with 100-foot-high sand dunes, where temperatures reach 100 degrees F. in the summer and plummet to sixty degrees below zero in the winter. The inland Eskimos live by seasonal subsistence, catching shee fish in the spring, netting salmon in the summer, and hunting the caribou along the river in the fall.

My duties as park superintendent were to protect the federal parks against environmental degradation, to provide for visitor enjoyment, and to manage subsistence hunting. The issues I faced in the Arctic differed from the classic tourist problems of the Teton and Yellowstone Parks. They centered on inventorying the extensive varieties of natural resources: flora, fauna, water, and land. We documented the cultural resources: archaeological sites, the ethnology of the Northwest Alaska Eskimos, oral traditions, and subsistence hunting practices.

No roads link these parks to the outside world; access is by boat, snow machine, or light aircraft. Travel is always risky, and Sheri could never count on my being home on the same day I left. On a stormy day in November, I flew with our native liaison, Jonas Ramoth, and our management assistant, Dave Mills, to the tiny village of Kivalina, about ninety miles north of Kotzebue. We were to attend a meeting on subsistence hunting, the major issue in the Eskimo community. Our work would take us to similar meetings in eight other villages.

Kivalina sits on a sand spit about a hundred yards wide along the windswept Arctic coast. A more exposed village is hard to imagine. Every aspect of the Arctic is magnified here. The plane landed in a 45-knot crosswind, sliding sideways down the ice-covered dirt strip. The pilot yelled into my ear, "How long will you be? I'll wait for you. Otherwise, I don't think I can land again and get you out of here!" I told him we would be all day, so he left in a flash. The frozen sea was polished smooth by the wind, and drifts of snow snaked across the streets in the minus-twenty-degree morning.

The meeting was to inform the local hunters of recent changes in the law. Due to the Alaska Supreme Court's decision that every Alaskan has equal rights to subsistence hunting, the federal government had assumed management of subsistence hunting on federal lands. This had major implications for the Inupiaq hunter, since it changed who would control his hunting practices and his livelihood. When we arrived in town, a call went out over the CB radio, and townsfolk came to the community center to listen to our short presentation.

The people asked questions, usually about seasons, bag limits, and other rules. Though it is difficult for us to think of hunting without rules, such concepts are foreign to a people who depend on opportunistic hunting. When the caribou cross the land, they are harvested. When the ducks fly north in the spring after a long winter, they are a source of fresh meat. When the whales swim north, the whaling crews go out in seal-skin boats to catch them.

After the meeting, we watched despondently as the few passing airplanes overflew the runway in the storm, leaving us in the village. But the Inupiaq Eskimo culture is based on sharing, and hospitality is absolute, so Enoch and Lucy Adams took the three of us into their home for the night. Conversation turned from subsistence to feasting as Enoch explained that he had just shot two caribou; there would be plenty of meat for dinner.

In the middle of the table steamed a large pot of caribou ribs and broth. Lucy took a rib and sliced the meat lengthwise from the bone with her ulu, the women's curved knife that fits into the palm of the hand. Enoch ate his meat using a traditional men's large sheath knife. With my Swiss Army knife, I was able to fit in.

After a few minutes, I noticed Enoch eating what looked like a grey-and-black lump from the meat pot and asked what it was. "Bible," said Enoch with a huge grin. "You guys wouldn't like it." Lots of giggling followed between Lucy and Enoch. I decided to try some. It was delicious, but I paused long enough to raise a smile from the couple. I asked Lucy what part of the animal it was from. "You don't want to know!" she laughed. After much coaxing, she admitted it was a piece of intestine just past the stomach. I asked how she prepared it. "Well, first you clean it . . . but not too good! . . ."

My wife was not pleased when we phoned to say we were spending the night in Kivalina. The next day was Thanksgiving, and we had invited twenty people to dinner. But the next morning, if you can call darkness morning, the weather was no better. By noon no planes had come. However, the basketball team was due home from Kotzebue, so one pilot at least would be attempting the trip and, if successful, would have room to take us back. The single-engine Cessna landed like a fly in a blizzard. The pilot never left the doorway of the plane and loaded us in a flash. The wind seemed to sweep us back to Kotzebue, just in time for a Thanksgiving dinner.

The Arctic is vast and seemingly untouched, yet I sense that this will not last. The Red Dog zinc mine, one of the largest in the world, has recently opened near Cape Krusenstern National Monument. A road to the mine winds across the monument's north end. Mining has been going on for five years, yet it has already begun to change the lives of the people in the region, who now work full-time as truck drivers, equipment operators, and managers. Copper and chromium await exploitation, and oil leases are pending just off the coast. Pollution from industrial countries in the Far East shows up as a brown cloud on the horizon, demonstrating that even the vast Arctic is small and fragile.

Wild lands have formed the character of these, my mentors. The faces in these stories cannot be separated from the land. Their days on the Arctic ice, or in high mountains, or on scorched deserts have made them tough. Their dependence on the land has taught them stewardship. The scarcity of resources has taught them to share. They have learned to kill and eat with respect and reverence. These very traits are likewise the heritage of my youth. The ingenuity, courage, and tight-knittedness of our ancestors were formed in the crucible of handcart journeys to the greatest wilderness in the American West. The stories of our pioneer ancestors continue to form the warp and weft from which we of this generation weave our lives.

The challenge to the pioneers was to conquer the wilderness. But the world of our forefathers and even our parents has changed. Wilderness no longer instills fear in civilized hearts. Rather, it has become a haven for recreation, rejuvenation, scenic wonder, and spiritual reawakening for a population increasingly pressed by the crush of humanity. The challenge for my generation and for me in particular has been to preserve the wilderness—our natural and cultural heritage. As a young Mormon boy I glimpsed the end of wild America. Now as an adult the memories of that wilderness heritage are the maps that guide me to a new vision of a wilderness, integrated into lives and relevant to the values of our generation.

Ralph H. Tingey is the deputy superintendent of the Alaska Support Office for National Park Service in Anchorage, Alaska.

"AND WO BE UNTO MAN THAT SHEDDETH BLOOD OR THAT WASTETH FLESH AND HATH NO NEED." (D&C 49:21.)

SPIRITUAL TRAILS
I HAVE TRAVELED:
THE INARTICULATE
SPEECH OF
MY HEART

CLAYTON M. WHITE

HE FIRST YEAR THAT I DROVE THE ALCAN HIGHWAY FROM ALASKA may have been the first time I experienced true solitude. I did so in the autumn of the year in 1964 accompanied only by our Siberian husky. The fireweed still carried some bloom; aspen and birch leaves were turning red, yellow, and subdued earth tones. The air was crisp and invigorating, snow topped some of the mountains in northern British Columbia and the Yukon Territory, and the sky changed constantly from crystal clear to rolling thunderheads. The trip took about eight days, so I had plenty of time to think. Solitude enables one to reevaluate beliefs and values, and I think some of mine—relative to man's place on the planet—were refined on that lone dirt road. I started to form my values of stewardship.

My feelings about landscape can be best described as "spiritual." Spiritual feelings are something I really can't define precisely nor quantitatively, but they are to me that which stimulates and educates the senses.

I keep a small flask of pebbles I have picked up from the countless unnamed beaches, gravel bars, and streams I have explored in my travels. When the routines of life become stressful, I finger the pebbles and remember how I picked them from bits of landscape where few have set foot, and I gain self-renewal. Several pebbles in particular came from beside a bit of melting glacial ice, cast upon a beach. The ice was from a glacier in Prince William Sound, Alaska, where I visited frequently during the *Exxon Valdez* oil spill. It was old ice with age numbered in thousands of years. It had seen a lot of history and now was seeing its last as it was peacefully being absorbed into the cold stark waters of the sound. It caused me to ponder my own passage through life. Perhaps it is the combined influence of heart-felt emotion and thought that we call conscience—that still small voice within. It is that voice which has given some of the best sermons about landscape that I have heard, all prompted from the pulpit of memory, to an audience of one—to paraphrase Neal A. Maxwell. This, then, is from where I take the second part of my title, from a song about inarticulate feelings of the heart by the singer and composer Van Morrison, which I listened to as I was traveling one of those spiritual trails.

One night in January 1993, longtime friend and colleague Bill Emison, who first worked with me on the U.S.'s underground testing programs in the Aleutian Islands in the late 1960s, was with me, researching parrots in western Victoria, Australia. We had finished a day's work; the sun-drenched clouds were all but gone, and sounds of night had begun. It was hot and humid. We were lounging on the porch of a cabin on a remote ranch, casting about experiences we had enjoyed together and trying to find meaning in them. For whatever reason, both of us had some forms of emotion close to the surface. It was in the late hours during that evening, with night birds such as frogmouths and nightjars and the chorus of frogs and insects calling, that I jotted down several scores of events, or spiritual trails. (If my trails can help you find a spiritual meaning in expressions of life's landscapes, then they will have had some value.) As my emotions carried me through those trails, I thought of the words of Rachel Carson in *The Sense of Wonder.* She tells of a child's world, full of wonder and excitement. She observed that it has been our misfortune that the clear-eyed vision for what is beautiful and awe-inspiring is dimmed and even lost before we reach adulthood. She remarked that if she had influence with the fairy God-Mother who presides over the christening of children, she should ask that her gift be a sense of wonder so indestructible as to last throughout life, an antidote against boredom and disenchantments of later years. It is not half as important to know as it is to feel; emotions and impressions of the sense of wonder are the soil in which feelings grow.

Scriptures from my culture relate that at the end of the creative periods, the Gods saw all that had resulted and proclaimed it "very good." It is consistent with the Mormon cultural concepts of creation to believe it was very good and that it pleased the Gods because there was some relationship in the interactions between earth's organisms. The scriptures then say, "I, the Lord, stretched out the heavens, and built the earth, my very handiwork; and all things therein are mine. . . . And if the properties are mine, then ye are stewards; . . ." (D&C 104:14, 56).

THE YUKON

My profession, working mainly with birds that are frequently rare or threatened, has carried me around the globe to many exotic and stimulating places. It is within these beckoning landscapes that many trails have taken me. And so, for more than thirty years Alaska has been a link for me—first as a student, then as a professional zoologist—with two of the most impressive of all bird species: the peregrine falcon and its somewhat larger relative, the gyrfalcon. The magical combination of geography, landscape, and falcons have been inseparable in my mind as a perfect union of environment and wildlife—the last remote American wilderness that holds this unique combination.

A falcon crag is one of those very special places on earth where humans have the opportunity to become peculiarly attuned to the oneness of living things and landscape. Aldo Leopold, who was more sensitive than most to this intermingling of land and life, gave expression to it in his writing about the ruffed grouse and the north woods. He called it a "numenon," in contrast to "phenomenon." As the ruffed grouse is the numenon of the north woods, so the falcon is the numenon of all those sheer, rocky habitats overlooking tundra, forest, river, and sea in Alaska. Remove the falcon from the scene and the whole landscape becomes diminished by more than the absence of a bird. The natural integrity—the rightness—of that particular piece of landscape is somehow distorted, and the cliff is never the same again.

In the 1960s and 1970s the peregrine falcon suffered large-scale but often regional reductions in numbers after having been affected by chemicals, mainly chlorinated hydrocarbons. Nesting domains were abandoned; thus, the later years of examining nesting-site use, especially within a historical framework, became bittersweet. Once, we camped across the river from a cliff and awoke to see the dawn from inside the forest. We crossed the river and, as we landed the boat beneath a nesting cliff, I was cloistered in a strange and surrounding quietness. An immense stillness mantled the forested landscape. Only the lap of water on the shore, the whisper of a light breeze pushing through the ragged spruce trees, and the occasional twitter of small birds along the river's beach could be heard. Except for a few old feathers, the falcon's nesting ledge was empty. As I sat on the sage-covered hillside above the cliff, overlooking the great river as it flowed noiselessly beneath me and the wide expanse of the forested landscape beyond, the outline of two falcons came into view. Their high calls, usually evoking in me a sense of wildness, freedom, and solitude, now seemed to carry with it a feeling of mournfulness and melancholy. They could not breed because of the synthetic poisoning their bodies carried. They were just there—sterile—victims of our toxic world, not theirs. I watched as the two ghostlike shadows drifted slowly off into the Arctic summer's twilight, and all again fell silent. Cold stones remained along the ledge rather than calls of life.

I remember a man named George McGregor, a prospector and trapper, already very old when I heard of him. He lived along the Yukon River in Alaska. He has been dead now three or more decades, but for many years he lived alone in a log cabin he built at the foot of a peregrine falcon nesting crag. Every year the falcons migrated back from the south, probably

Latin American, to nest on the rocks above his cabin. He did not disturb them, for he was a quiet man who blended serenely and unobtrusively into his surroundings and was part of the land just as much as the falcons, the river, and the spruce trees. Once, George saw a female falcon swoop out of the air and strike a marauding raven dead in midair over the river in front of his cabin, and his old eyes brightened when he told about it.

In recent years another man built his cabin by a falcon cliff not far downriver from George's now-crumbling cabin. This new man was loud, exploitive, cutting down excessive trees with a noisy power saw, and keeping a pack of howling sled dogs tied on short chains to their small square sheds at the base of the cliff. He operated a large creaking fishwheel right in front of the rocks where the falcons bred and where the river runs deep with salmon. He fervently tried to bring nature to his level with his rifle. No falcons returned to nest on the cliffs above his cabin. He too is gone now, and one can only guess how long it will be for the scars to heal. As I passed through his camp in later years, the mess he created along the serenity and solitude of the otherwise mighty river made my eyes moisten.

In reality, not too many people travel the Yukon River—but then not many want to. In fact, I suspect most people would not like true wilderness, given the chance to experience it. For although it stimulates a sense of wonder and is sometimes beautiful, it can also be threatening.

In 1971 my graduate student Steve Sherrod accompanied me to assess the potential impact on birds of a proposed dam to be built on the Yukon River at a place called the Woodchopper Volcanics. From that point, water could be backed up perhaps 120 miles, nearly to Dawson City in the Yukon Territory—our jump-off point on the river. During five days of travel downriver we saw no one. Finally, we came to a cabin on the right bank of the river (left and right are always determined by facing downriver), just down from the mouth of the Charlie River well into Alaska beyond the Yukon border. A broken-down raft-like thing made of oil drums supporting wood planks was tied to a willow at the riverbank, and smoke was coming from the chimney of the nearby cabin. I remembered the place as being deserted. I knew no one lived permanently along the river below Eagle until arriving at Circle, and so we investigated. In the cabin we found a confused young man, perhaps thirty-two to thirty-five years old. He was from New York and had come to Whitehorse and then to Dawson to "get away from it all." He had played in a band in New York City and had tried his hand at poetry. Nothing seemed to have turned out right for him. He built the crude raft in Dawson where the Yukon River flows past, and set off with some food and a sleeping bag. He had sustained an accident and ended up in the river but luckily (and miraculously) made it to that cabin where he had been living for a few days when we encountered him. He was almost out of food and without maps, with no idea even where he was. We offered to help. He said no thanks, that it was his "adventure" and he must take it alone. I alerted him to the fact that when he went on downriver, he had to stay on the left bank after passing the last cliff on the right or else he would miss Circle and end up somewhere in the Yukon Flats and lost forever. He tried to act brave as we departed, leaving him some canned food. But, you could tell that he was at the end of his rope. I have often wondered about him and whether he survived or not. Did he die there on the river as Steve thought he might have? We never learned nor did anyone I knew who traveled that part of the country hear of him after that. He was simply a passing moment.

One needs to love life, be high on it to avoid such tragedy. One needs to have a well-cultivated internal landscape. Today, four to five boats would have passed that cabin (which no longer existed by the time my wife and I went down the Yukon in the 1990s) each week, perhaps one a month when Steve and I were there. The days of "getting away" on the Yukon are gone, never to return.

THE ALEUTIAN ISLANDS

Living in the Aleutian Islands is like having the Arctic fever celebrated by Farley Mowat. There is no known cure for the fever and no one can find the "bug" that causes it, but it is real. The fever drives one over and over again to those Aleutian tundra landscapes, if only for brief moments. I will probably never travel the Aleutian trail again. Once, as I stood below a cliff housing a cormorant colony, birds flying in and out of the cliff and the incoming surf pounding at my very feet, I began to cry. Earthly facts were changed into transcendental spiritual expressions. I felt intensely alive. I was on Agattu Island helping with the Aleutian Canada goose transplant. The goose had been nearly extirpated from the Aleutian chain when the arctic fox, an efficient predator, was unwisely introduced on the islands some fifty years ago to provide fur trade for the native Aleuts. It was 1972 and I was one of the few people to visit that island in the past several decades. I was about to leave and knew that I would never return to this lovely, lonely, inspiring place of solitude.

The smell of salt-drenched air differs in those islands from its smell on tropical beaches, perhaps because the air and water are so cold. I really don't know, but to my mind, no place else on earth smells like it—home to the largest and darkest of all the peregrine falcons, rosy finches, and song sparrows; nucleus of the sea otter's range; former home of a giant, but now extinct, sea cow named for the first European to encounter it, George Wilhelm Steller; a chain of spectacular volcanoes on which the sea breaks its back. It is a unique place and, seen from a distance rising from the fog and mist-generated seas, the islands are more "illusions" than Aleutians, as noted by Cory Ford. They are magic.

We stayed in a cabin built by Aleut fox-fur hunters in the 1930s. It took some work to fix up. When the wind-driven rains were pounding against the walls and on the roof so hard we could not work, we would stoke the fire and listen to cassette tapes. Luckily the batteries lasted for the month I was there. One of the few tapes we had was the *Best of John Denver* and each time I hear it my mind travels again to that distant spot, especially when he sings that song about growing old being a turn-on.

Adjacent to Agattu, but separated by ninety miles and a very rough ride as waters rush back and forth from the North Pacific Ocean and the Bering Sea (one on the north and one on the south of the Aleutian arc), is Buldir Island—a tiny speck of lushly vegetated, jutting volcanic rock twelve miles in circumference. The island had not been visited since World War II when there was an outpost of a couple of soldiers, so we were truly on virgin ground there as we trod its hillsides looking for geese.

After that first visit I was privileged to take, Buldir became the stomping grounds for many goose biologists. I was among the first, however, and saw the deserted World War II water-cooled .30-caliber machine gun, all rusted and forgotten. An abandoned P-38 fighter aircraft that couldn't make it back to its base, probably Amchitka, belly-landed in the tundra—a lucky pilot, for there is not much flat space available on that island sitting in a featureless ocean—unclaimed by all, other than the weather, and forgotten to the world by all but a few. I walked on beaches few have trod since the Aleuts were slaughtered by the Russian sea-otter hunters of the late 1700s and early 1800s. My footprints in the black lava sands remained only until the tide rolled in. I often wonder how many footprints have been erased from those sands. The number is surely not great and probably episodic, but I feel that I have been on a piece of earth kept special. It was a spiritual experience. Holy ground.

ARGENTINA

My graduate student Sandy Boyce and I were in Argentina in 1984, collecting blood samples of birds for his dissertation. We had rented a car (a tiny Italian tin can of a thing) and were heading north to the Bolivian border some 800 miles away. One of the last Argentine villages we visited before touching the Bolivian border was Cuesta de Azul Pampa, reached only by a narrow rut-riddled dirt road winding up to 12,000 feet. It is among some of the most remote roads in southern South America. The bordering hillsides looked ancient, as though they had seen a lot of history. People doubtlessly walked over most of the slopes once, but now they are not visited because of their uninviting character. No footprints remained there. The rain began before we left Azul Pampa, and we slowly wound and clawed our way back down the muddy, puddled road. Rain had caused streams crossing the road to rise two to three feet. The force of the water on the steep gradient of streams forced boulders the size of basketballs to bounce along the streambed like so many Ping-Pong balls. We reached the last water crossing before entering the small valley below where we could get lodging for the night. The stream carried water that reached nearly to the bottom of the car doors. Besides the rumbling debris, the streambed was strewn with jutting boulders and rocks fixed in place. We had little way of navigating these fixed objects because of the water depth. If we didn't cross quickly, we would not get across for a couple of days, and there was no place to go to back up the road, which was now impassable.

"What should we do, Boyce?" I asked.

"Let's go for it before it's too late," he said.

The car washed and bounced down the stream several yards; we were about to go off the flat roadbed and on downstream just as we reached the other side. Gunning it, we made it the last few feet. Rain-battered, muddy, and cold, we reached a roadside hostel in San Salvador de Jujuy. That night in bed, covered by a worn, tattered but comfortable and warm quilt, I listened to the ethnically Incan music coming from the lobby below. Strains of "El Condor Pasa," "Canto al Altiplano," and "Mi Pueblo Azul" filtered up to the bedroom. My thoughts were not on the project nor the work still to be done, my thoughts were on landscape and family. I suspect when one is at peace within oneself, the thoughts that come are truly the most important, those thoughts to be trusted. I fell asleep to the gentle patter of falling raindrops as they softly danced on the tin roof, dreaming good peaceful dreams of landscapes I have loved.

NEW YORK CITY

I had been asked to be part of the 1991 spring lecture series at the American Museum of Natural History in New York. Dr. John Aronian, a medical doctor at Cornell Medical School and Hospital in New York, learned I was coming. He called to tell me he was a falcon aficionado, and would I spend some time with him the day following my lecture, looking at peregrine falcons nesting in New York City. "Sure," I said. That morning as I sat in my New York hotel room, there was a news story about a Latin live-in boyfriend killing a three-year-old girl with a fireplace poker while the girl's pregnant mother sat and watched. The mother had three other children from unknown fathers. At the hospital, which turned out to be the same hospital where my friend practiced, the dead girl was found to have cigarette burns on her body, healed scars from a life of beatings, and other signs creating a history of neglect.

Later that day, as Dr. Aronian and I ascended in the hospital elevator to the seventeenth floor, where we had to go to look down on the nest box with the peregrine in attendance, a pale and sickly fellow traveling with us kept trying to take imaginary "things" off his face. Arriving at our destination, we had to pass through the AIDS ward to get to the roof. Just as we entered the ward, where the fellow from the elevator was going as well, John was stopped by a colleague. John asked me to sit down for a few minutes while he talked to him. So there we were, right in the middle of the AIDS-ward waiting room. A dying Latin woman with her dying AIDS-infected child cuddled in her arms gazed with hollowness at me. A young Afro-American, perhaps seventeen years old, could hardly hold his head upright. Ten to fifteen people were surrounding me. It occurred to me that

I was among the walking dead. John and his friend proceeded to talk about the little girl I had mentioned earlier. She had been admitted to the hospital and John's friend was the attending physician. My emotions were ready to burst from my skin as I listened to them talk.

In the end we saw the falcon and then I left to go to the airport. At the airport I picked up a newspaper from a seat in the waiting lounge and read about another child, this time a four year-old Latin boy, living not far from the dead girl. According to the report, his father wanted him to throw a ball, and when the child tired of the game, the father beat him to death by smashing him against the wall.

What is happening to the world around us? Can this be the kind of life we were born to live? Are we becoming people who have misplaced the stewardship of both our external and internal landscapes? I fear many individuals' internal landscapes have not made the connection with the external landscape. The great philosopher Immanuel Kant understands this critical correspondence between the inner and outer worlds: ". . . Two things fill the mind with ever new and increasing admiration and awe, the more often and steadily we reflect upon them; the starry heavens above me and the moral law within me. . . . I see them before me and connect them immediately with the consciousness of my existence."

As I lay in bed that night, cuddled to the warmth of my wife's body and told her about what I had witnessed, I couldn't stop crying. I cried secretly all night long and part of the next day. My emotions were rent and riven apart. I pray that our dwelling places may be habitations of respect and stewardship. I pray that we may learn to give lasting embraces to the people and landscapes we love—to make them part of a landscape stewardship; to love for the sake of simply loving. Love, like science, is at its best when driven by passion and emotion. We are truly at our best when we create less dissonance between what we do for a living, how we think, and what we feel as creatures.

AUSTRALIA

I had wanted to get some peregrine falcons from my study area in Australia for a study program at Brigham Young University. In Australia peregrines nest not only on cliffs but also in the abandoned tree stick nests of other birds and in immense hollows in river red gum trees. One concept to study was the choice a falcon makes in picking a nest site. If born in a tree nest, and therefore presumably imprinted on trees, would the falcon return to breed in a tree nest when of breeding age or chose another substratum with equal ease? To get a young falcon from a usurped wedge-trailed eagle's nest, we went to the Mallee of northern Victoria. At one time, the Mallee was composed of short scrubby vegetation, much like the Great Basin landscape at the time of the first encounter by Europeans. Today it is mostly grape vines, or wine country, and citrus orchards. The charm of native vegetation is gone.

The flat land of the Mallee has lost its windbreaks. Winds and sand bulldoze their way through the countryside on frequent occasions. Our specific trip was during one of those times. The sky was darkened at midday. Constant winds were thirty to forty miles per hour. Sand was so thick in the air one could cut it. Temperature was 108 degrees Fahrenheit. As we tried to leave the Mallee in the station wagon with our prize captive baby falcons, we had to keep the windows rolled against the sand. The temperature inside the car was easily above 110 degrees. We had to hold handkerchiefs over our noses in order to breathe. Sweat streamed down our faces. My lungs ached to be full of fresh air. The wind was from the north and we were heading south at a snail's pace. Every five to ten minutes the car would heat up because we were not going fast enough to get air through the radiator (the wind was at our tail), and the air coming through the radiator was over 108 degrees. So, we had to turn the car around and face it into the wind at regular intervals. What should have been an eight-hour trip turned into twelve and then fourteen hours. I had recently read stories of numerous deaths in Australia from such sandstorms with intense heat. I did not think I would survive, and only Bill Bren, our Australian colleague who had been in such a sandstorm before, knew that we would probably be all right.

I truly tasted fear.

HOME

After all the years of trying to leave a mark on this planet through my profession as a biologist, I have now come to the conclusion that the only lasting mark I will make is to influence my children to be good and honorable people and to influence students to be good and honorable stewards, that the real quest is in trying to understand stewardship of all landscapes, internal and external. The landscapes I have come to know have been manifested directly in a variety of experiences, and it is those experiences that define perspective. Particularly important to me are the peak experiences that have punctuated the landscapes here and there, ones that are the "trails" I have traveled. Most frequently, my spiritual feelings usually take place as I am relating with or being absorbed into both the inside and the outside landscape. I think of the peregrine falcons—think of my family. All life's desire is not only to survive but also to flourish in the grace and beauty of this planet.

Clayton M. White is professor of zoology at Brigham Young University, and has studied endangered species worldwide for most of his professional career.

"Ye have seen what I did . . . how I bare you on eagles' wings, and brought you unto myself." (Exodus 19:4.)

MESSAGES FROM THE AERIE

Dorothy Allred Solomon

From the Perch

HEN I WAS A CHILD OUR GROUP OF FUNDAMENTALIST MORMONS sometimes went into the mountains to worship. This yearly pilgrimage to the wilderness salvaged our dignity and gave us a little freedom. On any other Sunday our ragtag little clan would be whispering hymns and taking the sacrament in my uncle's garage for fear of being caught and arrested. In the mountains it didn't matter so much that I was illegitimate, born into a marriage sanctioned only by spiritual ceremony. As vestiges of an era most Utahns would just as soon forget, "plygie kids" like me, born decades after the LDS Manifesto outlawed the Principle of Plural Marriage, were all the proof the authorities needed to break up our family. When another polygamous roundup threatened, my father gave off the bitter scent of violated freedom, the mothers kept the drapes drawn, and we children cringed whenever someone noticed us. And questions gnawed at me: Could our throwback lives be justified? If I could not be at home here in Zion, was there any place for me on earth—any way at all to be legitimate? In a land that guaranteed religious freedom yet imprisoned my parents for what they believed, where was my home?

The institutions of the Salt Lake Valley were not hospitable, so we kept to ourselves. We grew our own food. Women gave birth in their sister-wives' bedrooms. The sick convalesced and died in their own beds. The mothers in my family sewed our clothing and handed garments and toys down the long line of children. We lived a life of repair and invention in which nothing was wasted. Within the city, we could be caught wearing our shame. But above the city, where mountains stretched into more mountains, worn shoes and patched clothing had no bearing on the order of life.

Each time we met in the mountains I discovered something vital, something you could call the spirit of God. The warm white energy vibrating from tree to rock to flower and from one person to another didn't wend through our meetings in the Salt Lake Valley. Mountain meetings initiated my first moments of true worship: a reverence for life and a personal experience of divine that helped me grasp the roots of our religion.

We had to wait until the snow melted and the first wildflowers were out. One summer Sunday just after my fifth birthday, we caravanned up the narrow canyon. Here and there, bluebells nodded and alpine daisies smiled to let us know that somewhere on this earth we were welcome. In the voluminous backseat of my father's Hudson, we were tossed by switchbacks until someone got carsick. But I held white-knuckled to the door handle, my eyes on the steep ravine. At last we arrived at the high mountain valley, spilled from the car and stretched in the open. As more people arrived, we shouted our praises in song:

> *O ye mountains high,*
> *where the clear blue sky*
> *Arches over the vale of the free,*
> *Where the pure breezes blow*
> *and the clear streamlets flow,*
> *How I've longed to your bosom to flee!*
>
> *O Zion! dear Zion!*
> *land of the free,*
> *Now my own mountain home,*
> *unto thee I have come;*
> *All my fond hopes are centered in thee.*

—"O Ye Mountains High," *Hymns of The Church of Jesus Christ of Latter-day Saints,* pp. 34–35; text by Charles W. Penrose, music by H. S. Thompson.

Something happened in the mountains. Something I call soul or spirit triumphed over the dialectics of the ego—though of course I did not think this way back then. What I observed as a child was that the mountains were bigger than our biggest voices. The sheer cliffs echoed our choir to the sky, and the call went on forever. Here, where the heart of the sunflower opened the small truths of the sun, where constellations of wildflowers mirrored the milky paths of stars, my father's belief in the Celestial Order of Marriage and Eternal Family seemed possible.

This larger view brought my own way of seeing into sharper focus, yet I can't remember a single Sunday school lesson from those wilderness meetings. My favorite Bible stories—Esther Saving Her People, Daniel in the Lion's Den, Mary and the Angel—were learned in the city. I remember the shadows on my father's face as he stood beneath the trees, speaking to our congregation. But what he said was overwhelmed by birds whistling, quakies rattling, the brook burbling. I breathed deep, glad to banish some of the Bible heroes' power over my body and senses. As always, the mountains broke the shell of concept to reveal secrets of flesh and bone and blood. This gave me great relief, for even when I was young I knew some disappointing things about myself: that I could never be as good as Mary; that unlike young Joseph Smith, I would not receive personal visits from the Father and the Son; that if I should meet one of Daniel's lions in the mountains, it would likely tear me to pieces.

The overhanging cliffs cut the powerful brethren of the Priesthood Council down to size and gave my older brothers and sisters permission to throw off their starched shirts and petticoats to play. Even my father, patriarch of the family and spiritual leader of our religious group, ran wild on mountain Sundays. When meeting was over, he played horseshoes with such fervor that he forgot himself and swore. Then he got caught snitching the first slice of a double-layer cake from Aunt LaVere's tent. Aunt LaVere didn't talk to him until after our picnic dinner, although she was his sixth wife and in no position to be uppity. That day when the sandwiches were eaten and the corncobs gnawed clean, when the last of the cake crumbs had been lifted on the tip of a finger and the afternoon sunlight touched the river, my brother Jake took me to the base of a rocky trail. Jake pointed, and I sat on my heels and looked straight up. Through a ragged hole in the branches, I saw a flesh-colored promontory jutting out from the cliff, as though God were in the mountain, and His finger pointed a reminder . . . of what? That He was there?

"Let's go up there," I breathed to Jake.

He smiled. "You want to see the Eagle's Perch?"

Jake was happier than the rest of us, the only one of my brothers who didn't seem trapped in his own mind. Once when Jake was little, he tried to fly from the top of the silo, and the other boys called him an idiot. But Jake said he'd dreamed of flying, so he knew it could be done—he just needed practice. Jake didn't work for grades as though his whole life depended on it like most of my father's children. Everyone but my mother worried about his "lackadaisical attitude." My father lectured that we needed to prove we were solid citizens, and the other mothers said if Jake didn't keep up his grades, the district would send someone out and then the whole family would be in hot water. But Jake's eyes were like a lake that lets you see to the bottom. He already seemed to know about himself, and not to mind what he knew.

That day the other boys were challenging each other to dart out of the path of boulders set in motion from above. I think now that the game was a fitting activity for fundamentalist Mormon boys who must evade the big thumping realities that roll down from the mountain of authority.

Jake and I stood watching. "Go on. Do it, Jake," I urged. He shook his head. "Let's go on up the mountain."

We made our way through loose shale until we came to a clearing. I remembered a story my mother had told me, of a family in our group who left their toddler in a clearing, safe from the creek. The mother heard a rushing noise and turned, but the child was gone. No footprints, no sign of the kidnapper. The sheriff surmised that a large bird of prey, probably an eagle, had taken the child. I had seen an eagle grasp a ground squirrel in its talons and tear it apart with pitiless precision, piling bones and skin in a tidy heap as it consumed every shred of flesh. This made me scramble after Jake; I found him walking on the promontory of stone as if it was the route he took to school every day.

"Jake!"

"Come on, sis." He reached a hand toward me. His eyes were the same color as the afternoon sky. I shook my head. "Don't you trust me?" he asked.

A whirring filled my ears. I took a step toward his outstretched hand. At the second step, my foot slipped and I threw myself backward. Jake turned with the slow grace of an acrobat and came to help me up. He brushed the gravel off my butt, then stood back.

"Go on. It's easier to do it by yourself."

"No."

"Don't you believe me?" he asked.

I nodded, then shook my head.

"Then believe in yourself," he said. "Or believe in that." He gestured out at a mountain valley that sprawled like a giant palm with long curving fingers of canyon. I didn't know what he meant, but I stepped out the way you walk a curb or a fence-line, heel to toe, heel to toe. I reached the knuckle of the great pointing finger where I stood until my heart stilled. The stone wasn't as slender as it had seemed. I held my balance, then flapped my arms once. For the briefest instant I wanted to jump. I got down on my knees and crawled back to Jake. He sat down and put his arm around me, and we looked out at the valley for awhile.

We started down without talking. At the head of the trail, my brothers and sisters hooted as another boulder rumbled down. None of them but Jake knew that I had been on the Eagle's Perch. I made my way through the baskets and blankets to where my mother sat crocheting and talking with the other women, and put my head in her lap.

Perhaps I dozed, I don't know. But the next thing I knew, my mother was pushing my head off her lap, her voice shrill. She was running toward the rocky trail, toward the shriek of children. "Jake! Jake's been hurt."

I ran after her to where he lay at the base of the trail, a pool of vomit beside his mouth, a rivulet of blood from his temple staining the collar of his white shirt. My mother knelt in the dirt beside him, and then my father was lifting her up, bending over Jake.

He was our doctor and our spiritual leader, so we believed he always knew what to do. He gathered Jake in his arms and carried him to the green Hudson. My mother sat me on her lap while my father stretched Jake out in the backseat. "He's still unconscious," my father said. Just then Jake threw up again but didn't open his eyes. I'd never seen anyone throw up in his sleep; it scared me.

My father took the S-curves so fast, I got carsick myself, what with the smell of Jake and the smell of fear. I added my part to that sour ride, and my mother patted the front of my dress with her lace handkerchief. We arrived home as the sun was slipping toward the Oquirrh Mountains. I had never seen the white house so silent, so hollow. It was like glimpsing a dark tunnel that I wasn't supposed to know about, but there it was, whirling into tomorrow.

My father lugged Jake into the quiet house and put him on the living-room sofa. I sat on the floor beside him. I watched his eyeballs roll under blue-veined lids. I watched his lips lose their color. I watched the sun slip low. If he doesn't wake before the sun sets, I thought, he will never wake up again. I saw the tunnel again, a dark spiral in the corner of my eye.

Jake stirred at a sharp knock on the door. I heard Uncle Orvis and Uncle Lawrence in the hallway. I could hear them telling my father that Short Creek had been raided—all the men put in prison and the women under guard in some trailer camp, their babies and children parceled out to foster homes. What if they came after us, what should we do? And then my father's voice, strangled and scared, saying, "I don't know what to do."

Jake moaned. My father stood with his hands pressed against his temples. His worst fear had materialized: we would be cast out of our home. I knew that Jake had heard everything, but he wanted to slip into a dream and fly away. I didn't want to lose him. "Open your eyes," I whispered. "You have to stay here with me." I poked him until his eyelids fluttered open; I saw the endless blue, the ground too far for anyone to reach. Jake was barely there, a thin cloud you can see through. I had the sense of being lifted, of looking down at my father, my mother, our home from a great height. Once aloft, I wondered if I would ever find a place to land.

FROM THE NEST

Once we moved from the farm, we had no garden, no animals, no stream. Our refuge from the raid was a small Nevada town where we relied on the grocery store for the means to live. For the first time in my life, I understood what it meant to depend on money—in many cases, money others had gambled away. Jake and Saul worked after school at a service station. Danny and I sold newspapers in the saloons. My aunt waitressed in the casino known for its glass-encased polar bear. My mother played her beloved piano for weddings and funerals, for lounge acts and church services.

Nevada introduced me to spiritual as well as environmental drought. No mountains, no streams, no playmates or pets. No father to treat sicknesses of body, mind, or spirit. My mother succumbed to one of her depressions. My brothers withdrew from the family faith. At night, I lay awake and wondered what would become of us. Who was I without my sprawling family? Back home on the farm, there were rules: don't stand under the white circle in the barn; walk the furrows, not the mounds; put the tools in the tack shed, out of the rain. Back home, there were certain ways to behave: don't swear, don't drink coffee, don't hit people. In the Nevada town of gaming tables and red-light houses, where my aunt served coffee and my mother played in bars, where the children of blackjack dealers and bouncers cheated off my spelling papers and tripped me as I jumped rope, what were the rules?

Without rules, I was insubstantial as dandelion down, liable to be carried away by any breeze. During the long nights, I took myself to the Eagle's Perch and from there I could see our compound, frozen outside time like the kingdom of Sleeping Beauty. I held every family member on a slip of land no bigger than my body. And I knew that somewhere in the space between past and future, a real home waited.

The Nevada dust made me thirst for greenery. I tried to grow flowers in the bleached clay of the front yard, chipping at the hard crust, then sifting the soil and watering carefully with a Mason jar, but nothing sprouted. Saul watched me and worried; as with many oldest sons, he took on the duties of his absent father. Sometimes Saul invited me to go along when he hunted deer in the Humboldt Mountains or fished Wild Horse Reservoir. One day, we passed a row of power poles, and Saul screeched to a stop. He pointed out a huge nest crumbling on the crossbar and a mound of feathers at the base. He grabbed his fly-tying box and we ducked through the barbed wire.

Saul picked up the body of a bald eagle by its talons. A terrible stench made me back away. Maggots swarmed from the cavity and across the dark feathers. Saul turned his head and retched, but he didn't let go of the eagle's claws. The great wings spread stiffly, five feet across. Saul ducked his mouth and nose into the collar of his shirt and began to pluck tail feathers with an almost reverent touch. Each time he pulled a feather away, maggots squirmed and the stench grew strong. Saul turned and vomited, but he didn't quit. "It'd be a shame to waste these," he said.

He took six or seven feathers in all—a couple from the tail, one from each wing, and some smaller feathers from the body, setting each carefully aside. With a branch of sage he dug a hole and dropped the carcass in, then spread sand over it with the toe of his boot. He cleaned his hands with sand. He placed the feathers carefully in his fly-tying kit. "These will make great caddis flies. No telling when we'll see another bald eagle."

My fourth-grade teacher had taught us that it was illegal to kill eagles, so I asked Saul, with some anger in my voice, "Who killed it?"

Saul didn't think the bird had been shot. He guessed that maybe it had been electrocuted when its great wings touched the opposite ends of the power poles. "In a way, I guess we all killed it. In America, we think we should be able to throw a switch and have all the power we want." He looked up at the nest. "I wonder if there are eaglets in there." No sound came from the nest. Saul sighed. "Let's go."

After the dead eagle, I had a hard time getting myself back to the Perch.

The delicious terrifying freedom of standing on that finger of stone might as well be something I saw in a movie. As I learned the rules of the world outside—how to get better grades, how to win at hopscotch, how to get tips in the casino—I lost my desire to return.

But our six-year stint in Nevada ended and everyone but Jake (who stayed to marry a rancher's daughter) returned to "the old homestead" in Utah. The houses smelled of ruin and decay; we found broken windows, hanging screen doors, flooded basements. The animals were dead or stolen and the garden sprouted star-thistle and pigweed. The swimming pool that had doubled as our baptismal font was green and slimy with moss.

Looking back, I see that my soul cowered in a dark corner, lonely and unattended. I did not feel at home in Zion; I felt claustrophobic, as though everyone was watching me and judging. One Sunday when Saul came home driving a Ford hardtop convertible—used, but new to him—I longed for escape and asked him to take me up the canyon where we had once held our religious meetings.

The engine of his new car caught fire before we could reach the summit. Saul put out the fire with his jacket. An acrid smell told us that the engine was ruined and the wiring burnt. Saul kicked the fender and slammed the hood. When I worked up the courage to ask what was wrong, his rage gave way to tears and he confessed that he didn't know how he'd be able to stay in college. Our father had refused to help him, discouraging any learning that included "the Devil's doctrine of evolution." He expected Saul to pay board and help with family expenses as well as pay tuition, but he wouldn't let Saul file for a "head of household" exemption from military duty. Saul explained that if he had to leave school, he could be drafted and sent to Vietnam.

I saw my father's face in my mind's eye, his white shirt and clean fingernails. What good was his belief about God's law being more important than the laws of men? If Saul was drafted, he'd have to kill or be killed, whether the Ten Commandments or the Theory of Evolution was right. Doctrines would not repair the car or pay Saul's tuition. In sixth months he could be gone.

The tow truck arrived after sunset, when the mountains rang hollow with cold. Despite his grease-encrusted uniform, the driver brushed straw from the seat and made us welcome in his rusty truck. "So, what you gonna do?" the tow-truck driver asked Saul.

Saul shook his head. "It was a used car. The dealer won't fix it or take it back."

The driver smiled with sad eyes and pulled a pack of cigarettes from his shirt pocket. He offered one to Saul. Saul stared vacantly, then shook his head. I thought of Jake, who had started smoking when he fell in love with the rancher's daughter. Jake, who rode horses and cut sheep's testicles with his teeth. Jake, who had taught me about trusting. The tow-truck driver reminded me a little of Jake. He had corrupted the temple of his body with tobacco, but he wouldn't judge me the way our righteous Mormon neighbors did. His brawny shoulder pressed against me and opened on a larger world of drunks and whores I'd known in Nevada, the retarded girl who lived across the street, the neighbors from Arkansas who called themselves white trash—a world that included everybody. I pulled the smoky air deep into my lungs, inhaling the safety of kind hearts and modest ambitions. A nest, I decided, is any place you feel safe—even if it isn't home.

On Broken Wings

Saul did not have to go to war. The scar tissue surrounding a gunshot wound from his rabbit-hunting days got him a 4-F classification and he finished college. Despite this reprieve the war touched down like a tornado, entering through me perhaps because I was at war with myself. Jess was one of the casualties, along with my innocence and self-respect, a friendly young man set apart by his habit of protecting underdogs. I dodged his proposal until he joined the Marine Corps, then married him. Too little, too late. He shipped out to Vietnam soon after our wedding, and came home with combat coursing like a disease in his veins.

In 1973, experts predicted we would be out of Southeast Asia before the year was through. But I knew that the war raged on in my young husband, and in his foxhole-buddy, Stan, who had come to stay with us. They looked remarkably alike, these two, as though some force of nature had shaped all Marines at birth, made them all broad-shouldered and Roman-nosed, waiting for the years to overtake their ancient hearts and haunted eyes.

I couldn't get over the feeling that we had left part of ourselves in Vietnam, along with the POW's and MIA's. I sensed a change in our national character, a transmogrification from hero to bully. We had failed to combine the American dream with the moral imperatives of democracy. I longed to reach through the silk curtain and reclaim our innocence or acknowledge some responsibility—mine, Jess's, everybody's.

"We need to go back before it's all over," I said. "Or we'll pay into the next century."

The men laughed. "Go back?" my husband said. "What for? There's nothing left."

"Nothing but flies and bald mountains," Stan said.

"We bombed them into the dark ages," Jess said.

"That's about where they were when we started," Stan said. They shook their heads with that look of regret that seemed to be one of their features, like the drooping moustache or the long hair.

"Whatever happened to the Eagle, Globe, and Anchor?" Stan blew smoke at my rosebush.

It was awhile before my husband responded. "Even an eagle can't carry the weight of a lie."

"What lie?" I asked.

Stan smiled grimly. "A lot of people died so that your neighbor over there could have two cars and an RV."

"It was a war. People die in wars." I said.

Stan sucked his teeth. He lit one cigarette with the butt of another, pulling the smoke deep into his lungs and holding it there. His eyes burned as he looked at me, sending the message of the smoke, closing out all breath, all other possibilities.

"Tell me about it," Stan said, the smoke drifting on his words. "Go on. Since you know so much. Tell me about the war."

Jess narrowed his eyes. "Cool it."

Stan shrugged. "She doesn't know the first thing."

As if to educate me, Jess explained, "They sprayed this stuff called Agent Orange all over the jungles, the rice fields. In some places it'll be twenty-five years before they can grow anything."

Stan gave me a hollow-eyed grin. "See—the war isn't over."

Panic hit me, then guilt, two hard punches in the stomach. "How will the people survive?"

The men shook their heads in unison. "The worst of it is, we had no reason to be there. They didn't want us there. We had nothing to stand on," my husband said.

Stan nodded. "No place to stand."

I busied myself sweeping the porch so they wouldn't see the blood rising in my face, the tears springing into my eyes. In our strict Mormon neighborhood, I was again the anomaly, a dissident: I stood against the church's support of the war, against its racist practices, against its antifeminism. Like the veterans of Vietnam, I had no place to stand. I had left the fundamentalist group. Although I sent my child to the official church, I didn't go with her. Still, the habits of my childhood urged me to gather with others in the name of God. Maybe I could forgive the persecutions, erase the scars of paranoia. I asked my husband, "If I went to church, would you come with me?"

I must have known, even before I asked, his loathing of organizations. "Do you know what I've done for institutions—what I was ordered to do in the name of obedience?" His eyes had gone cold, hard.

I thought of the rumors that our soldiers had killed women and children in Vietnam. "What were you ordered to do?" I asked softly.

He stared at his feet, his eyes flickering wildly. He fumbled in his pants pocket for a wooden match. "When I realized the cost of blind obedience, I decided to keep as many people alive as I could. I'd get promoted for saving somebody's ass, and they'd give me a mission I had to refuse, so they'd bust me. Promoted and busted, eleven times over. Why would I want to declare my loyalty to another institution? Their walls are reinforced with bodies."

Stan nodded agreement. The two of them sat on the front porch smoking "squares"—as they called cigarettes made with tobacco instead of marijuana—while I walked my daughter down the street to the ward house and waved good-bye at the double doors. Church members coming up the walk looked away so that I would not see the pity or judgment in their eyes. Their painted porches and clean windows promised trust, communion, belonging. I wanted to believe it but did not. The perfect rows of marigolds and pansies could not silence my history.

The two men were still lazing on the front porch when I returned. Stan, who had grown up in the hills around San Bernardino, was amazed at our craggy mountains and wanted to spend the Fourth of July "up there."

"Independence Day," he said. "I'm ready to declare my independence." My husband and I looked at each other. Like so many Vietnam veterans, he was utterly alone. We worried that he might climb a cliff and jump, just to end the loneliness. But the next day we packed hot dogs and potato salad and sent our daughter to see fireworks with her grandmother. We traveled up the canyon and stopped at a campsite near the Eagle's Perch. I told Stan that my family had often camped here when I was a child. Stan said he lived by the beach as a child. "We had a picket fence," he said. "The waves took it. The waves took everything." Then he reached into his backpack and passed around little brown buttons shaved from a cactus in the Mojave Desert.

My husband lit a campfire, but as the peyote moved through my blood, my senses heightened and provoked a strong need to move. On the trail, I was enthralled by one thing, then another. Who knows how long I sniffed the primrose before I recognized the sweet and piercing fragrance of love? A doe stepped onto the trail, bent her head and nibbled. I took a sharp breath. She heard me and bounded away.

I returned to the fire. Flares lit my brain. I closed my eyes and saw huts burning, children with missing limbs, animals exploding above the trees. I imagined that my own house was on fire, and I ran up the hillside, hoping to find a vantage point. The Eagle's Perch, I thought, from there I can see home. The wind came up and the higher I climbed, the harder it blew. A black cloud blotted the last red lip of sun. Darkness blended rock and bush and shale until I stopped, cowed by the steep grade and gathering night.

I hunkered on a ledge, trembling. In the valley below, fireworks and lightning shot across the sky. Heat emanated from the clouds, and then I saw an eagle, wings locked, flying into the storm. The eagle disappeared, then reappeared above the black cloud. A few heavy drops splashed on my bare arms. Far below sat my husband, transmogrified by flame and distance. I felt my way down in the pitch dark, a tactilian creature grasping rocks and shrubs until I reached the fire. My husband motioned me to sit beside him. Stan was out in the night trying to find something he'd lost. I felt sad for all of us, scarred by the war and our own foolishness. Then I decided to trust; "All is well," I sang softly. "All is well."

That leap of faith gave me relief from exile. In choosing to love Jess just as he was in that moment, regardless of his guilt and pain and dark knowledge, I bridged my own gaps. I leaned against him. No matter how tattered his soul, I was committed to him. He lifted my chin and looked into my eyes with a kindness that made me think of Jesus. Something warm and sweet passed between us, and I felt my heart open, join with his, lock in place. With a pair of wings between us, we were strong enough to transcend the wreckage and ride into the storm.

FROM THE EAGLE'S FEATHER

My brother Saul was coming to visit from California, and I was a clash of joy and dread. How would I ever confess to him that I was expecting another child? He'd be hurt and angry that I'd gone against the creed he'd taught me, and I didn't know how to explain why.

Saul had been questioning what our parents had taught for as long as I could remember. To him, facts were truth, and truth was a machete to tame the wilderness of the mind. Saul regarded religions as massive machines invented by men for the purpose of manipulating others. He had toyed with atheism and agnosticism; now he whacked away at the thicket of beliefs that spawned us. He vented his frustration in painting and sculpture. Although he had been loving and supportive throughout my life, the rage in his work frightened me. Now that Saul was regional president of ZPG—Zero Population Growth—a new standard cast its shadow over me. As Saul had once prepared for his debates with my father, I now prepared myself to deal with Saul. It seemed I had always been trapped in their dialogues of spirit versus science. I tried to keep a middle ground where I could love both of them, but most of the time I felt pulled in half as they spurred their horses toward opposite poles.

I dimly understood that the conflict I felt with Saul echoed my own contradictions. I weighed these as I went through the house, dusting, vacuuming, shining mirrors. Saul prized order, and I wanted my house to be as clean as my mother's had always been. Still, I ached with a need to be justified.

"Mama may have . . ." I sang under my breath as I polished the refrigerator, "Papa may have . . ." I burnished the striker plates of the stove. "God bless the child who's got her own. Who's got . . ." My reflection stared back at me, confused and tentative.

Although I owed my life to my parents' conviction, I had little certainty when it came to matters of faith. When I was sixteen years old, my bishop in the official church had asked me to teach Sunday School to the seven-year-olds preparing for baptism. For an entire week I agonized over the calling, trying to find anything I could call truth. The next Sunday, I set the lesson books on the bishop's desk and said, "I'm sorry. I can't do this." Then I met a boyfriend at the park.

I stopped reading scripture and going to church. Later I enrolled in the university and my skepticism grew. When I began teaching school, my students wrote about mothers who slept in the next room with strangers, dads who disappeared, uncles who sold drugs and used cars. My embattled husband took off for days at a time. Such dense realities weighed on me and charged my dreams with dread. The old issue of my illegitimacy surfaced, more monstrous than ever. Now Saul's visit brought my doubts to critical mass and crystallized my fears.

We sat before the bay window filled with plants. Sun glinted off our coffee cups and pie plates. Saul was mourning the fate of his favorite fly-fishing stream when my three-year-old burst through the front door, cheeks flushed with sunshine, cornflower eyes dancing. "Uncle Saul!" She skipped over and took both his hands, holding them against her cheeks. "You love me."

He smiled. "Yes I do. And you love me."

After a bout of tickling and riding his knee, she went upstairs to play with her toys.

"What a doll," he said. "She's like you were at that age."

"Jess and I are thinking about giving her a brother or sister."

Saul's jaw tensed. "We have no business bringing more children into this world. And in this family, we have an obligation to make up for the sins of our father."

"What do you mean?" What would he think of his words when he learned I was pregnant?

"Technically, none of us should have children. Daddy had enough for all of us."

Since the Nevada years Saul had more influence on me than my father. He had unlocked the prison of polygamous patriarchy for me—urged me to think for myself and get an education. "Women are people, too," he had said, and my mind gaped hungrily as a baby bird. Now I felt pressured to exchange one credo for another, yet I knew whatever I chose had to be mine.

"I don't think I want to let ZPG or the EPA plan my family," I said.

Saul cleared his throat. He spoke intently, citing the natural resources a single person consumes in a lifetime. I knew his facts were accurate. But I also knew that life tyrannized by ideals can cripple every moment and distort the future.

"Other than making you a promise that I won't bear more children, what's the best thing I can do for the environment?" I asked.

"Well, actually, the best thing you could do for the environment . . ." Saul paused and his mouth twisted into a tender, bitter smile, ". . . would be to kill yourself."

Of course, he didn't mean it. He loves me and values my life, just as he loves my children. But he had denied himself more children in spite of his love for them, and he wanted others to toe the same line. He was as convicted in his way as my father was in his.

As I helped Saul pack his things in the station wagon, I made my confession. He flushed and looked at the sidewalk. Neither of us knew what to say. I hugged and kissed him good-bye, knowing that we had missed a chance to celebrate.

I had begun writing, and this helped me get perspective on my child-hood struggles. I realized that Saul must be haunted by similar phantoms, and why he spent all night behind a welder's mask as he blowtorched metal caricatures of dark humanity, keeping his vision sharp. One night, I finished a story beginning with my brother's birth and ending with my grandmother's death, a story arced by my mother's devotion and despair. It was a sad story, but I wept with the relief of telling the truth. I realized that truth offers real freedom—a torch that lights the wilderness as well as the path home.

In my writing class at the university, the professor required that we send our work to a publisher. Although I had cloaked my stories in the conventions of fiction, I knew that some members of my family would accuse me of betrayal. An adulterous generation asks for a sign, my father's voice recited in my head. But I was on my knees, a wanton need shivering up my spine, insisting on a response. Did my search for meaning matter to anyone but me? Would my writing legitimize my existence? In telling the stories of my people, was I indulging my ego or serving the highest good? I wanted God to speak to me, tell me personally if it was all right to mail the story.

A steel sky held the hush that precedes snow as I pushed the baby's stroller along the paths of the Tracy Aviary in Liberty Park. We approached the eagle's cage, and both eagles—the bald and the golden—rose up, circled the cage once, twice, and each dropped a feather at my feet just inside the fence. My baby girl reached a tiny hand through the wire, picked them up and handed them to me, smiling as if she knew what they were, what they meant, and that I should have them.

I took the feathers home and set them inside my Bible, and a deep well of peace opened inside me. It would be another twenty years before I learned from a Navajo medicine man that an eagle feather dropped at one's feet serves as divine confirmation of one's path. But even without this understanding, I found courage to carry the manila envelope to the corner mailbox. I let it drop and let loose a sob. In some ways, my life had just begun.

FROM THE GOLDEN EAGLE

I am stifled, silent. For two weeks now I have been unable to tell any-one what is going on inside me. Something yearns to be born, squirms and pecks at the shell of silence. I am tired of tiptoeing around my war-torn husband, tired of trying to please everybody. My short temper makes the children stop and stare. They bring me cards that say I love you in green and purple crayon, pictures of the family in red and orange: in their drawings I am only slightly taller than they; but their father is full-grown, his hair radiant, his fingers long. He can think; he can do things; I am undeveloped, fingers fisted at my side.

I know I am hell to live with. I try to make it up to my family by fixing a chicken dinner, and even then I can't resist banging doors and dishes. As

I set the roasting pan to soak, I notice that an eagle perches one-footed on the fence outside my kitchen window. While I'm swabbing the sink, I keep my eyes on the wind-bent willows, on the bird that seems unable to move. I worry that the poor thing has been wounded, so I call the bird refuge and the warden drives over to examine the bird. She reports that the bird is fine—not wounded at all—simply a young golden eagle afraid to fly into the high winds of October. She muses that perhaps the bird is lost, a fledgling in search of his own territory. The next morning I look out at the storm-laden sky; the bird is still there, clutching the post for dear life.

I go outside, lean against the fence, watch the young eagle. My hair blows across my face, my clothes whip tight around me, and I realize that I too am afraid to fly into the high winds of controversy, too frightened to publish my new book or face my husband with my feelings. What if my family ostracizes me; what if my husband leaves me; what if the church kicks me out?

The old fear of exile burns, a fire I thought I'd doused long ago. If those who share my life misunderstand or disagree, they could abandon me. If I go forward, I am accountable; I can blame no one. Still, the need to please others shrieks like a harpy: What if the chapters now piled neatly in the drawer mean nothing? What if publishing my book is the same as selling my soul? What if the Bridegroom comes and finds me sitting at the table of the Beast?

The years of warping truth for the family's safety has yielded an important lesson: letting fear rule is the biggest risk of all. Evening comes and I speak plainly to my husband. But as usual, we quarrel about small things: the volume of the radio, who will drive the children to school, who loves who the most. I turn my back to him, curl into myself, and perch at the edge of sleep.

I am swept into a dream: I am jailed in the Salt Lake City and County Building. Bats literally do live in the belfry of this old Gothic structure, and since madness prevails, I have to get out. At every door, stern guards stand with bayonets fixed. I find a kindly face and reason with him. I can do more good if you let me out, I tell him. Will you come back? he asks. And I assure him, yes, I will return. He unlocks the door and sets me free. Outside I sprout strong wings. I flap them once, twice, and updrafts carry me to the top of Mount Olympus where the wind blows wildly. The clouds crackle with a message and the words flow from my own mouth: *Brothers and sisters. We must be free. In order to really love, we must be free.*

I awaken in bed beside my husband, my mind lit up like downtown Saturday night. I look over at him sleeping soundly, his cheek crumpled against the pillow. I take the white Bible, tiptoe to the bathroom, close the door, and turn on the light. Now I will engage in what has become my secret delight, a habit of closing my eyes, letting the Bible fall open, putting my index finger on a passage. My husband calls it "Bible Ouija" and teases me about my superstitions. But in this small practice, I have found uncanny responses to questions I don't even know I have, a hunger fed at the instant of its sharpness. I remove the eagle feathers and the Bible falls open to Revelation. My finger lights on the passage about a woman "clothed with the sun, and the moon under her feet, and upon her head a crown of twelve stars." A woman of celestial poise in Judeo-Christian scripture? I can't think who she would be, or why I've never seen this scripture before. Is she God the Mother, the Queen of Heaven? With her twelve-starred crown, does she represent Israel? Perhaps she is Mary, mother of Jesus. Certainly she represents the feminine divine. I read on to find that the woman was with child, about to give birth, and the great dragon waited to devour the child; the woman took refuge in the wilderness in a place prepared by God while Michael fought the dragon.

This must be the war in heaven, the original clash of good and evil which set the parameters of the universe. I decide that the identity of the woman matters less than knowing she represents Life and that she gave birth in the midst of war. This, and that the earth is blessed and is a blessing—offering wilderness to protect the miracle of new life.

"And to the woman were given two wings of a great eagle, that she might fly into the wilderness, into her place, where she is nourished for a time, . . . from the face of the serpent."

I close my eyes; time rushes. A war in heaven, a war in Vietnam, a war in the last days. If peace is impossible, why were we sent a Prince of Peace? I remember the dream, the mountaintop, the message. My tangled feelings smooth. There is refuge in the wilderness. One eternal moment offering the seed of peace.

The next morning my young eagle has disappeared from the fence post. I venture outdoors, half-afraid that I'll find his body lumped at the foot of the post. The field glows in the morning sun; I turn toward a shriek to see my young golden eagle dive. He wheels like a king above the field. I feel unconscionably proud, as if I am watching one of my children perform.

I realize this: it is time for me to claim that which is mine. Time to return to the church without giving up who I am. The war has already been fought for my birthright; I will not relinquish my territory. I will not play the game of be right and make wrong, and I will not be buried alive in institutional walls—church or state, marriage or career. The key is in remembering that institutions are created to foster individual development and human connection, not vice versa. The deliberate choice evokes joy and fear and responsibility, but I am a citizen equal to the challenge. I will take who I am into my community and watch for a gathering of eagles.

From the Gathering

The day has grown long and thin, and my brain yearns for anything to catalyze change. The morning paper holds an announcement that Mormon scholars have been called to account by church authorities who question their loyalty. Specters of my past, phantoms for my future haunt me.

Among those targeted: historians writing on diverse subjects such as the church's polygamous epoch and Joseph Smith's flirtations with magic. Feminists are under specific attack for writing about spiritual abuse and for praying to a Heavenly Mother. Phone calls indicate that some of my friends could have their membership in the church questioned. Beyond my own claustrophobia, such narrowness saddens me. During the years I taught junior high school, I learned about the cruelty of adolescence; I am aware that institutions go through narcissistic phases and fits of immaturity, indulging in crusades, inquisitions, and witch-hunts. Will the doctrine of personal revelation survive the latest passage?

I bow my head and say a tiny prayer. I know that God helps those who help themselves, but the day slopes steeply, promising so little. My prayer burns bright and thin, refracted through the magnifying glass of my heart. I want to fly away, leave the house, leave the county, leave the state. But this is the community I chose. This is where I will stand.

I sit before the wide window in a small gray ranch house in the middle of nowhere. My closest neighbor is a mile away. Beyond the window, the hill unfolds a vermilion-and-russet tapestry as full sun falls on the golden field. A stream ripples past, the same that sings me to sleep each night. Despite the heartache of the morning paper, the view helps me believe the scripture, "Man is that he might have joy."

My eye is caught by movement in the high branches of the cotton-woods lining the stream—those large dark birds! What brought them here? I watch them carefully. Flying up, circling, soaring high, higher. My heart ascends with them, lifts to the pale sun. So many! Twenty, thirty, forty birds! What are they? Raptors, by the span of the wings, the way they swoop the field, then rise and circle before taking a place in the trees again. They are dark gray but they ride the currents like eagles. Intuition keeps niggling, whispering that I am beholding a phenomenon—and that I am blessed to be a witness.

I telephone my husband. The years of hunting deer before he went to Vietnam have left him with considerable knowledge of our mountain valley.

"Have you ever seen a gray eagle?" I ask him.

"No. Have you?"

"You should see these birds in the field. They fly like eagles. But they're the color of turkey vultures."

"How many?"

"About forty. They keep settling in the field, then going back to the trees."

"If it looks like a turkey vulture, then it probably is a turkey vulture. Especially a bunch of them together like that. Eagles usually hunt alone."

I rummage through my husband's sock drawer and find the binoculars. I examine one bird, then another through the high-powered lenses. Eagle head, eagle beak, eagle arrogance. Not the red hoods of turkey vultures I feared I would see.

I pull on boots and a jacket, and clump across the lawn, leg over the barbed wire. The gray birds have retired to the trees to watch me. I trek halfway across the field before I find the calf, dead only a few hours. The raptors have ripped the hide along the abdomen and at the throat; red flesh gapes here and there like various mouths. The calf seems a fitting sacrifice to the day, and these dark birds must be some kind of eagle I have never seen. At that moment, as if to confirm, a screech overhead makes me look out toward the pond to see three bald eagles circling slowly, their shrill cries stirring up the birds in the trees until all of them circle overhead and I am dizzy, spellbound in their ascending spiral.

It's like a puzzle I can't wait to get back and finish. I keep silent about what I have seen, setting up a pleasant dissonance—my heart knowing some magnificent secret, my brain probing and wondering. Doubt contends with the sense that I have seen something extraordinary. Perhaps I saw some kind of gray hawk or a buzzard I have never heard of before.

I carry the puzzle with me to Eastern Utah where, two years later, I am scheduled to read from my published work. After the reading, I am invited to dine with my hosts, the woman who heads the local Arts in Education program, and her husband, a wildlife biologist. The challenge of her job is to create a sense of artistic community among disparate groups—Mormon hog farmers, wildcat oil workers, the Ute Indian tribe. His job is to build migration paths for wildlife so that coal mines and oil fields don't banish the deer, the ferrets, the eagles. He tells me about his work and then about his guilt: During the war he was a Conscientious Objector; he escaped Vietnam. But now he feels that he let down his buddies and people like my husband. I know something about his guilt and I tell him that Vietnam was a good war to miss. We talk about the struggle of embracing peace. And then, on impulse, I confide about my gray eagles. He confirms my inner knowing—fledgling bald eagles, he says; a year or two years old—before their body feathers turn a rich brown, before their heads and wing tips have gone white.

"You mean I saw forty bald eagles at once?" I ask. "Forty-three," I correct myself, remembering the three adults stirring others to flight, the profusion of spirit in that winged circle.

"If adult bald eagles were present, there's your confirmation," he says. "The adults are like chaperons. Or tutors. They make sure the young birds know how to hunt."

He shows me a picture of a fledgling. Sure enough—it is the bird I saw through binoculars. This proof brings tears to my eyes. I have lived long enough to see the American bald eagle become abundant.

When the snow melts, my husband and I climb the mountain range west of our field. We struggle up the muddy slope, talking softly about the changes in the wind. The prophet has called us to create a kinder, gentler world. Coming from the prophet, it is a commandment, like "Love one another." A commandment I choose to obey. We smile and stop for breath,

Jess's arm propped on my shoulder. We each take a swig from the bottle of spring water. Then we continue, pushing through the scrub oak, scaling a bared fault line where the earth folded millennia ago. Among crags that make skiing impossible, we find what we are searching for: a great heavy nest reinforced each year, with annexes north and south. We keep our distance and we vow to keep the location of the aerie secret, grateful that no one has plans to build summer homes up so high that the air passes like fire through the lungs.

My husband climbs up for a closer look. He says he wants to scale the cliff above the aerie and climb all the way to the top. I am content to sit on my perch below, surveying the tender green valley, remembering those religious retreats of my childhood. I think of Jake, who first taught me about trust, and who struggles now, in the wake of his daughter's death, to trust in God. I think of my father, gone from this earth for many years. Yet he seems to be here now, his eyes misted with emotion as he stands with the wind riffling his patriarch's mane, reading from his tattered black Doctrine and Covenants: ". . . all things unto me are spiritual, and not at any time have I given unto you a law which was temporal. . . ." And I know from experience that what he taught us is true: life is eternal, stronger than death.

My Navajo friend, Jake, tells me that the animal guardian of spirit is the eagle. Perhaps the eagle's abundance offers a message of hope for our country and our world, a message Saul can believe in.

On occasion, the eagles direct us to a confluence where Saul and my father, science and religion, body and spirit converge. The eagles speak the language of sky, and we must discern their meaning with our hearts as well as our heads. They tell us the responsibility of freedom, and unfold a contract of creation where "true" and "real" are one and every illusion disintegrates. They tell us that when we observe the order of being, we align ourselves and our community with wilderness. One level of alignment begets another, moved by spirit to organize life into a form that serves function. The eagles warn that anything untouched by spirit becomes grist for the elements. My father, who stopped hunting when he was called to be a spiritual leader, seems to concur with modern biologists on a certain point: In the celestial order of Mormon being, as in supreme ecological balance, all life must be honored because everything is connected. Since diversity emphasizes an interrelated design in which every life-form is precious, nothing, no one is expendable. The eagles are the guardians of life, the purveyors of spirit, and they know.

"Listen to the voice of the wilderness," they scream. "Tether a true line to the sun."

In this high place where the newborn is protected from the serpent's tooth, I hear my own name called: daughter of earth, daughter of sky, child of woman, child of God. Here, I can span the paradox of my birthright.

In her first book, *In My Father's House* (1984), and in a collection of essays, *Of Predators, Prey and Other Kin*, Dorothy Allred Solomon shares her perspective as one of forty-eight children born to fundamentalist leader Dr. Rulon Clark Allred.

"AND NOW, BEHOLD, I SAY UNTO YOU, THAT THESE ARE THE GENERATIONS OF THE HEAVEN AND OF THE EARTH, WHEN THEY WERE CREATED, IN THE DAY THAT I, THE LORD GOD, MADE THE HEAVEN AND THE EARTH, AND EVERY PLANT OF THE FIELD BEFORE IT WAS IN THE EARTH, AND EVERY HERB OF THE FIELD BEFORE IT GREW. FOR I, THE LORD GOD, CREATED ALL THINGS, OF WHICH I HAVE SPOKEN, SPIRITUALLY, BEFORE THEY WERE NATURALLY UPON THE FACE OF THE EARTH." (MOSES 3:4–5.)

THE
NATURAL HISTORY
OF A QUILT

MARTHA YOUNG MOENCH

OT PURSUIT OF BUGS AND BUTTERFLIES WAS MY CHILDHOOD summertime passion on Commonwealth Avenue at the base of Pencil Point. I don't know who actually thought of the name Pencil Point, but for as long as I can remember, it belonged to the tallest mountain anchoring our neighborhood to the foothills of the Wasatch Mountains. Hiking Pencil Point was an unspoken achievement among all of us.

It was during such a hike, while resting on Red Rock, that one of the most beautiful butterflies of the summer of 1959 fluttered by. A tiger-tail, black and yellow. It was the biggest butterfly I'd ever seen, almost awkward. I didn't move; kept a solid watch as it gently floated downward, alighting on a rock, wings hypnotically beating. I could have sprung for it right then, but the colors and patterns were too intoxicating; black and yellow on a burnt red-brown rock. Intent on capture, I became captivated.

I feel the same about quilts.

Losing myself in the colors and repetitive patterns of quilting, the possibilities, the problems, I become a woman obsessed. The spiritual roots of all my quilt creations trace their genesis to the people I love. I turn to the natural world for images that allow me to speak. Seeds, germinating in my mind since childhood, sprout at night in the form of a quilt idea for my only daughter. What would I say to her? What clues about life would I stitch into a quilt to help her emerge? As moments of her childhood flutter through my mind, I try to place character traits in a quilt pattern. Which memories do I keep? Which do I let go? Maybe she won't know that I'm charting her metamorphosis stitch by stitch, but I'll know that someday she'll lie awake, tossing and turning, and this quilt will be her protective covering. Was it time to let all my bugs and butterflies go for her?

The Red Rock tiger-tail I did let go, but I caught plenty of others that summer. I used Mother's Kerr canning jars, and once the butterfly was caught, I'd slide on the lid and screw the ring tight. Screwdrivers and hammers were used to pound in holes for breathing. After a butterfly calmed down, I'd slide in a little grass for food.

A quilt on a frame was part of our basement furniture that year, providing a perfect canopy for keeping my insect collection safe in a family of nine children. Bottle in hand, I crawled under the quilt only to find my sisters already there. I gazed at its contents: an all-white butterfly with iridescent blue, fingerprint-size circles on its lower wings. Mother was using this oversized playpen as a babysitter for two-year-old Susie, who was contentedly stacking and restacking her blocks. Kathryn, just older than I, was looking for trouble.

Looking at me she asked, "What's in there?"

"A butterfly."

"Let me see it. What's the grass for?"

"Food."

"Butterflies don't eat grass."

"Well . . . it's not really eating the grass. It's eating antropes." I made up something quickly.

"You're lying. I mean it, you're lying. Cross your heart and hope to die, stick a needle in your eye?" she said.

Silence.

Louder she cried, "Cross your heart and hope to die, stick a neeeeedle in your eyeee!"

Susie started to cry while Kathryn, staring at me, crawled toward the edge of the quilt and stood up. For a few minutes all I saw were her legs. Then, brandishing a very large needle, she threateningly headed back our way.

"Okay, okay, there's no such thing as an antrope."

"Don't you know butterflies die without food? Why don't you let it go? Do you have to catch all the butterflies you see?" Pointing to another she said, "Look, this one's hardly breathing."

"All right, everybody out, we've got to roll this quilt," Mother said to her friends, gathered to make a bridal quilt. "At this rate, we could finish tonight. Secure all the needles and scissors and undo the clamps."

I scrambled to collect all my bottles of butterflies and began lining them up on the hearth. The women worked like shipmates, with mother as their captain. They took out the tacks, pulled the ends taut, and waited for her command. "Okay, everyone ready? Let's roll . . . good. Now clamp."

As Mother located her needle and began again, the eager chatter of women stitching with purpose resumed.

"I thought we'd never get to that last roll. How many stitches do you think we'll put into this quilt?" she asked.

"Hundreds of thousands. They say you can measure a quilter's worth by the number of stitches she takes per inch. A perfectionist wouldn't take less than ten," one woman commented.

Mother took her ruler and, measuring, said, "Well it looks like I'm about six. Right in the middle. Fine with me. Now is not the time of life to perfect my quilting stitch."

As Mother knotted the last stitch in her quilt early the following morning, Young family legend holds that at 2:00 A.M. she awoke Daddy saying, "Sherman, Sherman, we've finally finished. Come downstairs and take a look." Always the dedicated quilt enthusiast, Daddy assumed a commanding position standing on the couch, and pronounced, "Glorious!"

Heart's Desire, Cupid's Arrow, Thelma's Choice, Double Wedding Ring, Tangled Garter, Bridal Stairway, Honeymoon Cottage, Trip Around the World.

A few weeks into the summer of 1961, Mother decided I needed a summer project and offered to teach me how to embroider. "Eight years old is as good a time to start as any," she said. We got in the family station wagon and drove to Sprouse Reitz. There we picked out a set of eight blocks: a robin, a squirrel, a dog, a duck, a cat, a seal, a pair of canaries, and a rabbit. She let me choose the embroidery floss, needles, embroidery hoop, and a sewing box.

As beautiful as Mother was—dark hair, stark blue eyes, and translucent complexion—her hands made her mythic. They had well-defined muscles between every joint. Neatly aligning three strands of floss, she broke a piece off with her teeth, threaded the needle, and tied a firm knot. On a piece of scrap material she taught me the running stitch "backwards for left-handers," which I was, and I became immersed.

Eyeing my choices carefully, I began with the squirrel, smiling to myself as I selected the purple embroidery floss. Although sisters are always first to rise to another sibling's defense in the neighborhood, in the home they are fierce critics.

"I don't believe I have ever seen a purple squirrel," Carolyn, the eldest, announced one night at the dinner table.

"Purple squirrel, what are you talking about?" Mimi chimed in.

I forged on with my dinner. One never knows in a family of eleven how soon that much food will be centrally located again. The Young family food chain mimicked the natural world, and since Mother still habitually cut up food for both Robert and Susie, the youngest, as a middle child, I occupied the lowest rung on the ladder. Getting my fair share was serious business.

"Martha is embroidering a squirrel with purple thread. It's not too late to start over," Carolyn responded.

Kathryn: "There's no such thing as a purple squirrel."

Martha: "There is too. I saw one in the scrub oak by our fort."

Kathryn: "You did not. There are no squirrels in the scrub oak."

Martha: "If there are no squirrels, who are the acorns for?"

After dinner, I went to my room, shut the door, and looked through my embroidery blocks. Studying colors and subjects, I laid a skein of sky blue thread down next to the dog and smiled. A blue dog would be the next block I'd stitch.

During my first pregnancy, Mother surprised me by making a baby quilt from the embroidery blocks I'd sewn as a child. She framed each block with a blue border, sashed them together with white, and enclosed them all with a sawtooth border. Around the edge, she quilted double hearts symbolizing the pairs of hands that created the quilt: mine and hers. After presenting it to me in the hospital room, she carefully wrapped my first child in scenes from my childhood. For generations, a purple squirrel and a blue dog would endow newborn babies with the blessing of our handwork.

Baby Bunting, Tumbling Blocks, Sunbonnet Sue, Overall Sam, Clown's Choice, Duck & Ducklings, Catch-Me-If-You-Can.

I joined the Wasatch Mountain Quilters in the fall of 1993. At our bimonthly meetings, we're given a new pattern and invited to stitch a block by the next meeting. The stitched block is entered into a pool, a drawing is held, and the winner receives all the blocks stitched by class members. The first spring I was involved, Sandi Fox, our instructor, brought the butterfly pattern. By stitching more blocks than any other entrant, I banked the odds in my favor, convinced these creatures would be the pattern through which my daughter and I could communicate. I won the draw.

Eight butterflies, as varied as the women who stitched them, began our quilt. During spring break, I taught my daughter, Adrienne, and two cousins how to piece together a butterfly block using techniques taught me by their grandma and honed among the Wasatch Mountain Quilters. We measured and cut our fabric, choosing stripes for bugs' bodies and black for all heads and legs. Wings and body colors ranged from brightest jewel tones to palest iridescence. Aunt Kathryn brought fabric scraps covered with printed butterflies, saved from a newborn outfit she'd sewn for a great-niece. Cutting and reshaping the pieces, we stitched a new butterfly with another's wings. Adrienne had been remarkably vocal about fabric colors and selections.

At age four, Adrienne was asked to express her thoughts at our ward for a children's program called "I Believe in Being Honest." Microphone in hand she responded, "Telling the truth makes me sad. I don't like to tell the truth to my brother Pat because sometimes he gets mad."

I've tried to stay away from the George Washington and His Cherry Tree Theory of Honesty in raising my daughter. Women are not interested in hearing or talking about the whole truth at any age. Ask any community quilter. Every week at quilting group, I listen intently for what is unsaid, watching especially those older than I for guidance.

As our collection grew, Adrienne and I loved to ruminate together about each new creature.

"Mom, look at this butterfly. It has a tear drop on both wings. It looks like somebody who made it cried big tears. But it's the only one. Will you make another?" She selected the colors, and I made it a cousin.

By summer's end, we'd collected sixty-three bugs and butterflies, enough for a twin-size quilt. Stitchers included Grandma, aunts, cousins, and friends. I laid them out on the living-room floor, arranged in alternate rows of butterflies and bugs, trying to decide how to piece them together into one quilt top.

Adrienne asked, "Mom, have you ever seen material that goes from light green like the elm tree seeds to dark green like the rosebush leaves in the front garden? If we could find some, then you could sew a border around every butterfly and they would look like the green colors that they land on." I thought she might be onto something, so we took a trip to the fabric store. There she found exactly what she was looking for: a group of hand-dyed fabrics in eight different shades of green. From these, I constructed one-inch borders around each butterfly, stitched them together in rows, and then stitched all the rows together. Quilting traditions say that a vine bordering a quilt is symbolic of the quilter's wish for a continuous life. For that reason, I pieced together a continuous vine border surrounding all the bugs and butterflies.

As Sandi once said, the Wasatch Mountain Quilters stitch "for purpose and for pleasure in the same type of creative collaboration that characterized the quilted works of the last two centuries." To mark this anniversary, she curated an exhibit of our work to be shown at the University of Utah's Museum of Fine Arts, June through September of 1995.

November of 1994 at our bimonthly "quilting bee," Sandi viewed my completed bugs-and-butterflies quilt top. Taking me aside she said, "This quilt would be a stunning addition to our show. Is there any way you can have it completely quilted by next spring?"

With butterflies in my stomach, I said, "Of course."

I took my last stitch about 5:00 A.M. the morning my quilt was due at the museum. Although our house was unusually quiet, I felt giddy with the thrill of completion as I heard the birds outside begin to chirp, announcing a new day. Spread on the floor before me lay the fruits of my artistic longing stitched by threads of hope over a year's time.

My entire family attended opening night of the Wasatch Mountain Quilters exhibit—my husband, my children, my sisters, their families, and our parents. Because Mother had three daughters exhibiting—Carolyn, Kathryn, and myself—she could hardly wait to have her picture taken with each daughter standing in front of her work.

Adrienne walked into the exhibit, looked at the wall with all of our bugs and butterflies under lights, took me by the hand, and said, "Please, Mom, say it's mine!"

"It's mine, it's yours, it's Grandma's, it's Carolyn's, it's Kathryn's, it's Sandi's . . ." My mind began to drift.

Although Adrienne is now fifteen, I see her at age ten in her first dramatic role. She had taken an acting class at a local children's theater. On completion, the students performed *Alice in Wonderland* for their parents. I waited on the edge of my seat, anticipating which role my daughter had been cast in. During the performance, the suspense built for every parent until their own child appeared. The front rows began to laugh hysterically as a big blue caterpillar with kelly green stripes slowly inched its way over to Alice. Raising its head high and dangling itself back and forth, it finally came to rest, looking not at Alice but at me, smiling as it said, "Who are you?"

Looking at our quilt, I was overcome with an understanding of who we were: Mormon women—my mother, my sisters, my daughter, myself. Through patterns in our lives that we trace to each other, we offer a silent prayer for the next generation through layers of cloth they'll wrap their dreams in.

Taking hold of the quilt's corner I said to Adrienne, "For you, as soon as the exhibit comes down."

Morning Star, Friendship Knot, Daisy Chain, Swallows in the Window, Wild Rose, Star of Hope, Springtime Blossoms, Mother's Dream.

We knew Mother was hovering near the brink of death on October 9, 1996. That night as I slept, I dreamt of hordes of butterflies heralding her entry to heaven. At God's command their wings beat together, creating a great rushing wind.

The most relentless shock of Mother's death was our first picture of her lifeless body lying on a table in the basement of the mortuary. Still dressed in a hospital nightgown, she wore too many physical signs of her last nine days spent comatose in ICU. I had insisted that we, her daughters, should dress her body for the last time, and had rallied my sisters to the cause.

"It's her last earthly ritual," I said. "It should be performed by her daughters."

Kathryn turned away, saying, "I can iron her clothes."

Susie and Carolyn began to assemble her white clothing. We quietly wept. Someone gently pointed out that I was the one who had insisted we dress her. The observation was made that Mother's body was too heavy for two people to dress. It would require all of us. We all gathered around and, for the first time, looked at her hands. How many times had they dressed our wounds?

Mother died from complications due to a cerebral aneurysm, cocooned against pain through a coma. We found a curling iron and arranged her hair over stitches left from a shunt. We painted her fingernails. As Linda tied the bow in her blouse, Carolyn noticed we'd ripped a small hole in her sleeve. Susie said between sobs, "Let Martha mend it. She has the finest stitch." No one disagreed. We looked for a needle and thread. Thankfully, mortuaries are supplied with every earthly necessity. I broke off a bit of white thread with my teeth but couldn't see to thread the needle. I passed it down. It was passed again. Who knows which one of mother's seamstresses was able to thread that needle?

Autumn Leaves, Basket of Lilies, Alberta's Prairie Queen, Broken Circle, Bird of Paradise, Stars for Henrietta.

It has been almost three years since completion of the bug-and-butterfly quilt. We have given it a name: Earth's Whisperers. All that I am, and all that I hope for my daughter is stitched into its fabrics. Messages. Some nights, when sleep won't come, Adrienne and I argue about who will dream under its canopy.

Egg. Caterpillar. Chrysalis. Butterfly. Egg. Infant. Child. Woman.

Martha Young Moench lives in Salt Lake City, Utah, with her husband, Mark, and their three children—Patrick, Adrienne, and Matthew. Her current chosen profession is that of homemaker/quilter.

". . . THIS IS THE TOKEN OF THE COVENANT WHICH I HAVE MADE BETWEEN ME AND YOU AND EVERY LIVING CREATURE THAT IS WITH YOU, FOR PERPETUAL GENERATIONS." (GENESIS 9:12.)

BEARING WITNESS

MICHAEL DUNN

NE NIGHT ABOUT TWO YEARS AFTER I WAS ATTACKED AND NEARLY killed by a grizzly bear, I had just concluded a talk about the experience at a fireside for single adults. As I made my way out of the chapel I noticed a man working his way through the milling crowd, who seemed very anxious to talk to me. His manner suggested he had something very important to share.

"I got here a little late," he apologized as he met up with me and reached out to shake my hand, "but I just wanted to tell you that I really enjoyed your testimony. I came all the way across town tonight to talk to you about something I think you would be very interested in." With great passion he proceeded to chronicle the series of events leading up to what he felt was a major travesty—the reintroduction of wolves into Yellowstone. After making what he felt was an airtight case against the wolves, he went on to point out how I, a man who had been directly and unjustly affected by the mismanagement of wild beasts, would be the perfect spokesman for a group he was marshaling to repeal this outrageous act.

He had obviously arrived very late.

I paused at the conclusion of his railing and gave it a moment of polite consideration before responding.

"Uh, thanks, but there's only one problem," I said.

"What's that?"

"Well, I'm not really opposed to the reintroduction of wolves into Yellowstone. In fact, from what I understand about the issue, I think it's a pretty good idea."

For a couple of seconds he studied my face intently, searching for a clue that this might be some sort of sick attempt at humor on my part. Seeing no such sign, he suddenly backed away as if he had just discovered I had some terrible communicable disease.

"You've got to be kidding me," he said in a stunned tone. I shook my head slowly and was ready to explain my position but never had a chance because he quickly disappeared into the milling crowd with only a single disgusted look back. In his eyes, I was a wolf in sheep's clothing.

Speaking of his eyes, I will never forget the blazing look in them as he spoke of the villainous wolves and the unconscionable tree-hugging left who precipitated this action. It reminded me of a still-disturbing scene from an old black-and-white Frankenstein movie I had seen as a child, where the normally mild-mannered villagers, most of whom have never even seen the creature, are assembling in the town square to form the mob that will once and for all contain and then kill the mutant monster. In one particularly telling close-up, the flickering torches of the mob are reflected in one of the villager's wild glassy eyes. And it was obvious that rage has replaced any semblance of reason.

So it was with many well-intentioned people with whom I spoke shortly after the bear attack. For the most part they denounced the actions of this menacing creature and figuratively swore their willingness to be deputized and ride out of town with the posse. Even with assurances that it was an unfortunate but chance meeting between man and bear, people over and over again seemed more concerned with how and when the rangers were going to track down the bear and kill him.

Yet, oddly enough, retribution and revenge never crossed my mind.

From the moment I awakened in my hospital room on the morning after being found to see the sun streaming through my window and realize I was alive, I have felt nothing but profound gratitude for life and an uncanny affinity with bears in general. Which, frankly, was a highly unusual reaction, given my western-American male upbringing and pre-occupation with the concept of justice.

So why was it that the instinct of kinship prevailed over killing?

I believe there were many influences both of a physical and spiritual nature. But to fully appreciate my position, you first need to know more about this experience with the bear that forever changed my perspective on life. It is a story that begins the day before the bear attack.

It was still dark as I awoke to the relentless chimes of a Timex alarm watch. My eyes were too bleary from sleep to see how to turn it off, so I sort of smothered in the bottom of my sleeping bag until the beeping finally stopped. It was August 13, 1994, 5:30 A.M. The rest of my family was asleep in the tiny one-room cabin we were occupying during our vacation in Grand Teton National Park. My predawn wake-up call was so I could get in a long training run in preparation for the St. George Marathon. I pulled my arms back out and felt the cold mountain air. It took all my will to get the rest of my body out of that warm sleeping bag. But within five minutes I found myself out running on a cold, long, and very wet trail. It had rained the night before, making the trail very muddy. As I slipped and sloshed along I remember whining to myself about the miserable conditions and wishing I had listened to my weaker self and stayed in the sleeping bag.

Then I noticed something odd.

Glancing upward at the tops of the surrounding lodgepole pines, I saw something filtering down through their branches. It was light. The very first, almost indistinguishable light of what would become a stunning dawn. It was beautiful. In fact, a little too attractive. Looking upwards at it for a moment too long, I suddenly veered off the narrow trail and stumbled right into a pine tree. A very wet pine tree. The gooey, oozing sap on the branches slimed me but also did something else. The rustled pine branches kicked off that one-of-a-kind smell that began to awaken my faculties and turn me from an inward focus to an outward orientation. All my faculties seemed to vivify as I sensed the cool morning air, the rapidly lightening sky, and everything else around me in a greater degree of detail than I ever thought possible. I wiped my piny hands off, got back onto the trail, and began to run again towards an opening ahead of me. By the thinning trees I could tell I had reached the halfway point of my run.

But I could also tell that something preternatural was beginning to happen.

I noticed it as soon as I ran out into the open wind-swept jetty of land called Hermitage Point. Immediately below me, two sandhill cranes spotted my arrival and screeched their outrage as they took off in flight over Jackson Lake. I came to a stop and looked to my left. There on the eastern horizon was a magnificent sight. It was a fiery glow filtering through the lingering moisture in the mountain skies—moisture that blurred the solid color of yellow into a magnificent palette of orange, red, yellow, and then smeared them across the sky. My eye followed the colors to the western horizon where the sky deepened into an eerie cobalt blue. And there, framed in the blue and lit by a sunrise source half a sky away were the Tetons. Over the course of twenty years I had seen this mountain range in a variety of lights and situations. But never did it look as beautiful as it did on this morning. Adding to the beauty was a line of cotton-candy clouds that covered the middle section of the Grand's 13,777-foot summit, making it appear as if the midsection of the mountain had been cut away and the summit left to float on the billowy clouds. My eye next caught a near-perfect copy of the image I had just seen as I observed the reflection of the Grand Tetons in glassy Jackson Lake below me.

It was with these stunning images bombarding my senses that I suddenly felt a very odd need. It was not the sort of physical need for water or food that I normally experience during this part of a run. Instead this was a spiritual need that was so clear that I found myself dropping to my knees right there in the middle of the trail in the rocks, mud, and wet prairie grass. Then, closing my eyes I bowed my head and began to pray out loud, evoking a level of sincerity and integrity that can sometimes be missing in the routine of my silent prayers. It was a prayer that took me much by surprise—so much so that I found myself admitting to God that I wasn't even sure why I had initiated this high conversation. Then it came to me.

This was a prayer of thanks. I really had nothing to ask. Instead it was a prayer spurred by the overwhelming beauty of the sunrise, sky, earth, trees, and morning light. I thanked God for these everyday divine manifestations—manifestations that many years ago first let me know He was really there and that continue to be a reminder of His greatness and goodness.

Finally I ended my prayer and raised my head. Still awed by the incredible beauty surrounding me, I arose and started the run back.

Sleep came easy that night. Then, bright and early on August 14, 1994, I woke up and headed out on the trail again. My plan was for a much longer run—eighteen miles—and on a trail where I had never been before. Leaving that morning, I remember several subtle impressions. Specifically, I remember the uneasiness I felt as I crossed through that last open meadow, looking at the curtain of lodgepole pines looming just ahead of me. The feeling so unnerved me that I slowed down and walked for a moment. Then I stopped, held my breath, and listened while I looked in every direction. Other than a few birds in the distance there was nothing out there as far as I could tell. So I shrugged off the feelings and ran silently ahead into the forest.

It was not long before I knew what those feelings had been about.

Two hours into the run I suddenly heard a thunderous sound coming from the forest on my left. Even though I didn't initially know what it was, the sound set off every alarm in my body. Wheeling around to my left I saw it. From less than thirty yards a bear was coming out of the brush, heading for me at full speed. It was an incredible sight—teeth bared, growling, ears laid back. And then I spotted the hump, which told me this wasn't just a bear I was dealing with. This was a grizzly.

I screamed at the bear and had just enough time to brace for the impact. It hit me at full speed and then landed on top of me in a buffaloberry bush about ten yards off the trail. Instantly, slashing claws and teeth found their marks. I felt the first bite—down in my left hip—and screamed in pain and fear. But nothing seemed to faze the bear as I wrestled and struggled. It batted me around at will.

Several agonizing minutes later, I began to realize I was going to die. With the bear so enraged and with such a mismatch in size, I knew there was no way out. So I prepared myself to die, wondering what it would be like and when the fateful moment would come.

Then another blow came—quite literally. After chewing and clawing on my backside the bear suddenly took a swipe at my head. Fortunately he missed everything, except that one large claw found its way into my open mouth, then settled into the lower part of my jaw like a fishhook. The bear pulled so that my head began to twist backwards, almost as if he was going to take it off. I resisted the pull, straining with everything I had to keep my head forward. But the strength of the bear was beginning to win out. My neck muscles began to shake as they fatigued and I could hear what sounded like the small bones in the base of my neck starting to crack.

Then something remarkable happened.

Somehow, someway, the angle of the claw in my jaw must have opened up just enough, and not a moment too soon. Slipping out of the hold in my jaw, the claw came out with such torque that it detached part of my ear and nearly scalped me before exiting the back of my head. Blood was everywhere. Death was now not a question of *if* but *when*.

I prayed.

"God," I pleaded. "I need your help. And I need it now."

There was an immediate response to my supplication, not with a voice or vision or supernatural happening but by way of a simple impression—a clear impression entered my mind that consisted of just two words: *play dead*. Which is what I did. I stopped wrestling and struggling, and immediately put all my efforts into controlling my racing pulse and rapid breathing. I curled over on my right side, rolled into a ball, and tried to stay motionless.

As I lay there on the ground, trying to put all of my efforts into playing dead, I suddenly realized that the biting and clawing had stopped. I could still feel the bear on top of me and hear and smell his short choppy breath, but nothing else was happening. Summoning all my courage I peeked out of my hands and looked up to see a remarkable sight. What I saw was a bear who, just prior to my prayer, had been engrossed in killing me but was now totally disinterested. Instead he was very obsessed—spooked would be a more accurate description—by something in the forest. I watched as his head went from side to side looking into the trees and bushes. It was as if he could hear or sense something that really bothered him. I listened. I heard nothing. But there was definitely something out there, even though later official investigations would reveal that there were no other animal or human evidences in that part of the forest that day—proving, if nothing else, that angels really don't leave footprints.

Within moments, the bear left me and took off down the trail, which is when I really began to get scared. I was bleeding badly with gaping wounds all over my body and all alone on a wilderness trail. I prayed again. And once again He heard me and answered. Stumbling along on a shredded leg, I went the direction I felt was best—a direction that led me to my rescuers, a daring backcountry helicopter rescue, and the medical help that would ultimately save my life.

Or, more accurately, it was a prayer and a bear that likely saved my life.

That's not to suggest that a prayer from a dying man is that unusual. I'm convinced it's just the opposite, that in all times and ages and in a variety of dire circumstances—from burning buildings to battlefields to sinking ships—men and women have always felt an instinctive desire to look heavenward and cry out to God for help. For me, what is so unusual about this situation is that my prayer on that fateful morning was almost exactly twenty-four hours after a spontaneous prayer of gratitude, sparked by the beauty of the land around me. Yet, after this seemingly innocuous experience with prayer,

I'm convinced that the Spirit was schooling me with that unplanned prayer of August 13, preparing, teaching, and reminding me of the power and efficacy of personal prayer. As Ralph Waldo Emerson once wrote, "In the woods we return to reason and faith."

Then there was the bear, an unrecognized hero in this saga who never got to tell his side of the story, and who certainly is not the bad guy everyone immediately judged him to be. While most accounts focused on what the bear did do (sixteen major wound sites, 300 stitches, etc.), I instead marveled at what the bear did *not* do—namely, kill me, which he could have done at any time. But perhaps one can only fully appreciate the enormous raw power of these animals after having been in their clutches. I also believe, as do many others, that the bear was merely reacting to an uninvited surprise guest in his neck of the woods. In other words, doing what bears do when their personal space has been so rudely violated, which, ironically, means that it may have been fear on the bear's part that was responsible for both the beginning and end of the attack.

In an essay entitled "Subduing the Earth," Hugh Nibley points out that all creatures are awed by the presence of God's representatives, which makes complete sense if you believe that man was created in the image and likeness of God. If that's the case, then certainly there must be something in the genetic code of every animal that whispers deity every time a man or woman approaches. Similarly, God's high regard for animals has to be reflected in the fact that he brought them to earth even before mankind, that he gave mankind a special stewardship role over the animals, that he commanded a special prophet named Noah to preserve them from extinction during the great flood, and that it was an animal—a dove—that signaled the return of mankind to a cleansed and purified earth by greeting Noah with a highly symbolic olive branch.

Part of my lack of animosity towards the bear is because of the spiritual nature of having had my life spared. I had literally seen God intervene in my life and only felt a sense of reverence and awe for what had happened. Part of it may have also been because of the covenant.

In Genesis we read that God's covenant was not just with mankind but with Noah and all the animals, and that it extends to our day and for perpetual generations to come. This means that the statute of limitations has not run out. We as mankind are charged with a divine mandate to provide a symbolic ark, or refuge, for the escalating threat to species. I believe there is a much deeper connection here, a sacred three-way alliance between God, mankind, and the animal kingdom.

And it continues.

An ancient Hebraic text called the *Zohar* says, "Even the fierce beasts of prey fear man as long as he keeps his covenant, his kingly dignity, and his eye fixed on God in whose image he is." And from the book of Esdras in the Apocrypha: "Whenever man stands upright and lifts his eyes toward heaven, then all the animals raise their heads too, and look to man, fearing and trembling in his presence" (4 Esdras 8:47). Fascinating is the premise that we knew these creatures in a spiritual realm as part of the totality of creations, and that mankind is not merely the master but a proxy reminder of the great creator. It changes our role, warning us of the pitfalls of unrighteous dominion, as the proverb does that states, "As a roaring lion, and a ranging bear, so is a wicked ruler over the poor people" (Proverbs 28:15).

Throughout this ordeal I feared many things. There was the bear in the initial terrifying moments of the attack. Then I was scared of bleeding to death before being found. Lying on the trail in a pool of blood and unable to move, I desperately feared the bear's return. And after hearing from a doctor that the bear had clawed away an entire muscle group in my leg, I was afraid I would never run or even walk again.

Yet, this story is not really about what I feared but what I found— namely, a profound and renewed appreciation for the lushness of everyday life and a deeply concealed courage to take on some of the real bears in my head. From major career decisions to small personal challenges such as going back to the mountains to run alone again, I've been emboldened. Even more certain and permanent than the scars which crisscross my body is a deep and abiding respect for bears and the entirety of God's creation in my soul.

Henry Beston once wrote: "For the animal shall not be measured by man. In a world older and more complete than ours they move finished and complete, gifted with extensions of the senses we have lost or never attained, living by voices we shall never hear. They are not brethren, they are not underlings, they are other nations. . . ."

I celebrate and revere these nationals. Reminded again by an ancient sacred promise that the real issue isn't so much about finding a place for wolves, bears, and other living things in Yellowstone, it's really more about first finding a place for these majestic creations of God in our hearts.

Michael Dunn is an Emmy award-winning writer, producer, and director living in Salt Lake City with his wife, Linda, and their three children.

THANK THE CREATURES

JAMES ERICKSON

hank the creatures that feed us,
for you will notice the plague, the drought, and the famine
when the hunt has failed, when the animals are gone.

Thank the predator for preventing the overflow
of the plant-devouring creature.

Thank the herbivore for filling the plate
of the flesh-devouring creature.

A food chain reaction can be caused by one
too many trees cut down.

They served us unpaid,
and we should pay them back.

James Erickson is a fifth grader at Woodstock Elementary in Salt Lake City.

NAVIGATING THE ENVIRONMENTAL CRISIS: MENDING POLICY AND MYTHOLOGY

SAM RUSHFORTH

other of us all
Place of our birth
How can we stand aside and watch the rape of the world
—TRACY CHAPMAN[1]

November afternoon, school cut, a fast car, wild ride to the refuge. Tires screaming, car lurching at curves, stopping finally at lake's edge. In the midst of the noisy posturing of adolescent boys, a kit fox—on the mud near the edge of the lake. Ears up, back, then up. Eyes large, darting, nervous, aware he had made a terrible mistake to be seen, anxious to be away—back into the rushes that provided refuge, safety. But we were quick and the fox had ventured too far from cover. Curious at first, we cut off his path back to safe haven. Our own male eyes darting back and forth from fox to boy, questioning, what happens now? What should we do? How should we act? Don't foxes kill ducklings, don't they take eggs? And after all, weren't we hunters? Sportsmen?

The first rock missed, thrown almost as a question. But the fox understood and tried to pass. A quick move and he was turned back, another and he was turned again, another and he was circled back into our middle, eyes frightened now, reflecting perhaps a sad awareness or resignation, any curiosity gone. Survival alone his focus.

The first rock a crack in thin civility, an invitation for cruelty, brutality even. The rocks that followed crushing any hope for an understanding between boy and fox, any possibility of passing the terrible barrier between us, if only for a moment. Crushing, perhaps, in dominance and hierarchy even the hope for understanding between human and human.

The loss of a life? A lifetime? The death of the possible? Perhaps the central issue of our time . . .

The late twentieth century. Four or five million years into an experiment with an unusual upright primate. Two million years or so after the evolution of our own genus, *Homo*. A few hundred thousand years since becoming sentient as *Homo sapiens*. And maybe 50,000 years since obtaining nearly every human quality—speech, memory, reason, love, religion.

Homo sapiens variety *sapiens*—a new creation, a wonder in the universe, an organism with the ability to cast ourselves backward and forward in the net of memory and imagination, a being with the drive to understand the universe and our place in it. A species with the gifts of music, mind, memory.

> . . . *What a piece of work is a man! how noble in reason! how infinite in faculty! in form and moving how express and admirable! in action how like an angel! in apprehension how like a god! the beauty of the world! the paragon of animals!* . . . [2]

And in our short time here, where have we come? What have we learned to become with our noble reason and infinite faculties? Have we learned to live together in joyful cooperation? Have we discovered that peace is more than the absence of war? Have we cared for the poor among us? Do we know we are a part of the natural world—not apart from or above nature but owned and embraced by the sun, the water, the soil? Have we become stewards and caretakers? Are we, in fact, "admirable," "the beauty of the world," the "paragon" of life?

The late twentieth century. Six billion of us on the planet. More than half of all humans who have ever lived on this planet born in the past fifty years; perhaps six billion more in the next thirty. One hundred million babies born next year alone, most into poverty. Perhaps thirty wars occurring at any one time on our planet; more than 90 percent of the deaths in these wars civilians. Two hundred million war-related deaths this century alone. The richest countries on the planet selling more than $35 billion worth of deadly weapons to the poorest nations each year. At half that $35 billion, developing countries could initiate basic health services to save millions of their children's lives each year. Developed nations spending each year on armaments an amount equivalent to the entire income of the world's poorest two billion people.

The late twentieth century. Diarrhea kills at least five million children under the age of five yearly. Measles, flu, and respiratory illness almost as deadly. Perhaps one in six people in poor countries undernourished, malnourished, starving. Nearly one-fifth of all humans chronically hungry. More than twenty million hunger-related deaths each year—55,000 people per day, 2,200 per hour. Vitamin A deficiency blinding half a million children per year. Iodine insufficiency causing millions of children in tropical countries to lose their hearing or speech each year. Iron deficiency anemia affecting about 10 percent of men, one-third of women, and more than half the children in Earth's tropical regions.

The late twentieth century. Ninety-eight percent of streams in the lower forty-eight states degraded; about 20 percent of the world's freshwater fish species extinct or endangered; more than 80 percent of America's fish communities harmed or destroyed; 90 percent of our ancient or "old-growth" forests lost; 95 to 98 percent of virgin forests in the lower forty-eight states gone by 1990; 99 percent of virgin eastern deciduous forests logged; 97 percent of Connecticut's coastline developed; 95 percent of Maryland's natural barrier island beaches gone; nearly 100 percent of Ohio's bottomland hardwood forests lost; nearly 100 percent of Kentucky's native prairies destroyed; 98 percent of Southeast coastal plains' longleaf pine logged; 88 percent of southwest Florida's slash pine forests gone; 90 percent of tallgrass prairie disappeared; virtually all prairie in Michigan and Ohio gone; 72 percent of Minnesota's northern hardwood forests lost; 86 percent of Minnesota's red and white pine forests gone; 99 percent of California's native grassland gone; up to 98 percent of western Montana's old-growth forests and low-elevation grasslands lost; half of Colorado's wetlands gone; 90 percent of Hawaii's dry forests and grasslands gone.

The late twentieth century. Humans appropriating perhaps 40 percent of Earth's total yearly energy produced by green plants—the only energy available to sustain all living organisms on the planet. Eighty more years with the human population doubling and perhaps redoubling may leave nothing for any other animal species on Earth.

The late twentieth century. Ecosystems destroyed, communities disrupted or lost. Topsoil loss at critical levels and increasing throughout the world. Only 5 percent of the world's sewage treated before it is discharged into waterways or onto the land. Half of all humans living in areas with seriously polluted air. Much of the fresh water on the planet polluted.

And all of this for what? What has been worth the awful price we have paid for such unspeakable losses? Automobiles? Roads? Cheap paper products? Single-family dwellings? Television sets? Nuclear arms? Plastics? Pesticides? Fast food? Are we happier as individuals, more successful as a species? Have we made Earth a better, more habitable, or safer place for humans? Do we have hope for the future?

How can we live this way? What self-delusion, what demented vision of the future could allow us to live in this sort of rapacious orgy of self-destruction? What notions about Earth and ourselves could allow a sentient species to slowly and then with breathtaking speed destroy our planet, the very home we inhabit and profess to love—the home we must learn to love and protect if we are to continue to exist? How can we destroy Earth with no thought for our future or that of any future generation? What egotistical, bizarre worldview could allow us to look on our destructive path without horror? Without screaming for sanity? For wholeness? For peace? How is it possible that schools and religions have failed to warn us of the consequences of our actions?

What stories mold and make us—the stories we work the hardest to protect when they are challenged? The stories we believe so firmly and understand so deeply that we can hardly identify them? The stories that exist in our bones?

If we identify and understand our stories, can we chart a new course? If we find our old stories inadequate or malevolent, can we learn to tell new ones—stories of healing and renewal? If our old stories have failed us, can we learn new stories that may enrich, even save us?

Thomas Kuhn, in his fine book *The Structure of Scientific Revolutions*,[3] discusses our thinking about reality and how cultural stories develop and shape us. Kuhn suggests that several notions are important in understanding our modern shared stories. First, any people sharing a worldview share a broad, often unstated and untested set of assumptions about reality. Second, those sharing a worldview hold a common reality, a common set of assumptions and goals for their society. Third, shared assumptions about reality are accepted as the framework, the "rules of the road" for structuring society and solving problems. Fourth, those who share a worldview believe their "rules of the road" create the best possible framework for solving problems.

Such "rules of the game" make up the central core of the stories we tell and believe. Central assumptions, often unspoken and unexamined, are critical to our sense of who we are and how we behave. When we look at our creation myths, for example, we often share the notion that humans were created apart from nature and are in a separate and higher category than other species. This often leads to the notion that we have rights and prerogatives not given to our fellow species—that we alone can choose what species may live or die, which ecosystems may be destroyed, even what peoples should be chosen for elimination.

Sociologists Catton and Dunlap[4] suggest some of the "rules of the game" shared by many people with our Western scientific point of view. These include the following:

- humans are unique among all species of life on Earth and legitimately dominate all other life forms;
- humans are agents with the ability to develop and work toward individual goals;
- resources are not limiting for human agents;
- human history is linear, leading always toward progress;
- problems invariably have solutions; and
- human progress has unlimited potential.

Ecologist David Ehrenfeld[5] suggests some further assumptions of our modern worldview. According to Ehrenfeld, most of us believe that

- all problems are solvable by people;
- technology is the route to solving nearly all problems;
- problems resistant to technology can be solved by social means (i.e., politics or economics); and
- humans are clever enough to solve important problems before it is too late.

Is it possible that "rules of the game" similar to those identified by

Catton and Dunlap and Ehrenfeld could be the core of stories once useful but now failed? Is it possible that the terrible faith we hold in technology, in the human ability to solve all problems, in the belief of human domination over all of nature is terribly wrongheaded, even deadly? And is it possible that the general angst now permeating cultures across the planet is due to our failed stories?

What sort of organizing principles—new or old—may bring changes in direction, new thoughts, new possibilities for the human experiment? Do stories exist that could help us find a new way? Can we think of ways in which we could reorient toward Earth in more fulfilling ways—ways that could enhance our well-being and peace, and increase not only our own chances for long-term survival but for the survival of other species as well?

I think the difficult work of reframing our thinking about Earth and our relationships to each other has already begun. And, of course, the stories of some of Earth's peoples already seem to be more appropriate in many ways than our prevalent Western stories. Perhaps such beginnings can offer guidance.

The United Nations Declaration of International Rights, written nearly fifty years ago, suggests that fundamental rights exist for all people on Earth, no matter their ethnicity, creed, country or origin, or economic status. The document is an important and worthy attempt at defining the rights of individual humans on Earth but makes no attempt to define the relationship between peoples and Earth.

Some who work on issues of the relationship between people and Earth have made suggestions in the past few years of ways we might orient ourselves to live with less impact on our planet. Some such suggestions are draconian—the worldwide imposition of population control, for example. Others are less dramatic; for example, that developers, corporations, and governments must become more focused on the rights of individuals and the good of the planet rather than solely on profits.

Deep ecologists Devall and Sessions[6] suggest several core ideas that may cause us to craft new stories and design new ways of living on Earth.

- The well-being and flourishing of human and nonhuman life on Earth have value in themselves. These values are independent of the usefulness of the nonhuman world for human purposes.
- Richness and diversity of life-forms contribute to the realization of these values, which are also values in themselves, and humans have no right to reduce this richness and diversity except to satisfy vital needs.
- The flourishing of human life and cultures is compatible with a substantial decrease of the human population. The flourishing of nonhuman life requires such a decrease.
- Present human interference with the nonhuman world is excessive, and the situation is rapidly worsening.

- Policies must therefore be changed. These policies affect basic economic, technological, and ideological structures. The resulting state of affairs will be deeply different from the present.
- The ideological change is mainly that of appreciating life quality (dwelling in situations of inherent value) rather than adhering to an increasingly higher standard of living. There will be a profound awareness of the differences between big and great.
- Those who subscribe to the foregoing points have an obligation directly or indirectly to try to implement the necessary changes.

Several of the largest environmental organizations in the United States recently created an Environmental Bill of Rights stating that "every American has the right to a safe and healthy environment." The document urged ". . . all elected officials—local, state, and federal—to protect that right. We oppose any measures that would roll back the environmental progress of the last twenty-five years. We commit ourselves to support the following simple principles, and will hold public officials who represent us accountable for their stewardship of the planet."

The Environmental Bill of Rights contains five major provisions:

1. Prevent pollution. *Every American is entitled to air, water, food, and communities free from toxic chemicals. Government policies and regulatory standards must prevent pollution before it happens, expand citizens' right to know about toxics, and guarantee protection for citizens, particularly for the most vulnerable among us—infants, children, pregnant women, and the elderly.*

2. Preserve America's national heritage, wild and beautiful, for our children and future generations. *Wildlife, forests, mountains and prairies, wetlands, rivers, lakes, historic sites, urban parks and open spaces, oceans and coastlines are all part of our national heritage.*

3. End the give-aways of public assets, such as mineral, timber, grazing and fishery resources. *End the subsidies for oil and energy companies. Polluters should pay to clean up the mess they create. No one has the right to use property in a way that destroys or degrades the surrounding community. We reject the idea that good neighbors must pay bad ones not to pollute.*

4. Conserve America's natural resources by controlling waste, increasing energy efficiency, and protecting against overuse and abuse. *Encourage sustainable technologies that meet human needs without destroying the environment.*

5. Get the big money out of politics. *No more government for sale. Let's take our government back from the big campaign contributors and exploiters who control it today.*

Millions of Americans agreed with this document, signed it, and sent copies to Congress. The results certainly have not been felt yet. The 104th and 105th Congresses have perhaps the worst environmental records in the past twenty-five years. Even so, the notion that a very large number of Americans are disturbed with the environmental degradation around us is important. This is consistent with many recent polls that show that environmental protection is vital to more than two-thirds of Americans.

Still other ideas about changing "business as usual" require a substantial reorientation of our stories—a reorientation in the way we do development, harvest renewable natural resources, expend fossil fuels, dispose of wastes. Perhaps we need a new organizing framework for how we think about Earth.

Several organizations—including women's groups, the United Nations, the Ecological Rights Association, and even sovereign countries meeting at the Earth Summit in Rio—have suggested ways in which humans could reorient to make a substantial change in the way our lives impact Earth. For example, we must work to help peoples across the globe understand the interconnectedness of all life on Earth. Humans must recognize our dependency on nature. And we must understand that we can cause widespread and irreversible damage to the planet—damage on a scale greater than we ever before realized. We simply cannot continue to see ourselves as above and apart from nature. This sort of duality allows us to behave in ways that are reprehensible. It allows us to dominate and impose rather than converse and cooperate.

Several specific ideas for changing our worldview about our relationship to Earth have been proposed. For example, we should adhere to *anticipatory* and *precautionary principles*—we must make any impact on the environment with great caution. All development must be viewed as likely to cause serious environmental damage. Furthermore, it is the proponent of a proposed project or technology that must show the impact will not be detrimental and/or that the benefits of the project will outweigh the costs, including environmental and social costs.

With anticipatory and precautionary principles in mind, it is always critical to determine the *true costs* of any environmental action. To dam a river, for example, has many costs beyond the direct costs of excavation, construction, operation. Associated costs often include the loss of wildlife habitat, flooded agricultural lands, displaced families, altered downstream aquatic ecosystems, and a host of other site-specific costs. All must be included in determining whether the benefits of the project are worth the damage.

Until now, proponents of nearly any project or technology have often told a one-sided story—a story only of the benefits of their project. They have not faced a burden of proof to demonstrate that their action will not cause ecological or social damage. Such a burden has fallen to individuals or groups who believe the true costs of the project are unacceptable. Placing the burden of proof on developers may be an excellent instrument for improving our environment.

The above principles, among others, may have the potential to prevent substantial environmental degradation. Perhaps they also have the potential to help us think about nature in a different way. But other ideas may be even more important since they may ask us to change our stories in a more direct and fundamental way.

What if we decided as a people to affirm the story told by many native cultures that all generations of humans are equal, that future generations have as many rights to Earth's sustenance and resources as the present generation? Would we behave differently if we believed that we must be accountable for our decisions and actions not only in the immediate future but for hundreds of years to come? Would this lead to a worldview with a commitment to careful evaluation of proposed environmental changes? Would such a view change the way we think about biodiversity and sustainable use of our forests and prairies?

What might follow if we as a people decided that care of the Earth is correct and worthy of our commitment? Some have suggested we would eliminate weapons of mass destruction, phase out the use of nuclear power and mining of uranium, eliminate or drastically reduce military budgets, transfer military expenditures to environmentally sound and socially beneficial purposes, work to restore environmentally damaged or compromised ecosystems. In general, we would be committed to actions that would ensure the long-term survival of Earth rather than short-term behavior propelled by immediate profits without consideration or true costs of the future. We simply must change our stories—our fundamental beliefs about who we are—if we are to flourish in the years and decades ahead.

One thing is abundantly clear: as we move into the twenty-first century, the human experiment is in peril. Everywhere signs of degradation and decay crowd our senses and harm our spirits. We have created a world fraught with enormous ecological and social problems—an environment with the potential to create catastrophe on a scale unimagined.

The crisis of environmental degradation and destruction we face today is only partly a problem of air and water pollution, the extinction of species, and the ruin of ecosystems. It is perhaps more precisely a crisis of spirit and a loss of a sense of home. We have listened to the wrong stories this past century. We have been told that failure is success, that rapacious misuse is business acumen, that polluted streams and air are small prices to pay for progress. We have been told that the loss of biodiversity, the growing disparity between the world's rich and poor, the modification, loss, and ruin of ecosystems are all inevitable and small side effects of human development of Earth. We have been told we should be grateful for the terrible loss of beauty and sublimity, diversity and grace. We are told there is nothing we can do about the dreadful loss we feel, that diminished health and harmed spirits are the human condition in the late twentieth century, that greed and ugliness, poverty and hopelessness, squalor and violence are natural and inevitable.

Lies, all lies. The price we have paid is too high. The outcome of the industrial revolution has been the near ruin of our home. The technological drive to power we have seen this century may yet result in the collapse and destruction of many or most of the ecosystems on the planet. The greed and ugliness of spirit we see around us are not natural. They are by-products of wrong living.

Only by changing our stories, by rearranging our priorities, by rethinking the very core of who we are can we save ourselves and our home. Only by coming to see clearly the costs of our prideful and brutal attitude toward Earth may we change our course of self-destruction. Only with humility, love, and a connected full-blooded concern for all living things and all peoples do we embrace the possibility for a long-term habitation of planet Earth. Only by learning to tell new and truer stories—stories to help us live in peace and light—will we learn who we are, learn to become who we must. This may be the one task worthy of our best efforts, our greatest strength, our focused humanness.

Loren Eiseley wrote of his experience with a fox,[7] an experience pregnant in its meaning for us at this human crossroads.

> . . . It was a small fox pup from a den under the timbers who looked up at me. . . There was a vast and playful humor in his face. . . ."It has been said repeatedly that one can never, try as he will, get around to the front of the universe. Man is destined only to see its far side, to realize nature only in retreat.
>
> Yet here was the thing in the midst of the bones, the wide-eyed innocent fox inviting me to play, with the innate courtesy of its forepaws placed appealingly together, along with the mock shake of the head. The universe was swinging in some fantastic fashion around to present its face, and the face was so small that the universe itself was laughing.
>
> It was not a time for human dignity. It was time only for the careful observance of amenities written behind the stars. Gravely I arranged my forepaws while the puppy whimpered with ill-concealed excitement. . . .
> On impulse, I picked up clumsily a whiter bone and shook it in teeth that had not entirely forgotten their original purpose. Round and round we tumbled for one ecstatic moment. We were the innocent thing in the midst of the bones, born in egg, born in den, born in the dark cave . . .

As for me and millions of others, as we come to recognize our old failed stories and learn new ones, we will work for the preservation and restoration of forests and prairies, deserts and tundra across the planet. We will say with Barry Lopez, ". . . standing on farmland ankle deep in soil gone to flour dust, or flying over the Cascade Mountains and seeing the clearcuts stretching for forty miles, the sunbaked earth, the streams running with mud, . . . 'Forgive me, thou bleeding earth, that I am meek and gentle with these butchers.'"[8] And we will commit to ourselves and to each other not to be the butcher, not to bring harm.

We will look again for new chances to become the "innocent thing," to connect with each other and our fellow species in new and powerful relationships. We will commit to new stories—stories of renewal and atonement, new relationship to the Earth, new beginnings. We will no longer nor ever will again "stand aside and watch the rape of the world."

ENDNOTES

1. Tracy Chapman, "The Rape of the World," *New Beginning* (New York: Electra Entertainment Group, Warner Communications, Inc., 1995).

2. Shakespeare, *Hamlet*, act 2, scene 2, lines 314–18.

3. Thomas Kuhn, *The Structure of Scientific Revolutions*, 2nd ed. (Chicago: University of Chicago Press, 1970).

4. William Catton, Jr., and Riley Dunlap, "New Ecological Paradigm for Post-Exuberant Sociology," *American Behavioral Scientist* 24 (1980): 15–48.

5. David Ehrenfeld, *The Arrogance of Humanism* (New York: Oxford University Press, 1978).

6. Bill Devall and George Sessions, *Deep Ecology: Living as if Nature Mattered* (Salt Lake City: Peregrine Smith Books, 1985).

7. Loren Eiseley, *The Unexpected Universe* (New York: Harcourt, Brace, Jovanovich, 1969).

8. Barry Lopez, *The Rediscovery of North America*. (Lexington: The University Press of Kentucky, 1990).

Sam Rushforth is a conservation biologist working to protect cultural and biological diversity.

"WE WILL GO DOWN, FOR THERE IS SPACE THERE, AND WE WILL TAKE OF THESE MATERIALS, AND WE WILL MAKE AN EARTH WHEREON THESE MAY DWELL; AND WE WILL PROVE THEM HEREWITH, TO SEE IF THEY WILL DO ALL THINGS WHATSOEVER THE LORD THEIR GOD SHALL COMMAND THEM." (ABRAHAM 3:24–25.)

LATTER-DAY SAINTS, UTAHNS, AND THE ENVIRONMENT: A PERSONAL PERSPECTIVE

THOMAS G. ALEXANDER*

LTHOUGH I GREW UP IN OGDEN, AS A YOUNG BOY I USED TO SPEND a couple of weeks each summer on the farm owned by my grandpa, Mormon Bird, in Mendon, a small Cache Valley farming town nestled against the Wellsville Mountains west of Logan. At the time I attached a sort of romanticism to the farm in Mendon not unlike that which many environmentalists today connect with wilderness. In many ways, I still do. The farm offered a place of refuge fifty miles and a quarter century away from the unchecked growth and gut-wrenching change of World War II and postwar Ogden.

On the farm, life moved at a decidedly different pace—not easier, but different. I learned to ride horses, drive a team hitched to a hay mower and a dump rake, irrigate the vegetable and berry garden, follow the cows back and forth between the pasture and the barn, pick fruit, and hoe weeds. One year, I even whitewashed the chicken coop.

By current agribusiness standards, Grandpa owned a small outfit, perhaps 130 acres all told. He owned the property surrounding his old carpenter Gothic house, including the adjacent garden, the alfalfa field, the barnyard, the chicken coop, the pig pens, and perhaps an additional twenty acres, which he planted to sugar beets. East of town toward the Little Bear River—what local people called the Muddy—Grandpa owned a five-acre pasture and an additional ten acres, which he often planted to wheat. On the foothills of the Wellsville Mountains west of town, he raised wheat on an eighty-acre dry farm. If I completed the chores around the yard, Grandma would let me go over to Uncle John Hughes's. If I helped Uncle John with the chores, he would often let me ride his horses. Bishop of the Mendon Ward, Uncle John also scratched out a living on a farm slightly larger than Grandpa's. As I remember, he also ran a few cattle on the Wellsville Mountains west of Mendon in a pattern followed by many Mormon farmers.

Both Grandpa and Uncle John were conservative Republicans. I never really sympathized with their politics, but I shared their love of the land and of the beauty of the mountains and of Cache Valley.

Uncle John, especially, understood how people and livestock could abuse the land. He and others like him wanted to protect their farms, their homes, and the mountains. Before the Great Depression, overgrazing had denuded mountain slopes, and summer thunderstorms had inundated communities along the Wasatch and Plateau Fronts from Box Elder to Sanpete Counties with rock-mud floods. Such floods had plunged down on communities stretching from Sanpete to Box Elder Counties.

By the early 1930s Uncle John and his friends knew that the Forest Service had begun active watershed management and that forest scientists had experimented at the Great Basin Station in Ephraim Canyon and on the Davis County Experimental Watershed with new techniques to restore and preserve the land. They knew also that forest range managers had begun to reduce the large numbers of livestock that had destroyed plant cover on the mountain slopes. In management of the watersheds by the Forest Service they saw the salvation of the Wellsville Mountains and of their valley homes and farms.

In 1933, several years before I was born, Uncle John had joined together with others, including Robert H. Stewart of Brigham City and William Lathum of Wellsville, to try to acquire lands for watershed protection. Encouraged by their early success, these men organized the Wellsville Mountain Watershed Protective Association in 1936. In their campaign to protect the watersheds, they collected money from the depression-induced poverty of their friends and neighbors to purchase private lands, which they donated to the Forest Service for watershed rehabilitation. They may have seen watershed protection as a mission not unlike those they had served in foreign lands, in building the Logan Temple, or in constructing the local ward house. They also joined others in lobbying successfully with Congress to enlarge the boundaries of the Cache National Forest to encompass the lands they had purchased. Congress helped purchase other lands by allowing the Forest Service to use receipts from commercial activities such as grazing and timber sales to buy critical watershed lands within the extended national forest boundaries.

Thus, the labors of Cache Valley farmers like Uncle John and caring management by the Forest Service facilitated protection of these lands and preserved the beauty of the Wellsville Mountains. In 1984, the Utah Forest Service Wilderness Act designated an area called the Wellsville Mountain Wilderness on land that Uncle John and his friends had helped to shield and rehabilitate. Today, the Wellsville Mountain Wilderness stands as a fitting memorial to the efforts of such Latter-day Saint farmers as my uncle, Bishop John O. Hughes, who worked to protect their farms and homes and to preserve the beauty of the mountains around them.

Farmers like Uncle John were not the only Mormons who loved the land and sought to preserve its beauty. In the old Ogden 29th Ward where, as a young boy, I sat through many a long and boring sacrament meeting, I regularly saw a tall, balding man named Chester J. Olsen. Chet, as his friends called him, had been born and raised in the central Utah farming community of Mayfield. After graduating from Utah State University, he served as a ranger on forests in Nevada and Utah until 1936, when he transferred to the regional office in Ogden as an assistant regional forester. He continued to work in the Forest Service's intermountain regional office, eventually serving as regional forester from 1950 through 1957.

Shortly after World War II he helped to stop what contemporaries called "The Great Land Grab," a movement not unlike the current efforts in Utah, Nevada, and New Mexico to transfer ownership of the public lands to the states or to private interests. Along with many others, he believed that the Forest Service could provide more environmentally sensitive management for these lands than private owners.

Some stock raisers and their backers supported the transfer proposals. In the mid-1940s a band of western congressmen and senators—including Joseph C. O'Mahoney, Edward V. Robertson, and Frank Barrett of Wyoming, and, at times, Nevada's Pat McCarran—promoted legislation to meet the stock raiser's demands. In its alternative forms, the various bills would either have transferred the surface rights of national forest lands to the states for sale to stock raisers or, alternatively, have prohibited the Forest Service from reducing the number of livestock on grazing allotments.

Awakened to the goals of this movement, a group of environmentalists led by Bernard DeVoto, Lester Viele, and William Voigt began in 1946 and 1947 to publish articles opposing the land grab. Angered at the negative publicity their proposals had engendered, congressmen such as Barrett and Robertson blamed Chief Forester Lyle Watts, who had previously served in Utah, with feeding information to DeVoto and others in an attempt to thwart their efforts. In 1947, Barrett conducted hearings throughout the West in support of the legislation. At the hearings, he paraded favorable witnesses who told heartrending tales of Forest Service abuse. The *Denver Post* called the hearings "Barrett's Wild West Show."

Contrary to the congressmen's assertions, Lyle Watts probably did not feed information to DeVoto, but Chet Olsen certainly did. DeVoto, a native of Ogden and son of a Mormon mother and Catholic father, had cultivated a long-standing friendship with Olsen. During DeVoto's travels through the West in 1946, Chet, and probably others, talked with him about the land transfer proposals, and Olsen gave him copies of the stockmen's resolutions in support of Barrett's legislation. As a result, as Wallace Stegner put it in his biography, "DeVoto went West in 1946 a historian and tourist. He came back an embattled conservationist." Following that visit, DeVoto wrote more than forty articles about the West, most of them on environmental issues.

Chet Olsen did not stop after he helped convert Bernard DeVoto, however. Stung by the success of Barrett's efforts in Wyoming, he and his associates prepared for congressional hearings in 1947, especially in Salt Lake City and in Ely, Nevada. In the hearings, Latter-day Saints such as Mayor Earl J. Glade of Salt Lake City and Professor Vasco Tanner of Brigham Young University testified in opposition to Barrett's proposals, supporting the testimony of national forest officials and of other citizens. A former Forest Service official, who asked to remain anonymous but who accompanied Olsen as he attended the hearings, told me that Chet organized the Forest Service's response brilliantly. As the two men followed the hearings from place to place, Olsen spent countless hours on the phone recruiting support and encouraging people to testify. Partly as a result, witnesses representing city and county governments, mining interests, chambers of commerce, sports associations, the Boy Scouts, and labor organizations praised the Forest Service and condemned the proposed transfer. By October 4, 1947, when Barrett held his last hearings in Ely, his show had mired in the chuckhole Chet Olsen had helped to dig.

Hooked off the stage by these efforts, Barrett's committee made their recommendations to Congress in 1948, proposing simply to codify existing Forest Service multiple-use policy. Instead of proposing to transfer national forest lands to the states or even to prevent the Forest Service from reducing numbers of livestock on national forest ranges, they recommended that Congress amend the Forest Service's organic act. In a proposal that followed existing national forest policy, and which Congress incorporated in the Multiple-use Sustained Yield Act of 1960, Barrett's committee recommended that national forest management include grazing, recreation, and wildlife along with timber and watershed protection among its legitimate functions.

As his activities in the environmental movement intensified, Bernard DeVoto continued to cultivate his friendship with Chet Olsen. DeVoto died in 1955. Acceding to his wishes, his family contacted Chet. Taking charge of the body, Olsen made arrangements to have it cremated and the ashes scattered on some of the national forest land the deceased conservationist had labored so long to protect. To this day, the brass tag that had accompanied DeVoto's body on its return journey to Ogden remains housed with Chet Olsen's papers in the Weber State University archives, a symbol of the bond that tied these two environmentalists together in life and in death.

Uncle John Hughes and Chet Olsen were not the first Mormons in the twentieth century to champion environmental causes. As a senator from Utah, Elder Reed Smoot, the only member of the Council of the Twelve who has served as a United States senator, offered virtually unwavering support for the efforts of Theodore Roosevelt and Gifford Pinchot to regulate livestock grazing and timber harvesting on national forest lands. Believing that national forests offered necessary protection to such resources and to valuable watersheds, Smoot regularly supported appropriations for the Forest Service.

Moreover, he also worked to preserve the president's prerogative to encompass endangered watersheds and forests in national forest lands without congressional approval. In 1907 Smoot joined with the congressional delegations of California, Washington, and Nevada to thwart the efforts of some congressmen and senators who wanted to prohibit the president from designating national forests in their states. As it passed, the legislation required an act of Congress to designate national forests in Oregon, Idaho, Montana, Wyoming, and Colorado, but in Utah and the other states mentioned, the president could designate them by executive proclamation. Roosevelt recognized Smoot's commitment to the environmental cause by appointing him as chairman of the forestry section at the National Governor's Conference on Conservation in 1908.

Continuing his efforts for conservation, Smoot worked to support America's national parks. Along with such environmentalists as John Muir, he opposed—futilely as it proved—the Hetch Hetchy Act, which took a part of Yosemite National Park to fill a reservoir for San Francisco. Following failure with success, he placed his brand on the National Park Service Act in 1916. Working with Stephen T. Mather and Horace M. Albright, Smoot threw his strong support behind the bill introduced by Congressman William Kent of California to set up the National Park Service. The House of Representatives had included an amendment allowing grazing in national parks, which Smoot insisted on deleting. After passage of the legislation, the Wilson administration invited Smoot to be a guest speaker at the inauguration of the Park Service in January 1917. Afterward, Smoot worked successfully for designation of Zion and Bryce National Parks in Utah.

Why should a farmer and bishop such as John Hughes, a Latter-day Saint Forest Service officer such as Chet Olsen, and a general authority such as Reed Smoot have concerned themselves with the environment? Smoot, of course, tried to represent the interests of his constituents. The professions followed by Uncle John and Chet Olsen kept them in contact with the soil, the plants, and the animals. Each of these men loved the land on which they lived.

On a deeper level, however, all three men carried a Mormon religious heritage of environmental consciousness. As Mormon theologian Hugh W. Nibley, geographer Richard H. Jackson, and others have shown, nineteenth-century Mormons treasured a reverence for the land grounded in the theology taught by Joseph Smith and Brigham Young.

Strongly communitarian, Mormons sought to build the Kingdom of God on earth. In Utah, they expected to refashion the arid West first as an earthly home where they could live as God's stewards and as a fit place for Christ's Second Coming. They understood that Christ would not return to clean up the mess unmindful people made of the earth. Human beings had the responsibility to care for God's creation themselves.

To accomplish these goals, they attempted to subordinate the Euro-American entrepreneurial tradition to the gospel of Jesus Christ. Returning to the Puritan practice, they reenvisioned entrepreneurship as an aspect of the sacred; in a word they resacralized it.

At the same time Latter-day Saints extended the Christian environmental ethic, regrounding it in the teachings of men they followed as living prophets who could reveal God's word. In prophetic revelations, Joseph Smith taught the sanctity and unity of all living things. From an outlook with an affinity to that of many Native Americans and modern Gaians (native religionists who see the earth as a self-regulating ecosystem), and quite heretical to many nineteenth-century Christians, Joseph taught that animals and plants, like humans, had eternal spirits. In a revelation of March 1832, he wrote, "that which is spiritual being in the likeness of that which is temporal; and that which is temporal in the likeness of that which is spiritual; the spirit of man in the likeness of his person as also the spirit of beast and every other creature which God has created" (D&C 77:2). In a sermon on April 8, 1843, Joseph taught that beasts have souls and that God would save them in heaven. Speaking for the Lord, he said that, unlike the majority of humans, these creatures lived righteously and would eventually enjoy "eternal felicity." He said that the earth, the "mother of" all humans, possessed a soul, pained by "the wickedness of" her "children" (Moses 7:48).

On the way west and after the saints had arrived in Utah, other LDS Church leaders elaborated on these teachings. Brigham Young rebuked members of the pioneer company for killing more animals than they could eat. Apostle Orson Pratt—arguably the preeminent mid-nineteenth-century LDS theologian—taught that God had created "the spiritual part" of the earth and all earthly animals and plants in heaven "before their temporal existence," and that this creation sanctified them. Heber C. Kimball, a counselor to Young in the church's First Presidency, urged the Latter-day Saints to extend mercy "to the brute creation," since animals have spirits and God will resurrect them along with the earth and human beings. Only after the saints had learned to live in harmony as stewards with one another and with the earth, Young said, could they expect to inherit it, presumably as exalted beings, from the Lord who owned it.

As the Mormons settled Utah, Young and his associates restated and elaborated on these teachings. Young taught that the earth belonged to the Lord and that humans could hold no real title to the land and resources.

Landholders might manage God's estates but only as stewards. Moreover, Young said that if stewards did not oversee the land as good managers, the Lord required them to relinquish it to someone who would. Apostle Orson Hyde warned of the damage that overgrazing had done to the valleys, and he chastened the saints for their "inordinate desire for wealth and extensive possessions."

At the same time, Young proposed an unusual interpretation of the biblical injunction to multiply and replenish the earth. To accomplish this goal, Young urged the saints to conserve native plants and animals but also to increase the diversity of God's creations since they were "all designed to be preserved to all eternity." In view of this belief, Young fostered the importation of large varieties of alien flora and fauna to the intermountain region, while, at the same time, he urged the people to protect the species already here.

In addition to the spiritual unity of humans, the earth, and its nonhuman inhabitants under the fatherhood of God, church members drew on a holistic concept of the relationship between the temporal and spiritual to regulate settlement and the utilization of resources. In prophetic statements repeated by Brigham Young and other church leaders, Joseph Smith had taught the unity of the temporal and the spiritual. Speaking for the Lord, he said that "all things unto me are spiritual, and not at any time have I given unto you a law which was temporal" (D&C 29:34). From a theological perspective, then, the Latter-day Saints lived in an undifferentiated temporal and spiritual world, building God's kingdom on earth and in heaven under the leadership of divinely commissioned prophets. In the most profound sense, prophetic leaders expected the Mormons to reweave entrepreneurship and stewardship into a seamless garment.

Some Latter-day Saints seem to have forgotten these teachings. Willing to trade environmental protection for a mess of pottage labeled immediate gratification, too many have abused the land that they manage for God by redubbing themselves owners rather than stewards. Often, however, as the examples of Uncle John, Chet Olsen, and Reed Smoot show, Latter-day Saints have recaptured the vision of the theology taught by Joseph Smith and Brigham Young. They have recognized that we are brothers and sisters with all of God's creations, sharing with each an eternal spirit and the promise of eternal life in His presence. As sentient beings created in His image, they acknowledge that the Lord assigned humans a special stewardship—to care for His creations.

*Thomas G. Alexander: "I appreciate the assistance of a number of people on the research and thinking that underpins this article, particularly Harvard Heath, Bruce Westergren, Jennifer Lund, Sondra Jones, Andrea Radke, David Hall, Jessie Embry and her transcribers, Sharon Carver, Philip Johnson, Floyd Iverson, Stan Tixier, James Jacobs, William Hurst, Hardy and Sunny Redd, Gibbs and Catherine Smith, and William Smart."

Thomas G. Alexander is Lemuel Hardison Redd, Jr., Professor of Western American History at Brigham Young University.

"AND OUR GLORIOUS MOTHER EVE, WITH MANY OF HER FAITHFUL DAUGHTERS WHO HAD LIVED THROUGH THE AGES AND WORSHIPED THE TRUE AND LIVING GOD." (D&C 138:39.)

W E S T   O F   E D E N

TERRY TEMPEST WILLIAMS

N APPLE IS A GIFT TO A TEACHER FROM HER PUPIL. EVE SEES AN apple hanging from the Tree of Knowledge. Eve admires the fruit. God tells Eve, "You shall not eat of the fruit of the tree that is in the middle of the garden, nor shall you touch it, or you shall die." The serpent slowly wrapping itself around the tree says to Eve that if she takes a bite of the apple she will not die, "for God knows that when you eat of it your eyes will be opened, and you will be like God, knowing good and evil." Eve listens to the serpent, plucks the fruit in her desire for wisdom, and eats the apple. Eve's eyes are opened. She is naked. Adam is naked. She tastes death and hands the apple to Adam. Adam eats the apple with Eve. The serpent disappears. Adam and Eve witness the illusion of paradise, cover themselves and walk out of the garden into the wilderness.

Somewhere west of Eden, I hold in my hand a red apple like a burning globe. Eve is my teacher. I bite into the apple and partake of the fruit of the Mother. Eve's wisdom burns inside me.

I listen to the words of the Creation and imagine our own.

In the beginning God created the heaven and the earth.

Her hands hold the dust of stars and the cracked clay of the desert.

And the earth was without form, and void; and darkness was upon the face of the deep. And the Spirit of God moved upon the face of the waters.

Slowly the clay moistens with her tears and takes shape, round like her belly.

And God said, Let there be light: and there was light.

The sun rose at dawn, lifting the slickrock canyons out of darkness.

And God called the light Day, and the darkness he called Night. And the evening and the morning were the first day.

The heat reverberated from the sandstone walls like a heartbeat; the small round ball of clay began to bake on the edge of a blue pool that reflected the sky.

And God made the firmament, and divided the waters which were under the firmament from the waters which were above the firmament: and it was so. And God called the firmament Heaven. And the evening and the morning were the second day. And God said, Let the waters under the heaven be gathered together unto one place, and let the dry land appear: and it was so.

On the edge of the wash were tall green grasses, horsetails, that when broken created whistles. She picked one stalk, pulled the segments apart and blew through one end.

And God said, Let the earth bring forth grass, the herb yielding seed, and the fruit tree yielding fruit after his kind, whose seed is in itself, upon the earth: and it was so. . . . And the evening and the morning were the third day.

The green flute filled the canyon with joy until the sun set and the moon rose over the sheer cliff walls as the Milky Way poured starlight onto her bare shoulders.

And God made two great lights; the greater light to rule the day, and the lesser light to rule the night: he made the stars also. . . . And the evening and the morning were the fourth day.

As her eyes relaxed with the night, she watched an owl perched in an old cottonwood tree. The owl was silent, waiting, watching for the slightest movement on the sand. In a flash, the owl swooped down on a kangaroo rat darting from one sage to the next. Death was certain.

And God said, Let the waters bring forth abundantly the moving creature that hath life, and fowl that may fly above the earth in the open firmament of heaven. . . . And the evening and the morning were the fifth day.

She had fallen asleep and was now awakened by the sweet stirrings of the wind. It was morning. There were tracks circling around her like a script left on the sand to be read by one who knows the language of animals.

And God said, Let the earth bring forth the living creature after his kind . . . and every thing that creepeth upon the earth after his kind: and God saw that it was good.

It was good, she thought, that she was not alone but surrounded by beauty. She walked down to the river and bathed in the cold clear water of the desert that ran downcanyon like the veins of her own body, pulsing, throbbing, and delighting in the movement of life. She watched swallows dip down in the water to drink. She raised her hands to them.

And God said, Let us make man in our image, after our likeness: and let them have dominion over the fish of the sea, and over the fowl of the air, and . . . over all the earth.

She knelt down on the sandy red banks of the canyon to pray. The morning was still and peaceful. When she looked up she saw a man she knew, also naked, who spoke to her, and she was not afraid.

So God created man in his own image, in the image of God created he him;

male and female created he them. And God blessed them, and God said unto them, Be fruitful, and multiply, and replenish the earth . . .

The woman and the man walked through the canyon noticing each tree, each flower, bird, lizard, and frog. They stopped at a small pool of water to drink. They saw each other's reflection, touched the surface, watched it ripple, settle, then ripple again.

And God saw every thing that he had made, and, behold, it was very good. And the evening and the morning were the sixth day.

The couple in the desert drank and ate and found shelter in the safety of a fern-lined grotto. As the day drew to a close they slept in one another's arms and dreamed their future into being.

Thus the heavens and the earth were finished, and all the host of them. And on the seventh day God ended his work which he had made; and he rested on the seventh day from all his work which he made. And God blessed the seventh day, and sanctified it: because that in it he had rested from all his work which God created and made.

The Creation of the World is sacred.

The Marriage of Woman and Man is sacred.

Perhaps I heard my first love poem in Genesis when Adam addressed Eve upon seeing her, "This is now bone of my bones, and flesh of my flesh." Could it be that the story of the Garden of Eden is a story of love and imagination, our sincere consent for transformation, to bite into the raw experience of life and be physically and spiritually engaged in our own creation, even in the creation and sustaining drama of the earth. To separate ourselves from the presence of God is to face the illusion of paradise and embrace change in all its dimensions, the difficulties and gifts of what we discover on our own and in partnership.

Within Mormon doctrine we are told that Eden is not simply a metaphor but a place, a very large place with mountains and valleys, known as *Adam-ondi-Ahman*, meaning the place or land of God where Adam dwelt. We are also told a revelation was given to Joseph Smith on May 19, 1838, that Eden was in truth, a place in North America, specifically located in Daviess County, Missouri, named Spring Hill by the Lord. "Adam-ondi-Ahman, because, said he, it is the place where Adam shall come to visit his people, or the Ancient of Days shall sit, as spoken of by Daniel the prophet" (D&C 116).

It is believed that this is where one of the greatest spiritual gatherings of all ages took place some 5,000 years ago when Adam was blessed by the Lord and called Michael, the prince, the archangel. Adam bowed humbly before the congregation of prophets and seers and offered sacrifices upon an altar built for this occasion. It is believed a remnant of that altar remains today.

We are also instructed that another gathering of great spiritual significance will occur here again, this time, the Second Coming of Christ when

He will make the final preparations to personally reign upon the earth at the time of the Millennium.

One of the emblematic tenets of Mormon religious belief is that at the Second Coming of Christ, "the earth will be renewed and receive its paradisiacal glory." The earth will be returned to its Edenic state just as we will be returned to our physically exalted states. A belief in the resurrection, where our bodies will be restored in full from the ravages of death, is also extended to the earth.

William W. Phelps wrote these verses to an Edenic hymn during Joseph Smith's day:

This earth was once a garden place
With all her glories common,
And men did live a holy race,
And worship Jesus face to face,
In Adam-ondi-Ahman.

Her land was good and greatly blest,
Beyond old Israel's Canaan;
Her fame was known from east to west,
Her peace was great, and pure the rest,
Of Adam-ondi-Ahman.

Hosannah to such days to come—
The Savior's second coming,
When all the earth in glorious bloom
Affords the Saints a holy home,
Like Adam-ondi-Ahman.

As a writer and naturalist, I do not know whether or not the Garden of Eden was a true place, even in North America, although it is a fantastic idea. (I would say I have experienced Eden not necessarily in Daviess County, Missouri, but in the red-rock canyons of southern Utah or in the Tetons and the Yellowstone Plateau of the Northern Rockies.)

What I do believe in, however, is the divine Creation, that the earth is holy, created out of an intelligence we may only begin to glimpse through the lenses of science: astronomy, geology, and physics. Perhaps my original impulse to pursue an understanding of biology and the ecological relationships that bind us together as living organisms was my desire to come that much closer to an understanding of God, even the love of God.

Thinking about the Garden of Eden from another vantage point, it becomes a poignant story of our separation from Creation, the acknowledgement that all the dazzling fruits that dangle from the Tree of Knowledge will not give us the wisdom we long for regarding our relationship to the earth. We must taste it for ourselves—the delicious, spontaneous, beautiful, terrible omnipotence of nature. The earth is the physical face of God in all its majesty and terror. I do not blame Eve for choosing to bite into the apple. I thank her. I thank her for opening our eyes to our limitations and what it means to be human. We are all complicit in the Garden of Good and Evil.

God said, "Don't." The Serpent said, "Do." Eve said, "I will find out for myself," and she shares her experience with Adam. Together in partnership, with open eyes, they turn their backs on the illusion of Eden as paradise and walk into the desert, a landscape that will dream them into good stewards simply by their desire to drink water. Their survival and the survival of future generations will depend on this marriage of righteous intention. Eve leads us into a redemptive relationship with the natural world through humility.

> *And Eve . . . heard all these things and was glad, saying: Were it not for our transgression we never should have had seed, and never should have known good and evil, and the joy of our redemption, and the eternal life which God giveth unto all the obedient. (Moses 5:11.)*

A sustainable relationship with the earth nurtures a sustainable relationship with God because we acknowledge and honor the power of reciprocity, that there are, in fact, limits and consequences of what we desire. If we act on the premise that we are not alone, that other individuals and creatures have wants and needs, that our definition of community is not just human-centered but creation-centered, then we begin to engage in a spiritual economics that promises to be more unselfish than our present relationship to Other. We cannot continue to simply take from the earth without giving back something in return, even if that means drawing on principles of restraint, generosity, gratitude, and compassion.

We cannot return to Eden. We know too much and we care too little about the complexities of our collective past. But perhaps we can find our way toward a *new genesis,* a wiser relationship toward Creation that is founded on the sacred principles of love and respect and empathy.

How do we remain mindful of the divine nature of the earth?

How do we honor the Creation through our actions?

How is an ecological ethic that considers the health of the land as our own adopted within our families and communities?

The Book of Revelations tells us that what has been broken can be healed.

One fall morning while I was writing in a tiny cabin at the base of the Tetons, a bluebird, female, hit my window as she was flying with her mate. I opened the door, walked out on the porch and found her stunned, lying on her back. I picked her up, gently cupped her limp body in my hands, and sat down on a willow rocking chair. Her breathing was labored, her beak open, her left eye bulging. Slowly with each breath her head lowered until she rested her chin on my fingers. Her feathered body pulled itself in like a triangle.

Time.

In time, she became stronger, her breathing more regular. I loosened the cradle of my hands, straightened her left wing and folded it gently over the other across the back of her tail, then held her farther away from my body like an offering to the sky. With a cock of her head, her large black eye watched me and stared. I bowed my head, not to frighten her but to acknowledge that I meant her no harm. A flock of kin were circling the cabin like wind. Her head straightened, her gaze strengthened, her left eye seemed to relax. Her breathing slowed down and I began breathing with her, her little body rising and falling with each breath, rising and falling, my hands rising and falling with her, no thought, just breathing, a bluebird and a woman breathing, the depths of her eyes steady on mine—and then her posture changed.

In an instant she flew—she flew almost vertically until suddenly, she was met by her mate, who extended his wing and lifted her, carried her with his wings, upward; they circled the golden meadow wet from morning dew and then swooped down into the grasses. A chattering, a fluttering of wings ensued as if to tell each other their private longings—and then they rose once again over the meadow, banked south, and joined the flock of blue-birds who were still circling, waiting, on this day of migration in the fall.

Balzac writes, "The union of a spirit of love with a spirit of wisdom lifts the creature into the divine state in which the soul is woman and the body man." Could the Garden of Eden reappear each time this marriage of Creation occurs?

I believe in our reconciliation with nature. I believe that we can engage ourselves in small simple acts that loom large in a day, that there is a reci-procity that occurs when we allow ourselves to touch and be touched by Creation. I do not believe we are indifferent to the world's pain, nor is the world indifferent to our suffering. We simply have forgotten how deeply connected we are to nature, especially our own divine nature reflected in the eyes of Other.

When God said, "and it was good," after each day of Creation, perhaps He was offering us a clue as to our own sense of purpose, the importance of reflection, of spending time appreciating beauty, its inherent capacity to heal and bring forth joy and the realization that order out of chaos is the manifestation of our own creativity.

We are not passive inhabitants on this earth. We are capable of extraor-dinary acts of faith that we can exercise on behalf of life. And in these quiet gestures of hope, we can advance a theology of the earth that is compatible with the dream of Adam-ondi-Ahman, that here, even in Zion, we might gather spiritually to carry the fire of Eve's desire for intimacy with all Creation, and honor the humility housed within her heart that recognizes our place in wildness.

Terry Tempest Williams is a writer who lives in Salt Lake City, Utah. Her books, which reflect her intimate relationship with the natural world, include *Pieces of White Shell: A Journey to Navajoland* **(1984),** *Coyote's Canyon* **(1989),** *Refuge: An Unnatural History of Family and Place* **(1991),** *An Unspoken Hunger: Stories from the Field* **(1994), and most recently,** *Desert Quartet: An Erotic Landscape.*

"THEY SHALL ABUNDANTLY UTTER THE MEMORY OF THY GREAT GOODNESS, AND SHALL SING OF THY RIGHTEOUSNESS." (PSALMS 145:7.)

THE MEMORY OF LANDSCAPE

HUGH W. PINNOCK

 NE OF GOD'S GREATEST GIFTS TO EACH OF US IS MEMORY. TO BE able to recall experiences that we have had, even beginning at a young age, is an endowment of immeasurable worth. Most of my feelings for our Heavenly Father's world are based on experiences I had with my father and our special friends out of doors. My earliest recollections in life are of peering with my dad into the streams such as the Provo, Weber, Logan, and Bear that tumbled from the Wasatch and Uinta mountain canyons, those diamond-clear streams that eventually found their way to the Great Salt Lake, creating the extensive wetlands that circle it like emeralds.

My father and I loved to hear the noise and smell the pungent odors found in the mudflats and marshes as thousands of ducks, only a few geese back then, snipes, pelicans, gulls, curlews, and coots would paddle about or fly overhead. I can still remember the beautiful autumn days breaking open with the golden eastern sky filled with black silhouettes of ducks flying south.

Once as a little boy in the third grade, I looked up at recess and saw the Vs of migrating geese, so high in the sky they were almost indiscernible, making their way south to warmer climates. At about the same time, a lovely elderly lady would take a friend of mine and me to the Audubon lectures that were held at Kingsbury Hall at the University of Utah. She loved to teach us about birds.

I remember another occasion when my friend and I were walking to this same woman's home and discovered a pyracantha hedge filled with noisy elegant brown birds. We ran to her house, knocked on her door, and asked her what kinds of birds these could be, with top notches and such smooth brown-and-orange feathers with yellow dots on them. We had never seen them before. She enthusiastically explained that they were cedar waxwings traveling through Salt Lake City from Canada on their way to a warmer place.

217

Years later, one of our sons and his wife spotted these same beautiful birds migrating north and stopping for a snack in their berry bushes. They had never seen them before. They called me to inquire what they might be.

"Waxwings," I replied, recalling my same boyhood discovery.

Now they too will carry the memory of this special species of bird.

Since those early memories, I have continued my love of nature, floating some of the great rivers of the world looking for fish, birds, moose, and other animals. And I persist in loving the wonders of the earth in which we live as new memories are created with friends and family.

I have learned while fishing a stream, hiking a rocky trail, or climbing a mountain, that most individuals with whom I come in contact in nature are among the most honorable folks in the world. Have you noticed how a continual exposure to nature seems to make one a better person? Perhaps it is because in being closer to nature we become closer to the nature of God.

If the natural world affects us in such special ways, perhaps it would be wise to penetrate deeply the reasons this is true. In our childhood, each of us was introduced to Adam and Eve and the Garden of Eden when a parent, relative, or Sunday School teacher would read us stories from the Bible. We became aware of the power of nature as Noah sailed away with his gopher-wood ship full of animals that God had asked him to transport in order to save from drowning. Or perhaps, in our mind's eye, we see Moses splitting the Red Sea so his little band of Israelites could escape from the Egyptians. Or maybe we turn to Ezekiel who spoke of the importance of being good shepherds not only of animals but each other. In the simple wisdom of Bible stories, birds and animals are central to the teachings of compassion and humility.

We are not alone.

The number of birds and animals found in the scriptures are noticeable to anyone who takes a moment in their musings to observe them. Birds occupy center stage with sparrows, eagles, vultures, grebes, kites, pigeons, owls, pelicans, nighthawks, cuckoos, swans, bitterns, ravens, hawks, hurons, storks, lapwings, cranes, and swallows, to name just a few.

Animals and reptiles such as lions, bears, wolves, camels, leopards, elephants, deer, snakes, adders, and turtles are also written about by those designated as prophets or teachers.

The natural world is part of our spiritual imagination and education.

Parley P. Pratt, drawing upon his memory, wrote about spring in a devoted manner while expressing his deep love of nature.

'Tis the spring of the year,
All the fountains are full,
All nature is pregnant with life and love;
A chorus of voices ascend from each pool,
A myriad of songsters enliven the grove.

To her nest in the Andes, the condor retires,
    The winds from Magellan no longer prevail,
And Sol, with the north breeze returning,
    Inspires new life on the zephyr, and love on the gale.

The forest is clad in its robes of fresh green—
    Where the dove sings an anthem, his mate to decoy.
The orchard is dressed as a holiday queen,
    And the rosebud is bursting with fullness of joy.

The orange, the olive, the fig and the vine,
    Are clothed as in Eden, with innocent bloom:
The earth is an altar of incense divine,
    Exhales a sweet odor of richest perfume.
—Parley P. Pratt Autobiography, p. 362

Again, through personal experience and memory, we come to a sweet contemplation of nature and our place within Creation.

Another early Mormon leader, President John Taylor wrote,

But as an intelligent being, if I have a mind capable of reflection, I wish to contemplate the works of nature, and to know something of nature's God, and my destiny. I love to view the things around me; to gaze upon the sun, moon, and stars; to study the planetary system, and the world we inhabit; to behold their beauty, order, harmony, and the operations of existence around me. I can see something more than mean jargon, those childish quibbles, this heaven beyond the bounds of time and space, where they have nothing to do but sit and sing themselves away to everlasting bliss, or go and roast on gridirons. There is nothing like that to be found . . . in the world. Whether you look at birds, beast, or the human system, you see something exquisitely beautiful and harmonious, and worthy of contemplation of all intelligence. What is man's wisdom in comparison to it? I could not help but believe there was a God, if there was no such thing as religion in the world. (Journal of Discourses 1:151–52, June 12, 1853.)

Nature and memory. Memory and nature. How thankful I am that we live within a society that understands, at least in part, our great blessings pertaining to nature and our responsibility to assist others in appreciating this part of our heritage.

Brigham Young, displaying his own remarkable memory and feelings about nature, calls for an environmental education among our youth with his counsel:

Then let there be good teachers in the school rooms; and have beautiful gardens, and take the little folks out and show them the beautiful flowers, and teach them in their childhood the names and properties of every flower and plant, teaching them to understand which are astringent, which cathartic; this is useful for coloring, that is celebrated for its combination

219

of beautiful colors, etc. Teach them the lessons of beauty and usefulness while they are young, instead of letting them play in the dirt, making mud balls, and drawing mud in their hats, and soiling their dresses, and cultivate their mental powers from childhood up. When they are old enough, place within their reach the advantages and benefits of a scientific education. Let them study the formations of the earth, the organization of the human system, and other sciences; such a system of mental culture and discipline in early years is of incalculable benefit to its possessor in mature years. Take for instance, the young ladies now before me, as well as the young men, and form a class in geology, in chemistry or mineralogy; and do not confine their studies to theory only, but let them practice what they learn from books, by defining the nature of the soil, the composition or decomposition of rock, how the earth was formed, its probable age, and so forth. All these are problems which science attempts to solve, although some of the views of our great scholars are undoubtedly very speculative. In the study of the sciences I have named, our young folks will learn how it is that, in traveling in our mountains, we frequently see seashells— shells of the oyster, clam, etc. Ask our boys and girls now to explain these things, and they are not able to do so; but establish classes for the study of sciences, and they will become acquainted with the various facts they furnish in regard to the condition of the earth. It is the duty of the Latter-day Saints, according to revelations, to give their children the best educations that can be procured, both from the books of the world and the revelations of the Lord. If our young men will study the sciences, they will stop riding fast horses through the streets, and other folly and nonsense which they are now guilty of, and they will become useful and honorable members of the community. (Journal of Discourses 17:45–46, April 18, 1874.)

One of my favorite retreats now for our family—our children, and our grandchildren—is our cabin near the edge of Bear Lake. To the north, acres upon acres of wetlands abound with the grace of shorebirds, ducks, and geese. I think of my father. I think of our children and their children and the great continuation of nature. We are bound by memories of landscape, even wings as these blessed birds fly above us generation after generation.

Through the years, we have kept a checklist of the birds we have seen so that we might cherish and remember them. I share with you a list that we compiled at Bear Lake in just a few days one time we were there. Their names and diversity is a reminder of this glorious Creation and our humble responsibility toward all God's creatures:

Avocet
Barn owl
Red-wing blackbird
Yellow-headed blackbird
Brewer's blackbird

Great blue heron
Bufflehead
Canadian goose
Chinese pheasant
Common nighthawk
Coot
Bronze-headed cowbird
Crow
Long-billed curlew
Red-shafted flicker
Ferruginous hawk
Grackle
California gull
Franklin gull
White-faced ibis
Kestrel
Killdeer
Mallard
Magpie
Marsh hawk
Western meadowlark
Mourning dove
White pelican
Pintail
Raven
Red-tail hawk
Robin
Sandhill crane
English sparrow
Grasshopper sparrow
Song sparrow
Spoonbill
Starling
Bank swallow
Barn swallow
Cliff swallow
Cinnamon teal
Green-wing teal
Western grebe

Hugh W. Pinnock has been a General Authority for The Church of Jesus Christ of Latter-day Saints for the past twenty years, serving as a Seventy.

> *"AND IT PLEASETH GOD THAT HE HATH GIVEN ALL THESE THINGS UNTO MAN; FOR UNTO THIS END WERE THEY MADE TO BE USED, WITH JUDGMENT, NOT TO EXCESS, NEITHER BY EXTORTION." (D&C 59:20.)*

WILDERNESS IN THE HAND OF GOD

WAYNE OWENS

N THE BEGINNING GOD CREATED THE HEAVENS AND THE EARTH, and now much later it's up to us to see whether we save any of that original creation. The debate over wilderness preservation has always had religious overtones. John Muir wrote, "John the Baptist was not more eager to baptize the sinners in the River Jordan than I am to baptize mine in the glory of the wilderness." But there's been a deep ambivalence in Christianity's view of nature and wilderness, although the balance has been shifting during the last two centuries in favor of the wilderness argument, and a much closer tie has been established between God and wild nature in most people's minds. The connection between things natural and things divine among Mormons has generally followed what has happened among many other Christian groups.

Historically, wilderness has been characterized as a fearful place for much of religious thought, at least in the Judeo-Christian ethic. Eastern religions seem to have a closer relationship and a greater reverence with the natural world. They have not been burdened so much perhaps with the notion of man's dominance over nature. A *himsa*, a main tenet of Hinduism, is translated into English as a reverence for life and is the cornerstone for Aldo Leopold's land ethic in his *Sand County Almanac*. My relationship in recent years with many believers of Islam has led me to the conclusion that Moslems hold natural things in very high regard.

In the Judeo-Christian ethic, "wilderness" is interchangeable in the Bible with the word "desert," and "desert" has traditionally implied spiritual and physical deprivation. On the other hand, water and gardens mean physical and spiritual health, as in baptism and the Garden of Eden. Making the desert, or wilderness, bloom with flowers and plant life then meant changing the characteristics of wilderness and bringing God's approbation upon the land by making it green and fruitful. Not until the Israelites journeyed into the wilderness for forty years did wilderness as a concept begin to take on some positive attributes as a place of refuge, freedom, purging, testing, and spiritual growth. Elijah and John the Baptist found strength in the wilderness. The Psalms of David exude peace as they describe the hills and still waters. The tops of the mountains have traditionally been a place of refuge for prophets, particularly as they seek communion with the Lord. The Savior himself spent forty days and forty nights in the wilderness. To him, apparently, it was the place of greatest strengthening as he prepared for his ministry.

On the other hand, we are told that the natural man is an enemy to God, and has been since the beginning. Adam was instructed that man is to exercise dominion over the earth. Perhaps this freed Cotton Mather and other preachers to frighten their New England congregations in the early 1700s with the tales of "the rabid and howling wolves of the wilderness which will make havoc among you and not leave until the morning." Wilderness frightened the churches in colonial America because morality and social order disappeared where wilderness began. Nathaniel Hawthorne's *Scarlet Letter* was representative of the belief that the forest harbored sinners and devils. Perhaps the relative anarchy in the wilderness was unnerving because, as Robert Frost wrote, "We fear our own desert places, the wild parts of our souls, we fear our own instincts." The taming of the wilderness and the spread of Christianity went together across the continent and much of the world.

But sometime in the mid-1700s, positive views of wilderness began to emerge. Roderick Nash, writing in *Wilderness in the American Mind*, notes that American society began to relate godliness and beauty with the wilderness that had been spiritually terrifying. The romantic period swept Europe and then America, and wilderness appreciation was an important component. Rousseau popularized the *Noble Savage* and advised Europeans to return to their primitive roots. By 1918 Estwick Evans in the United States was writing, "There is something in the very nature of wilderness which charms the ear and soothes the spirit of man. There is religion in it."

We all remember Lord Byron who wrote in 1860, "There is a pleasure in the pathless woods, there is a rapture on the lonely shore, there is society where none intrudes. I love not the man less, but nature more." Deists with nature at the core of their belief as the best way to approach God, arose in New England. Transcendentalists such as Emerson and Thoreau popularized the idea, now widely accepted, that God's essence was best perceived in his untarnished creations.

In this age, and partly under these influences, Mormonism was born in Thoreau's and Emerson's New England. Mormonism, as a recipient of these influences, and Joseph Smith were both more closely aligned with appreciation of nature and wilderness than most other Christian faiths were. For example, Mormon theology teaches that the earth itself has a spirit. This goes well beyond even St. Francis of Assisi, who was branded as a heretic for trying to save the souls of animals. We believe the earth groaned and the rocks were rent at the crucifixion of Jesus. We sing hymns about earth and her ten thousand flowers and all the creatures of our God and King. The Doctrine and Covenants counsels us not to waste flesh if we have no need. Our concept of the creation as expressed in the Pearl of Great Price depicts a universe that was not created ex nihilo (out of nothing) but organized from existing matter according to natural laws.

Numerous latter-day prophets have been inspired by the beauty of God's creation and have expressed similar environmentally progressive thoughts. In the earliest written account of the First Vision, Joseph Smith recorded that he was inspired to seek God in large part by the beauty of nature. In the march of Zion's camp, he counseled respect for all creatures, even rattlesnakes. Spencer Kimball spoke of not shooting the little birds, and David O'McKay and Heber J. Grant expressed consistent thoughts on this subject to the church membership. Brigham Young taught remarkably prescient and enlightened doctrines about man's relationship to the natural world. This comment by Brother Brigham is one I like the most:

> There's only so much property in the world. There are elements that belong to this globe and no more. We do not go to the moon to borrow, neither lend to the sun or any of the planets. All our commercial transactions must be confined to this little earth and its wealth cannot be increased or diminished.

Brigham Young's granddaughter Marianne Morgan Young, when age ninety-two, wrote me an emotional and touching letter in support of my wilderness proposal with two insightful quotes from her grandfather, both documented in the *Journal of Discourses*. "The soil, the air, the water, are all pure and healthy. Do not suffer them to become polluted in the wilderness." And secondly Brother Brigham asks, "Are you not dissatisfied and is there not bitterness in your feelings the moment you find a canyon put in the possession of an individual and power given unto him to control the timber, wood, rock, grass, and in short, all its facilities?"

The Mormon exodus, so similar to the exodus of ancient Israel, provided our own tests of strength and added to our special perspective on the wilderness.

Our doctrine is enormously progressive as it relates to the environment, but our cultural interpretation has not followed suit. Our theology has not translated politically into a powerful environmental ethic. Some hope is found, however, that the Mormon public is increasingly sensitive to things environmental. Why this reticence on the part of so many to preserve God's greatest handiwork? How can this be?

It seems to me there are at least two reasons. First, Utah is two-thirds federally owned and our red-rock wilderness is located in the areas of the state with the least economic vitality. Traditionally, the wilderness has represented in people's minds an untapped source of local wealth. Wilderness appreciation runs counter, or at least secondary, to the pioneers' need for the earth to be placed in the service of man. Wilderness is not generally harvested, mined, or worn, and man's economic and survival interests collide to some degree with the idea of preservation. Struggling pioneers and other colonists have not often waxed eloquent about the wilderness. Mormon pioneers focused almost entirely upon the difficulty of carving out a basic life in the wilderness. Not surprisingly then, support for the wilderness movement in Utah has always come from the urban areas where there is precious little wilderness quality left.

Second, perhaps Mormon reticence to worry about preserving the wilderness and wildness came with one interpretation of man's stewardship over the earth. Some believe that the earth must be used by man or it will go to waste. This view, which was never official Mormon doctrine, is giving way to the view that wise stewardship requires, or at least permits, conservation. This planet is one of the greatest gifts given to man, and what we do with it is one of our greatest tests. As we believe, this earth will receive a place in the celestial kingdom and will be the residence for those who receive a celestial glory. The scriptures prophesy that the desert would blossom as a rose. Surely this has come to pass in Utah, where natural water supplies make our desert one of the few that are irrigable on a sustainable basis, and where the blossoming desert provided sustenance for the Saints seeking refuge from persecution. But the prophecy does not mean that every desert must be made to "blossom" according to the view of developers and other unsustainable users. There are clearly times when the desert should blossom as a desert.

None of this means that wilderness is not to be used by man. Our view of wilderness does not preclude use; in fact, such a view would find practically no popular support. Wilderness preservation in America reflects more precisely a preference for nonconsumptive use over consumptive use, which is a reversal of the historical order. Wilderness preservation is not altruistic and disinterested. The movement and the law exist to serve man's purposes. We preserve wilderness because it brings important spiritual and restorative benefits to us and, secondarily, to other living things. Our citizens want access to unspoiled areas, and the Wilderness Act was a political, not biological, decision based on genuine human need, although there are biological benefits from protection of the wilderness.

Perhaps other ideas also give rise to an anti-environmental mind-set on the part of the Mormons and other Christians. The belief that the earth is doomed to destruction anyway before Christ's Second Coming, no matter how we take care of it, is a subtle argument against wilderness preservation. James Watt, the fox who was left to guard the henhouse at the Department of the Interior, publicly used that rationale to explain his anti-environmental positions. Gratefully, this idea does not seem to have been given much place in the Mormon mind. As we anticipate the return of our Lord, it makes sense to prepare the earth by preserving its beauty, not despoiling it. Who in their right mind messes up the house on purpose before receiving an important guest?

Some Christians resist the philosophical underpinnings of the theory of evolution, and this may also play a part in their perception of the natural world. Such persons may feel less kinship with the rest of creation, thus treating it with less respect and less affection. Hopefully this view is weakening. Whatever one thinks of evolution, we know that our Heavenly Father is so powerful and all-knowing that he cares when a sparrow falls. It seems safe to assume that he sorrows when a species becomes extinct. Yet none of this displaces the human from the potentially exalted position as a literal child of God. Mormons, of all people, should understand that it is not necessary to destroy nature to gain God's attention for humanity.

When I visit the canyon country of southern Utah where I grew up and where I ran cattle as a teenager, when I contemplate its extraordinary blend of sandstone shapes and colors, I am unfailingly inspired and lifted up by that experience. To me, it is a religious experience. I cannot believe and my mind cannot accept that this remarkable, unmatched beautiful product of ages and ages of natural sculpting was intended by God to be changed irretrievably by man in his thoughtless, relentless search for economic gain or his egotistical need to conquer and subjugate. I do believe that with the preponderance of doctrinal evidence on our side, we are finally, in fact, moving towards a deeper appreciation of wilderness as a religious concept.

We know that Jesus considered the lilies of the field, how they grew. Sigurd Olsen was right when he postulated that "each of us has a spiritual need for wilderness at the core of our being no matter how urban or how urbane we may be." We need wilderness for our spiritual health. We need it, as Frederick Jackson Turner and Bob Marshall believed, to maintain our national character, which was, as Turner wrote, "born in a forest wilderness." Wilderness brings us strength and vitality. It is no coincidence that the movement began in earnest in the early 1900s, just when the nation began to feel sapped and weakened by severe urban degradation. Interest in wilderness has tended to peak during times of societal disillusionment and discontent, just as the wilderness movement has subsided during periods of complacency and contentment. The discord of the sixties and seventies is indicative of the former, and the self-satisfaction of the fifties and the eighties is illustrative of the latter. If we see little of the degradation of the city, we will not be moved by the contrast with the purity of the wilderness, and if we cannot experience the natural beauty in the wilderness, we will not be as offended by the failures of city life.

Some of those who live in Utah's wilderness areas do not share my enthusiasm for wilderness protection, though they too love the land and want much of it to stay in its natural condition. Where you stand on wilderness protection often depends on where you sit. We must recognize the need of these local people and their right to live on and with the land. Most of all we must avoid any appearance of an argument that the land must be preserved and protected for the recreational or restorative use of those of us who have moved to the cities where naturalism has been sacrificed already to permit us to make our own livings. However, there are some natural places left that are so unusually beautiful, so extraordinarily and magnificently different that they must be preserved for the benefit and enrichment of all men and women and children for generations to come, whether they live in the city or the area involved.

The love of wilderness represents a powerful homing instinct we will never relinquish. John Muir wrote, "Going to the woods is going home." There is a love of wild nature in everybody—an ancient mother love showing itself, whether recognized or not. When cities were rare and wilderness common, the obvious goal was to conquer and civilize the earth. But now, as cities and development predominate and wilderness is overwhelmed, the equally obvious solution is to preserve the wilderness that remains. Americans and Mormons need to be touched by the spiritual value of wilderness, to be aware that wilderness is a place of holiness, refuge, and challenge. Edward Abbey said, "We should treat our wilderness with deference, for it is a holy place." John Muir agreed, "The hills and groves were God's first temples." Wilderness is a window on the Creation; it's the only place to see the Creation anew. Once again John Muir expressed this thought succinctly, "I used to envy the Father of our race, dwelling as he did in contact with the new-made fields and plants of Eden. But I do so no more because I have discovered that I also live in creation's dawn. The morning stars still sing together, and the world not yet half made becomes more beautiful every day."

Sometime ago I had occasion to drive through the same wilderness where the Savior spent his forty days and nights. It is unchanged from the days when Jesus taught there, according to the geologists. It is brown and colorless and lacking in the magnificent sweep of color that is the glory of Utah's wilderness. It is also, to my eyes, harsh and inhospitable. And yet the Savior loved it. He found strength and solitude and peace in it. I stood on a hillside there and, as the hot winds blew, I tried to imagine what the days and nights were like in that barren land of hills and valleys when the Savior was there. I found I could relate—it was wilderness and it went on as far as the eye could see, and I could sense how one could love it and come to find oneself in it.

We should never give up the privilege of enjoying and relating to wilderness or permit our children, our grandchildren, or their great-great-grandchildren to be deprived of it. Whether we are talking about the state or about the planet, once gone, wilderness can never be replaced—never.

I believe in God, I feel His existence, and I am profoundly influenced by my absolute conviction that He is alive and that this earth is among his great achievements. I view its beauty and magnificence as evidence that He loves us, for He gave us such an exquisite place to live. Wilderness is a window on creation. It is the easiest, clearest way to see the hand of God. We should not and we will not give it up without a fight.

Wayne Owens served in Congress for eight years, representing Utah's Second Congressional District and fulfilling an appointment to the Foreign Affairs Committee, where he chose to concentrate his efforts on the Middle East. He is now president of the Center for Middle East Peace and Economic Cooperation.

"AND OUT OF THE GROUND MADE I, THE LORD GOD, TO GROW EVERY TREE, NATURALLY, THAT IS PLEASANT TO THE SIGHT OF MAN; AND MAN COULD BEHOLD IT. AND IT BECAME ALSO A LIVING SOUL. FOR IT WAS SPIRITUAL IN THE DAY THAT I CREATED IT; . . . " (MOSES 3:9.)

WHAT I HAVE LEARNED AND HOW I LEARNED IT

GIBBS M. SMITH

COME HIKE ALONG WITH ME

 LL I KNOW IS WHAT I KNOW. I'VE TRIED OCCASIONALLY OVER THE years to act out of another place that is not from the bedrock of what I know but from what I thought would be socially acceptable or popular or what someone else wanted me to say or think. My experience has taught that for me this never works. However, if I get in touch with what I really know, then I can act out of confidence and my actions and words are not hollow.

What I'm attempting in this essay is to speak about what I really know about being a Mormon and an environmentalist, and to do this with a sincere heart. My goal in this essay is to send a message to other people who may know the same things I know. If you know what I know, I urge you to speak up and influence events. This is a time when many wonderful things related to environmental issues can happen, and we must let ourselves be heard.

Like many people, I went through a period of feeling generally alienated. For a while my desire was to oppose the status quo and be alienated from every aspect of my life: church, government, school, all except my family. My family was my base. My parents always loved me unconditionally and trusted me and gave me the support and freedom to find my own way. I actually enjoyed the feeling of alienation because it is a definite feeling of being alive. I believe it is also an indication one is evolving into the person he really is. But in my soul I knew that I didn't want to stay alienated. It was a place to move through and out of, not to stay in for one's whole life.

There is something about me that always knew that I need and long for spiritual harmony and peace. And the way I first discovered this harmony and peace was through nature. I intuitively knew that the natural world was, for me, an avenue to God. So nature became a school of experience that has been a great solace spiritually.

My spiritual development through nature began on walks with my mother. These are some of my earliest recollections. We lived in Oakland, California, and our walks were around Lake Merritt, where we fed water fowl, and around the well-manicured neighborhood of the Oakland hills.

Often on these walks, my mother would rub my hand over the bark of trees. I learned some are smooth, like the sycamore, and some are rough, like the pine. I learned the names of trees. My mother would pick up stones and hand them to me. We liked to put small smooth ones in our pockets. I learned to love the smell and feel of rocks heated by the sunlight. We would pick up leaves and look at the veins, shapes, and colors. My mother would ask me to look at the color of the sunlight at different times of day. My favorite sunlight was the pale and soft light of Bay Area mornings. On our walks, we could feel the cool moist air on our cheeks.

That was the beginning. I learned to feel at home outdoors, observing and delighting in nature. I learned that I could stop thinking and just be still. I learned that I was happy. Long walks still smooth out my mind and make me happy.

Moving to Utah with my family as a child was a shocking experience. Gone was well-manicured nature. When we moved to Kaysville, Utah, in 1948, most of the paved roads ended just out of town and turned to dirt. The sidewalks were mostly overrun with weeds or nonexistent. The sunlight was harsh, and the air was dry. The winters were cold. The summers were hot.

But gradually, I came to know and love the raw beauty of Utah. I liked becoming aware of how nature made patterns and how nature harmonized colors. My teachers were the mountains rising to the east and west of my home. Over many years, I observed the mountains in various seasons. Sagebrush, oak, and maple grew in pleasing patterns on the mountain slopes. Snow melted in patterns that were quite regular and predictable year after year. Colors changed with the seasons. Storm clouds often sliced along the face of the mountain in a clear and definable line. The natural drama of the mountains became part of me. Especially during uncertain teenage years I was helped by mountains.

I grew up east of Antelope Island. As a child, year after year I could keep my eye on the island from the second floor of my old grade school. It became a teacher as I watched storms roll in over the lake and envelop the land. Sometimes lightning struck the Junegrass and burned the island. I learned to measure the severity of winter storms by measuring the snow line on Antelope Island. I could tell spring was coming as the sun moved back between two of the island's peaks. I could tell my directions by noting where the island was.

The island, the lake, and the mountains became my psychic lodestones as a child. I knew where I was and who I was, partly by positioning myself with them.

Until I was out of college, I knew little of southern Utah. Few of my friends ventured out to explore; and although I met new friends who lived as far into the southern "wilderness" as Richfield, they seemed to be glad to have escaped to urban Salt Lake City.

Occasionally in a geology or history class, I heard references to events that had occurred or to unusual geologic or geographic features in the south. I was involved in vague discussions about how the growing Glen Canyon Dam would eventually flood Glen Canyon.

But it was not until several years later, after I married my wife, Catherine —and after I had moved back to Utah following seven years in Santa Barbara, California, where we started our publishing company—that I ever really went to southern Utah to look at it and experience it. During these years, I kept up the pattern of walking and observing. As we had little money, we started exploring Utah for recreation. We hiked and camped over a good portion of it. That was our peace and our solace during the difficult years of starting a company.

How I Used What I Know

Finally, by the early 1980s, we had enough confidence in our economic survival to consider adding another dimension to our lives. We felt the urge to become involved in other commitments and to contribute to the society in which we lived in other ways. My choice was to become active in the Sierra Club. I had long been a dues-paying member but had done nothing else. After this decision, I started attending chapter meetings where I knew no one, somewhat apprehensive of the time commitments I might be drawn into. I worried that it was more than I could handle. Gradually, I became acquainted and took on small tasks such as participating in mailing parties, calling people, raising money, and helping to organize chapter events.

Also, there was hiking and camping with Sierra Club friends. As we knew the land from our own experience, we were confident we could talk and walk the land with anyone. We liked the people we met. One's religion was not an issue. But gradually I became aware that I was about the only Mormon involved.

Over the years, we've become very good friends with the group of people who were and still are Sierra Club activists in Utah. We met people who, in their professional lives, held very responsible professions by day and in the evenings and weekends attended Sierra Club meetings, to organize mailings, testify at public hearings, organize others, and work on issues such as air quality, water quality, wilderness preservation, and more. I learned to love my Sierra Club friends while working with them on issues that affect the quality of life for everyone.

It was on hikes and camping trips that I learned my fellow Sierra Club activists were like me and had also learned on their own to feel at home in nature. We love the smell of sunshine on rocks in the desert, the smell of thundershowers on desert vegetation, the color of shadows in the high plateaus, the bite of chill air during winter hikes on clear cold sunlit days. And yes, we sometimes even hug trees!

Our young daughter began going on these hikes. On a memorable hike down Ashdown Gorge, east of Cedar City, I carried her on my shoulders all day, crossing exposed ridges and jumping from rock to rock down a streambed. Steadily over the years she increased her strength and ability, and now, at seventeen, she hikes up front with the best and strongest.

For many years, I have also been involved with SUWA, the Southern Utah Wilderness Alliance. I joined their first board of directors because I thought it was important that the group was started to protect Utah wilderness and that it was headquartered in Utah. SUWA has expanded its membership nationally, and I sense the same dedication and selfless service in the organizers and current leadership of SUWA as I feel in the Sierra Club. In fact, many are the same people.

Over the years as I have worked in these organizations—becoming, for a five-year period, the chapter chair of the Sierra Club in Utah—I found few fellow Mormons among my environmentalist friends. I have never understood why.

This thought was shared by other isolated Mormons working independently on environmental concerns. Why, we wondered, did the undoubted enthusiasm of our Mormon acquaintances for the outdoors not translate to attending hearings on clean air, saving wilderness, voicing concern over the building of highways or over the quality of our natural life? Were people too busy to get involved? Perchance did they actually believe that environmentalists were crazy extremists as voiced by shortsighted local political leaders? Would a nudge by the general church leadership to be actively engaged in good causes produce devotees and activists?

Consider the thoughtful statement by Elder Jeffrey Holland: "Jesus died for us, and only the mountains that trembled and the sun that darkened seemed to understand the gift that was being given."

Or Moses 3:1, 5, 9 in the Pearl of Great Price:

> Thus the heaven and the earth were finished, and all the host of them.
> . . . And every plant of the field before it was in the earth, and every herb of the field before it grew. For I, the Lord God, created all things, of which I have spoken, spiritually, before they were naturally upon the face of the earth. . . .
>
> And out of the ground made I, the Lord God, to grow every tree, naturally, that is pleasant to the sight of man; and man could behold it. And it became also a living soul. For it was spiritual in the day that I created it; for it remaineth in the sphere in which I, God, created it, . . .

Or, our own Thirteenth Article of Faith, parroted by members from early youth: ". . . If there is anything virtuous, lovely, or of good report or praiseworthy, we seek after these things."

So, Where are the Mormons?

So, where are the Mormons? And why should they be speaking out for the environment at this time?

Over the last twenty years, most countries of the world have accelerated the integration of environmental thinking into national policy. This evolution of thought is rapidly creating a new sense of reality in terms of public policy, and the Mormon tradition has much to contribute. As the West, including Utah, is rapidly changing from a rural to a highly urban region, enormous economic expansion and accumulation of wealth are pushing rampant development into beautiful corners that have heretofore been ignored. In Utah as well as many other areas, small communities look with horror at the growth of neighboring towns in the throes of rapid change.

In Utah and other Rocky Mountain states, our politicians play a cynical game, pitting constituency groups against each other instead of providing leadership and vision on environmental issues. It doesn't need to be this way. Utah, with its strong Mormon population and magnificent landscape, should lead the nation in developing wise environmental policy and protection of open space and the natural world. We should demand sensitivity of elected officials and be willing to build constituencies to elect those with enlightened environmental vision. It is a certain truth that if enough people care about an issue, politicians in both parties will follow.

We should elevate to public consciousness an awareness that there is a strong environmental ethic in the Mormon tradition—the elements of which are pervasive in our theology. We are taught that:

• Our destiny is linked to the earth, as is our health—physical, spiritual, and emotional. We are sustained by the earth. Our theology encourages us to be good stewards and to replenish. It reminds us that the earth will be the celestial home of those who progress to that level.

• The earth is God's creation and handiwork. The hues, colors, textures, varieties, and types found in the natural world, besides having value in themselves, are also created for man's enjoyment and inspiration.

• All we see and experience as the earth is, in its essence, spiritual. All creation is spiritual, and spirit communes with spirit. Some who have developed a heightened sense of communing with the spirit of a place find that their lives are enriched, and, in a very real way, their ability to know God is expanded.

• Our behavior matters to the earth. The earth groans under the weight of the sins of its inhabitants, as it rejoices in their righteous, balanced, and harmonious living. The religious traditions of Native American people recognize this truth. One of a Native American spiritual leader's greatest responsibilities is to help keep balance, harmony, and natural rhythms operating in healthy ways. Their participation in ceremonial life helps maintain this balance and order in the natural world.

Likewise, I feel Mormon efforts are important in sustaining not only the earth's well-being but also our own. Living our tradition with a sincere heart, obeying the commandments, and providing service and love are important in ways we may not fully realize for sustaining the earth's well-being. We are taught that a few righteous people can have a great effect in staving off calamity on the earth. The positive effects of millions of righteous people is clearly enormous, and I feel the earth must rejoice when this occurs.

> *Yea, all things which come of the earth, in the season thereof, are made for the benefit and the use of man, both to please the eye and to gladden the heart; Yea, for food and for raiment, for taste and for smell, to strengthen the body and to enliven the soul. And it pleaseth God that he hath given all these things unto man; for unto this end were they made to be used, with judgment, not to excess, neither by extortion." (D&C 59: 18–20.)*

You Come, Too

I've always liked camping and hiking. And it has taken me along a road "less traveled" by many in my faith. As I've traveled, I've realized the tremendous power that dedicated individuals can exert for good in their own lives and for the future of this most wondrous earth.

So, why not hike along with me? Let's share the rejuvenating sense of play that I find in my environmentalist friends. Let's hike to the top of a mountain just for a view, then return to defend it. Let's squeeze through a slot canyon in the middle of winter to enjoy the feel of sandstone on our hands and bodies and the press of rocks. Then let's applaud and support efforts to protect this place and this experience. Let's meet at night for a warm meal together and meet again for another hike to do it all over again in a different place. Walking, talking, celebrating, the rhythm smoothing out one's mind . . . no need for religious instruction here, other than the trance of feeling and observing.

Together we can issue the joyous invitation of Robert Frost,

> *I'm going out to clean the pasture spring;*
> *I'll only stop to rake the leaves away*
> *(and wait to watch the water clear, I may)*
> *I shan't be gone long.—*
>
> > *You come too.*

Gibbs M. Smith is a book publisher and painter in oils.

"And the Lord God took the man, and put him into the garden of Eden to dress it and to keep it." (Genesis 2:15.)

COWMEN AND THE
ENVIRONMENT

Mackey Hedges

FTEN, YOU HEAR IN RANCHING CIRCLES THAT "COWMEN ARE THE *true* environmentalists" and "ranchers care more about the land than anyone else because their livelihood depends upon how well they manage it." The truth is, there are many ranchers who are good stewards but there are also those who are bad ones. During my lifetime, I have known and worked with some of the most knowledgeable and devoted range managers, ones who dedicated their time and efforts into improving or maintaining the condition of the land not only for monetary reasons but also because they felt it was their God-given duty.

My father, who was not a Mormon, was the first person to teach me about our duty to respect the land. His grandmother was a Native American, and she brought him up to believe that everything—the plants, the animals, the land—had a spirit and was to be respected. To my father, the earth was his spiritual mother and the animals that shared the land with him were his brothers. He had probably never heard of the word *environmentalism,* and if he had I doubt that he knew what it meant. But his love and understanding of the land were tremendous.

Shortly after we were married, my wife and I lived next to the Owyhee Reservation in northern Nevada where I spent many of my formative years. Later I took a job managing an LDS Church-owned welfare ranch that bordered the Temok Reservation near Lee, Nevada. One of my closest friends at that time was Raymond Yowell, the head of the Western Shoshone's Sacred Land Council. This group is both a political and religious organization striving to maintain traditional practices and struggling to regain some of the original land granted the tribe in the treaty of 1863. Even though many of Raymond's religious ideas conflicted with my LDS beliefs, it was from him that I was able to understand my feelings about the land. During this time, I came to realize that my father had a great deal of influence on me as well.

When I was about thirty-five I went to work for Kent Howard on his ranch at Rowland, Nevada. Even though he didn't know it by that name, Kent Howard was a pioneer in the use of Alan Savory's Holistic Resource Management. Years of careful observation had taught him that short-term, intense grazing improved the quality of his range and increased the quantity of available forage.

He accepted the principle of "multiple use" on his federal lands, and was more than willing to share his range with other groups, such as hunters, sightseers, and miners. He also felt that his LDS Church teachings made it *mandatory* for him to be a good steward of the land he had been entrusted with.

The terrain in the Rowland area where Kent ran his cattle is steep and rocky, with only a few good trails leading to the canyon bottoms. Yet at roundup time Kent Howard never let his cowboys drive cattle downhill in the same place two years in a row, no matter how inconvenient it was to find another trail. He knew that defined and heavily used trails would wash and erode with the spring runoff. Salt grounds were established in many areas that were accessible only by packhorse. Even though it cost him more for labor, Kent knew that this had to be done to distribute his cattle more evenly and to lessen the animal impact. He also salted his cattle in areas where tourists and sightseers would never have to see them congregated. This was done out of respect for their right to share the land with him.

Kent had never heard the popular buzzwords *biodiversity* and *species diversification*, which environmentalists and eco-preservationists like to use. All he knew was that if he grazed his land correctly, the number of different plant species increased, and as they increased in number, so did the different varieties of animals that shared the range with his cattle.

About 1988, Ken Howard was nominated for the Excellence in Grazing Award by the Society of Range Conservationist for his summer Forest Service allotment. Surprisingly, that was the same year that he did battle with a young local Forest Service range conservationist who wanted to cut his permit because of "overgrazing." After the award was presented, the proposed cut by the young ranger was quietly dropped.

In 1991 the Howard family sold their property at Rowland to the Rocky Mountain Elk foundation, and it ceased to be a working cattle ranch. At first my family and I were devastated. After almost seventeen years we had come to feel that Rowland was our home. Two of my three boys were born there. We had our own little herd of cattle. My sons had a band of brood mares that they ran with Kent's stud and his mares. None of us had even dreamed of leaving, and yet, suddenly, it was all over.

I don't know how the other family members handled it, but for me I went through all the symptoms of someone who has lost a loved one. At first there was denial. I kept believing that at anytime the deal would fall through or that the foundation would lease the ranch back to another party who would keep us on. Then blame set in. I blamed the sale on everyone from the Forest Service to the sportsmen. I blamed the whole environmental movement. I grouped every person who had ever voiced as much as an ecologically supportive whisper into the groups of "tree huggers" or "bunny breeders." I hated them all.

Finally came acceptance. It's true we had known that the Howards had had the ranch up for sale for some time, but I was sure that because of the ruggedness of the country and the isolation, whoever bought the place would have to keep us on. *After all*, I thought, *who is the new owner going to find who will know the country and will be willing to live 125 miles from town in a house that had no TV or radio, and had electricity only when the generator was running? How many women could the new owner find who would be willing to teach their children at home, chop their firewood, and pack water part of the winter?* As it turned out, with the sale to the Elk Foundation, none of this mattered.

We finally had to face the fact that we were not only going to be out of a house and a job but we were also going to have to sell our livestock and move—soon.

But blessings come in many shapes and sizes. If the Howard Ranch had not sold, I never would have worked for the Deseret Land and Livestock Company, which was run by Bill Hopkin and Gregg Simonds, two of the most knowledgeable and dedicated stewards of the land who ever lived.

With a little over 200,000 acres of deeded land, the Deseret Land and Livestock Company near Woodruff, Utah, is the largest tract of privately owned land. It was purchased by The Church of Jesus Christ of Latter-day Saints in 1983, and today it is known worldwide for its innovative range-management practices. People come from all over the world to study the way Hopkin and Simonds integrated their livestock program with their wildlife operation.

Gregg Simonds is a graduate of Utah State University with a master's degree in range science. He is known throughout the West for his knowledge of Holistic Resource Management and his many new ideas. Bill Hopkin is a Weber State graduate with a degree in biology. He was born and raised on a neighboring ranch and has spent his entire life in the valley where the Deseret Ranch lies.

Where Simonds was a visionary with a mind that is unrestricted and brimming with contemporary ideas, Hopkins was more conventional with a wealth of common sense and practical experience. Together they were an unbeatable team. Simonds would come up with new, wild ideas and Hopkin would figure out the means to implement them. Together they were able to take a ranch that had not made a profit in twenty years and turn it into a well-managed, smooth-operating machine capable of producing top-quality cattle while maintaining one of the best-managed wildlife programs in the world.

Both Simonds and Hopkin understood the principle of "time and timing grazing," that it was not the number of cattle that were put in a field that caused overgrazing, it was the time of the year that the animals were in the pasture and the length of time that they were left there. They knew that fifty cows left in a field for the summer would do more damage to the plant community than 500 head would do if moved in and moved out in ten or fifteen days.

For this reason the Deseret Ranch is now divided into about 100 different pastures. On a normal year each of these units will be grazed at least once and in some cases twice, which requires over 150 different cattle moves annually.

Both Hopkin and Simonds had taken classes in Savory's Holistic Resource Management, learning that there is a definite factor of mutual benefit between livestock grazing and range improvement, that it takes heavy animal impact and grazing to improve and maintain the quality of the land and plant community, which is the underlying precept for the success of this program.

In a presentation at the BYU Livestock Symposium, I once heard Bill Hopkin tell a group of listeners,

> To say that running more cattle in a controlled area for a controlled length of time improves plant growth so that you can turn around and run even more livestock would be an oversimplification. Grazing exposure also has to be controlled or limited in such a way that each plant has an opportunity to grow and compete to stay healthy. For instance, on any given day during the time of rapid plant growth, all Deseret cattle are on less than 10 percent of the range, giving the remaining 90 percent of the country time to grow and develop. At this time of the year the cattle are being moved every four to five days. This gives the grazed areas a chance to recover. As the season progresses and the time of rapid growth decreases, the cattle will be left in the individual fields longer.

By their understanding of the principle "time and timing," Simonds and Hopkin were able to change the structure of the plant community, thickening the stands and broadening the number of species that grew in the area. With the increase in plant species diversification came an increase in animal species diversification and an overall increase in the animal population.

When seen in these uncomplicated terms, it seems almost too simple to believe, yet the Deseret Ranch is working proof that the concept works. To spend a September day riding in the mountains on this fantastically beautiful ranch is to get a glimpse of what heaven must be like. Crystal-clear mountain streams alive with trout and beaver, the air filled with the high-pitched whistle of bugling bull elk, lush mountain meadows surrounded by heavy stands of fir and broken patches of quakies—these are the rewards that all Deseret cowboys are able to enjoy.

These pictures etched in my memory, and the fact that I learned more about range management at the Deseret Ranch than I ever did in college, were the gifts that I took with me when I left.

Mackey Hedges, author of the award-winning western novel *Last Buckaroo* (1995), has spent most of his life working, ranching, and appreciating God's handiwork in the West.

". . . AND THEY SHALL PLANT VINEYARDS, AND DRINK THE WINE THEREOF; THEY SHALL ALSO MAKE GARDENS, AND EAT THE FRUIT OF THEM." (AMOS 9:14.)

STEWARDSHIP IN THE BACKYARD

G. MICHAEL ALDER

ROM THE PERSPECTIVE OF HALF A LIFETIME'S CAREER AS A PLANT ecologist and of working and playing close to nature, I have come to a profound conclusion: There is no finer avocation than making compost.

One reason is the satisfaction of being part of the solution to one of the problems plaguing our planet. Today's unprecedented scale of consumption puts us at risk of losing touch with reality. We think that what we buy will be available indefinitely. We forget where it comes from. We also forget where it goes—into burgeoning landfills that within a few years will be full. As a citizen of the United States, I create more waste than a citizen of any other country. I'm not proud of that, but it's a fact.

Recycling aluminum cans, paper, plastic, and glass is an honorable and effective way to restore some sense of stewardship, but it lets me participate in only part of the process. By recycling the lawn clippings and edgings, weeds, and fallen leaves that otherwise would be hauled off by the garbageman, I sense more fully my stewardship. I am the sole author and executor of a process that, instead of turning my waste over to others to handle, turns it into a useful product in my own backyard. The volume of such waste in a typical city is enormous; the operator of the local landfill says he needs a third more staff and trucks to haul off the stuff during the warmer months.

So an important reason I compost is that it makes me feel good; I've done something worthwhile. In a recent speech, Mayor Daniel Kemmis of Missoula, Montana, said of cities that "wellness begets wellness." It seems to work with individuals as well. On Saturdays of LDS conference weekend I love to work around the house as I listen to the messages of our leaders; it improves my concentration. So, last Saturday, turning the radio down just enough to avoid offending the neighbors, I cleaned the garage. As I finished, a feeling of righteous well-being began to develop.

The weather was beautiful, so in the afternoon I strolled out to my backyard garden plot. Cleaning out last year's weeds and debris seemed overwhelming for such a day, but next to the garden is my compost pile; I decided spreading compost seemed do-able and appropriate for a conference afternoon. The annual miracle was about to unfold. With my wheelbarrow, shovel, and digging fork, I approached the pile. The first task was to remove the top layers that had not had time to create compost. They were pushed aside to begin a new pile for next season. There it was, just as last year, the dark, mostly decomposed, fine granular material called compost. I loaded the wheelbarrow and headed for the strawberry patch. Nothing loves compost more than strawberries except maybe raspberries, which quickly got the next load. Then came the garden spots; each is now coated with a dark brown, rich-looking layer that is ready to be tilled in prior to planting. Talk about a feeling of well-being; my spirit is uplifted with conference, my garage is clean, and my garden is fed.

And that leads to the next reason I compost: to feed the garden. More than a century ago, Kârel Kapek wrote in his Czech book *The Gardener's Year* words that echo in my subconscious. We rush about, he wrote,

> . . . *and at most one notices what beautiful clouds there are, or what a beautiful horizon it is, or how beautifully blue the hills are; but one does not look under one's feet to note and praise the beautiful soil that is there. You must have a garden . . . to know what you are treading on. Then, dear friend, you will see that not even clouds are so diverse, so beautiful, and terrible as the soil under your feet. . . .*
>
> *And if you have no appreciation for this strange beauty, let fate bestow upon you a couple of rods of clay—clay like lead, squelching and primeval clay out of which coldness oozes; which yields under the spade like chewing-gum, which bakes in the sun and gets sour in the shade; ill-tempered, unmalleable, greasy, and sticky like plaster of Paris, slippery like a snake, and dry like a brick, impermeable like tin, and heavy like lead. And now smash it with a pick-axe, cut it with a spade, break it with a hammer, turn it over and labour, cursing aloud and lamenting.*
>
> *Then you will understand the animosity and callousness of dead and sterile matter which ever did defend itself, and still does, against becoming a soil of life; and you will realize what a terrible fight life must have undergone, inch by inch, to take root in the soil of the earth, whether that life be called vegetation or man.*
>
> *And then you will know that you must give more to the soil than you take away.*

That's what composting is about—giving more to the soil than you take away. I know no better way than composting to make soil that is, as Kapek describes it, "puffy like pastry, warm, light, and good like bread, and you will say of this that it is beautiful, just as you say so of women or of clouds."

It is a simple process, composting. This is how you do it. First, find a place that is convenient to get to and yet a bit hidden, since composting, while important, cannot be described as attractive. My compost is hidden behind a large flowering shrub. There are clever commercial composters you can fill and rotate and have compost much faster; they also deserve a spot out of the way because they are not attractive either. The least expensive way to compost, though, is to simply pile up the organic waste and occasionally stir with a digging fork. Make sure the spot is large enough for the volume from your yard and, perhaps, waste you invite the neighbors to contribute. My volume is plenty large, but when I see neighbors with bags of leaves out on the curb for the garbage man, I invite them to bring them over.

Next, make a decision on what will go in your compost. Mine generally includes only lawn clippings, leaves, weeds before they go to seed, and lawn edgings. Occasional watermelon rinds or some corn husks get thrown in, but nothing that would attract pests. And nothing, such as prunings from woody plants, that would take a long time to decompose. These can be included if chipped or shredded, but for that kind of work you need a machine and a tolerance for noise.

You can be very scientific with compost, but I recommend you keep it simple. I always have a shovel nearby to scatter a little soil over each fresh layer of lawn clippings or leaves. There are about 40,000 living microorganisms in soil the size of a sugar cube. Those microbes begin immediately to break down the new garden waste. Within a week, if the temperature is warm and the pile is moist, the volume will be reduced by half. I often throw a few handfuls of nitrogen fertilizer onto the pile to feed the microbes so they will work faster. The pile needs a little moisture, but not a lot. A soggy compost pile may smell a bit from anaerobic bacteria that grow in environments without oxygen. If so, stir it up, let in some air, and the odor will quickly disappear.

Depending on the season, compost will be ready for use in a few weeks to a few months. You will be able to tell. The fiber and form of the raw material has disappeared, and a dark, granular, soft organic top dressing for soil will be your reward. Simply haul it from the pile by bucket or wheelbarrow to all locations where you want your soil to be richer. Use only an inch or two at a time; if you get too enthusiastic, plants may be robbed of nitrogen while the spoil bacteria finish breaking down your too-abundant top dressing.

I must share a story about what this "brown gold" will do. One year we threw a moldy Hubbard squash onto the pile and forgot it was there. Next spring a bunch of squash seedlings appeared in the middle of the pile. My twins begged me not to disturb them, to see what would happen, so I started another pile and left that one alone. The plants grew at an incredible rate. By summer's end there were squash vines forty feet in every direction. The neighbor inquired what he might expect from the huge vine that had invaded his yard. My yard looked like a scene from *Invasion of the Body Snatchers*, the movie where aliens came in pods from outer space. On the bathroom scales we weighed the squash and found we harvested 360 pounds from that one hill on the compost pile.

Compost is a reservoir of nutrients for plant growth. By the time it is finished the microbes that produce it have turned it into complex chemicals called *humates*. Humates give the dark color to fine topsoil. They make the nutrients locked up in organic matter available for healthy plant growth. If you add compost to your soil every year, it will become steadily richer and more fertile. Soil is a fundamental source of life on this planet. By working with it, improving it, you will stay in touch with where food comes from, will more completely understand your stewardship, may even feel a small sense of partnership with the eternal Giver of life.

G. Michael Alder, born in Denver and raised in Salt Lake City, was founder of Native Plants, Inc. (1973), was a recipient of the first Governor's Medal for Science and Technology in Utah (1987), and was appointed to head the Office of Business Creation for the State of Utah (1989). He is currently the executive director of Emerging Technology Partners in Alabama.

"... IT IS REQUIRED OF THE LORD, AT THE HAND OF EVERY STEWARD, TO RENDER AN ACCOUNT OF HIS STEWARDSHIP, BOTH IN TIME AND ETERNITY." (D&C 72:3.)

SKIPPING THE GRAND CANYON

STEVEN E. SNOW

N 1861, PRESIDENT BRIGHAM YOUNG CALLED MY GREAT-GREAT-grandfather, Erastus Snow, to leave his comfortable home and farm on City Creek in Salt Lake City and help colonize the St. George Valley in southwest Utah. Although the southern Utah of 1861 was even more scenic than now, Erastus and his fellow pioneers had little leisure to appreciate its beauty. Their time and attention were dedicated to survival in land first described by Parley P. Pratt in 1850 as he stood with his Mormon exploring party on the Black Ridge and stared south into what is today Washington County and the Arizona Strip:

> *The great Wasatch Range along which we traveled our whole journey here terminates in several abrupt promontories. The country southward for eighty miles showing no signs of water or fertility . . . a wide expanse of chaotic matter presented itself, huge hills, sandy deserts, cheerless, grassless plains, perpendicular rocks, loose barren clay, dissolving beds of sandstone . . . lying in inconceivable confusion. (Parley P. Pratt Autobiography, pp. 365–67.)*

The early settlers felt the same way. The land they were called to tame was tough, harsh, unforgiving. To accomplish their mission, any use of the land, no matter how damaging, was acceptable. That attitude was carried down through the generations until prosperity and leisure caused many of us to look anew at our surroundings.

Grandfather's journals are conspicuously absent of any reference to the beauty of Dixie. They focus more on the temporal and spiritual affairs of an early church leader. There are entries about church conferences, reports of various business enterprises (including frustration with operation of the cotton mill in nearby Washington), summaries of counsel given his Mormon followers, events in the lives of his four families living in St. George. Nowhere is described the color of the hills during an October sunset, or the majesty of Pine Valley Mountain. We will never know how he felt about the sights, sounds, and smells of an August thunderstorm, only his concern that the Virgin River dam might be washed out once again.

I think of a story involving my younger brother Paul. At age eighteen he was working at Tom's Texaco Service in St. George on what was then old Highway 91. A car with New York license plates pulled into the station and the driver asked for a fill-up. While Paul was washing the windshield (they used to do that in those days), the man asked how far it was to the Grand Canyon. Paul replied that it was 170 miles.

"I can't wait," the man said. "All my life I've wanted to see the Grand Canyon. What's it like out there?"

"I don't know," my brother answered. "I've never been there."

The man was incredulous. "You mean to tell me you live two and a half hours from one of the seven wonders of the world and you've never been there?" Paul assured him that he had not.

"Well, I guess I can understand that. My wife and I have lived in Manhattan for over twenty years and we've never visited the Statue of Liberty." Paul looked up with a grin. "I've been there," he said.

Human nature is like that. We yearn for far-off places of beauty and excitement, ignoring what lies at our own feet. To my brother, driving by the turnoff to the Grand Canyon on the way to see the Statue of Liberty seemed perfectly normal. The country he had grown up in was there, little-changed, mostly unyielding. For generations it had been used by a very few of my forefathers and their neighbors. The open, undeveloped desert real estate seemed endless. Except for some exploring for minerals and oil, the outside world had shown little interest in southern Utah. We were pretty well left alone to enjoy almost unfettered use of a seemingly inexhaustible resource.

How quickly, dramatically, irretrievably that has changed!

Golf courses, luxury homes, shopping malls, trailer courts, and auto dealerships cover those once-empty lands. The land itself is redefined. It was different with our forefathers. They built where nature allowed. They learned quickly that the sandy banks next to rivers and creeks was no place to be, that the rocky slopes of the surrounding mesas were too steep, too rugged, too far from water. Out of necessity they became stewards of the land they settled. Certain locations were reserved for development, other areas precluded. Agricultural lands, the foundation of the economy, were carefully preserved.

No longer. Developers find no obstacles in rocky slopes and arid valleys. Sandy plains become filled with lakes and artificial streams. Hills can be flattened; roads can be built virtually anywhere. Housing units on rocky slopes long thought unsuitable for development leave ugly scars seen for miles. Water-thirsty lawns and shrubs replace desert plants.

It's a paradox. Though early settlers didn't appreciate the beauty of southern Utah, they preserved it. Though present residents were attracted here by that beauty, many of them are complicitors in destroying it. Seriously threatened is the sense of stewardship for the land that was so important to its early settlers.

Also threatened, if not lost, is a sense of community. Like other early Mormon towns, St. George had a well-defined town center where the church, the school, the courthouse, and a few business were clustered. Residences were grouped around this center, with fields and farms located outside of town. It was important to be close to neighbors so families could assist and serve one another in times of hardship, celebrate with one another during times of joy, and especially worship together. For the first 100 years, this changed little; I recall as a youngster being able to walk easily to church or school or almost every business in town. Today, urban sprawl with shopping malls scattered around the valley has pulled apart our community and greatly weakened our tradition of caring for each other.

As a people it is important to keep in mind two important principles. First, no matter where we choose to reside, whether in southern Utah, southern California, or northern New Jersey, the Lord has given us much for which to be grateful. He wants us to appreciate these blessings; he wants us not to miss the Grand Canyon on the way to the Statue of Liberty. I do not believe it pleases him when we constantly search for happiness elsewhere.

Second, I believe the Lord expects us to act as good stewards. We have many stewardships, not only in our family, church, and citizenship responsibilities but also in temporal things. That principle is clear in LDS scripture:

> *I, the Lord, stretched out the heavens, and built the earth, my very handiwork; and all things therein are mine. . . .*
>
> *Behold, all these properties are mine, . . . And if the properties are mine, then ye are stewards; otherwise ye are no stewards. (D&C 104:14, 55–56.)*
>
> *. . . it is required of the Lord, at the hand of every steward, to render an account of his stewardship, both in time and in eternity. For he who is faithful and wise in time is accounted worthy to inherit the mansions prepared for him of my Father. (D&C 72:3–4.)*

As Mormons we tend to focus on our ecclesiastical and family stewardships, which is well and good. But I believe we will also be held accountable for how we treat one another, the community in which we live, the land that surrounds us, even the earth itself.

That stewardship was never more urgent. Our generation, more than any other, has the ability to irretrievably change the land. Financial rewards provide tremendous pressure to unleash our technology to reinvent our surroundings. There will be growth; change will come. But failure to care for the land on which we live means turning our backs on a heritage laid down carefully and at such great cost by our forefathers—and will leave us immeasurably poorer.

Steven E. Snow is a native of southern Utah and practices law in St. George, Utah. He recently served as a mission president in southern California.

"AND IT CAME TO PASS, AS THE VOICE WAS STILL SPEAKING, MOSES CAST HIS EYES AND BEHELD THE EARTH, YEA, EVEN ALL OF IT; AND THERE WAS NOT A PARTICLE OF IT WHICH HE DID NOT BEHOLD, DISCERNING IT BY THE SPIRIT OF GOD." (MOSES 1:27.)

COMMUNION:
A FAMILY RESPONSE

JOSEPH AND LEE UDALL BENNION, ZINA, AND LOUISA

"ALL MEN AND WOMEN ARE IN THE SIMILITUDE OF THE UNIVERSAL Father and Mother and are literally the sons and daughters of Deity."
—THE FIRST PRESIDENCY, *Improvement Era*, November 1909

COMMUNION
Joseph Bennion

I am a potter, a husband, and a father. I find my approach to these roles connected, defined, and shaped by my faith. In turn my work in the home and the studio has built my faith and brought me closer to my Creator. In all of this I feel a profound connection to Earth.

I once saw an old English slipware platter by the potter Thomas Toft which bore the inscription; "Earth I am it is most true, despise me not for so are you." This truth has always been evident to me. My religion teaches me that "the spirit and the body are the soul of man" (D&C 88:15). Therefore this soul, which in the resurrection becomes eternal, is made of material from Mother Earth and spirit from Heavenly Father. This understanding teaches me to see Earth as part of me and me as part of Her.

Just as a tiny growing fetus cannot live without its mother's blood, our bodies cannot live for very long without our eating and drinking the food and water that Earth provides for us. Our connection to Earth is mandated by our biology. In this light I like to think of eating as a ritual of communion that renews our relationship to Mother Earth. In this daily ritual the vessels of communion are the clay pots formed by the potter. The primary ingredients of clay are alumina, silica, and water, which are the three most common ingredients in the surface of Earth. The vessels used in the meal are the umbilical cord through which Earth feeds us. I feel that the pottery I make for the family meal are mundane in the finest sense of the word.

In the creation and expulsion story contained in Genesis and Moses we see our first parents driven out of their garden paradise into a world fraught with dangers and trials. As they are cast out they are given instructions on how to live in this world. I see these instructions as parallel and complementary. The woman is told that "in sorrow thou shalt bring forth children." Her task, which will be hard, is to produce bodies for her children from the earth materials she eats. The man is told to till the earth and "in the sweat of thy face shalt thou eat bread." His task is to provide for the woman and her child. Both forms of work bring life from Earth. Both are very sacred. Working together the man and the woman nurture and teach the child as it grows.

In a lecture titled "Indian Pottery and Indian Values," the Pueblo potter Popovi Da said: "We Pueblo people eat gently, recognizing with inner feelings that the corn or the squash were at one time growing, cared for, each plant alive, now prepared to become part of us, of our bodies and minds, quite sacred." As I was growing up, gardening was central to our household. I have always felt a deep spiritual and physical satisfaction in putting my hands into the soil. The oft-repeated admonitions of prophet leaders to practice a provident lifestyle have sounded to me as an invitation to engage in a cyclic ritual that connects body, spirit, and earth with heaven in much the same way that the temple does. If this were not the case, why did Spencer Kimball suggest that urban dwellers grow even one plant in a window sill and eat its produce? Everyone needs the experience of eating something they have cared for and loved. Thus activity invites us into sacred space.

For me the craft of gardening, making vessels for the meal table, procreation, and child nurture are confluent practices that bring me in touch with creation and to the edge of the sacred work that a woman practices with her body.

As our three daughters have come to us I have marveled at the glory they come clothed in. I have delighted to see them unfold according to the divine pattern that is in them. As part of my responsibility to teach them, and because it is so much fun, I have gone with them and their mother to the wild and beautiful places in the canyons and deserts that surround our Utah home. I want them to learn what the Colorado Plateau has been teaching our family for five generations. I am pleased that they feel connected to these sacred places. When they return to us from their distant college studies they always go to the desert as soon as it can be arranged. I delight in looking at their drawings and reading their poems and stories that draw from red-rock wells. When I go to these places alone I am always reminded of them. When I look into their faces I see the landscape shining and the rivers flowing in their eyes.

Much as I value the wilderness experience we have shared as a family, I feel that our most important connection to Earth and to our spirituality is in our bodies and how we maintain them in working and eating. As I sit down together with my wife and daughters and join hands to give thanks for the food we have raised carefully from our garden to the table, where it rests on dishes taken from the same native soil, I sense a deeper kind of environmentalism manifest that involves body and spirit, heaven and earth, as well as male and female.

RECOGNITION
Lee Udall Bennion

A few years ago, I was showing slides of my paintings to a group of women and was asked a question about a certain visual theme one woman had noticed in my work. She pointed out that a number of my paintings depict interiors with windows or that look out on vivid landscapes. Often a female figure appears in front of the window, sometimes looking out, and sometimes looking towards the viewer. I had never been asked about this before, and hadn't thought about what these paintings meant in my conscious mind.

I fumbled for a few seconds, groping for some explanation. Suddenly, with swift clarity, I knew how to verbalize what I already understood on a subconscious level about these paintings. At the time I was doing these paintings, my daughters were young, and my life was very tied to the domestic interior of our home. This was not something that I resented or disliked, but it was not always easy. It is a huge change in a young woman's life when she takes on the role and responsibility of being a wife and mother. The interior of these paintings represents this time of my life. The window with the landscape represents my past and my future, a time when life was and will be less tied to the interior.

It isn't that simple, though.

Somehow I see the interior window with the landscape as a sort of blending of these two ways of life. At present, I happen to be spending the majority of my time still with interior spaces, but that landscape beyond, the wilderness, is still present. The windows in my paintings seem to have no glass, and afford the viewer a landscape that almost comes in and becomes part of the interior. Although I may physically be inhabiting the interior space, the external landscape is still within me, ever present. It is a part of who I am.

As a young girl I remember being under a night sky, high in the Sierra Nevada. I was not far away from friends or family but far enough in that pitch-black, star-studded night to feel alone. Looking up into the Milky Way, I felt very small, insignificant, and scared. I felt like running back to the cabin, to be inside where it was light, warm, and familiar. But I stayed a few moments longer, wanting to try to understand the source of these feelings of fear. I continued to gaze up at the stars and as I did a feeling of recognition washed over me. I suddenly felt as if I had seen God's creation for the first time and that I was a part of it. I recognized who I was in a new way. This was the closest I had ever felt to God; I felt like a new creature.

This feeling, this recognition of who I am, has come to me at other times and places in my life. Without exception these epiphanies have come to me in either one of two places: within the interior of my home, specifically in my relationships with my family, and in the landscape of wilderness. I find that the night sky or a pristine tract of land experienced in solitude is my most direct route to these feelings of recognition.

It is interesting to me that both home and the wilderness have so many similarities. The environment, the creation I like to call it, is not always an easy place to be. Its glorious elements can be intimidating, powerful, and lethal. On the other hand it can be still, quiet, and nurturing. So, too, is the interior of family life. On the outside, family life appears so safe and easy compared to life in the wilderness; yet living with others, particularly those whom you love, can be frightful, dangerous, and, at worst, lethal to one's soul.

Perhaps it is in this common ground of wildness and family that spending time in the outdoors with my husband and children has been as necessary and important to me as the ordinances of faith I also hold dear, such as baptism and temple work. This lovely and sometimes violent creation that we are a part of helps me to see and feel my God, myself, and my family with divine clarity. The layers of protection and self-image dissipate in the desert heat. In the wilderness I have felt completely stripped down to physical and emotional bedrock, and then born again. I think that this experience is harder to come by in the physical comfort and pleasant mundane quality of my home. Yet, in that physically safe environment there are times when the disappointment, despair, and turmoil of family life are comforted and soothed by a walk under a starry night sky.

I see these paintings of interiors and windows as self-portraits of my soul. The wilderness of the landscape helps me to navigate the wilderness of my family life and recognize myself as a part of God and his creation, and likewise my family and God have helped me to survive and be in the wilderness that I love.

DREAM
Zina Bennion

I once had a dream in which I found myself standing before a huge mirror. As I peered into the depths of it I found that my reflection was not a body of flesh and bones but a deep, rich red wall of sandstone. I stood staring at this alien reflection and felt, ever so slowly, my feet push deeply into the ground, forming a solid thick base that not even the strongest earthquake could budge. I became acutely aware of each individual particle of sand that made up my body and of the importance of these tiny granules. I felt secure, yet subject to changes and growth brought on by the forces of time and nature. I felt ready to give and receive; I felt beautiful.

I awoke slowly, only to see another wall of red sandstone before my eyes with the early morning sun rays peeping over its edge. I was on a weeklong backpacking trip with my father and several other friends in one of the many desert canyons of southern Utah. Growing up in central Utah has allowed me to take countless trips like this one, backpacking and river running through some of the most beautiful and isolated wilderness areas in all of America with my family and friends. These trips and the experiences they have given me have played a strong part in forming the person I am today.

It has been during my experiences in these desert places when I have felt the greatest fear, joy, exhilaration, and introspection of my life. I have found that it is when I am in the quiet of nature, far away from the hustle and bustle of our modern world, that the true Zina Bennion emerges easily, shedding off layers of stress, anxiety, frustration, and anger that build up during the day-to-day pressures of homework, deadlines to make, money to earn, tests to take, and problems to work out in relationships with fellow Homo sapiens. When I sit in these tabernacles of limestone and sandstone I am overcome with the amazing force of nature, the billions of years it took to form these convoluted yet perfect canyons and landscapes. I realize the relative smallness of the human race in comparison to these wise ancient oracles of water, wind, and rock. I have learned to respect the wisdom of these wilderness places. I have found that they have much to teach us about the cycles of life, of being built up only to be worn down and starting this cycle of change all over again.

RIVER ROCK
Louisa Bennion

The river is trying to tell me about the rocks beneath its belly. It crawls over them and polishes them like pearls with its silty underside. It sings out their songs, writes their histories and the shapes of their faces on its surface.

I trail my fingers in the water and I wonder what kind of shape I'd make if I tumbled out of my boat, face-forward like a stone, and sank slowly to the bottom.

I think I would roll with the current until my sharp edges and rough places were ground smooth. Then I would find a place to wedge myself between two other rocks and I would turn my face to the surface, dreaming of the sky and canyon walls.

My skin would become fluted and black as the currents combed over it. The water would coil around my nose and ears. High above, a still, dark, white-edged fold would appear, echoing my curves.

The floods would come and I would be moving again through strong creamy water. My arms and legs would break away and I would become round, scoured like the moon.

I would pound deep into the dense sand below the river; I would burrow toward the source of fire. And finally, in a moment when the weight of all the past came to bear upon me, I would become my core, I would fuse to the bedrock of this planet, and the earth and its waters would shine for that moment like a birthing star.

Joseph Wood Bennion (born 1952, Salt Lake City, Utah) is a father, husband, and studio potter. His work can be found in collections around the globe, and he also is in demand as a guest artist/teacher for workshops, colleges, and universities.

Lee Udall Bennion (born 1956, Merced, California) is a mother, wife, and painter. She lives and works in the small central Utah town of Spring City.

Zina Lenore Bennion (born 1979, Mt. Pleasant, Utah) is a daughter of Joseph and Lee Bennion. She is a first-year student at Sarah Lawrence College, Bronxville, New York, focusing on studying the visual arts.

Louisa Bonelli Bennion (born 1977, Provo, Utah) is a daughter of Joseph and Lee Bennion. She was first published in *Stone Soup* at age eleven and has since then won many awards and recognition for her writing. She is studying writing at Cornell University, Ithaca, New York, where she is in her third year.

"Counsel with the Lord in all thy doings, and he will direct thee for good, yea, when thou liest down at night lie down unto the Lord, that he may watch over you in your sleep; and when thou risest in the morning let thy heart be full of thanks unto God; and if ye do these things ye shall be lifted up at the last day." (Alma 37:37.)

THROUGH THE VIEWER: THIS IS MY PLACE

Emma Lou Thayne

ll things
are too small
to hold me,
I am so vast
In the Infinite
I reach
for the Uncreated
I have touched it,
it undoes me
wider than wide
Everything else
is too narrow
You know this well,
you who are also there.

How did she know the vastness, Hadewijch II, seven centuries ago in Antwerp? The infinite, the Uncreated—how did she touch it? How did she allow the blessed undoing, wider than wide? And how did she know that I, these eons later, might know it too?

I do know. Because I grew up knowing it in my childhood in our Utah Mt. Air Canyon. There sprouted the expansion that cannot be circumscribed by convention, let alone learned from the experience of others. Our life in the mountains was simply ours. And with it came the vastness, the knowing, the traveling into it unperplexed, uninhibited, expectant in the way a child can awaken to morning or gravitate to night like a bird on the sky.

251

I was a little girl, lucky to grow up in the canyon during the Great Depression of the 1930s. We went there the day school was out for summer and stayed until it started in fall. Most richness came as it might to a creature of the earth. To be part of it was as simple as making mud pies, digging an underground, shinnying the powder white trunk of an aspen, or climbing to the giant rock armchair on the highest ridge to look for forty miles in any direction, all of it and us shimmering in 95 dry degrees on a Twenty-fourth of July.

At home in the cabin, some of the same rare opulence came by way of Mother's stereopticon viewer. At eight I'd never seen a movie. Living-room television was more than two decades away. Imagination and a sturdy sense of belonging wherever they led allowed me into the stories Mother and Father told and the books they invited me into.

As that little girl I begged Mother to bring out the stereopticon. Held with a straight handle against my face it fit my forehead and eyes like an aviator's goggles. From the eyepiece extended a slim wooden holder on which to slide the viewer for focus. One by one I slid cardboard-backed pictures into the slot on its top. Magic indeed. Two photographs of the same scene from slightly different angles could present in three-dimensional sepia a looking up at New York City skyscrapers or looking down into the Grand Canyon of the Yellowstone or looking out on Theodore Roosevelt in Cuba, waving his big stick. In the viewer the Rocky Mountains rose invitingly above the valley of the Great Salt Lake. Expanded, I fell into any scene as if part of it, my ringlets and dimity dress made by my mother to pronounce me thoroughly grounded in little girlhood, giving way to wind fingering my hair and pants tucked into my boots. I belonged in the vastness of wherever the pictures took me. But I always made sure to end in the Rockies. Back home to where everything took off from. Unconventional, unplanned, wider than wide.

Through the years, the stereopticon in my now-grey head, wherever I am, lets me travel inward, lets the scene appear: east of the valley of the Great Salt Lake, the Wasatch Mountains, humped, rocky, towering, some ribbed into gullies of green, others a soft relief map covered with the cowhide bronzing of summer sun, the hills of home nudging the valley with fluted reminders of Lake Bonneville's slapping waves 10,000 years ago.

In that mind viewer come my people, as much there as rocks on the 8,000-foot ridges above the timberline. At the mouth of that one gully of the Wasatch, Parley P. Pratt invited pioneers with their wagons and goods to rest before entering the valley. Two miles up, in Maple Fork, still stands the white cabin built by my grandfather Stephen L Richards in the late 1890s, where we lived every summer, where Mother kept her stereopticon and the Victrola. We'd wind its handle and then hear out of its megaphone on its one-sided, thick scratchy record, "Our mountain home so dear, where crystal waters clear flow ever free, . . ." One switch in my viewer and the breathy pumpings of the organ spill out "For the strength of the hills we bless thee, our God, our fathers' God; . . ." On a screened porch under giant pines are singing at Sunday school the sometimes sixty relatives living in the canyon, now grown up and old, for me at seventy-three more than half of them gone, another half still becoming, still singing across the green arena of the canyon, "The Spirit of God like a fire is burning! . . . We'll sing and we'll shout. . . . Let glory to them in the highest be given, . . ." And oh, we gave it, the glory. And receive it still from those mountains. And from those dear rugged and refined people, lasting as the landscape we all belonged to. "Henceforth and forever, Amen and Amen!"

Because this is my place. Every view lets me in on the created and the uncreated.

This is my place. Derivative? Of course. As I am. Intimately and in touch, folded into this, my landscape. Here is my solace as well as my joy. Here is where sky meets earth and the infinite, which undoes me wider than wide. Now forty years since, I can call up that day in 1956, my first encounter with death, a new need for the canyon.

That morning in September went stammering off without me. "She died fifteen minutes ago." No! So alive. Sick only forty-eight hours. Only twenty-eight years old. Last time I looked, it was 6:44 A.M. The voice from the polio ward at the County Hospital: "Are you family?" "No, just a friend." Just a friend. My friend so close I would pick up the phone after her funeral and dial her number. That day my husband and our three daughters under five slept a Sunday morning sleep, the house for me suddenly a suffocation. In my stupor, into my mind's stereopticon, my canyon. My rescue. Beyond the leaden garage door, I was in the car, driving, my way, my only way. Against the east, my comfort, my mountains holding up the pale sky saying, "Come."

On the road, behind my empty eyes my friend rose to meet them, my mountains. Our ten years of being in on each other's lives melted into this one Sunday morning, the mountains opening around me, their arms holding me on the curves following Parley's Creek to the gate guarding our Mt. Air Canyon. She and I were again playing tennis, introducing each other to the boys we married, confiding the coming of babies, singing "In Our Lovely Deseret" in sacrament meeting, skiing the hills, teaching at the same school, laughing, laughing, laughing.

Into that canyon familiar as a face just out of sleep beside me, I drove the winding narrow road the two miles farther toward our cabin. In the cottonwoods a whippoorwill let go her name. Car windows down in 1956, creating our own wind, the car and I were drawn by a pulley insistent as the need to swallow. Maples, birch, pines, kinnikinnick reached for each other, for me in a tunnel of green, the slim brown road singing its dirge under my tires, new air rushing mint and the mulch of my thirty-one summers into my breathing, every half breath into a sigh.

Passing other cabins, I remembered other voices singing on the screened porch at Sunday school erupting over the years, "Our Mountain Home So Dear." The green tunnel twittered and waved me by, my journey flight to, from, the years tugging at my face, tears scalding inside with not letting go. I could hear her sextet singing ". . . in the same way then, but I can't remember where or when . . ." Through the crest of trees, mountain rose out of mountain, great green humps rounded into higher ones, redrock faces jutted from underbrush splotched with orange and red. The sky became the purple blue of sadness holding its own, us, in the palm of God. Continuations of canyon swells and sinews spilled into the shores of each other like mounting convulsions of desire. Up through the tops of trees the vastness moaned, Cry, Cry, please, the balm of tears.

Even as I traveled, into my stereopticon came my cousins, my brothers, my husband and children, my friend, crisscrossing the hillsides, the ridges, sage tangy, sego lilies and Indian paintbrush bursting from the crackle of rusty saxifrage at the end of summer, no climb too steep, no descent resistible, my legs crashing through chest-deep bushes, bounding. I remembered a doe and her two fawns by the high deer lick running as we surprised them, their white bottoms a blur of escape. Now I was beseeching the infinite, "Let it be me. Open the green, the blue, the cool hand for me to come home." In my stereopticon, her small children bewildered before me, two struggling on short understandings to find her, the baby unyielding in others' arms, their father disappearing into his disbelief. How ever to let their loss, mine, fade into trees of my childhood, the tinge of autumn telling its time. Maybe with snow, I thought, surely the snow just weeks away would level the pain, give silence to the creek that would weep under its ice, send all creatures to frosty sleep. How inevitable the passing death of the seasons. How alive with the thousand colors of green waiting.

I knew this would be only the beginning of the dying. How to fathom the others to come? The disappearance of who was there? With the scent of those mountains I could see the climbing of those who would be gone. Their voices as children called for me, took off from Echo Point and Castle Crags, Pine Top and Mt. Air Peak. "Lullaby and goodnight . . ."

Into the grassy-centered driveway, across the wooden bridge, at the foot of great hovering Castle Crags, the car stopped at the brown cabin, the whole canyon alive with its tremblings and songs. In some familiar distance I heard what I'd learned in seventh grade chorus, "Mother's there, 'spectin' me, Father's waitin' too, Lots of folks gathered there, all the friends I knew," widening, welcoming. And they weren't even there yet.

I was sobbing. The mending had begun. In my canyon and beyond.

Through my forty winters since and the departure of another and another and another, the landscape has furnished me with what I need to know. Everywhere now is a dead and a living place. Now my own children and theirs occupy me and it along with those still attending to wherever I am. Into my soul or onto a page I have learned to smuggle the sun and trees, the white ski hills and magenta foliage, the bursting of creatures in the red rocks and chartreuse spring, or the songs of cousins around a summer bonfire. Utah mountains, in some crooked nook of time, travel with me, they and their holdings, scribbled over anywhere else I land. My own stereopticon imaginings let me always be at home. From the Amazon forest to the Trans-Siberian Railway, from Alaska to Florence, from Israel to Acapulco, Istanbul to Edinburgh, Bucharest, Helsinki, or Honolulu, whenever I leave them I am awakened only more to why I will return, why I will live and be buried here. I'm expected here as I know I will be expected there soon in forever Light. The voices of my dears and the infinite, swoop down on me in my place. I want to write books full of them, full of their history, mine, full of the Utah never idle inside me, its vastness.

Of course "For the strength of the hills [I] bless thee, [my] God, [my] fathers' God"—and my mothers' God. My husband's and our children's and grandchildren's. God of my grandfathers and grandmothers who came here, Richards, Stayners, Warners, Candlands, Longstroths, and, three generations back, Emma Turner, my namesake, who marks my path as surely as my friend did hiking with me and disappearing into forty years ago. But it is *my* God to know and to worship.

In my greying years I go more and more to my canyon where I know so well the vastness after that first death and the bliss of childness before it. In my viewer I go to Echo Point, completely surrounded by higher mountains, where a "yoo-hoo" in any direction brings back seven yoo-hoos. The desert lifts its dryness 7,000 feet up to send us crashing down through the "bushes" we never knew the names of, only the feel of leaping like those deer through them, still yahooing, to the creek for a drink of the then-drinkable, always-icy water, laughing itself around rocks and down falls and into still pools in the cool shade of Lovers' Lane, where we'd lie down on hands and stomach to suck up sweet wetness like the woods creatures we had become.

That daring and that naturalness have led me to a life rich with people and what matters for them. The poignant death of a friend decades ago was only a hint of the need for solace in my mountains. And much of that need has had to do not only with me but with my community and sense of it. I headed for those hills about twenty years ago after seeing nearly 14,000 women at the IWY Conference in the Salt Palace mobilized to reject their own rights, succor, and offerings. I invited others there, too, to regain focus and try to begin healing.

I've taken my realizations and friends to the canyon to find answers together, to have fun, returning refreshed for another try at some coming together or mending of fences in dealing with the biases of the very traditions I honor or the systems I continue to be part of.

My canyon harmony has become "Let there be peace on earth and let it begin with me." I hear "Amazing Grace" among strangers linked by a mutual cause as well as among my family and friends. Others come to our place in the mountains, invited in the same way that I go alone to the green rescue. They are as various as the green itself moving with the seasons. I see them blazing their own inroads, flinging themselves through the bushes of trivia and prejudice, finding themselves renewed, and then offering their own voices to do the same for others.

Even as I take my Mormon Relief Society sisters there, I also go to mourn with AIDS mourners and sufferers, to struggle hand in hand with those who give their strength to unpopular peace or survival of the very rocks and trees that offer the harmony of my canyon. I would bless the strength of the hills and give ardent and vocal thanks to my God, my father's God. And the best way I know how is to let that strength feed whatever truth I have learned away from those hills and through my faith in God. Those who so richly people my past cry to me to find trails of my own, to let my echo ring with unfearful praise of those alike or different from me or in either more or less favor with earning or spending.

Now another generation holds sticks with melting bronzed marshmallows over the new fire pit below the sentinel Castle Crags looming above the gully. I can see where the single rope swing dared us to fly, its knot anchoring a seat, a thick branch of mountain mahogany. Through my viewer I can be taking off from a platform on the mountain to sail between two huge pines, forty feet out, to whoop at a sudden taking in of the tops of aspen and birch and sandstone giving way to wildflower-scented marshes around the spring, and the mouth-drying tingle of willing a look, head back, feet pumping into circles, becoming the wind, an eagle declaring its rights to the sky, my wanting never to land, singing "Oh, he flies through the air with the greatest of ease, the daring young man on the flying trapeze" and "Oh ye mountains high, where the clear blue sky arches over the vales of the free, . . . All my fond hopes are centered in thee." The mix, the sturdy brew of the earthy and the eternal, the spirited and the spiritual. I am still sent forth "with joy, [to] be led forth with peace: the mountains and the hills . . . break forth before [me] into singing, and all the trees of the field . . . clap their hands" (Isaiah 55:12). The peace of the sacred binds me and my people like bark on the same tree but still frees me to find my own way and clap my own hands for what I see. If I became an earth creature in my growing up, I also came to know that "all God's critters got a place in the choir." And from my place in the mountains I will celebrate the valid offerings of whoever comes into my view, in Utah or across the globe.

Finally I can bring up a picture of light taking its time leaving the steep green of Pine Top. My watching is from an ancient wicker rocker on the cabin porch as the sun pulls away its touch like a reluctant lover, as if ignited from within the mountains, its now subtle brilliance inching skyward.

Yesterday and still today I put into my stereopticon the natural coming and going of sun, dark skies, lightning and thunder, forest fires and chill snow double the height of a man, sunlight turning to crepuscular the silhouettes of cottonwoods, pines, and maples. Behind any of it looms the intimate outline of mountains on sky, black on black. I can see the moon too, somewhere waiting to stream into the long window by the bed where we wait for it before sleep, seeing stars without names, all as familiar as "Abide with me! fast falls the eventide; . . ." I need that abiding. I live by it.

Since an accident on the freeway eleven years ago and a death experience

I can now see without any viewer but my own knowing, I can see to the infinite that Hadewijch II saw those centuries ago. I can sing in my soul, "When I leave this frail existence, when I lay this mortal by, Father, Mother, [I will] meet you in your royal courts on high . . .", the royal courts surely some filmy vestige of my hills of home, the mountains I'll be looking to and beyond.

In the family cemetery where Mel laughed with my three brothers picking out a site twenty years ago, we will be buried. Instead of my ashes scattered over the hillside above our cabin and Castle Crags that looks down on it, tradition will have its way. But next best will be to bring the canyon to the valley. A great slab from the granite face of Castle Crags sloughed off a million years ago has been brought out from its steep slope by my canyon cousin who has the say at the cemetery. The shadow Mel and I will leave over our grave will be a bench rough hewn from that rock, with a full view over trees to Mt. Olympus, nestled near it the canyon Mel has learned to love as I do, above it cobalt blue Utah sky. Beside our names, inscribed on the bench will be what I wrote twenty years after the death of my friend, telling the story above our pine stairs at the cabin, what will continue to come to pass:

MT. AIR

This is my place.
Finally I have turned away
and walked into the morning.
It is as I knew it was.
I do or I don't do.
At last that is not the thing.
All that is is this:
I am here
and whatever is calling in the crags
knows.

What is calling in the crags is the softer music of the inner life, what sustains me in any skimpiness of vision or limiting by self-righteousness. Everything else is too narrow. The vastness, the expansion is there. What's too often missing in cluttered, peopled, commercialized, urban skylines and lives. What's too often missing in what the soul can perceive, in what the eye can span, the ear hear, the lungs breathe, or the imagination encompass—the sense of God's hand handing, what the human race evolved from. The "it is very good" of any man or woman realizing the full measure of that creation. What can be visible with the primordial eyesight of the thirteenth century, the 1930s, or the 1990s. For me, growing up Utahn lets me in on the uncreated that lies beyond even my mother's stereopticon viewer.

You know this well, you who are also there.

Emma Lou Thayne, a writer of fiction and nonfiction, is a poet, lecturer, outdoors person, and champion of many causes—artistic, environmental, social, and civic.

"Now faith is the substance of things hoped for, the evidence of things not seen." (Hebrews 11:1.)

MORNING WALK

Natalie Taylor

ROM MY MOTHER'S GARDEN I GATHER ROSES: DAINTY BESS, ANGEL Face, and Peace. I tie them together with a lavender ribbon and call for Haley, my three-year-old.

"Can you hold these for me, sweetie?"

I buckle her in and drive my old Subaru through the gates, honking the horn. I get out of my car and look back at my parents' house. A set of white ceramic doves chime in the breeze.

I run back into the mother-in-law apartment, which has been our home for the past two years since my divorce, to find the plastic bag full of sandwiches, some apples, and juice, and wave to my mother.

"Come on, get off the phone!"

Quinn, my three-year-old nephew, comes running out of the house. "Can I come too?" he asks.

We are all waiting when finally my mother comes running out. "What took you so long?" she teases. "I've been waiting for you."

We drive up Big Cottonwood Canyon to the Brighton ski resort and park at the entrance to Silver Lake.

My best friend, Becky, meets us at the trailhead with a bouquet of white wildflowers wrapped in clear cellophane. We hug.

"They're lovely," I say, "what are they?"

"I don't know," she answers, "but they reminded me of her."

I brush a tear away, glad for the distracting voices of Haley and Quinn, enthralled in the meadow of wildflowers. Chasing the half-tame squirrels under the boardwalk, the children keep their eyes alert for the glimpse of another bushy tail or fat gray stomach.

We walk slowly. Mount Millicent is reflected in the slow ripples of Silver Lake.

"It's been a year today," my mother says quietly. "Are you still angry at God?"

Part of me is still in shock; the clouds move overhead as easily as I move through time.

"I guess she's not coming back." I say. "For so long, even after the memorial service I kept expecting the hospital to call and tell me that there had been some terrible mistake and she was there, well, waiting for me to come pick her up." I'm crying now, the children far ahead with Becky. "I just thought she'd visit more," I say. "You know, when I dream of her she's still a baby, still fifteen months old; she doesn't walk or talk but she's not sick, no machines, no drugs, no scars, just Olivia . . . normal. I'm dressing her or the girls are playing or I'm taking them down to Millcreek in the wagon. I just can't believe she's gone."

Boys are fishing from the platforms. The fish are tiny, not worth fishing for at all, and when caught are mostly thrown back. We walk quietly until my mother interrupts.

"Did you look at her face just after you changed the trach tube?"

I shake my head. That morning one year ago today is crystal clear.

I heard the nurse suction her and take her outside to look at my mother's gardens. They were blooming now as they were last year. Olivia loved to have mimosa tufts rubbed on her cheek. They must have done that. I got out of bed and started to get dressed to go for a run. The nurse and Olivia must have walked past the eremurus lily. This was my mother's talisman that Olivia would come home from the hospital. It was blooming its strange pink blossom next to the hibiscus. The nurse came inside and I heard her put Olivia in the crib. My front room looked like a hospital room. She fiddled with the oxygen tank while Olivia played with the tubes that snaked across the crib. The nurse walked down the hall to put the dirty diaper away.

I walked downstairs to see my baby. From across the room I saw her leg, like a slab of marble, mottled and still. Simultaneously, I saw my mother and father coming through the gates, back from their morning walk. I did not panic; I remembered what the trach CPR classes had told me. I called to my mother for help. I dialed 911 and recited her birth defects: "We need an ambulance, fifteen-month infant, dextro-cardia, agenesis of the right lung, specialized trach tube. We have home-care nursing but we've lost a pulse." In the time it has taken for me to call, my small apartment is full of family. I handed the phone to my sister Nan and pulled sterilized gloves on. The nurse is trying to start her heart. I had never changed her trach tube before. But my baby is not breathing. So I did what I thought I could not do. I took the collar that held her trach tube in place and pulled out the clogged tube. I put the clean one in and refastened the Velcro collar. Just like they did at the hospital. The paramedics have arrived and they put her limp body on the floor. One of them cut the nightgown my mother made for her to match Haley's down the front. Her chest is still red with scars, one runs the length of her Adam's apple to her sternum. He plunged an emergency IV through her shinbone as I turn up the oxygen. We had spent four and a half months at the ICU unit; we were accustomed to crisis situations. We would cry later. For now, we were keeping her alive. But she was already gone.

From the fog of my memory I hear my mom's voice, "She opened her eyes and kind of smiled, and then she waved her hands—like she did when she said bye-bye. I think she was waving to the angels, or maybe to us."

"Mommy, Mommy. Hey, Mommy!" Back to the land of the living and the exploration of a beaver dam the kids had found. Becky tells them about the entrances a beaver builds; there is always an escape route, a secret entrance. They try diligently to sit quietly as only toddlers can, but no beaver appears. A squirrel scolds us from the safe perch in the fir tree and a falling pine cone scares them into our arms. We move on through the forest and into a clearing of wild columbine, bluebells, cranesbill, and monkshood.

"I'm tired, Mamaw," Haley says, so we find a bench to let the toddlers rest.

"This is easier than I thought it would be, coming here I mean."

My mom begins, "I've never forgiven myself for not bringing her here that night we had planned."

"Mom, she was home eight days. There wasn't enough time. Besides, Drew said it was hailing that night up here."

She has that faraway look in her eyes and I can tell that my words are of no comfort to her now.

We are sitting a few feet away from where I took Olivia's ashes out of the plastic baggy and laid them in cobalt blue silk. Just the family and a few close friends were there after the service. We gathered wildflowers then and laid them on top of the ashes, pastel amber, lavender, pink, even a touch of blue on a beige chip. They are not fine like sand, like the ashes of a fire; they are like small shells on the beach. Then we gathered in a circle and held hands while my father prayed. A sense of well-being and peace surrounded the grieving.

The clouds roll overhead, the past and present undulate like wisps of cumulus. Haley and Quinn are ahead of us again, chasing a blue dragonfly that hovers over them, then darts out of sight. Last year at Haley's third birthday party all the kids stopped suddenly in the midst of the Halloween mayhem to watch a copper-colored dragonfly buzz around the lights. The dragonfly stayed through the party and when Haley asked, "Mommy, why didn't Olivia come to my party?" the dragonfly hovered over her right shoulder. A few days later I found the dragonfly dead on the smallest pumpkin, the one Haley had painted for Olivia. Now this one, flying just out of reach, disappearing for moments, only to return. "Hi, baby," I thought.

"When my dad died," my Mother begins, "I was so angry he didn't visit me. I even asked him, too, before he died and he told me he would if he could. But he never has. One day I was hiking by myself and I got a little frightened. Suddenly, I was overwhelmed by this sweet feeling, and an incredible peace came over me. I knew then that Christ lives, and what we've been told about him is true. I knew that before, I'd been married in the temple, had you and your brother and a third on the way. But nothing as powerful as this. Maybe that was what I needed, more than to see my dad."

"Come quick," Becky calls. The kids had spotted a brown trout hiding in the mossy rocks. It was about three inches long but it was a monster to the little ones. After the memorial service a family friend had offered her cabin at Fish Lake so the whole family could do some quiet grieving. The first night I was there I watched an osprey fishing. I was struck by its beauty and fatal grace. It flew away after a stunning dive, with a trout swishing frantically between its curved beak. Life and Death. The circle never ends.

The morning adventures have worked up the children's appetites, so we head back for the car and the sandwiches. Once again we pile in and I drive up past the sloped roofs of the ski chalets and the new additions to the lodge. We drive on the granite road until we come to the amphitheater. Solid granite steps formed from boulders, halved logs lain in the crooks of the rock served as benches. This is where her memorial service had been. No one had objected to a Sunday service on the mountain, the air scented with morning rain, the chords of an acoustic guitar floating over the fir cones to the still-white patches of glacier snow steady on the granite. It was unorthodox. But then, it is unnatural for a baby to die. Her body had been her coffin and it was time to set her free. The service had been a celebration of her life; she had lived with courage and joy. It was her choice to go, I would honor that. I place the bouquet of roses in the center of the granite. She will know.

We sit far away from each other, the intimacy of shared pain unbearable. Becky eats only a few bites, the sandwich held limply in her hand between her knees. Tears flow across her cheeks. Behind her sunglasses, my mother's eyes are closed. She is praying. I wait for a sign, some sense of Olivia, a perfect flower, the dragonfly, a wild mourning dove to land on my shoulder. The name Olivia means peace. Doves are the symbol of peace. It never comes. What I really want is her. I am aware of the sun's heat on my shoulders; and the children frighten me, they play so close to the edge.

Driving down the canyon my mother starts again. This woman, who has raised eight children solely on intuition and a fierce love, knows about grief and healing. "Massa, your grandmother, has visited a couple of times—at her funeral and once when you spoke at church after you came back from Europe. But I never sensed her. Maybe I wanted it too much. But at Nan's baptism I could tell you exactly when she came and when she left. The bishop said, 'We have special visitors tonight.'"

My mother had a dream about Olivia shortly after her death, and I was very jealous of it. She told me Olivia had come to meet her after she died. Olivia was a young woman, beautiful, with long hair, and she spoke in a melodious voice. "And those eyes," my mother trembled, "those magnificent eyes. I had a sense that she is at peace. She is busy but happy. She isn't being tortured anymore, she is released from her pain." My mother had once told me that when she looks back on any one of the procedures, the drugs that kept her paralyzed and sedated, the ventilator that breathed for her, the way her body looked lost after her open-heart surgery, it made her sick. "I ache for her and can't understand how we ever did it, went up to the hospital in shifts, you and I so Olivia wasn't alone, day after day, month after month. Praying harder and faster after each setback, regaining our hope only to have another relapse." She weeps, then speaks through the tears, "But, if I look past the horror and see Olivia's life as a whole, it was profound, however brief. She affected so many people who were charmed by her charisma. She was a rare soul, a gift to you. We were honored to be her caretakers. I know she loves you, I sense her nearness, she is mindful of you. I believe this."

In the backseat the children collapse against each other. I can see Haley's ribs through the thin cotton shirt. She has not had it easy, this one. I spend more Sundays in the woods than I do at church, but I pray just the same. I pray Olivia is well and knows I cherish each second spent in her presence, however painful. I pray she visits me and that the power of my love can span an eternity. I pray I can have the privilege of raising her in heaven. I think Haley would like that too.

Back at home I find the quiet of the patio comforting. I swing back and forth using my big toe for leverage. Behind me is a strip of earth where I planted white Olivia lilies, forget-me-nots, and angel tears. A few new wildflower petals are dropped in the blue urn my sister Nan made, which has a white dove flying on top. We spent hours on this swing, Livvy and I. It was the only thing that would calm the tears. The rhythmic movement, the shade, the garden's colors and smells lulling her to sleep. My father finds me and asks if he can sit down.

"I had a dream last night I wanted to tell you about," he says. "It was the day she was born; we all went up to see you and your new daughter. I looked at her and said, 'We have a special visitor.'" His warm arm wraps around my shoulders and we sit there swinging in the heaviness of a summer afternoon. Mother comes around the corner, carrying a spade, her eyes glowing. "Look," she says, pointing with a clump of weeds, "up there." We look. In the middle of a huge pine tree, hidden in the branches, is a pair of wild mourning doves, nestled together.

Natalie Taylor is a freelance writer living in Salt Lake City, Utah.

"THEY THAT REMAIN, AND ARE PURE IN HEART, SHALL RETURN, AND COME TO THEIR INHERITANCES, THEY AND THEIR CHILDREN, WITH SONGS OF EVERLASTING JOY . . ." (D&C 101:18.)

SUSTAINABILITY: WILL THE CHILDREN RETURN?

DAN AND BONNIE JUDD

N THE SAWTOOTH MOUNTAINS OF IDAHO LIES REDFISH LAKE, named for the darting, crimson shapes of sockeye salmon that once crowded in by the thousands to spawn. Last year, a single wild salmon returned.
—THE HERALD JOURNAL (Logan, Utah), September 8, 1995

When the insulating depths of winter cover summer memories, our children begin to ask, "Mom, Dad, when are we going back to the cabin?" The place they long for is a log-and-chinking summer cottage first acquired almost a hundred years ago by our great-grandfather, Heber J. Grant, as a gift for his wife, Augusta. The cabin is located in Utah's Wasatch Mountains at the head of Big Cottonwood Canyon, situated in a glacial bowl known as Brighton. Brighton is a place that has retained a sense of its past. Cabins that dot the landscape are for the most part thirty, forty, or more years old. Aspen and Indian paintbrush still hold their own. It is a place one wants to return to and a place one still can.

Last summer we arrived at Brighton well after midnight. Headlights tunneled through the aspen and Douglas fir, as the children slept, parkas for pillows, in the back of the van. Approaching the cabin, our minds moved ahead to a scene unchanged by the passing years. The great room—rafters overhead and peaked ceilings above lending spaciousness, woven blankets on log walls, and Navajo rugs on pine floors providing coziness. Awaiting family and social gatherings, the massive wooden table surrounded by straight-backed oak chairs joins the rust-colored sofa and bent rocker facing the stone hearth. There will be no sounds of television or telephone interruptions here, only the sounds of Big Cottonwood Creek, conversation, and children's games. We return here to reflect.

Our plan was to carry the children undisturbed to their beds, but the kids had other ideas. Lights were turned on and so too the excitement. Shouts of "We're here! We're here! We're at the cabin at last!" reverberated. Pillows were flung into the air in jubilation. After more than an hour of delight and rediscovery, the enthusiasm conformed to the late hour. The twisted, aspen-branch banister along the back wall supported the children's ascent up the slatted stairs to the loft—that treasured place where the dreams of night and day run together.

Once the kids were settled, we carried the bags to the back bedroom. Passing by the wall below the stairs, we paused to look at the framed photos, some black and white and some brown and white. These were the faces of those who in the past laughed together and fed their families around this table.

A whispered reminiscence ensued, "I remember the first time I saw these faces. You brought me here on our second date. Your mom met us at the door and began introducing everyone, 'This is Dan's sister, Carlie, and brother, Steve.' Without hesitating the introductions continued at this wall. 'This is Dan's great-grandmother, Augusta, as a young girl, and here is Dan's great-grandfather presenting a book of braille to Helen Keller.' I remember being struck by the connection your family felt to their forebears. There seemed to be no differentiation between the living and the deceased. I had never been introduced to ancestors before. What I remember most, however, was the letter."

We lifted the framed letter from Heber to his wife, Augusta, off the wall. Together we read it once again:

Salt Lake City, August 14, 1899

My Darling Gusta,

You will recall that I promised you that I would make you a present on your birthday of a place in Brighton. Well, Dearest, I have made good my promise and the deeds will be made out at once. I have paid two hundred and fifty dollars for the Romney place, and I am told by Brother George Pyper that he thought it was a cheap place at three hundred. Odell tells me it is the finest place there . . .

All is well and I send to my love my fondest love and all the sweet kisses she wants, or that it is possible to send by mail.

I shall be glad to be at Soda again.

Lovingly yours,

Heber

Odell has agreed to repurchase the place next year if we do not want it.

Heber and Augusta seemed to be reading over our shoulders. It was good to be back with them again.

This letter marked a beginning. Since its writing a century ago, members of our family have returned here to Brighton—returned to wander along the shores of Silver Lake, to climb Sunrise Peak, to watch summer's wild geranium give way to violet fireweed and autumn's aspen gold. Like salmon, we are inherently drawn to return.

The cabin is a haven for each generation, providing a base from which to discover the canyon. Each summer we come here to reunite with the earth and with the family. As we walk trails with fathers and cousins, mothers and nieces, aunts and brothers, we seem to be accompanied by our loved ones from the past; and though we have never met them, this place familiarizes and holds us together.

How does this relationship transpire? How is it that these ancestors remain in the hearts of their great-grandchildren? The answer, in part, is in Brighton, our refuge in the natural world. Would we know these people without this place? We may know them as names on a genealogical chart, but there is more. Rocks, water, and trees convey not just natural history but a human story.

As children, it was here in the canyon we fell into an affinity with nature. Discovery drew us. Self-discovery now draws us to the past. A bridge that spans the years is traversed as we return to this place in the natural world.

In essence, this is what sustainability means, that the children are able to return. As Mormons, we seem to reach for what may be called "spiritual sustainability," a way to transcend the generations to influence the lives of our children's children. How can this be done? In response, the words of author-ecologist C. A. Bowers resonate with our experience: "Transgenerational communication is a characteristic of ecology-centered cultures." We understand Bowers to be saying that people who esteem the environment are given a means to converse across generations. Our experiences with Brighton affirm that ecology-centeredness in our families promotes communication over time. Spiritual messages can be lastingly transferred through the language of a natural place. Place to person, person to past—the landscape delivers the message:

> And may the timber and grass, the vegetation of every description, growing in this little valley in the tops of these mountains be blessed and we consecrate and dedicate it to Thee for the benefit of Thy people; for their happiness, that they may rest here and be safe.
> Jedediah M. Grant
> Dedicatory Prayer of Big Cottonwood Canyon
> July 24, 1856

This excerpt is from a prayer blessing the canyon, given by our great-great-grandfather at a Twenty-fourth of July celebration here in Brighton. The celebration commemorated the arrival of the Mormon pioneers to these mountains. This dedicatory prayer was delivered just five months before his death and just one year prior to the electrifying news that Johnston's Army was advancing on the Mormons. Today, we face another kind of advancement: the onslaught of the media, the pressures of time, the insistence of getting. Are rest, safety, and happiness even a possibility? How can this blessing be fulfilled? For us, we discover their realization here, in Brighton. The benefit of which he speaks is not in lumber but in fir and pine. In the *life* of this place, we find our rest.

Growing with each generation, love for Brighton gathers like the waters of Big Cottonwood Creek from the experiences of each child. The cabin was ultimately gifted by Heber's wife, Augusta, to her daughter, Mary Grant Judd.

> *My Dear Mary,*
>
> *. . . I would like you to have my cottage. You have been in it so much with me, and I **expect you always to be with me here** and help me. So this is in the nature of my "last will and testament," that I would like you to have my cottage and a strip of land with it for yourself and family, and I hope you will never sell it.*
>
> *Your loving mother,*
> *Augusta W. Grant*
> *Brighton*
> *July 22, 1918*
> *[emphasis added]*

Like her mother, Mary felt an abiding love for this place. Like us, she deepened her relation with grandparents through Brighton. Mary never knew her grandfather, Jedediah M. Grant; he died when her father, Heber, was only nine days old. At the request of her father, and to feed her own understanding, Mary Grant authored a biography of Jedediah. His canyon blessing touched her emotion as it did ours. She concluded her biographical tribute to him with these words:

> *Because much of the writing of this biography was done in Big Cottonwood Canyon, at Brighton, I felt closer to my grandfather when I learned that he, too, loved that mountain retreat. . . . [His] lovely prayer will mean much to the great number of people who know and love Brighton, and perhaps will encourage those who have not experienced the beauties of this lovely spot to go there and enjoy the exhilaration and spiritual uplift which are to be found.*

The spiritual uplift continues to be felt by her great-grandchildren. It was energetically expressed by our five-year-old, Skye, upon rising the morning following our midnight arrival. The aroma of pancakes on the griddle beckoned her down the stairs. Bundled in a blanket, she headed for the outdoor porch to warm up. The early morning light was just cresting the mountain. After a moment, with a flurry of slippers and blankets, she was back inside. "Dad," she exclaimed, "we've *got* to eat breakfast outside! It's *glorious* out there!" Where does a five-year-old come up with a word like "glorious"? From an experience of heaven, or God's mountains.

Our week was one of reunion with familiar places. By Thursday, we were planning a midweek hike to Twin Lakes. Grandma Louise drove up from the city to join us. With our one-year-old, Daniel, in the backpack, and Mimi encouraging her three granddaughters, we climbed, reveling in wildflowers. Spring was unusually wet, producing an unseasonal abundance of blossoms. The breadth of the south-facing slope above Twin Lakes spangled as yellow arnica caught sunshine and bluebells clustered under aspen.

The purpose of our hike connected mountains and spiritual life. Our intent was to give our children a before-school blessing. Such a blessing is customary in many Mormon households; this year we chose an uncustomary setting.

Locating a secluded spot under the trees near the shore, each child sat in turn on the bent trunk of an aspen. The midday sun shone on the water. From the far side of the lake, a mountain breeze carried the light in ripples across the surface toward us. The children were blessed.

Spirit. Oneness. Message. The moment spoke of living eternally with our God, not only in the afterlife but "here." In the experience of nature, we find Him "now."

In prophetic vision even our identity as a people was shaped by these mountains.

> ... the very gathering of this people to these mountains is a direct fulfillment of the promises made through the Prophet Joseph Smith ... that the Latter-day Saints would yet come to the valleys of the Rocky Mountains and become a great and prosperous people.
> Heber J. Grant
> Salt Lake Tabernacle
> January 26, 1896

What does it mean to be great and prosperous? Is prosperity only material? Brighton reminds us that "peace in our souls" is prosperity. We prosper from the quiet, the rest. In the natural world we find not a way to happiness but a recognition that happiness is the way.

On the last day of our trip, we returned to "these mountains." That Sunday morning on the trail to Lake Mary, we had in mind a family testimony meeting for the afternoon. As we stood at the edge of a cliff overlooking Brighton, the mountain bluebells at our feet gave way to a gradient blue sky resting on plummeting green. Our soon-to-be-six-year-old, Lauren, was asked if she had been thinking about her testimony. She answered assuredly, "This," as if to add, "of course." Her hand swept outward, "This is my testimony."

Not one word, not a thousand words, could better testify. Her words echo those of her forebears and display a knowledge they would want her to have. The desire to whisper spiritual messages to the souls of great-grandchildren can be realized. Find a place for your family—a place in the natural world. Revere it and return to it. Share your message. Your Father in Heaven's creations are the convincers.

What messages hold the most meaning for us? Is there anything in the lives of our grandparents that could aid us in our efforts to preserve the places we care about?

Heber J. Grant was certainly not one to hesitate in taking a stand on vital issues. Yet he had the uncommon wisdom to bring together opposing factions in the process. His biographer, Francis M. Gibbons, names as one of his greatest accomplishments the mending of division among Utahns due to religion. His eighty-second birthday was the celebration of this most effectual message:

> ... the general chairman of the event was John F. Fitzpatrick, head of The Salt Lake Tribune, the local paper that, in President Grant's earlier years, had been so unrestrained in its criticism of the LDS Church and its leaders. An editorial appearing in the paper, reporting on the [birthday] banquet, eloquently reveals the dramatic change in the climate of Mormon-gentile relations that occurred during the life of one man:
>
> "There was something more than individual tribute in this bond of friendship. In all of Utah history there is no signal of unity more poignant with peaceful understanding than this one. To attain such a goal is the work of generations devoted to all that is good in civilization. . . . To be the medium for such an expression was pleasing to the venerable church leader, loved and admired by all his associates without regard to religious ties."
>
> The Salt Lake Tribune, November 1983
> As quoted by Francis M. Gibbons
> in Heber J. Grant: Man of Steel, Prophet of God

Heber J. Grant was a pivotal person. Returning to the intent of his father's canyon blessing, his desire was that all God's children find "happiness, rest, and safety" here. A bitter struggle was mitigated through his wisdom and emphasis upon another returning—the return of mutual understanding. A more cohesive community is the result.

This past summer, it was our family's turn to close up the cabin for the season. As we swept the floors, the unsettled dust found rest suspending in the amber light of afternoon. Calmed, our eight-year-old daughter, Corinne, paused to look out the window at the trees that shelter the cabin. "Mom, I'm glad Augusta didn't give the cabin back. Aren't you?"

I mused at her first-name relationship with her great-great-grandmother and asked, "What do you mean?"

"You know . . . the letter!"

"Oh," registering her reference to the letter from Grandpa Heber to his wife, Augusta, "you mean you're glad she didn't sell it back to Odell."

"Yeah!"

"Yes," I bent down to smooth a wrinkle in the bedspread. "I am very glad she kept the cabin."

"Mom," she hesitated, "would there ever be a reason why we couldn't come back to the cabin?"

Forming my answer, I swept and thought of Augusta sweeping and then her daughter Mary. "Only if we don't take care of it," I said. "The cabin means too much to all of us. I'm sure we would never sell it."

"I'm glad."

"Me, too."

As we packed the last backpacks into the minivan, bolted the cabin doors, and piled the kids in the car, we experienced that moment of regret at parting.

The cabin disappeared, hidden behind the massive trunks rising up on each side of the winding asphalt that carried us back to the city. I thought once again of Augusta and Mary, Heber and Jedediah. "Would there ever be a reason our children's children could not come back here—here to our place in the natural world, this place of kinship, place of rest?"

Words of promise came with the wind through the window.

"Return to the message."

"In returning, the blessing is fulfilled."

Dan and Bonnie Judd's roots in Utah reach back to the early settlers. This essay is dedicated to their legacy.

BIOGRAPHICAL PROFILES

G. MICHAEL ALDER graduated from the University of Utah with a B.S. in botany (1967) and an M.S. in biology (1970). He served an LDS mission to England and then spent time as a military reservist in the medical corps. In 1973, Mr. Alder founded AgriDyne Technologies (originally, Native Plants, Inc.), serving as its president and chief operating officer through 1983 and its vice chairman until 1988. During his five-year tenure as head of the Office of Business Creation for the State of Utah (1989–94), he directed a program that helped to create ninety-two companies and over 2,000 industry and university jobs in the state. He then cofounded the Grow Utah Fund, a technology start-up group, in December 1994. Currently he is chairman of the board of Westcamp and executive director of Emerging Technology Partners, a private for-profit limited-liability company formed in Alabama in 1997 that takes responsibility to design and develop business aspects of new joint ventures, freeing the scientist/founders to focus on technology issues while the company is being formed.

His essay on conservation, "Earth, A Gift of Gladness," appears in the July 1991 issue of the *Ensign*. He is currently writing a book, *The Measure of Their Creation*, concerning a Mormon's perspective of conservation and living on the earth in modern times. His service in the LDS Church includes a five-year calling as bishop in his Salt Lake City ward. He and his wife, who make their home in Birmingham, Alabama, have five children and five grandchildren.

THOMAS G. ALEXANDER specializes in Utah history, western history, environmental history, and Mormon history. Some of his books include *Things in Heaven and Earth: The Life and Times of Wilford Woodruff, A Mormon Prophet* (1991; 2nd ed. 1993); *Mormonism in Transition: A History of the Latter-day Saints, 1890–1930* (1986; 2nd ed. 1996); and *Utah, the Right Place: The Official Centennial History* (1995; 2nd ed. 1996). A graduate of Weber State and Utah State Universities, he earned a Ph.D. in American history at the University of California at Berkeley (1965). He has won a number of prizes, including the David and Beatrice Evans Biography Award. He has served as president of the Mormon History Association and of the Utah Academy of Sciences, Arts, and Letters; and the Utah State Historical Society. He and his wife, the former Marilyn Johns of Ogden, live in Provo and are the parents of five children. He currently serves as a chair of the Provo City Landmarks Commission and as first counselor in the Edgemont 11th Ward bishopric.

MARILYN ARNOLD's life and energies have always been divided among libraries, classrooms, and the out-of-doors. She is an emeritus professor of English at BYU, having also served as assistant to former university president Dallin H. Oaks, as dean of Graduate Studies, and as director of the Center for the Study of Christian Values in Literature. She received the Karl G. Maeser Award for research and is an internationally known scholar on Willa Cather. A widely published writer and speaker in academic circles, she continues her scholarly work through the Women's Research Institute at Brigham Young University, where she is working on several projects: editing a dictionary reference companion to the Book of Mormon, coediting a book of women's poetry on peace, and serving on the editorial board for the Journal for Book of Mormon Studies. Currently, she is teaching a BYU class on Willa Cather at the LDS Institute at Dixie College in St. George, Utah. At the same time, she makes her heart's home in the red-rock desert surrounding St. George, where her spare time is spent hiking and playing tennis year-round. Recently, Dr. Arnold launched a career as a different sort of writer, as attested by her recent publications—*Sweet Is the Word: Reflections on the Book of Mormon, Its Narrative, Teachings, and People* (1996); *Pure Love: Readings on Sixteen Enduring Virtues* (1997), and her first novel, *Desert Song* (1998). Her love of scripture and her abiding love for the restored gospel are reflected in her lifelong service to her church.

JOSEPH AND LEE UDALL BENNION, ZINA, AND LOUISA: Joseph and Lee Bennion met while engaged in undergraduate studies at Brigham Young University in Provo, Utah, married in June 1976, and settled in Spring City, Utah, the following April, where they began their family and careers in art. At this writing the family is still there.

The Bennions feel a deep connection to the land of Utah through the pioneer families they descend from. On every line of their family tree are pioneers who opened Utah and the surrounding area for the establishment of the LDS faith. These early pioneers include Jacob Hamblin, John D. Lee, and Zackariah Decker of the Hole-in-the-Rock party.

In addition to their daughters Zina and Louisa, Joseph and Lee have a ten-year-old daughter named Adah Lee. As early as each girl was able, she was taken into the mountains and deserts of Utah for backpacking and river trips. Wilderness experience has always played an important role in the Bennion family, as has their connection to nature through the garden where they take a large portion of their sustenance.

Joseph and Lee have been recognized throughout the West for the quality of their artwork. Louisa and Zina have also gained substantial acclaim, both winning scholarships to their respective colleges. The Bennion family was the subject of an award-winning documentary film, *The Potter's Meal* (1992), made by Steve Olpin of Springville, Utah.

VON DEL CHAMBERLAIN was born in Kanab, Utah, in 1934, where he attended public school until his senior year. He graduated from Granite High School in Salt Lake County, and was inducted later into the Granite High Hall of Fame. He obtained a bachelor of arts degree with a major in physics from the University of Utah in 1958, then a master's degree in astronomy from the University of Michigan. He has worked at the McMath-Hulbert solar observatory, the Robert T. Longway Planetarium and the Abrams Planetarium, all in Michigan. In 1973 he joined the staff of the National Air and Space Museum at the Smithsonian Institution, where he directed the Albert Einstein Spacearium (planetarium), administered the giant-screen IMAX theater, and developed educational programs. In 1984 he became director of Hansen Planetarium in Salt Lake City, a post he held until he retired in 1996. Mr. Chamberlain was the founding member of both the Great Lakes Planetarium Association and the International Planetarium Society. In addition to developing education programs in classrooms and planetariums, he has encouraged "sky interpretation" in outdoor visitation areas, and lectured widely in outdoor settings, on cruise ships, and elsewhere. He is known for his research on Native American ethnoastronomy, cohosting the first world conference on that topic. He is the author of many papers as well as a book titled *When Stars Came Down to Earth: Cosmology of the Skidi Pawnee Indians of North America* (1982). Currently, he teaches university classes, lectures, and writes. His writing includes a newspaper column, "Looking Around," published twice monthly.

LARRY CLARKSON is president of Clarkson Creative, a Salt Lake City design and marketing communications consulting firm. He has won more than 300 professional design awards and has been published in many major design publications, including *Communication Arts, Print,* and *Graphis.* He holds a graduate degree in design and marketing, and has taught design at the University of Utah, Brigham Young University, and Westminster College. Larry is cofounder and past president of Entrada, an institute that celebrates Utah's landscape through the arts, and is founder of Friends of Capitol Reef. When he isn't exploring the high plateaus and desert canyons with his family near their second home in Grover, Utah, he spends his free time painting and writing poetry.

CORDELL CLINGER was raised and educated in Utah. He has been a member of the Salt Lake Symphony and has appeared in several productions of the Utah Opera. Currently, he is a member of the Mormon Tabernacle Choir, and treasures the profound experiences this calling has played in his life for the past fourteen years. His studies in Russian history and East European Jewry with Dr. Anita Baker at the University of Utah prompted his decision to study in Israel. The desert landscapes of Israel and Utah have been and continue to be a source of wonder, awe, and spiritual nurturance to him.

MICHAEL DUNN is an Emmy award-winning writer, producer, and principal for Dunn Communications, Inc., a Salt Lake City advertising agency. Numerous national awards given to Mr. Dunn include two gold medals from the New York Film Festival, several Clios, and two Emmy nominations—one for public service in 1992 from the national Academy of Television Arts and Sciences. He has also written and produced two documentary films: *Shared Vision* (1994) focuses on a group of doctors serving a humanitarian mission in a remote African nation, and *In Those Days* (1997) explores life in Utah during the depression era.
Graduating cum laude from the University of Utah, where he also did his graduate work, Mr. Dunn began his career as a freelance journalist, then moved to radio broadcasting as a reporter and producer. Prior to opening his own advertising agency, he spent thirteen years as a senior writer and producer for Bonneville Communications and Fotheringham & Associates in Salt Lake City. Community board service includes the University of Utah Alumni Association, the Bennion Center, Pioneer Theatre Company, Odyssey House, and the Utah Advertising Federation. He also serves on the editorial review boards of two magazines: *Continuum* and *This People.* Miraculously he survived his un-bearable experience and shares it with national television audiences and in a forthcoming book. He and his wife, Linda Poulson Dunn, are the parents of three children—Jeff, Brady, and Emily.

EUGENE ENGLAND was raised on a dryland wheat farm near Downey, Idaho, and, as a teenager, in the eastside suburbs of Salt Lake City. He graduated from the University of Utah, served in the Air Force as a weather officer, and did his Ph.D. at Stanford University. There he was a founding editor of *Dialogue: A Journal of Mormon Thought*, the first independent journal of Mormon arts and letters, and began to publish his personal essays and poetry as well as literary criticism. He taught literature at Stanford and in the experimental Paracollege at St. Olaf in Minnesota, where he also served as Dean of Academic Affairs.

After two years of teaching Institute for the LDS Church, he joined the faculty of Brigham Young University in 1977, where he has taught creative writing, American and Mormon literature, and Shakespeare. He has authored four collections of personal essays, a biography of Brigham Young, and a critical study of the American poet Frederick Goddard Tuckerman; he also has edited or coedited eight collections, including anthologies of Mormon poems, stories, and literary essays. He and his wife, Charlotte, have six children and twelve grandchildren; they like to dance, go to the theater, and walk in the woods. He goes fly-fishing a lot.

JAMES ERICKSON is a fifth-grader at Woodstock Elementary in Salt Lake City, Utah. With an inborn appreciation for the natural world, James loves the wilderness and wild animals. He imaginatively creates animals and uses them in his writing. He also enjoys writing about science fiction.

VAUGHN J. FEATHERSTONE has served as a General Authority of the LDS Church, as Area President in five different sections of the world, as Mission President in the Texas San Antonio Mission, as Young Men's General President, and twice as a counselor in the Young Men's Presidency. He has served on the National Executive Board of the Boy Scouts of America and on the National Advisory Council, has represented the Boy Scouts of America in World and National Jamborees, and has traveled extensively around the world on behalf of youth and the Boy Scouts of America. As a youth himself, he achieved the rank of Eagle Scout and received the Ranger Explorer Award. He has six sons, all of whom are Eagle Scouts.

DONALD L. GIBBON works in industrial energy and resource conservation, particularly in materials microcharacterization. In earlier incarnations he received a Ph.D. in geology at Rice University, spent a couple of years in the Corps of Engineers in France, taught geology at Guilford College in Greensboro, North Carolina, and worked for Ferro Corporation in Cleveland. In 1969 his sister gave him a membership in the Sierra Club, which, except for his marriage and then joining the LDS Church in 1974, turned out to be the most expensive thing in his life. Now a life member, he devotes much of his time to "environmental education," which he takes to mean as helping the rest of the world to see things Muir's way.

LYMAN HAFEN has chronicled the history, culture, and personality of southern Utah in hundreds of articles and essays over the past fifteen years as founding editor of *St. George Magazine*. He is the author of five books, including *Over the*

Joshua Slope (1994), *Roping the Wind: A Personal History of Cowboys and the Land* (1995), and *Mukuntuweap: Landscape and Story in Zion Canyon* (1996). He is a graduate of Dixie College and Brigham Young University, served an LDS mission in Argentina in 1975–76, and has been a bishop. A former state champion bronc rider, Hafen now lives a more down-to-earth life with his wife, Debbie, and six children in Santa Clara, Utah. He has served as chairman of the board of the Zion Natural History Association.

P. JANE HAFEN teaches minority literatures at the University of Nevada, Las Vegas. She is the recipient of a Frances C. Allen Fellowship from the D'arcy McNickle Center for History of the American Indian, Newberry Library, and has published articles on various topics in Native American literature. She is the mother of four children.

MACKEY HEDGES has spent his life working on ranches in Nevada, Idaho, Oregon, Montana, and California. He works rough country, builds great horses, and takes pride in his ability to rope and work cattle. He is presently managing the Double J Ranch out of Calleo, Utah, an environmentally sensitive cattle operation in the West Desert that takes in a limited number of guests each year to participate in these environmental activities. He strongly supports the Western Shoshone Defense Project in their efforts to preserve the environment and to encourage the U.S. government to recognize the Ruby Valley (Nevada) Treaty of 1863, which gave the Shoshones control of the northern part of Nevada at that time. Hedges is also the author of the much-acclaimed book *Last Buckaroo* (1995), a western novel that draws from Mackey's firsthand experiences in cowboying and ranching. He has been married to Candace Kidd for more than thirty-one years and has three sons—Buck, Jed, and Sam.

DAN AND BONNIE JUDD are both originally from Salt Lake City. Individually they were drawn to Big Cottonwood Canyon, where each acquired a love for Brighton. In 1983, it was Brighton that brought them together, and they were married in the spring of 1984. They now raise their family of four children in Smithfield, Utah, but return to Brighton whenever the season or opportunity permits.

JAMES B. MAYFIELD is an internationally recognized authority on the problems and challenges of third-world development. He is a professor of political science at the University of Utah (1967–97) and has been a management consultant with USAID, World Bank, UNICEF, and other donor agencies for the past twenty-five years. His areas of expertise include issues of third-world development, comparative public management training, Middle East studies, political economy of peasant societies, and survey research methods and data analysis. Dr. Mayfield is presently chairman of the board for CHOICE (Center for Humanitarian Outreach and Inter-Cultural Exchange), a humanitarian organization committed to improving the quality of life in the villages of Africa, Asia, and Latin America. He has published various books and scholarly journal articles, including *Rural Politics of Nasser's Egypt* (1971), *Go to the People* (1985), and *One Can Make a Difference: The Challenges and Opportunities of Dealing with World Poverty* (1997).

NATALIE CURTIS MCCULLOUGH has taught literature and writing courses in a variety of settings, has volunteered in the English as a Second Language Program, has been the guest discussion leader for Human Pursuits: The Western Humanities Concern, and is a frequent public speaker around the Salt Lake Valley. Natalie, who was born and educated in Salt Lake City, and her family live in this area.

MARTHA YOUNG MOENCH lives in Salt Lake City, Utah, with her husband, Mark, and their three children—Patrick, Adrienne, and Matthew. Her current chosen profession is that of homemaker/quilter.

RON MOLEN was born in 1929 in Hammond, Indiana, attended Indiana University before an LDS mission in Switzerland and Austria, then graduated from the University of Utah with a BFA in architecture. He practiced architecture for over thirty years, designed four small communities, and designed housing for the planned community of Columbia, Maryland. His book *House Plus Environment* (1974) addresses many of the social aspects of community. Recently he attended the world conference on sustainability at Findhorn, Scotland, and he is presently writing a book on the sustainable village. Many of his designs have appeared in national publications, and he is a guest lecturer at the university on the topic of planning for sustainability.

He has served on a variety of boards—Utah State Fine Arts, Friends of the Marriott Library, Utah Council for Crime Prevention, and Utahns Against Gun Violence. He and his wife, Norma, have four children and eight grandchildren. They both paint oils in their home studio, and he writes fiction. His first published fiction is called *My New Life* (1996). He has had articles published in *Catalyst, Sunstone, Dialogue,* and *UTNE Reader.*

HUGH W. NIBLEY graduated summa cum laude from the University of California at Los Angeles, and completed a University Fellow Ph.D. at the University of California at Berkeley. He taught at Claremont Colleges in California and served in the military intelligence in World War II before joining the faculty of Brigham Young University. In 1959–60 he returned to the University of California at Berkeley as a visiting professor. The David O. McKay Humanities Award is just one of many honors he has received. He also served as a missionary for the LDS Church in Switzerland and Germany, concluding his service in Greece. He and his wife, the former Phyllis Draper, are the parents of eight children.

WAYNE OWENS and his wife, Marlene Wessel, have five children and eight grandchildren. He has given six years of full-time service to the LDS Church, has practiced law in Utah and Washington, D.C., and is a member of the Utah State and U.S. Supreme Court Bars. Prior to his eight years of service in Congress, he worked for a dozen years on the staffs of three U.S. senators: Frank Moss of Utah, Robert Kennedy of New York, and Edward Kennedy of Massachusetts. He was appointed in 1980 to the National Commission on Resource Conservation and Recovery Board by President Jimmy Carter.

In 1989, while a member of Congress and the Foreign Affairs Committee, Mr. Owens and his friend S. Daniel Abraham, a New York and Florida businessman, organized the Center for Middle East Peace and Economic Cooperation to support and promote the peace process and to help build economic interaction between Israel and its Arab and Palestinian neighbors. They established a working relationship with almost all of the leaders of that region. Mr. Owens became vice-president of the organization in 1993, and assumed the responsibilities of president in 1995.

In 1994, he was appointed to the Utah Reclamation Mitigation and Conservation Commission by President Bill Clinton, and recently served as chair of the Southern Utah Wilderness Alliance and as a member of the boards of Defenders of Wildlife and The International Crisis Group.

HUGH W. PINNOCK is a lifetime resident of Salt Lake City but has lived in several other places as well, including Colorado, Indiana, California, Pennsylvania, and, lastly, England for three years. After graduating from Granite High School and the University of Utah, he spent a short time in the U.S. Army as a finance officer. For twenty years, he was a businessman specializing in life insurance management. He was then called as a General Authority for The Church of Jesus Christ of Latter-day Saints, and has served as a Seventy for the past two decades. What spare time he has is spent enjoying his family, reading, and writing. He fishes periodically, having caught seventy-two different species during his lifetime.

PAUL H. RISK holds a bachelor's degree in botany and biological science from California State University at Los Angeles, a Lifetime Secondary Teaching Certificate from the State of California, a Master of Science in entomology from the University of California at Davis, and a Ph.D. in wildlife biology with an emphasis in speech communication from Michigan State University, where he developed their first curriculum in environmental interpretation. He taught interpretation, environmental issues and attitudes, and environmental science at Penn State University and the University of Maine at Orono, and has written numerous articles and other publications in these fields.

His environmental career as an arboretum naturalist at Descanso Gardens in La Cañada, California, was followed by work as a seasonal ranger-naturalist at Grand Canyon and Lassen Volcanic National Parks, as a mountain-rescue specialist with the County of Los Angeles Sheriff's Department, and as a teacher of outdoor safety and wilderness survival. Over the past thirty years, he has been an environmental communication and public contact consultant to U.S. and Canadian park, forest, and fish and game agencies.

He is currently bishop of his ward in Nacogdoches, Texas. He and his wife, Rosalie, have three sons—Bradley, Christopher, and Thomas—and five grandchildren.

KRISTEN ROGERS, associate editor of the *Utah Historical Quarterly* and prizewinning author, loves all things spiritual. She likes writing (after it's done), being with her very amazing family, learning new things, playing piano and fiddle, doing anything outdoors, teaching, growing things, discussing ideas, and getting to really know people. Things that make her angry include poor urban and rural planning, billboards, shortsighted politicians, wasted resources, bulldozers, VIP mentality, and her own hypocrisies.

SAM RUSHFORTH has been active in national and local environmental causes for the past twenty-five years. He has worked on issues of air and water pollution and has done research on aquatic ecosystems throughout western North America. During the past several years he has focused on land-use alternatives and wilderness protection. Rushforth currently teaches university courses in conservation biology, ecology, and conservation ethics.

WILLIAM B. SMART was born in Provo and reared mainly in Utah. After graduating Phi Beta Kappa from Reed College in Portland, Oregon, he worked forty years with the *Deseret News* as reporter, feature writer, chief editorial writer, executive editor, and, finally, editor and general manager.

Following retirement from the *Deseret News*, he served with his wife, Donna Toland, a two-year LDS church-service mission as director of public affairs for an area covering Eastern Canada, New England, and upstate New York. Other church callings include service as a bishop and on the general boards of the Sunday School and the Young Men's Mutual Improvement Association, where he was chairman of the Explorer committee.

He was president or chairman of the Provo-Jordan River Parkway Foundation, the Utah Foundation for Technological Innovation, and the Institute for Studies in the Humanities. He has been director of such organizations as the Western States Arts Foundation, Snowbird Institute for Arts and Humanities, Hansen Planetarium, Utah Symphony, Pioneer State Theater, and Salt Lake Chamber of Commerce. He is deeply involved in conservation issues, currently serving as a director of the Grand Canyon Trust for responsible conservation of the Colorado Plateau, the Southwest Heritage Foundation, and as environmental representative on the Utah Resource Advisory Council of the BLM.

DENNIS SMITH is a native-born Utahn who lives in Highland, Utah. His bronze sculptures of children have long been a familiar feature in Utah's urban landscape, as well as his lighthearted, though less conventional, welded sculptural assemblages. Significant aspects of his work in recent years have been his paintings and his writings. Author of a book of poetry, *Star-counters* (1971), his most recent publication, *Meanderings* (1995) is a collection of personal essays gleaned from his weekly columns in the *Deseret News*.

GIBBS M. SMITH is a book publisher, a painter in oils, and the author of the book *Joe Hill* (1969), which was made into a film. A long-term Sierra Club activist, he functioned as the chair of the Utah Chapter for five years, served on the board of directors and the advisory board for Southern Utah Wilderness Alliance. He was a member of the board of the Western Folk Life Center, which promotes the preservation of family ranch culture in the West, has been a member of the board of the Utah Humanities Council, and is currently chairman of the board of the Mesa Foundation. He is an active member of the Barnes Park Ward in Kaysville, Utah.

STEVEN E. SNOW was born and raised in St. George, Utah. He graduated from Utah State University in 1974 with a degree in accounting, and from J. Reuben Clark Law School in 1977. He is a senior partner in the St. George law firm of Snow, Nuffer, Engstrom, Drake, Wade, and Smart. Involved in community service, he has served as president and member of the Washington County School Board, chairman and member of the Utah State Board of Regents, chairman and commissioner of the Western Interstate Commission of Higher Education, and chairman and trustee of the Grand Canyon Trust, a regional conservation organization. He has been active in church service, having held such positions as bishop, stake president, and full-time mission president in Southern California. He and his wife, Phyllis, have four sons.

DOROTHY ALLRED SOLOMON is twenty-eighth of forty-eight children born to Dr. Rulon Clark Allred, a Mormon fundamentalist leader practicing the outlawed Principle of Plural Marriage. Her first book, *In My Father's House* (1984), a winner in the Utah Original Writing Contest and the Utah State Publishing Prize, recounts her family's history of exile and persecution, culminating in the murder of her father in 1977. *Of Predators, Prey, and Other Kin*, a first-prize winner in the Utah Original Writing Award, draws on her fundamentalist background to explore the imperatives of environmental/nuclear threat and to encourage a transcendent awareness of "the natural man." The essays suggest that as we take responsibility for our inclination to be predator and/or prey, we are more likely to attain the encompassing love and reverence for life associated with God. Dorothy has published stories, essays, articles, and poems in a variety of periodicals and anthologies, and has received several writing awards. She lives with her husband of thirty years and their four children in Park City, Utah.

NATALIE TAYLOR graduated in 1989 from the University of Utah with a BFA in creative writing. Her writings have appeared in *The Sun* and *Northern Lights*. She currently works as associate editor for *The Inkslinger*, a local newsletter.

EMMA LOU THAYNE, the much-honored poet and author of thirteen books, is probably best known for the lyrics she wrote for the Mormon hymn "Where Can I Turn for Peace?" Translated into many languages, this beloved hymn has been sung and recorded by a variety of groups worldwide, including the Mormon Tabernacle Choir. An English teacher on the university level, she has also been a member of many academic, religious, arts, business, and civic boards of directors, and served as the only woman on the *Deseret News* board for seventeen years. She and her husband, retired realtor Melvin E. Thayne, have five daughters and nineteen grandchildren.

RALPH H. TINGEY, a native of Utah, lives in Chugiak, Alaska, with his wife, Sheri, son Thor, and daughter Daphne. He is an avid mountaineer, skier, and boater. For ten years he raced long-distance sled dogs across Alaska and Canada. He started his career as a mountaineering ranger at Grand Teton National Park. In 1981 he and his family transferred to Alaska, where he served as assistant superintendent at Denali National Park, and as superintendent at Northwest Alaska Areas in Kotzebue, Alaska, and at Lake Clark National Park and Preserve. He is currently the deputy superintendent of the Alaska Support Office in Anchorage.

ARDEAN WATTS is best known as a former associate conductor of the Utah Symphony and a music educator at the University of Utah. He has been an active environmentalist, serving as a board member of Hawkwatch International and as founder of the Mushroom Society of Utah.

CLAYTON M. WHITE did graduate work at the University of Alaska, Fairbanks, received a Ph.D. from the University of Utah in 1968, and taught at the University of Kansas and Cornell before joining the faculty of Brigham Young University. He was an advisor for the National Science Foundation's Office of Polar Programs and a technical representative working on arctic oil development with the U.S. Department of Energy. He runs an active graduate program and has published over 150 articles. He was recently an expert witness during the *Exxon Valdez* oil spill.

TERRY TEMPEST WILLIAMS is a native of Utah, having grown up within sight of the Great Salt Lake. She has served as naturalist-in-residence at the Utah Museum of Natural History, where she worked for fifteen years. She is currently the Shirley Sutton Thomas Visiting Professor of English at the university. A recipient of the National Wildlife Federation's Conservation Award for Special Achievement, Ms. Williams was recently inducted into the Rachel Carson Institute's Honor Roll. She has served on the Governing Council of the Wilderness Society in Washington, D.C., and is currently a board member of the Southern Utah Wilderness Alliance. She has received fellowships in creative nonfiction from the Lannan Foundation as well as the John Simon Guggenheim Foundation. Besides her previously mentioned books, she has collaborated on a variety of notable anthologies, including *Great and Peculiar Beauty—A Utah Reader* (1995), edited with Thomas J. Lyon; and *Testimony: Writers of the West Speak on Behalf of Utah Wilderness* (1996), edited with Stephen Trimble. She lives with her husband, Brooke, in Emigration Canyon.

TED WILSON is a native of Salt Lake City, Utah. Having lost his father at the age of fourteen, Wilson says, "It was the mountains—skiing in the winter, climbing in the summer—that saved my soul. The world would be a better place if every kid had the Wasatch Mountains for a playground." He went on to teach at Skyline High School for seven years and to serve as chief of staff to Congressman Wayne Owens in Washington, D.C. Elected mayor of Salt Lake City in 1975, Mr. Wilson served in this position until 1985, when he left to become the director of the Hinckley Institute of Politics. He remains active today in both politics and mountaineering.

LARRY YOUNG has focused his environmental activism during the 1990s in two primary areas: as cochair of the Utah Wilderness Coalition—a group of 155 national, regional, and local environmental organizations seeking to protect Utah's pristine wild lands—and as a founding member of Mormon Peace Gathering, which organized Mormon participation in the Franciscan-led faith-based witness against nuclear testing at the Nevada Nuclear Test Site.

Professionally, he is associate professor of sociology at Brigham Young University, where he teaches courses on macro-institutional forces shaping modern societies. He currently is coordinator of Graduate Programs in his department and acts as a faculty advisor to *Voice*, the campus feminist club. He has served as president of the Mormon Social Science Association and as an elected member of the Council of the Sociology of Religion Section of the American Sociological Association. He has published numerous articles and book chapters and is coauthor of *Full Pews and Empty Altars: Demographics of the Priest Shortage in United States Catholic Dioceses* (1993), which received the Distinguished Book of the Year Award from the Society for the Scientific Study of Religion, and *Goodbye Father: Power and Patriarchy in the Roman Catholic Church* (forthcoming, 1999). He also coedited *Contemporary Mormonism: Social Science Perspectives* (1994), and edited *Rational Choice Theory and Religion: Summary and Assessment* (1996).